The First Thousand Years

The First Thousand Years

A GLOBAL HISTORY OF CHRISTIANITY

ROBERT LOUIS WILKEN

Yale

UNIVERSITY

PRESS

New Haven and London

Yale University Press books may be purchased in quantity for educational,
business, or promotional use. For information, please e-mail sales.press@yale.
edu (U.S. office) or sales@yaleup.co.uk (U.K. office).

Designed by Nancy Ovedovitz and set in Galliard Oldstyle type by
Keystone Typesetting, Inc. Printed in the United States of America.

The Library of Congress has cataloged the hardcover edition as follows:
Wilken, Robert Louis, 1936–
The first thousand years : a global history of Christianity / Robert Louis Wilken.
p.   cm.
Includes bibliographical references and index.
ISBN 978-0-300-11884-1 (hardback)
1. Church history—Primitive and early church, ca. 30–600.
2. Church history—Middle Ages, 600–1500. I. Title.
BR162.3.W55 2012
270—dc23   2012021755

ISBN 978-0-300-19838-6 (pbk.)

A catalogue record for this book is available from the British Library.

10 9 8 7 6 5 4

To Carol

Always fair
And young to me

Contents

Acknowledgments   ix

Introduction   1

1. Beginning in Jerusalem   6

2. Ephesus, Rome, and Edessa: The Spread of Christianity   17

3. The Making of a Christian Community   28

4. Divisions Within   37

5. Constructing a Catacomb   47

6. A Learned Faith: Origen of Alexandria   55

7. Persecution: Cyprian of Carthage   65

8. A Christian Emperor: Constantine   75

9. The Council of Nicaea and the Christian Creed   88

10. Monasticism   99

11. A Christian Jerusalem   109

12. Emperor Julian, the Jews, and Christians   118

13. Bishop and Emperor: Ambrose and Theodosius   127

14. Architecture and Art   136

15. Music and Worship   145

16. The Sick, the Aged, and the Poor: The Birth of Hospitals   154

17. The Bishop of Rome as Pope   163

18. An Ordered Christian Society: Canon Law   174

19. Augustine of Hippo   183

20. The Great Controversy over Christ   195

21. Egypt and the Copts; Nubia   205

22. African Zion: Ethiopia   214

23. Syriac-Speaking Christians: The Church of the East   222

24. Armenia and Georgia   229

25. Central Asia, China, and India   238

26. A Christian Empire: Justinian   246

27. New Beginnings in the West   257

28. Latin Christianity Spreads North   269

29. The Sacking of Jerusalem; More Controversy over Christ   279

30. No God but God: The Rise of Islam   288

31. Images and the Making of Byzantium   297

32. Arabic-Speaking Christians   307

33. Christians Under Islam: Egypt and North Africa   316

34. Christians Under Islam: Spain   324

35. An Emperor in the West: Charlemagne   333

36. Christianity Among the Slavs   344

Afterword   355

Chronology and Maps   361

Suggested Readings   373

Translations   377

Index   381

Illustrations appear following page 182

Acknowledgments

This book has been a long time in writing, and I have consulted and corresponded with many people along the way. Now is the time to thank them for their advice, comments, and corrections of what I had written. I am deeply grateful to Thomas F. X. Noble, who read the entire manuscript, offered constructive criticism, and helped me see more clearly what I was about. R. R. Reno also read the manuscript and offered helpful observations. Robin Darling Young was very generous in pointing me in the right direction when I was dealing with the Syriac-speaking East and Armenia and Georgia and answered many questions on specific points. Others helped me with bibliographical matters, addressed questions of interpretation, and clarified specific historical issues. The list is long, and I hope I have not overlooked anyone: Joseph Amar, Gary Anderson, Monica J. Blanchard, Thomas E. Burman, Ann R. F. Burns, James Campbell, John Dobbins, Paul Corby Finney, Elizabeth Digeser, Harold Drake, John Hall Elliott, Harry Gamble, Sidney Griffith, Russell Hittinger, Caroline Humfress, David Hunter, Blanche Jenson, Sandra Keating, John Peter Kenney, Judith Kovacs, David Kovacs, William Mahrt, Bernard McGinn, John McGuckin, Kevin O'Brien, Ute Possekel, Leslie Rahuba, Cristina Riggs, Dorcas Schudlich, Bryan Stewart, Mohammed Sawaie, Mark Swanson, Richard Bishop, Robert Taft, S.J., Augustine Thompson, O.P., Daniel Weiss, Daniel Williams, and John Yiannias. I am grateful to each for advice.

In spring 2010 I spent a stimulating month at the Center for World Catholicism and Intercultural Theology at DePaul University. I am grateful to Peter Casarella for the invitation and for conversations when I was in residence. As I was finishing the manuscript I was visiting professor at Providence College in Providence, Rhode Island. It was a congenial atmosphere in which to work. Members of the faculty helped to clarify my thinking on a number of matters, and the library staff obtained books I needed from other libraries. Katherine Bruno and Noah Curtis, graduate assistants in the Department of Theology, helped me with technical matters preparing the manuscript for publication. My thanks to all at Providence College who made my stay pleasant and productive.

Finally I wish to thank my editor Jennifer Banks, who has encouraged me at every stage in the process. Piyali Bhattacharya, editorial assistant at Yale University Press, helped bring the project to a conclusion, and the two outside readers provided invaluable criticism and suggestions. Suzanne M. Tibor negotiated the world of images for the book, William Nelson prepared the maps, and Phillip King cleared up many things in copy-editing the manuscript. Nathaniel Peters prepared the index, and Meghan Duke corrected the page proofs. I am grateful to all.

Introduction

"What power preserves what once was, if memory does not last?" These words from the Polish poet Czeslaw Milosz kept coming to mind as I was writing this book. The past doesn't vanish at once; it dies slowly. But if remembered, the dead maintain their ground and live among us.

Historical memory, like all memory, is selective, and there are many claimants to the telling of Christianity's early history. The Christian Church has a long and crowded past, and whether by design, forgetfulness, or ignorance, its history will be remembered in different ways. Our knowledge of the past is not objective but personal and participatory. In writing the history of the first thousand years I have chosen to highlight those events and persons that, in my judgment, are worthy of remembrance at the beginning of the third millennium.

In many books on early Christianity the accent falls on the first several centuries. And for good reason. The formulation of the Church's central beliefs, the development of its distinctive practices, and the establishment of its most enduring institutions took place during the first five centuries. Christianity did not come into the world full-blown, and these years will have a resonance without parallel in any account of Christian history. The story of beginnings, however, requires a wider horizon. Only toward the end of the first millennium did the form Christianity took in history come fully into view. I begin with Jesus of Nazareth in the first century and end with the baptism of Vladimir, the Rus prince in Kiev at the close of the millennium in 988. By the year 1000 the map of the early Christian world was largely complete.

The emergence of Christianity brought about one of the most profound revolutions the world has known, and the principal theme of this book is the slow drama of the building of a Christian civilization. The Church's history is more than the history of a religious community. Christianity is a culture-forming religion, and the planting and growth of Christian communities led to the remaking of the cultures of the ancient world along with the creation of a new civilization, or more accurately several new civilizations.

One mark of culture is language, and as I read the ancient sources afresh I marveled at the primacy of language—Greek, Latin, Syriac, Coptic, Armenian, Slavonic, even Arabic as Christians in the Middle East adapted to the rule of Islam—in the spread of Christianity. Christianity has no sacred tongue, but it cannot exist without books. In some cases, among the Armenians or Slavs, it was Christians who first wrote down the oral languages of the new Christian peoples.

Culture has to do with the pattern of inherited meanings and sensibilities embedded in rituals, institutions, laws, practices, images, and stories of a people. But it also includes tangible products of human activity that can be seen and touched. In the first two centuries Christianity was largely invisible to the inhabitants of the cities in which Christians lived. But by the beginning of the third century the first signs of a Christian material culture appeared in Rome. The Christian community bought a plot of land and constructed the catacomb of Callixtus, an underground columbarium where Christians buried their dead and gathered to worship. About the same time small oil lamps with Christian designs and figures began to be produced. In the fourth century the construction of churches presented a very public face in the ancient cities, and those who stepped inside beheld pictures of Christ, the Virgin Mary, and scenes from biblical history in vivid color.

Christians created laws to govern the life of their communities and established the first hospitals to care for the sick. Music, too, was a sign of the new culture, and one of the most far-reaching developments was the invention by Christian monks of a system of notation to write down musical melodies. Until that happened, what was sung could be transmitted only by memory from one singer to another, a fallible undertaking. With the invention of the staff (stave) it was possible to learn a melody without having heard it sung by someone who knew it.

In much writing on the early history of Christianity theological ideas play a major role, especially in accounts of the great controversies over the doctrine of the Trinity and the person of Christ. That is right and good. But institutions were vitally important, and the three that figure large were the office of the bishop, monasticism, and kingship (or imperial rule). Whether one is speaking about Gaul, Egypt, or Persia, one always finds bishops and monks. And as new peoples, such as the Ethiopians or the English or the Bulgarians, embraced Christian faith it was a king or queen who opened the way for the introduction of Christian practices and beliefs. Religion was not a private affair, and moderns forget that in ancient times the world was ruled by emperors and kings. There was no future for Christianity that did not include the blessing of temporal rulers.

When the Roman emperor Constantine converted to Christianity in the fourth century, the Church was no longer a small association living in the shadows; it was a vibrant and visible community with resourceful leaders, a network of communications, a keen sense of its own tradition, and a large constituency. As the Church's rituals became civic celebrations, its way of life changed the rhythms of society. For Rome, the alliance with Christianity came late; outside the empire, in Ethiopia or Armenia and later in early medieval Europe, the Christian mission began at the top and the king became the head of the Christian people. Conversion was not a warming of the heart, but a change of public practice.

The account of the early centuries, however, would be incomplete without the stories of the many memorable persons who give life and vigor to the narrative: the indomitable missionaries who set out to preach the gospel among new peoples, Boniface the apostle to the Germans, or Augustine to the English; Macrina, who influenced the form of monasticism in Asia Minor, and the empress Theodora, who sent missionaries to Nubia in black Africa; the translators who wrote down the oral language of new Christian people to make possible translations of the Bible and the liturgy, Cyril and Methodius among the Slavs, Mashtots the Armenian; Anthony of Baghdad, who translated Christian texts into Arabic; poets such as Ephrem the Syrian, Romanos Melodos the Greek, Prudentius the Spaniard; the bishops, popes, and patriarchs who guided the Christian people, Cyprian bishop of Carthage and martyr, Ambrose of Milan, Pope Gregory the Great, and Timothy *catholicos* (patriarch) of the Church of the East in Baghdad; deeply original thinkers such as Origen of Alexandria, Augustine of Hippo, and Maximus the Confessor; Basil, bishop of Caesarea, who built the first hospital; monks who formed enduring religious communities, Shenoute the Copt in Egypt and Benedict in Italy; emperors who gave form to the new civilization, Constantine, Justinian, Charlemagne; scholars who transmitted ancient learning, Cassiodorus, Isidore of Seville, and Photius of Constantinople; Abu Qurrah, the first Christian to write theological works in Arabic. All these persons and many others have a place in the narrative.

I have made the rise and spread of Islam integral to the history. No event in the first millennium of Christian history was more catastrophic than the Muslim conquest of Christian lands, and none more consequential. For centuries Christianity had spread around the Mediterranean Sea, throughout the Middle East, and farther east to Central Asia, India, and China. But in the seventh century most of the lands on the southern coast of the Mediterranean and all of the Middle East and Central Asia swiftly came under Muslim rule. Today this large geographical area is still ruled by Muslims, and Christianity has either disappeared, as in Algeria and Tunisia (ancient North Africa), or been gradually reduced to a minority of the population, as in the Middle East. The extraordinary success of Christianity in the first millennium must be set alongside the dramatic rise of Islam and the decline of Christianity in historic Christian lands. If the story of Christianity is told solely from the perspective of the West, an essential element is ignored.

To give the reader a sense of the magnitude of the impact of the Islamic conquest on Christians, I devote four chapters to the rise and spread of Islam and the momentous changes Muslim rule brought to Christian communities in the Middle East, North Africa, and Spain. In each geographical area the story takes a different course. In greater Syria and Iraq, Christians adopted the language of their conquerors as their own and created a large and diverse body of Christian writings in Arabic. In Egypt, Christians held on to their native language, Coptic—while at the same time eventually adopting Arabic—and were able to maintain a unique identity in a Muslim society. Today, the Copts are the largest Christian community in the Middle East. In North Africa, Christianity disappeared and no indigenous Christians remain in countries such as Libya, Tunisia, and Algeria. Some Christians in Spain adopted Arabic, but others held on to the traditional Latin culture. Significantly, the first translation of the Qur'an into Latin took place in Spain.

I have subtitled this book *A Global History of Christianity*. When I began to do research I wanted to show the wide geographical reach of Christianity in the first millennium. But only as I read more broadly and learned more about Christianity in such regions as Armenia, Persia, Ethiopia, Central Asia, India, and China did I realize how energetic and enterprising the mission to spread the Christian gospel was and what a vast reach it had in the early centuries. For example, there is a first-hand testimony to the existence of a Christian community in Ceylon (Sri Lanka), and Timothy I, the catholicos of the Syriac-speaking Church of the East in Baghdad, commissioned a bishop for Tibet. The fourth to tenth centuries were a remarkable age in the history of Christian missions.

Christianity is transcultural and migratory, and each interaction with a new people and language brought changes in how Christians practiced their faith. At the same time, Christian rituals such as baptism and the Eucharist, the Bible, the Nicene Creed, the office of bishop, and monasticism bound Christians in a spiritual unity that transcended the deep cultural differences.

The date 1000 is not sacrosanct. It works well for the Byzantine and Slavic East because the Rus prince Vladimir was baptized at the end of the first millennium. In the Latin West, however, I have brought the story to a close with the reign of Charlemagne. By the early ninth century when he died Christianity in western Europe had assumed the shape it would have for the next eight hundred years. In the Middle East, I end with the first flowering of Arabic Christian literature in the ninth century, a time of extraordinary intellectual creativity in the East beyond Jerusalem.

I have written for the general reader who may have little background in the history of Christianity. The chapters are short and I have sought to keep the narrative moving. There is a vast body of scholarship on the early history of Christianity, and the interpretation of many of the topics I discuss continues to be debated by historians. But that discussion belongs properly in scholarly articles and monographs. My aim is to depict the central developments in early Christian history with an eye to the form of Christianity that spread around the ancient world and endured into the Middle Ages. The notes are few, but I have included a selection of books for further reading and a list of translations of works from which many of the quotations are taken. In the case of quotations from the Bible, most use the Revised Standard Version, but in some cases I have translated from the ancient original versions, such as the Latin.

Beginning in Jerusalem

In the centuries before the birth of Jesus, Rome, a city-state on the Italian peninsula, had gradually extended its rule not only over Italy but also over Gaul (modern France), Spain, and North Africa (modern-day Tunisia and Algeria). In the first century B.C. the Romans conquered large territories in the eastern Mediterranean, Greece, the Balkans, the ancient kingdoms of Asia Minor, Egypt, greater Syria (including the land of the Bible), and beyond. As the empire grew, and the earlier republican form of government proved ill-suited to the new challenges, the order and stability of the empire were invested in the hands of one man.

This man was Octavian, the adopted son of Julius Caesar, and after a series of civil wars and the defeat of his principal rival, Mark Antony (and his lover Cleopatra, queen of Egypt), at the battle of Actium in 31 B.C., he became master of Rome and the territories it had conquered. On his return in triumph to the city of Rome with the full military might of the empire at his disposal, he inaugurated a constitutional revolution, reshaping Roman political life in light of its growing responsibilities as ruler of many lands and peoples. In 27 B.C., the Roman senate conferred on him the title of Augustus, the "majestic one," and from this date the beginning of his reign as emperor, and hence the commencement of the Roman Empire, is marked. Caesar Augustus ruled for forty-one years, until A.D. 14, and the empire he founded lasted in different forms until the fall of Constantinople, the "second Rome," to the Turks in 1453.

Under Augustus, for the first (and last) time in history the lands around the Mediterranean Sea, including the land of Israel, the ancient homeland of the Jews, were joined together under one political authority. By the first century Rome's empire reached from the Euphrates River in the east to the Atlantic Ocean in the west, from the olive groves and vineyards of North Africa on the southern coast of the Mediterranean to the great rivers of the north, the Danube flowing into the

Black Sea and the Rhine into the North Sea. All the major cities of the empire—Carthage, Alexandria, Caesarea, Antioch, Ephesus, Rome—were located on or near the sea, and the most vital lines of communication lay by sea, *mare nostrum,* our sea, as the Romans called it. Ideas, goods, and technology (architectural style, for example) all moved easily upon its waters. Restrictions on travel were almost unknown, and merchants and traders could journey from the Euphrates in the Fertile Crescent to the Thames in Britain without crossing a border or being asked to show a passport. Never before had so many different peoples enjoyed such a measure of security and freedom of movement. As Rome conquered the world, it made the world welcome.

Rome's ancient experiment in government, to rule many peoples under one authority, did not break down the cultural and linguistic diversity of the lands surrounding the Mediterranean, nor did it temper the regional loyalties of its peoples. Egyptians spoke Coptic and Syrians spoke Aramaic. But the spread of the Greek language after the conquests of Alexander the Great three centuries earlier, and its use as a lingua franca in the cities of the eastern Mediterranean, provided a common language for communication, trade, education, and intellectual life. The term used to refer to the culture of the Roman Empire in this period is Greco-Roman, widespread use of the Greek language under the umbrella of Roman political institutions. The world was changing, and as the ruins of Roman buildings in Tunisia in North Africa, Jordan in the east, and Turkey to the north bear silent witness, men and women in lands distant from one another became part of a single confident civilization.

Although Christianity, like Judaism and Islam, arose in the Middle East, unlike Judaism and Islam its destiny came to be yoked to the vast empire centered in the great city far to the west, the city of Caesar and Cicero and Augustus, mighty and eternal Rome, which "carries her head high above other cities," in the words of Virgil the Roman poet. The events that gave rise to Christianity were auspicious not only for what they brought about but also for where and when they took place, in the Roman Empire during the reign of the first emperor. When the Christian evangelist Luke introduced his account of Jesus's birth he made a point of recording that he was born in the Roman Empire during the reign of emperor Augustus. "In those days a decree went out from Caesar Augustus that all the world should be enrolled" (Luke 2:1). And it was in the cities of this cosmopolitan and multicultural society that the first Christian communities were established.

The story, however, begins in Palestine, for it was there in a hidden corner of the earth that Jesus was born among the Jewish people in the land they called their own. Their principal city was Jerusalem, located some forty miles from the Mediterranean Sea on the edge of the desert leading down to the River Jordan and the Dead Sea. In Jerusalem stood the temple, an "immensely opulent" building, in the words of the Roman historian Tacitus, the center of Jewish religious life, where sacrifices were offered daily and faithful Jews came from all over the land to celebrate the major festivals. In the towns and villages, however, Jewish worship took the form of a service of readings from the Torah and the prophets, exposition of what was read, singing of psalms, and recitation of prayers in a synagogue, usually a modest rectangular building.

Once Israelite kings had ruled the land from Jerusalem, but over the centuries the Jewish kingdom had been conquered by the Assyrians and the Babylonians, its single temple destroyed, and many of its people taken into exile in Mesopotamia. In the fifth century B.C. some of them returned and the temple was rebuilt, but only for a brief period were the Jews able to gain their independence as a people. Then in the first century B.C. Rome conquered the region and incorporated the territory of the ancient Jewish kingdom into its empire. The Jews, however, never lost hope that they would one day drive out the intruders and restore Jewish rule. For some this hope led them to believe that in the near future God would intervene to change the course of history. Jesus was born at a time when this hope was fervent.

In our earliest sources Jesus's birthplace is given as Bethlehem, a few miles south of Jerusalem. But his family came from Nazareth in Galilee, in the north of the country, and it was there that he passed his years as a child and young man. Not until Jesus was almost thirty years old and baptized by John the Baptist does he come clearly into historical view. John was an itinerant prophet who proclaimed that God's rule was at hand and exhorted the Jewish people "to practice justice towards their fellows and piety toward God," as an ancient historian has it. He was a solitary prophet and an ascetic who lived on honey and locusts in the desert between Jerusalem and the Jordan River, yet people from the towns and villages flocked to the parched hills and dry riverbeds to heed his preaching and to be baptized in the waters of the Jordan.

Jesus was among those who came to the region of the Jordan to hear John and to be baptized by him. After his baptism he traveled around Judea urging his fellow Jews to repent, and, according to the reports of some, also baptizing (John 3:26). However, the evangelist John says explicitly, and the other gospels confirm, that Jesus did not baptize, only did his disciples (John 4:2). After John was arrested, Jesus began his own ministry to his fellow Jews.

The Gospel of Mark introduces Jesus's ministry in this way: "Now after John was arrested, Jesus came into Galilee, preaching the gospel of God, and saying, 'The time is fulfilled, and the kingdom of God is at hand; repent, and believe in the gospel'" (Mark 1:15). The phrase "kingdom of God," the most characteristic feature of Jesus's teaching, signified that in the near future, so near that the time is at hand, God would act in surprising and unfamiliar ways to save his people, right wrongs, render judgment, and bring about a new age. Although the term "kingdom of God" could have political overtones to signal the restoration of a Jewish kingdom, these associations are largely absent from Jesus's preaching. In the Acts of the

Apostles, an account of Christian beginnings, after his resurrection his disciples are reported to have asked: "Lord will you at this time restore the kingdom to Israel?" (Acts 1:7) But there was little in Jesus's sayings to support such hopes. The accent was on repentance, on living with one's face turned toward God, on warnings of the tribulation to come at the end of time leading to resurrection and judgment. Everything that Jesus says about how one is to live in the present depends on what God is doing and will do in the future.

Though Jesus began as a disciple of John the Baptist, unlike John he was neither a solitary nor an ascetic; he carried his message to the towns and villages of his native region of Galilee, to the territory of the Decapolis, ten Hellenized cities to the north and east of the Jordan, and finally to Jerusalem. Jesus met people close to their homes, in the places where they lived and in the synagogues where they gathered for prayer. In the Gospel of Luke his first public gesture was to read and expound a passage from the prophet Isaiah in the synagogue in his hometown of Nazareth. What is most conspicuous about this story is that Jesus takes the prophecy (Isaiah 61:1–2) to refer to himself! The kingdom of God, he says, is already present in his person.

In the passage already cited from the Gospel of Mark, Jesus says that the kingdom of God is "at hand" (Mark 1:15), and in the Gospel of Luke he is reported to have said the kingdom of God is "in the midst of you." This sense of "already" but "not yet" gave his sayings and his parables a mysterious depth. Once Jesus was asked why the disciples of John fast while his disciples do not fast. To which he responded: "Can the wedding guests fast while the bridegroom is with them? As long as they have the bridegroom they cannot fast." In other sayings the coming of the kingdom lies in the future, and before it arrives nation will rise against nation, earthquakes and famines will terrify and plague the world, the sun will be darkened and the moon will give no light, and on the last day only the elect will be gathered in. Jesus urges his disciples to "take heed and watch, for you do not know when the time will come" (Mark 13:33).

Almost everything we know about Jesus comes from the accounts of his life and teachings in the gospels, Matthew, Mark, Luke, and John, written by different authors a generation or more after his death. The events they narrate and the parables and sayings they record were drawn from traditions passed on orally in the early Christian communities, adapted to local interests in the process of transmission over the decades, and shaped according to the aims of each author. Nevertheless, taken as a whole, the four gospels present a compelling portrait of his person and teaching.

Jesus's message was centered on the God of Abraham, Isaac, and Jacob, the God who had created the world and delivered the Jewish people out of bondage in Egypt to lead them to a land flowing with milk and honey, who had sent prophets to censure their unfaithfulness and lift their hopes, and was now calling his people to repentance, to renewed devotion and a life of holiness. He sought to rescue the commandments from being a quotidian set of rules by raising up what was central in Jewish teaching, to love and serve God whose goodness is the source of all good. "You must be perfect," he says, "as your Father in heaven is perfect" (Matthew 5:48). Jesus called for resolute and steadfast obedience to the will of God. When someone said to him, "I will follow you, Lord, but let me first say farewell to those at home," Jesus responded: "No one who puts his hand to the plow and looks back is fit for the kingdom of God" (Luke 9:57–62).

Echoing the words of the psalmist, "Incline my heart to perform thy statues" (Psalms 119:112), Jesus made the will, not the mind or the intellect, the agent of the heart. He spoke directly to the wellspring of human action, the desires and passions of the heart. Evil does not have to find a place in men and women—it is always lurking within the human breast. "It is not what goes into a man from outside that can defile him," Jesus said, "It is what comes out of a man that defiles him. For from within, out of the heart of man, come evil thoughts . . ." (Mark 7:18–21). What we love drives our lives. "Where your treasure is," Jesus said, "there will your heart be also" (Matthew 6:21). In the Sermon on the Mount, Matthew's summary of Jesus's teaching, one finds nestled among his sayings on humility, justice, mercy, and peacemaking the startling words: "Blessed are the pure in heart for they shall see God" (Matthew 5:8).

As an observant Jew, Jesus went regularly to the synagogue on the Sabbath, he celebrated the Jewish festivals and kept the food laws, he asked a blessing before breaking bread, he approved of gifts and offerings in the temple, and, according to the Gospel of Mark, he even urged obedience to biblical laws of ritual purity. He once told a leper who had been healed to show himself to the priest and make an offering as commanded by Moses (Leviticus 14:1–2; Mark 1:44). Some scholars believe that he wore tassels on his garments as observant Jews do today. His message was addressed to wayward Jews, to the "lost sheep of the house of Israel" (Matthew 15:24), and the language, imagery, and historical allusions are all drawn from Jewish tradition.

Jesus was a sage, not a philosopher, who spoke about what gives life value and purpose. He taught that the things that most delight our frail hearts bring no ultimate satisfaction. True wisdom begins in the fear of God and has as its goal the love of God. Hence the summary of his teaching, what is called the great commandment, makes love preeminent. "You shall love the Lord your God with all your heart, and with all your soul, and with all your mind. This is the great and first commandment. And a second is like it, You shall love your neighbor as yourself" (Matthew 22:37–39). Even when Jesus lays down concrete examples of how his disciples should act toward others (turn the other cheek, or love your enemies [Matthew 5:39, 44]), he is no moralist. Love of neighbor begins with love of God.

He spoke little of religious ideas. His teaching had to do with how one was to live among family, friends, and neighbors. He praises meekness and humility, he exhorts his followers to forgive those who have wronged them, to return good for evil, to reach out to the poor and needy, to show mercy and compassion to all men and women. Among the best known and most beloved of his parables is the tale of the good Samaritan. In answer to the question "Who is my neighbor," according to the Gospel of Luke, Jesus told this story: "A man was going down from Jerusalem to Jericho, and he fell among robbers, who stripped him and beat him, and departed, leaving him half dead. Now by chance a priest was going down that road; and when he saw him he passed by on the other side. So likewise a Levite, when he came to the place and saw him, passed by on the other side. But a Samaritan, as he journeyed, came to where he was; and when he saw him, he had compassion, and went to him and bound up his wounds, pouring on oil and wine; then he set him on his own beast and brought him to an inn, and took care of him. And the next day he took out two denarii and gave them to the innkeeper, saying, 'Take care of him; and whatever more you spend, I will repay you when I come back.' Which of these three, do you think, proved neighbor to the man who fell among the robbers? He said, 'The one who showed mercy on him.' And Jesus said to him, 'Go and do likewise'" (Luke 10:29–37).

What Jesus taught was not bound to time and place. Its winsome simplicity is as appealing to those who read the gospels today as it was to those who heard him two thousand years ago. Even the prayer he taught his followers is crisp, concise, and devoid of ornament: "Father, hallowed be thy name. Thy kingdom come. Give us each day our daily bread; and forgive us our sins, for we ourselves forgive every one who is indebted to us; and lead us not into temptation" (Luke 11:2–4).* Notice,

---

*The Lord's prayer (Our Father) is given in two forms in the gospels: Matthew 6:9–13 and Luke 11:2–4. I have cited the version from Luke, which is probably closer to the original. The more familiar version in the Gospel of Matthew may reflect the form that came to be used in the worship of the earliest Christian communities:

> Our Father who art in heaven,
> Hallowed be thy name.
> Thy kingdom come.
> Thy will be done,
> On earth as it is in heaven.
> Give us this day our daily bread,
> And forgive us our debts,
> As we also have forgiven our debtors;
> And lead us not into temptation,
> But deliver us from evil.

The doxology, "For thine is the kingdom and the power and the glory," was added later, following David's prayer in 1 Chronicles 29:11–13.

however, the telling phrase "Thy kingdom" in the midst of the prayer. Jesus's message cannot be divorced from his belief that God's reign is imminent. Though it must be said that many readers of the gospels have selectively picked and chosen what suits their taste. Thomas Jefferson, for example, pruned the gospels of everything he found objectionable and turned Jesus into a simple moralist in a little book titled *The Life and Morals of Jesus of Nazareth.*

Jesus taught through parables, simple stories with a pungent, sometimes enigmatic moral. He once told the story of a man who hired laborers for his vineyard. After agreeing with the workers for a day's wage, a denarius, the landowner sent them into the vineyard. A few hours later he needed other workers and promised to pay them "whatever is right." Several hours later he did the same, and again later in the day he took on more workers; finally as the day was ending he hired yet others. When those who had been hired at the end of the day came forward for their wages they were paid a denarius, and when those who had been hired first came forward, they too were paid a denarius. Naturally they grumbled that they had been treated unfairly. "These last worked only one hour, and you have made them equal to us who have borne the burden of the day and the scorching heat." But the owner of the vineyard said: "Friend, I am doing you no wrong; did you not agree with me for a denarius? Take what belongs to you, and go. I choose to give to this last as I give to you. Am I not allowed to do what I choose with what belongs to me? Or do you begrudge my generosity? So the last will be first, and the first last" (Matthew 20:1–16). God's ways are past knowing, and as a master teacher Jesus knew that the way to understanding was often oblique, seldom direct.

At times Jesus's rejoinders to questions are sharp and biting, and his hearers turn away disquieted. When a young man asked what he could do to gain eternal life, Jesus told him to sell everything he owned and follow him. On one occasion he told the crowd: "If any man comes to me and hates not his own father, and mother, and wife, and children, and brethren, and sisters, yes, and his own life also, he cannot be my disciple" (Luke 14:26). At another time he said: "Do not think that I have come to bring peace on earth; I have not come to bring peace, but a sword" (Matthew 10:34).

On hearing Jesus one did not say, "That was interesting," and return to one's business. He made a claim on those who heard him and invited a response. In a parable about a man who had given a great banquet, when the host realized that his guests had spurned his invitation and nonchalantly gone about their affairs, he ordered his servant to go into the streets of the city and bring in whomever he might find, the "poor and maimed and blind and lame." The servant did as he had been commanded, but still there was room. So the master said to the servant: "Go out to the highways and hedges, and compel people to come in, that my house may be filled." To which Jesus adds, "For I tell you, none of those men who were invited shall taste my banquet" (Luke 14:16–24).

Nevertheless people listened with astonishment, for he taught "with authority," as the evangelist Matthew has it. Though his sayings and parables can stand on their own as a singular body of spiritual and moral teaching (and have often been taken as such), it was his bearing among those who knew him that left the deepest impression on his contemporaries. Jesus lived a simple life (owning no property) and moved among men and women of little means and status. He was a person of great tenderness, compassionate to the sick and needy, kind to outcasts, gentle with the handicapped, understanding of children. But he was a formidable adversary, quick and clever in debates, ready with an apt verse from Scripture to disarm his critics.

Jesus made himself part of his message. The proclamation of the Kingdom of God ended with the invitation: "Follow me." If one was to turn to God, to trust and love God, one had to come to terms with him. "Everyone who acknowledges me before men, I also will acknowledge before my Father who is in heaven" (Matthew 10:32). A decision about God was a decision about Jesus. Understandably, this did not go down well with the religious authorities in Jerusalem.

Jesus had the gift of healing, and when people heard he was near they brought their sick to him. The most affecting stories in the gospels are about men and women in desperate need seeking help. Once a leper kneeled before him, begging, "If you will, you can make me clean." Jesus, "moved with pity," stretched out his hand and touched him and said, "I will; be clean" (Mark 1:40–42). In another case friends of a paralyzed man, unable to reach Jesus because of the crowds, broke through the roof of a house to let him down where Jesus was teaching (Mark 2:1–12).

Jesus sought solitude and often retreated by himself to be alone with God in prayer. In the course of three chapters the evangelist Luke says that Jesus went off to be "alone," departed for "a lonely place," "withdrew to the wilderness and prayed," and went to "the mountain to pray" (Luke 4:42, 5:16, 6:12). Mark reports that after healing many people, the next morning Jesus rose "a great while before day and went out to a lonely place and there he prayed" (Mark 1:35). More than anything else the frequency and intensity of his prayer gives evidence of his closeness to God, whom he called Father. Yet from the outset of his ministry he was always in the company of others, not only men but also women, most notably the strong and independent Mary Magdalene. He had a close group of friends whom he loved deeply, and he enjoyed the warmth of the home of his friends Martha and her sister Mary and their brother Lazarus.

Jesus addressed his message not only to individuals; he also formed a disciplined community of followers. According to our earliest record, the Gospel of Mark, after he was baptized the first thing he did was call together a group of twelve disciples, recalling the twelve tribes of Israel. They accompanied him as he moved among the people teaching and healing, and would become leaders of the new community formed after his death and resurrection. His disciples were no anonymous company. Each is identified by name as he is called to follow Jesus, and at one point in the gospels their names are given: "Simon whom [Jesus] surnamed Peter; James the son of Zebedee and John the brother of James, whom he surnamed Boanerges, that is, sons of thunder; Andrew, and Philip, and Bartholomew, and Matthew, and Thomas, and James the son of Alphaeus, and Thaddaeus, and Simon the Cananaean, and Judas Iscariot who betrayed him" (Mark 3:16–19).

After teaching and healing in Galilee for almost three years, Jesus made his way to Jerusalem. When he goes up to the holy city the account in the gospels becomes more solemn and resolute, as the prophet and sage of Galilee embarks on the decisive moment in his young life. From this point on everything is seen in light of his impending death. Planning to celebrate the Passover in Jerusalem, Jesus arrived in the holy city as the festival was approaching. He wished to spend some time teaching in the city and in the temple. His reputation went ahead of him, and as soon as he entered the city he attracted crowds, but sharp exchanges with some Jewish teachers provoked resentment and sparked suspicion that he was subversive. Before long he was challenged by priests and scholars in the temple: "By what authority are you doing these things?" they asked. To which Jesus replied, "I will ask you a question; answer me, and I will tell you by what authority I do these things." When they refused to answer, he said, "Neither will I tell you by what authority I do these things" (Mark 11:27–33).

On the evening before his death, Jesus had a final meal with his disciples. In Christian tradition it is known as the Last Supper, and for many the scene is imagined as it is depicted in Leonardo da Vinci's painting by that name. It is not, however, possible to reconstruct precisely what took place, much less to envision the setting. The evangelists report that in the course of the meal Jesus took bread, blessed it, and said, "Take, eat, this is my body." In the same way he took a cup, and when he had given thanks he gave it to them and said, "This is the blood of the covenant, which is poured out for many. Truly I say to you I shall not drink again of the fruit of the vine until that day when I drink it new in the kingdom of God" (Mark 14:22). The meal anticipated Jesus's death.

Though the occasion was most likely a Passover meal, the gospels say nothing about the traditional elements of the Passover ritual, such as the eating of bitter herbs, the recitation of the account of deliverance of the Israelites from Egypt, the Passover lamb. Instead they focus on the blessing of the cup of wine and the blessing of bread (both of which are part of the Passover ritual) and link these directly to Jesus's death. The use of the phrase "blood of the covenant" suggests sacrifice and echoes the ancient Jewish practice of ratifying the covenant with blood. Even Jesus's final words to his disciples at the Passover meal, "I shall not drink again of the fruit of the vine until that day when I drink it new in the kingdom of God" (Mark 14:25), foreshadow his imminent death.

Once supper was ended Jesus and several of his disciples left the city for the

Garden of Gethsemane, a secluded area outside the city walls on the western slope of the Mount of Olives, east of Jerusalem. There he was arrested (seized would be more accurate), abandoned by his disciples, and left to face alone what lay ahead. Here the story picks up pace. In less than twenty-four hours, Jesus would be dead. After being taken captive he was brought before an unusual night sitting of the chief priests and elders of the temple. The charge was that he was a false prophet. Some testified that he had said: "I will destroy this temple that is made with hands, and in three days I will build another" (Mark 14:58). But the witnesses did not agree. Jesus kept silent and made no defense. Then the high priest asked him whether he was the Messiah, to which Jesus gave an enigmatic response: "You have said so" (Matthew 26:64). The authorities took his response to be blasphemous and worthy of death. That would have meant stoning. But the next morning they decided to turn the matter over to the Roman governor, Pontius Pilate.

Early on Friday morning Jesus was brought before Pilate. Pilate had heard about Jesus and did not want to be drawn into the affair. So he sent him to Herod Antipas, the tetrarch, the local ruler of the region. His headquarters were in Galilee, in the north of the country, but like many others he was in Jerusalem for the Passover. Pilate's move seemed shrewd, but Antipas did not want to get involved either, and sent him back to Pilate. So the Jewish leaders laid their accusations before the Roman authority, Pilate, charging that he was a Messianic pretender and insurgent. Pilate was unconvinced. In the end, however, he gave in and ordered Jesus executed. That afternoon at Golgotha (which means place of the skull), a hilltop just outside Jerusalem, Jesus of Nazareth was crucified. It was the eve of Passover, and most of the city was occupied in getting ready for the festival, but a small group of Jesus's followers, including his female disciples, kept vigil at the cross. They took down his body, and with the help of Nicodemus, a prominent and devout member of the sanhedrin, the council of Jewish elders, he was laid in Joseph of Arimathea's tomb hewn out of rock.

Our perspective on Jesus's crucifixion is so shaped by what happened afterward that it is hard to imagine what his death meant to his followers. The gospels give us only a few hints of their mood, but what they report is revealing. Overwhelmed with grief and despair, those who had been at the foot of the cross made their way to their homes. Their hopes had been shattered. Some of the disciples hid "in fear" (John 20:19), wondering whether they would be sought out by the authorities. In the Gospel of Luke, Cleopas, a disciple of Jesus, speaks of Jesus in the past tense. "We *had* hoped that he was the one to redeem Israel" (Luke 24:21). So swiftly had the end come that they were thrown into confusion and disarray. Memories could not console, for everything he had done and said was darkened by the terrible events leading up to his crucifixion and death. The disciples were certainly not of a mind to spread stories about Jesus being raised from the dead.

Yet within a short time it was reported that Jesus had appeared alive to some of his followers, who told others of the astonishing sight they had seen. Although the gospels give us a narrative account of the discovery of the empty tomb, our earliest record of the resurrection comes in a letter by Paul that focuses entirely on the appearances of Jesus to his disciples. In the days immediately after his crucifixion, Jesus presented himself to those who knew him in a way that he was recognized. "For I delivered to you as of first importance," wrote Paul, "what I also received, that Christ . . . appeared to Cephas [Peter], then to the twelve. Then he appeared to more than five hundred brethren at one time, most of whom are still alive, though some have fallen asleep. Then he appeared to James, then to all the apostles. Last of all he appeared also to me" (1 Corinthians 15:3–8).

These words were written down two decades after the death of Jesus, but the formulaic language used by Paul, "I delivered . . . what I also received . . . ," indicates that he is handing on a communal memory that went back to the days immediately after Jesus's death. A personal encounter with the living Christ gave his followers the confidence and the courage to go forth from Jerusalem to proclaim the gospel ("good news"), that the God of Israel had done an extraordinary new thing in Jesus of Nazareth.

2

Ephesus, Rome, and Edessa:
The Spread of Christianity

In his *Annals,* an account of the Roman Empire in the first century, Tacitus the Roman historian had this to say about the early spread of Christianity: "The name Christian came from Christ who had been executed by Pontius Pilate, the governor of Judea during the reign of Tiberius. But in spite of this temporary setback the deadly superstition had broken out afresh, not only in Judea (where the mischief had started) but even in Rome. All degraded and shameful practices collect and flourish in the capital."

I've always been fond of the phrase "temporary setback." For Tacitus, Christ's death marked failure and defeat, and he was surprised that the followers of Jesus were able to overcome their disappointment and disillusionment to come together as an energetic and enterprising community carrying on the mission of their late lamented leader. For Christians, however, Jesus's death was the culmination of his life, the cross a token of glory, and the resurrection the beginning of a new age. The knowledge that he had risen from the dead transformed their lives and changed how they thought about his person.

Tacitus may have gotten his theology wrong, but his historical sense is sound. For in saying that the Christian movement (the "deadly superstition") had "broken out afresh" after a "temporary setback," he recognized that those who carried on Jesus's mission in spite of his death were the same men and women who had followed Jesus during his lifetime. This is a point of capital importance for understanding the origins of Christianity and the Church's nascent self-understanding.

The first Christian community was made up of men and women who had known Jesus and were "witnesses" to his resurrection (cf. Acts 2:32, 5:32). "Witness" did not mean bystander, like someone who happened on an automobile accident or a passing parade. It designated those who had known Jesus, hearkened to his teaching, served as his disciples, and seen him alive after his death. This group, called the apostles (those who are sent), was the foundation upon which the new community was built. Now, however, they knew Jesus in a new way, no longer simply as a teacher and healer who had lived among them, but as the risen Lord held in memory by stories about him and collections of his sayings circulating in their communities and present among them in the blessing of bread and wine.

All of Jesus's disciples were Jews, and they remained faithful to the ancient traditions and customs of their people, observing the Jewish law, which meant circumcising their male children, abstaining from certain foods, and keeping the Sabbath and holy days. They had no thought of breaking with Jewish ways, nor did they have a mandate to invite non-Jews into their community. At one point in the Acts of the Apostles, Christians are identified as the "sect of the Nazarenes," a tiny band of Jews who worshiped the God of their fathers, revered Jesus's teaching, and awaited with eager hope the resurrection of the dead. They did not constitute a new religion but a "way" among the Jewish people (Acts 24:14).

At first the movement spread among Jews in Jerusalem and the surrounding regions, Judea, and Galilee to the north, but soon there were communities in Lydda and Joppa on the coast, to the east in Damascus in modern-day Syria, even north up the coast in Antioch, the home of a thriving Jewish community. Jerusalem, however, remained the center. During Jesus's lifetime Peter had been the acknowledged leader and spokesman for the disciples. He was one of the first to heed Jesus's call, and his name always stands at the head of the list of disciples. After Jesus's death he continued in that role, but he also shared authority with James, identified in the Scriptures as the "brother" of the Lord (Galatians 1:19; Matthew 13:55).

James does not figure in the accounts of Jesus's ministry in the gospels, and his ascendancy after the resurrection is puzzling. But there is no doubt of his standing among the first Christians. When Paul gave a list of those to whom the Lord appeared after his death, the only name he mentioned besides Peter was James (1 Corinthians 15:7). Later, when Paul made his first trip to Jerusalem, it was to confer with James and Peter (who was called Cephas [Galatians 1:18–24]). It seems that along with Jesus's closest disciples, the leadership of the nascent community fell to a respected member of his family.

Paul was a third prominent figure in the first decades. Unlike the other apostles, Paul had not known Jesus as teacher or mentor. He was born early in the first century A.D. among Jews living outside the Land of Israel, in what was called the "diaspora." His home was Tarsus, a Greek-speaking city in the southeastern corner of Asia Minor (modern-day Turkey). Jews had long lived in other parts of the world, most notably in Babylonia (modern Iraq) and Egypt, and in the centuries before the rise of Christianity their numbers had grown in the cities that were now part of the Roman Empire, cities such as Alexandria on the coast of Egypt, Antioch in Syria close to the Mediterranean, Ephesus and Sardis in western Asia Minor, Carthage in North Africa, and of course Rome.

Paul boasts that he was "circumcised on the eighth day, of the people of Israel, of the tribe of Benjamin, a Hebrew born of Hebrews" (Philippians 3:5). His Jewish credentials were impeccable. As a boy he was educated at home by his father, and later he may have studied in Jerusalem. A zealous adherent of Jewish traditions, Paul, or as he was known then, Saul, first comes into view as a persecutor of Jews who had embraced Jesus as the Christ, the Messiah of the Jews. The term *Christ* is the Greek translation of the Hebrew *Mashiach,* the "anointed one."

In A.D. 34–35, five years after the resurrection, when Paul was a relatively young man (though we have no certain information about the date of his birth), his life was turned around through an encounter with the risen Christ on a trip from Jerusalem to Damascus. According to his own account Jesus Christ "called" him to abandon the persecution of Christians and to preach the gospel among the gentiles (Galatians 1:1–17). After his conversion the first thing he did was to "go away into Arabia." Where Arabia was located is uncertain, but it seems to refer to the region around Petra, southeast of the Dead Sea in the southern part of present-day Jordan. Why he went there is also unclear, but Petra was a non-Jewish city and he may have set out to preach the gospel to gentiles. He met with little success and soon returned to Damascus. His sojourn in territories east of Jerusalem, however, is not without significance. For it shows that the Christian mission spread not only westward into the cities of the Roman Empire surrounding the Mediterranean Sea, but eastward into greater Syria and ancient Mesopotamia, the area between the two rivers, the Euphrates and the Tigris, where the population spoke Aramaic (a semitic language spoken in the Middle East), not Greek. Paul's journey east was a portent of the future.

In Damascus Paul seems to have learned a trade, most likely as a "tentmaker" (Acts 18:3). This was a portable skill always in demand that allowed him to support himself on his travels as he went about preaching the gospel and establishing new communities of converts. After three years, however, Paul had to flee to Damascus, and he made his way to Jerusalem. It was a journey with consequences. After his conversion he had assumed the mantle of an apostle, "without conferring with flesh and blood," as he put it (Galatians 1:16), meaning without receiving the blessing of the authorities in Jerusalem, Peter and James. In an extraordinary statement written later he says: "Am I not an apostle? Have I not seen Jesus our Lord?" (1 Corinthians 9:1). Paul's rapid emergence as a commanding presence in the early Christian community changed the dynamic of its leadership and enlarged its vision.

Paul's purpose in going to Jerusalem was twofold. First, from the leaders in Jerusalem he sought legitimation of his mission to the gentiles. Peter had already made some tentative efforts to reach out to non-Jews, but Paul was the first to give the gentiles an equal place in the emerging Church. Second, he wanted to learn at first hand more about the life of the churches in Judea (Galatians 1:22). He also knew very little about Jesus's life and teaching, and people in Jerusalem had known Jesus in the flesh and had put his sayings and parables to memory. Already something like the account of Christ's life that we know from the gospels was circulating orally.

After winning the support of Peter and James, Paul set out to carry the gospel of the living Christ to other parts of the world. He traveled north into Syria and then headed westward to Cilicia, his native country where Tarsus was located, in southeastern Anatolia (Asia Minor), then to the island of Cyprus and on to Greek-speaking cities in central Asia Minor, Iconium, Lystra, and Derbe. He even reached the southern coast of the Black Sea before traveling across the Aegean Sea to Corinth in mainland Greece. This itinerary is based on the Acts of the Apostles, a historical account of Christian beginnings written at the end of the first century, not Paul's own writings, and it may give us a more schematic account of his activities than was actually the case; but from his letters we know that he established churches in western Asia Minor (including Ephesus), Macedonia (the lower Balkans), and Greece (such as in Corinth).

Paul's unbounded confidence, irrepressible energy, directness, and personal charm were irresistible (though not to all), and soon there were tiny Christian communities scattered throughout the region. He was an indefatigable traveler. Given the difficulties and dangers of travel in those days and the extent of territory he covered, his success as a missionary is astonishing. The tiny band that had gathered in Jerusalem only two decades earlier was on the way to becoming a religion not only for Jews but also for gentiles—a form, as it were, of Judaism for the nations.

But there were difficulties. During the first decades most Christians were Jews, and Jewish synagogues in the cities of the Roman Empire were the nurseries in which the seeds of the gospel were first planted. When Paul came to a city he proclaimed the good news of Jesus Christ in the local synagogue. These synagogues often included groups of gentiles, "godfearers" they were called, who had been attracted to the Jewish way of life. In Paul's hands the gospel of Christ became compelling to gentiles as well as to Jews, and the churches he founded were composed of Jews and gentiles—a social and religious fact that would provoke the first great controversy in Christian history. However, it should not be forgotten that Paul remained very much a Jew who believed that becoming a Christian meant being joined to the "commonwealth of Israel" (Ephesians 2:12). Christianity was not a revolt against Israel.

After working as a missionary for a decade and a half, Paul went to Jerusalem with a co-worker, Barnabas, a Jew from the island of Cyprus, and a Greek convert named Titus. Apparently some Jewish Christians, called the "circumcision party," had opposed his mission to the gentiles. At issue was whether gentile converts who joined the Christian "way" must be circumcised and take upon themselves the obligation of observing the Jewish law. Titus had not been circumcised, and Paul held that circumcision was not a condition of membership in the new community. Paul's unwillingness to circumcise Titus provoked a heated dispute. The leaders in Jerusalem argued that the Jewish law was still binding. Jesus had taught that "not an iota, not a dot, will pass from the law" (Matthew 5:18). But Paul retorted that if he were compelled by the authorities in Jerusalem to circumcise gentile converts he would have "run in vain" (Galatians 2:2).

Peter acknowledged that God's Spirit was present among gentile Christians (Acts 15:8). The admission of gentiles was God's choice and not his to reverse. In other words, the decision to reach out to the gentiles had already been made. In truth, he adds, "there is no distinction between us and them" (Acts 15:9). Their hearts have been cleansed "by faith" and the distinction between "clean" and "unclean" no longer held. According to the book of Acts, to resolve the dispute James proposed a concrete solution including four points: (1) Gentile Christians should have nothing to do with the pollution of idols, meaning they cannot eat meat that was offered to idols; (2) they should observe Jewish practices with respect to marriage and sexual relations; (3) they should eat only meat slaughtered according to Jewish law; and (4) they should not ingest animal blood. In short, gentiles should observe the law as it had been imposed on "strangers among the Jews" (Leviticus 17:8, 10–13) in the Torah. His was a solution along Jewish lines.

A letter was prepared setting forth the terms of the agreement and dispatched to the Christians in Antioch and elsewhere. Paul makes no mention of this letter, but he does say that James and Cephas (Peter) and John, the brother of James, another of the "pillars" in Jerusalem, "gave to me and Barnabas the right hand of fellowship, that we should go to the Gentiles and they to the circumcised" (Galatians 2:9). Significantly, the leaders in Jerusalem also requested that Paul and his co-workers take up a collection among the new churches for the poor in Jerusalem, a practice that was well established among Jews. By contributing to the material needs of Jewish Christians in Jerusalem, the new gentile Christians in Asia Minor and Greece bound themselves to their needy brothers and sisters in a close-knit fellowship transcending ethnic boundaries.

The agreement, however, did not hold. Its shortcomings became apparent early in matters of food, or how to deal with table fellowship between Jewish and gentile believers. Could Jewish Christians who observed Jewish law, such as abstention from pork and not mixing meat and milk dishes, eat with gentile Christians? Soon after the meeting in Jerusalem, Peter had journeyed to Antioch, home to a Christian community composed of Jews and gentiles; according to the book of Acts, the followers of Jesus were first called "Christians" in the city of Antioch (Acts 11:26). Initially Peter followed the local custom of eating with gentile Christians. But some Jewish Christians, complaining that they could not abandon the laws on food, sent a delegation to inform James in Jerusalem what was being asked of them. In response James sent emissaries to Antioch with this message: abandoning the food laws was not what he had in mind when he signed off on the agreement with Paul. When they arrived, Peter broke off fellowship with the gentile Christians. Even Barnabas, Paul's companion, went over to the Jerusalem side. Paul realized that if Jerusalem carried the day his mission to the gentiles would be undermined. So he challenged Peter: "If you as a Jew live in gentile, not Jewish fashion, how can you compel the gentiles to live like Jews?" (Galatians 2:11–14). The break had to be clean; there was no way to hold on to some practices of the law and dispense with others. Obedience was owed only to Christ.

It is easy, looking back from the far side of Christian history, to see only Paul's side of this controversy and to slight the arguments of the leaders in Jerusalem. Their insistence on keeping the Jewish law seems alien to the "freedom in Christ" (Galatians 2:4) celebrated by Paul. But the dispute shows that the first Christians were pious and observant Jews, not renegades. For them the law was a good and holy thing, a gift from God that gave grace and beauty to their lives and lifted their hearts to the praise and adoration of God. Their faithfulness to the Jewish law (in matters that still define Jewish observance) was a sign of a living faith. It is tribute to their faithfulness that they were unwilling to jettison the ancient ways of their people without a vigorous defense of their traditions. Even when the matter came to a decision at a meeting in Jerusalem (Acts 15), according to the Acts of the Apostles, they proposed a solution in traditional Jewish terms. In the end, however, signs of the presence of the Spirit among gentile Christians set the Christian "way" on a different course.

Paul then resumed his missionary work in the west. He returned to Corinth, where he had founded a congregation, and from there he sailed to Ephesus on the Aegean coast of Asia Minor, where he remained for several years. In Ephesus he wrote several letters to the church in Corinth. Next he headed to Troas, a city in northwestern Asia Minor where he hoped to meet up with Titus, who had been in Greece overseeing a collection for the poor in Jerusalem. Titus had already left, but Paul caught up with him in Macedonia. He sent Titus on to Corinth and later joined him there. Over the winter (in A.D. 55 or 56), while staying in Corinth, he wrote a letter to Christians in Rome.

The Epistle to the Romans is Paul's weightiest and most influential letter, and it reminds us that he is significant not only for what he did but also for what he wrote. He is sometimes regarded as the first Christian theologian, for he began the daunting task of interpreting the life and teaching of Jesus of Nazareth in the light of his resurrection from the dead, the central conviction of the young community. In Paul's letters we see how after the resurrection Jesus was confessed as the Son of God, and Christian faith came to be centered on his death and resurrection. Jesus was not one thing and Christ another. The Christ of Christian faith was the same person as the Jesus of Nazareth who proclaimed the kingdom of God, prayed to God the Father, healed the sick, and was crucified outside Jerusalem. Paul makes this clear in the opening paragraph of the epistle: Christ was "descended from David according to the flesh" and "designated Son of God in power according to the Spirit of holiness by his resurrection from the dead" (Romans 1:3–4).

Paul taught that all human beings have sinned and turned away from God, but through his death Christ has made peace with God. "God shows his love for us in that while we were yet sinners Christ died for us." For "if we were reconciled to God by the death of his Son . . . how much more shall we be saved by his life" (Romans 5:9–10). One of his favorite expressions is "in Christ." In one of the most arresting passages in the book of Romans, Paul says that those who have been "baptized into Christ Jesus were baptized into his death." If one is buried with him in baptism, Paul writes, so "we believe that we shall also live with him." All who have been united to Christ share in his life.

For Paul to become a Christian meant being joined to a body of persons in intimate union with Christ. His thinking is profoundly corporate. "We are to grow up in every way into him who is the head, into Christ from whom the whole body, joined and knit together by every joint with which it is supplied, when each part is working properly, makes bodily growth and builds itself up in love" (Ephesians 4:16). Reading Paul's letters one understands why as a missionary he was not content to "convert" individuals; he established local churches that were bound together by their fellowship with Christ and with other believers.

At several places Paul speaks of Christ as the "image" or "likeness" of God. He believed that Jesus Christ, though he was born of a woman and lived a fully human life, shared in God's life and was to be venerated as "Lord." In a memorable passage in his letter to the Philippians, Paul quotes an early Christian hymn that praises Christ who, though "in the form of God, did not count equality with God a thing to be grasped." He took on human form and "became obedient to death, even death on a cross." Therefore God highly exalted him and gave him a name above every name, so "that at the name of Jesus every knee should bow . . . and every tongue confess that Jesus Christ is Lord to the glory of God the Father" (Philippians 2:5–11).

This exaltation of Christ to divine status is not unique to Paul. Another early writing that bears his name, though it may not have been written by him, the letter to the Colossians, uses even more elevated language. Christ is called the "image of the invisible God, the first born of all creation, for in him all things were created. . . . He is before all things, and in him all things hold together" (Colossians 1:15–17).

And the Gospel of John, written at the end of the first century, begins: "In the beginning was the Word [Christ], and the Word was with God, and the Word was God" (John 1:1). In these and other passages early Christian writers always present Christ's divine status in relation to God the creator.

In other passages Paul mentions a third divine reality besides God the Father and Christ: the Holy Spirit. His second letter to the Corinthians ends this way: "The grace of the Lord Jesus Christ and the love of God and the fellowship of the Holy Spirit be with you" (2 Corinthians 13:14). "Spirit" is a translation of the Greek term for breath, or wind, and signifies the life-giving power of God. Through Christ, says Paul, believers have been justified and have access to God, and through the Holy Spirit God's love has been poured into their hearts (Romans 5:1–5).

In these early Christian writings (which became part of the New Testament) one can discern the lineaments of the distinctively Christian teaching, that the one God has a mysterious triune, or threefold, nature. It took centuries for Christian thinkers to work out the implications of such terms as "Father," "Son," and "Holy Spirit," as we shall see in later chapters. Here I wish only to note that trinitarian language is found in the earliest Christian documents.

These ruminations on Paul's thinking were prompted by his letter to the Romans. Besides its rich theology, the letter to the Romans is significant for another reason. Unlike the churches his other letters were addressed to, in Ephesus, Corinth, Thessalonica, and others, Paul had never visited Rome. The church there, as in Antioch in Syria, was founded by someone else. This letter is evidence that there were other emissaries of the gospel at work in the cities of the Roman Empire besides Paul. The impression one receives from the New Testament (and from the maps of Paul's missionary journeys that are sometimes included in Bibles) is that he and his co-workers were the principal missionaries in the early decades. But the existence of a church in Rome shows that others had gotten there before him, and it is certain that Christian communities had been established in other metropolitan areas. At the end of the letter Paul wrote that he not only wanted to visit the Christians in Rome, he also hoped to journey farther westward, even to Spain (Romans 15:24). But first he had to return to Jerusalem with the "collection" for the poor that he and his co-workers had been gathering from the churches he had founded.

Because of his powerful personality, and the historical information contained in Paul's letters, it is tempting to follow out the rest of his story. If we wish to keep before us the larger picture, however, we cannot allow the charisma and glamour of Paul's life to overshadow what was happening elsewhere.

It is very likely that the Christian gospel reached Alexandria on the coast of Egypt in the first century. This glittering cosmopolitan city was the home of a large Greek-speaking Jewish community, and it was easily accessible by sea from Palestine. Paul's co-worker Apollos was a native of Alexandria, and early Christian tradition venerates the evangelist Mark as the founder of Christianity in Egypt. There is no hard evidence from the first century of a Christian community there, but archaeologists have found fragments of papyri in Egypt with verses from the Gospel of John dating to the early second century. By the middle of the second century Christianity was well established in Egypt, and Alexandria was to become one of the premier Christian cities, along with Antioch and Rome.

The Christian mission also made converts east of Jerusalem. Before Paul's conversion a Christian community had been established in Damascus, a Greek-speaking city located in the midst of a large geographical area in which the populace spoke Aramaic. One of the principal cities in the region was Edessa (modern-day Sanliurfa in eastern Turkey), some 150 miles northeast of Antioch on the Silk Road leading to India and China. The city was pleasantly situated among a ring of hills and surrounded by a fertile plain at the head of the crescent formed by the Tigris and Euphrates Rivers and linked to the Mediterranean by a string of towns. Edessa was the home of a flourishing Jewish community, and the city had been drawn into Rome's orbit during the century before the birth of Christ.

The gospel may have been carried there by Jewish merchants from Antioch. But the Christians of Edessa had a much more colorful tale of how Christian faith came to their city. According to a fascinating legend recorded in the first church history, written by Eusebius of Caesarea in the early fourth century, it is said that the king of Edessa, Abgar, "monarch of the peoples of Mesopotamia," was dying from a terrible disease that baffled his physicians. Hearing about a Jewish prophet who had the power to heal, he sent a letter requesting Jesus to come to Edessa. According to the legend, Jesus responded with a personal letter and promised to send one of his disciples to Abgar. In his letter Jesus wrote: "As to your request that I should come to you, I must complete all that I was sent to do here, and on completing it must at once be taken up to the One who sent me. When I have been taken up I will send you one of my disciples to cure your disorder and bring life to you and those with you."

After Jesus was "taken up," or ascended into heaven (Acts 1), so goes the story, the apostle Thomas sent Thaddeus, another apostle (cf. Matthew 10:3 and Mark 3:18) to Edessa. Thaddeus healed many people in the city and the surrounding region, and the king sent for him. When Thaddeus appeared before him, the king saw a marvelous vision on Thaddeus's face, and he "bowed low before the apostle." Abgar asked whether he is a disciple of Jesus, and Thaddeus said that if you believe in him he will cure you. Abgar said: "I too have believed in Him and in his Father," and Thaddeus laid his "hand on him in His name." At once Abgar was cured of the disease. Then Thaddeus asked Abgar to call together the people so that he could preach to them "and sow the word of life." In gratitude Abgar offered Thaddeus gold and silver, but he refused, saying: "If we have left our own property behind, how can we accept that of other people?"

The story is legendary, but when read in light of other evidence it suggests that

Christianity came early to the region. It is also very likely that early in the second century there were Aramaic-speaking Christians farther east in Adiabene (modern Arbil) in northern Iraq. In the early years as Christianity was moving westward into the cities in the Roman Empire it also spread eastward. This historical development has great significance, as we shall see in later chapters. The gospel was brought to Central Asia and to China by Syriac-speaking missionaries. There were other linguistic worlds, those of the Copts up the Nile River in Egypt, the Nubians (of present-day Sudan), the Ethiopians farther south, the Armenians east of Asia Minor, and the Georgians between the Black and Caspian Seas, but the three most important Christian languages in the early centuries were Latin in Italy, North Africa, Spain, and western Europe, Greek (and later Slavic) in the eastern Mediterranean and eastern Europe, and Syriac in the Middle East. Already in the early centuries Christianity had the makings of a global religion.

The first Christian leaders in Jerusalem were Jews. Even though they confessed that Jesus of Nazareth was the Messiah of the Jews, they had not given up their Jewish ways, and they shared the fate of their people. Jerusalem had been conquered by the Romans in 63 B.C., and over the course of the next hundred years the Jews living in Palestine were ruled by procurators (governors) from Rome or by kings appointed by the Romans, most famously Herod the Great. The Jews, however, lived with the memory of the time when they had their own kings and Jerusalem was the capital of a Jewish kingdom. During Jesus's lifetime and in the decades after his death, organized bands of Jews had provoked and challenged Roman authority. On occasion the yearning to cast off Roman hegemony broke into open rebellion. By the sixties these insurrections had become bolder and more persistent, and Jews were able to overpower Roman garrisons in certain towns, such as Jericho in the Jordan Valley and Masada on the Dead Sea. In 66 the Jews even minted their own coins with the inscription ISRAEL'S SHEKEL YEAR I and HOLY JERUSALEM, marking the years from the "liberation of Zion" [Jerusalem].

In response to Jewish resistance, Emperor Nero sent one of his ablest generals, Vespasian, to crush the revolt. Given command of three legions, about forty thousand men in all, in the spring of 67 he advanced down the Mediterranean coast from Antioch to Palestine, subduing Jewish towns in the north of the country and the area around Jerusalem. But Nero committed suicide in June 67. At first Vespasian, the heir apparent, bided his time as other generals swore allegiance to him. Then he returned to Rome to be acclaimed emperor. His son Titus was given charge of the campaign against the Jews.

The siege of Jerusalem took place in the spring of A.D. 70. Although Jewish leaders were determined to fight to the end, they were divided among themselves, weakening their defense. Nevertheless they heroically withstood the Roman siege engines for several months. In August, however, Roman legions broke through the city walls, destroyed the Antonio fortress, a military barracks in the city, and on

August 10 (9 Ab by Jewish reckoning) set the torch to the most hallowed place in the city, the Jewish temple. By early September Jerusalem lay in ruins.

Vespasian issued coins to commemorate the triumph with the inscriptions IUDAEA CAPTA (Judea captured) and DEVICTA IUDAEA (Judea conquered). Sometime after A.D. 81, a large triumphal arch was constructed in Rome to commemorate the victory. One of the friezes depicts the large solid gold seven-branched menorah (lampstand) held aloft on two horizontal staffs borne by Roman soldiers as it is being carried out of the temple. This arch is still standing, and even today the melancholy scene of Jewish defeat and humiliation stirs visitors who pause to look up at it in the Forum in Rome.

The fall of the city of Jerusalem and the destruction of the temple changed forever the life and institutions of the Jewish people. Without the central sanctuary of Jewish religion there could be no priesthood and no sacrifices, pious Jews could no long travel to Jerusalem to celebrate the annual religious festivals, or offer the first fruits of grain and produce to God, and the high priest could no longer enter the Holy of Holies on the Day of Atonement. The Romans made Jerusalem off limits to the Jews, and those who did make their way to the city came no longer to pray in the temple but to mourn the city's destruction and weep over its ruins. In the generations and centuries that followed, Jewish leaders gradually adapted their ancient traditions to the new facts of Jewish life. The result was a profound transformation that led to the religion we know today, Judaism centered on the synagogue whose life is ordered by the Talmud, that enduring collection of Jewish law gathered in the sixth and seventh centuries A.D.

For the Christians in Jerusalem the fall of the city and the destruction of the temple were no less momentous. Some fled the city and settled in a town called Pella east of the Jordan. But not all. A nucleus remained in the city and, according to one early source, Christian life in Jerusalem continued without interruption. One writer in the second century even provided a list of bishops, Christian leaders in Jerusalem, up to the year 135, all of whom were Jewish. The list may be fictitious, but it does suggest that the Christian community in Jerusalem survived through the turbulent years following the Roman conquest.

In the wake of the Roman conquest the early structure of authority in Jerusalem gave way to new forms of leadership in the churches founded by the first generation of missionaries. Jerusalem came to be celebrated more in memory than in fact; in the central narrative of Christianity's history during the first two centuries, Jerusalem was a minor player. Only in the fourth century, with the building of the Church of the Anastasis (Church of the Resurrection, today known as the Church of the Holy Sepulcher) over the tomb of Christ and the mounting stream of pilgrims who came to worship at the holy places, would Jerusalem assume its historic place as the "holy city" of Christians.

3

The Making of a Christian Community

Early in the second century, Ignatius, bishop of Antioch, a metropolis in ancient Syria (southeastern Asia Minor) near the Mediterranean coast, was arrested during a persecution of Christians in the city. He was sent to Rome under guard of a cohort of ten soldiers. Along the way his keepers picked up other prisoners to be taken in chains to the capital. From Antioch they sailed to the southwestern coast of Asia Minor, where they planned to make their way to Ephesus, but instead they headed northeast to Philadelphia. While in Philadelphia, Ignatius was allowed to meet with a group of Christians in the city. Then the company of prisoners journeyed west to Smyrna (modern Izmir), on the Aegean coast, where Polycarp was bishop. Decades later as a very old man Polycarp would be martyred there.

In Smyrna, Ignatius received visitors from Christian communities in Ephesus, Magnesia, and Tralles, Greek-speaking cities in the western part of the peninsula. He also wrote a letter to the church in Rome to inform the Christians there that he was being taken to the capital under guard. Fearing that some might intervene on his behalf to have him freed, he urged them to let things run their course. "Grant me nothing more," he wrote, "than to be poured out as a libation to God while an altar is at hand."

Then the company traveled to Troas, near the Hellespont, where the waters of the Sea of Marmara flow into the Aegean. While in Troas he learned that the persecution in Antioch had ceased and "peace" was restored, but that did not win his release. Still, he was able to write letters to the churches in the cities he had just visited, to Philadelphia and Smyrna and also to his fellow bishop Polycarp. Next the tiny group made its way to Neapolis, the seaport of Philippi in Macedonia at the head of the Aegean Sea, where Ignatius again met with members of the Christian community. Finally the band of soldiers and prisoners headed westward via the

Egnatian Way to Dyrrhachium on the Adriatic coast (in modern-day Albania) to board a ship sailing to the eastern coast of Italy. From there they made their way overland to Rome.

This was no ordinary journey of no ordinary man. Even though Ignatius was shackled to one of his guards, his slow peregrination to Rome was a triumphal procession played out before Christians in Asia Minor and Greece. He was to become one of the most celebrated martyrs in the Church's early history. After the paucity of information about Christian leaders during the first generations (save Paul), Ignatius is the first major figure to come clearly into view. His letters reveal a man whose mind and heart were passionately devoted to Christ. His intense and fervid piety, his affecting witness, his florid images, and the evocative language of his prose have endeared him to later generations.

The power of his person is evident in his description of the journey. "I am fighting wild beasts from Syria to Rome, by land and sea, by night and day, bound to ten leopards. . . . By their mistreatment I become more of a disciple though 'not for that reason am I justified' (1 Corinthians 4:4). May I benefit from the wild beasts prepared for me, and I hope they will make short work of me. I shall even entice them to eat me up at once and not hold off . . . ; and if they are reluctant, I shall force them. Indulge me; I know what is to my good; now I begin to be a disciple. Let nothing of things visible and invisible stand in the way of my reaching Christ. Let fire and cross, packs of wild beasts, the wrenching of bones, the mangling of limbs, the grinding of my whole body, cruel punishments of the devil on me—my only wish is to attain Jesus Christ." Someone who wrote this way is not easily forgotten.

Ignatius's vivid and flamboyant imagination was displayed in very public letters he had every reason to believe would be read aloud in the communities that received them and even preserved to be copied and read by others after his death. They display a studied awareness that the journey to his death offered an unparalleled opportunity to instruct and edify the churches. Again and again he urges his fellow Christians to look below the surface—someone in chains being led to almost certain death—to the deeper meaning of his trial. By his sufferings he wished to bear witness to the suffering of Christ, for he yearned "to die in union with Christ's passion."

His letters are valuable for another reason. They allow us a rare first-hand glimpse of the inner life of the Christian community as it was taking form at the beginning of the second century. The churches in Asia Minor were not isolated circles of believers existing independently of one another; they understood themselves to be part of a larger body bound together in a mysterious spiritual unity. Ignatius is the first to use the term "catholic church." This expression would grow in meaning as the centuries passed, but already it carried some of its later overtones, namely that the churches formed an organic fellowship belonging to a single and undivided communion united to Christ. The sign of this unity was the person of the bishop. As Ignatius puts it in one of his letters: "Wherever the bishop is, there one finds the fellowship; just as wherever Jesus Christ is there is the catholic Church."

Christianity came into the world as a community, not a casual association of individual believers. How the internal life of the churches would be ordered was a matter of more than pragmatic arrangement. I deliberately use the word "ordered" rather than "organized," because in Christianity authority and governance are never simply a matter of function. Order implies a point of reference beyond itself. For the early Christians leadership was an affair not only of how things work or what is most efficient, but of the faithful transmission of the teaching of the apostles. There was a spiritual affinity between oversight and teaching, between leadership and divine authority, as the letter to the Hebrews has it: "Keep in mind those who have been placed over you who *spoke* to you the word of God" (Hebrews 13:7). The letters of Ignatius provide an occasion to look at the early stages of what would become a distinctive and enduring Christian "institution," the office of the bishop. In the early history of Christianity the bishops are often the central players.

In the first generation leadership rested on those who had been disciples of Christ during his lifetime and were witnesses of his resurrection. Authority was yoked to memory. The task of the first leaders was to preserve and transmit the teachings received from Jesus and the traditions about Jesus. In the first decades the two figures to whom the churches looked were Peter, the leader of the disciples during Jesus's lifetime, and James, the "brother" of Jesus. Even as charismatic and strong-willed a person as Paul was deferential to these "pillars" (Galatians 2:9) in Jerusalem. After his conversion he made a special trip to the holy city to ensure that his mission to the gentiles had the blessing of Peter and James.

New communities were, however, established not only in Palestine but also in Syria, in Asia Minor, in Greece, and even as far distant as Rome in Italy. The founders of these churches did not reside in their congregations. Paul was always on the move and kept in touch by letter, visiting the churches he founded only intermittently. He was not a resident pastor. In his absence (and after his death) many questions arose: Who would be responsible for handing on the traditions about Jesus? Who would oversee the affairs of the church? Who would lead the congregation in prayer and preside at the communal meal? Who would baptize converts? Who would deal with matters of discipline? In Corinth, a congregation Paul had founded, the community became divided as different persons vied for authority. Some said, "I belong to Apollos," and others, "I belong to Paul" (1 Corinthians 1:11–17).

Eventually the first missionaries had to allow the young communities to fend for themselves, and the Acts of the Apostles, written toward the end of the first century, sheds some light on the transition from the first generation to the next. According to Acts, in his final visit to the church in Ephesus, Paul called together the "elders [*presbyteroi*] of the church" to bid them farewell and to ready them for the tasks that lay ahead. He urged them to continue the work he had begun: "Take heed to yourself and to all the flock in which the Holy Spirit has made you overseers [*episcopoi*] to care for the church of God which he obtained with the blood of his own Son" (Acts 20:28).

Note that the terms "elder" (*presbyter*) and "overseer" (*episcopos*) are used interchangeably. In time the term *episcopos* would become the Greek word for "bishop," and *presbyter* would become "priest," but at this stage the two terms were used without distinction for members of a council of elders. The invocation of the Holy Spirit implies not only that there was a process of selection but also a ritual for setting the elders apart for their distinctive service. Unlike ancient Israel, Christianity had no hereditary priesthood passed on in certain families. Among the Jews, only those belonging to the tribe of Levi could serve as priests in the temple in Jerusalem. In the Church the ministers had to be chosen from mature and able members of the congregation and invested with authority. From letters written toward the end of the first century we know that this took place through the "laying on of hands" (1 Timothy 4:14).

By the beginning of the second century, in some regions the system of elders had begun to give way to a single office, that of the bishop, who acted in concert with a council of presbyters. Ignatius is an early witness to what is called the *monoepiscopos,* one bishop as head of the local church. But it took some time for this way of ordering the Church's life to establish itself as the norm across the Christian world. In other regions, particularly in the larger cities, there was a constellation of small groups each with its own elders. In the course of the second century, however, the principle of one bishop for a city gradually took hold, and by the end of the century it had become almost universal.

The reasons were several. The single bishop was the sign of the unity of the Church. As Ignatius put it, there is one Eucharist, one altar, one cup, one Christ, and one bishop. There could be no liturgical celebration, no communal action, no public teaching except in fellowship with the bishop. Unlike the pagan priest whose function was chiefly ritualistic, the bishop was overseer of the community (hence the title *episcopos*) and teacher, as well as priest. He was responsible for the care of orphans, widows, and the poor. The bishop kept in touch with other bishops through correspondence, and later, as church-wide disputes arose, bishops came together (in what came to be called a synod or council) to resolve conflicts. Strong leadership was indispensable for unity and stability, even for survival. As the Church grew in numbers and influence the bishop became the public face of the Christian community. In the office of bishop we can discern the beginning of a kind of constitution for the

Church as a distinct society with its own form of governance. As the churches began to lay down rules on matters such as admission, liturgical practices, and discipline, the bishop was charged with seeing that rules that governed the Church's life were carried out. Because the office conferred a status that transcended his person and abilities, the love and affection of the faithful came to rest on the figure of the bishop.

Of course the bishop was assisted by the presbyters and deacons. In a rhetorical flourish Ignatius writes: "Let the bishop preside in God's place, and the presbyters take the place of the apostolic council, and let the deacons (my special favorites) be entrusted with the ministry of Jesus Christ." Over time the offices of presbyter and deacon were defined more precisely. In the absence of the bishop, presbyters consecrated the Eucharist, preached, and baptized; the deacons served at the altar, read the gospel in worship, and cared for poor and needy, the aged and infirm, and widows. By the third century other minor "offices" had come into being, lector (reader in the liturgy), subdeacon, acolyte (servers at the altar), exorcist, doorkeeper, but there was a distinct hierarchy and the bishop was the acknowledged head of the community. Order requires hierarchy, a truth that Shakespeare put well in *Troilus and Cressida:* "Take degree away, untune that string, and hark! What discord follows."

A principal responsibility of the bishop was to "offer the gifts"—that is, to preside at the celebration of Eucharist. A second was to receive new members into the community through baptism. It is not "permissible," said Ignatius, "either to baptize or celebrate the 'love feast' apart from the bishop."

The word "baptism" comes from a Greek term meaning to immerse in water, and in Christianity baptism designates a solemn washing with water. Ritual cleansings with water were practiced in Judaism, such as washing one's hands before eating, the high priest bathing his body before entering the Holy of Holies, women bathing after menstruation. But Christian baptism has its origin in the practice of John the Baptist, who immersed in water those who responded to his proclamation of the kingdom of God. Jesus was also baptized by John, and the gospels give his baptism a prominent place in his life. They do not, however, tell us why Jesus was baptized, and this caused some puzzlement in the early Church. In the account in the Gospel of Matthew, for example, John at first refuses to baptize Jesus and only relents after Jesus says that it was necessary "to fulfill all righteousness," apparently meaning that his baptism is part of God's plan. Whatever the reason, Jesus's baptism in the Jordan River became the model for Christian baptism. In the words of Ignatius, "Christ submitted to baptism so that by his passion he might sanctify the water."

Christian baptism differed from traditional ritual washings in Judaism in two ways. First, one did not perform it on oneself; baptism was administered by someone else. Second, it was done only once, although in the third century there was a dispute over whether someone who had been baptized in a schismatic group should be rebaptized on being received into the catholic Church. Baptism was the ritual by which one entered the Church, the way "we dedicated ourselves to God when we were made new through Christ," as one early writer put it.

We cannot be certain what words were used for the rite of baptism in the early decades. It is possible that some baptized "in the name of the Lord Jesus," but the formula that became standard was this: "I baptize you in the name of the Father and of the Son and of the Holy Spirit." As for the method, baptism was always by full immersion in water, not sprinkling or pouring. Later, when Christians began building receptacles to hold the baptismal water they constructed good-sized pools with steps on either end so one could go down into the water at one end and exit on the other.

The person to be baptized went down into the water unclothed and, while in the water, was asked three questions. "Do you believe in God the Father Almighty?" "Do you believe in Christ Jesus the Son of God?" "Do you believe in the Holy Spirit and the holy Church?" After each question, he or she answered, "I believe," and was fully immersed. After coming up from the water those who had just been baptized were anointed with oil and the bishop laid hands on them as he prayed: "Lord God, you have made them worthy to deserve the remission of sins through the washing of regeneration; make them worthy to be filled with the Holy Spirit, send your grace upon them that they may serve you in accordance with your will; for to you is glory, to the Father and the Son with the Holy Spirit in the holy Church both now and to the ages of ages. Amen." Baptism was a rebirth, the beginning of a new life.

Christians also celebrated a communal meal called the Eucharist or the Sacrifice. The Eucharist had its origins in the Last Supper, the meal that Jesus celebrated with his closest disciples the night before he died. In the early decades it took the form of a meal with eating and drinking and concluded with the blessing of bread and wine. By the end of the first century a ritual meal had begun to be celebrated separately, though at one place Ignatius refers to the "love feast," by which he apparently meant a meal followed by the blessing of the bread and the cup.

The words spoken over the bread and wine were taken from the accounts of the Last Supper in the gospels. The precise form varied but it was similar to what Paul handed on in his first letter to the Corinthians. "For I received from the Lord what I also delivered to you, that the Lord Jesus on the night when he was betrayed took bread, and when he had given thanks, he broke it, and said, 'This is my body which is for you. Do this in remembrance of me.' In the same way also the cup, after supper, saying, 'This cup is the new covenant in my blood. Do this, as often as you drink it, in remembrance of me.' For as often as you eat this bread and drink the cup, you proclaim the Lord's death until he comes" (1 Corinthians 11:23–27).

By the second century the blessing of bread and wine had become part of a service that included readings from the Scriptures interspersed with psalms or canticles. The readings were followed by a homily or sermon in which the bishop explained and interpreted what had been read and applied it to the lives of the faithful. After the exposition of the reading, the congregation offered prayers for their needs and the needs of others and greeted each other with a kiss.

Then bread and wine and water were brought forth. We are not certain as to why water was included, but the practice of adding water to the wine was widespread. In the third century a Christian bishop insisted that the practice went back to the apostles. The bishop took the bread and wine mixed with water and offered thanksgiving "to the Father of the universe through the name of the Son and of the Holy Spirit."

In Greek the term for "thanksgiving" is *eucharistia,* hence the popularity of the word Eucharist for the principal service of Christian worship. In the early years the prayer over the gifts was extempore, but over time it was written down and took a fixed form. *The Apostolic Tradition,* an early "church order"—a collection of directives on liturgy and administration—gives us the words of a prayer used most likely in Rome in the third century.

> We give thanks to you God, through your beloved child Jesus Christ, whom in the last times, you sent to us as savior and redeemer and angel of your will, who is your inseparable Word through whom you made all things and who was well pleasing to you. When he was handed over to voluntary suffering, in order to dissolve death and break the chains of the devil . . . he took bread and giving thanks to you he said; take, eat, this is my body which will be broken for you. Likewise with the cup saying: this is my blood which is poured out for you. Whenever you do this, you make me present among you. Remembering therefore his death and resurrection, we offer you this bread and cup, giving thanks to you because you have held us worthy to stand before you and minister to you as priest. . . .

As this prayer makes clear, the Eucharist was understood to be an offering, and what was offered were not simply words of thanksgiving and praise but the consecrated bread and cup. Already in the New Testament, Saint Paul drew an analogy between the bread and cup of the Lord's Supper and the sacrifices in the Jewish temple and pagan sacrifices (1 Corinthians 10:14–22). Ignatius calls the table on which the bread and wine were offered an "altar," a term that implies sacrifice. Two generations later, in commenting on a passage from the prophet Malachi—"In every place incense shall be offered to my name and a pure sacrifice (Malachi 1:11)"—Justin Martyr, an early Christian philosopher, said that here the term "sacrifice" refers to "the sacrifices which are offered to God by us gentiles, that is the bread of the Eucharist and likewise the cup of the Eucharist." Accordingly "sacrifice" or "the sacrifice" was used to designate the Eucharist.

In the ancient world religious worship without sacrifice was inconceivable, and the most esteemed form of sacrifice was the roasting and eating of an animal. This was as true of the Jews as of the Greeks or the Romans. The Scriptures are filled with sacrificial language, and the book of Hebrews presents the death of Christ as a sacrifice. "[Christ] entered once for all into the Holy place, taking not the blood of goats and calves but his own blood, thus securing an eternal redemption" (Hebrews 9:12). When Christ blessed the cup he spoke of the "blood of the covenant" (Mark 14:24), and Paul called the cup "communion with the blood of Christ" (1 Corinthians 10:16), implying sacrifice.

The term "sacrifice" comes from the Latin, *sacrificium,* "to make something holy," that is, to set it apart from common usage and offer it to God. Many things could be offered—grain, wine, honey, flowers, cheese, fruit, milk—but the highest form of sacrifice was the killing and roasting of an animal. In contrast to grain or wine, an animal was a living thing and its blood carried the principle of life. In the sacrifice, after the animal was roasted, its vital parts—those that gave life, the heart, liver, kidneys—were offered to the gods, and the other parts were consumed by the people.

The Christian sacrifice differed, however, from pagan sacrifices in one very significant way. It did not involve the actual killing of an animal. In the language of the ancient Christian liturgies, it was an "unbloody sacrifice," meaning no blood was shed. But it was a sacrifice nonetheless, because it celebrated Christ's death, in which blood was shed. Hence Christians believed that in eating the consecrated bread and wine they were eating the "flesh and blood" of Christ. "The Eucharist is the flesh of our savior Jesus Christ who suffered for us," wrote Ignatius. In the blessing of bread and wine the Church offered to God what it had first received, the Christ who had come into the world to offer his life for sin. Through eating and drinking the body and blood of Christ, Christians believed they had communion with the living Christ.

The early Church was a community with a distinct anatomy; it was not simply an aggregate of individuals who believed the same things. Of course Christianity was also defined by its beliefs. Outside observers knew that a unique feature of the Church was, as a Roman governor put it at the beginning of the second century, that Christians worshiped Christ—a human being—as "god." But to be baptized meant becoming part of a society within society with its own rituals and rules, governance and discipline. The office of the bishop, baptism, and the Eucharist gave shape to the community. There would be other things, such as creeds, fixed formulations of Christian belief, and a collection of authoritative writings, a Christian sacred Scripture. But I single out these three at the beginning to stress that what set Christianity apart was not simply its beliefs but also the architecture of its communal life. At this stage the Church as a corporate body was relatively invisible to the larger society, but within its life it moved to the rhythms of a well-ordered and purposeful fellowship, a Christian "commonwealth," as one early writer put it. This hardly meant the churches were free of controversy. Now it is time to turn from the somewhat benign portrait of Christian life sketched in this chapter to several of the disputes that divided Christians in the second century.

4

Divisions Within

It is tempting to romanticize the early Church and imagine a golden age of peace and harmony. In truth there was never a time, even in the first decades, that Christians had no differences. Because Christian faith holds that certain things are true (there is one God, creator of all that exists), controversy over what is to be believed as well as how the faith was to be practiced was present from the beginning. Sharp divisions arose during the first decades over whether the Jewish law should be observed by non-Jewish converts. At the end of the first century this debate was still alive in Antioch, where Ignatius was bishop. Others had begun to ask whether Christ was fully human or only "seemed" to have a human body. They were called "docetists," from the Greek word for "seem," and held that Christ was a bodiless divine spirit who only appeared to be a human being. In this view he did not actually suffer and die. Ignatius challenged the docetists with the argument that if Christ did not truly suffer and die, there was no resurrection and hence no hope.

These were not just local disputes. The place of the Jewish law in Christian life was at issue in those communities where Jews had become Christians and also where Christians lived alongside Jews—which was the case in many cities. As late as the fourth century, particularly in greater Syria, some Christians attended the synagogue on festival days and were attracted to Jewish rites. Docetic ideas sprang up in different forms across the Christian world in the early centuries.

But there were other controversies, and none more far-reaching and divisive than fixing the date on which the death and resurrection of Christ would be celebrated. Calendar is a defining mark of a religious community. Think of the place of the Sabbath in Jewish life, the uniqueness of Sunday in historic Christian countries, or the monthlong fast of Ramadan among Muslims. To be a Jew is not simply to believe certain things, for example that there is one God, it is to *do* certain things, such as to keep the Sabbath and celebrate the annual cycle of festivals, the New Year

(Rosh Hashanah) and the Day of Atonement (Yom Kippur) in fall and Passover (Pesach) in spring.

When Christianity came on the scene the Jewish calendar had been in place for centuries, and even those who were not Jews knew when the holy days came round. Jews would close their shops, buy special foods, and gather in the synagogues and homes for communal and family celebrations. Christians had no religious calendar. They did, however, gather on Sunday, the first day of the week, "to break bread" (Acts 20:7), and already in the book of Revelation Sunday was called the Lord's Day (Revelation 1:10). Sunday, wrote Ignatius, was the day on which "our Life" (that is, Christ) "arose." It had replaced Saturday, the Jewish Sabbath, as the Christian holy day, and even outsiders observed that Christians gathered on a fixed day for worship.

By the second century Christians had begun to celebrate an annual festival on a day in the spring at the time of the Jewish Passover. Unlike the later Christian festival of Easter, the ancient celebration marked not simply the resurrection of Christ from the dead; it was a solemn observance of Christ's passion (suffering), death, and resurrection—a kind of Good Friday and Easter combined—called the Pasch, from Pascha, the Greek transliteration of the Hebrew term for Passover, *pesach*. The Paschal celebration, which included the reading of the account of the first Passover in Exodus 12, began in the evening and ended early the next morning with the offering of the Eucharist.

But there was no agreement as to when the fast that preceded the celebration should end. Some thought it should end on the 14th of the month of Nisan, the date of the Passover in the Jewish calendar; others thought the celebration should fall on a Sunday, the day of Christ's resurrection. The churches in Asia Minor and some parts of Syria reasoned that Christ, the true paschal lamb, had died at the beginning of Passover. Accordingly they ended the fast on the 14th of Nisan, whatever the day of the week, and celebrated the Eucharist early the next morning when it was still night. They came to be called Quartodecimans, from the Latin for 14th day (*quarta decima*) and claimed that their practice went back to the apostle John. Other parts of the Christian world, such as Rome, Alexandria, and Jerusalem, held that the Christian festival should be observed on the following Sunday, that is, on the Lord's Day that came immediately after Passover.

This difference in regional customs, some churches celebrating the Pasch on 14 Nisan, others the Sunday following, led to a spirited dispute among bishops from different parts of the Christian world. According to the ancient sources, at first churches "remained in communion with one another." The bishop of Rome in the mid second century, Anicetus (d. 166), even invited Polycarp, whose church in Smyrna followed the Asian custom of observing the Pasch on 14 Nisan, to celebrate the Eucharist in Rome. But two decades later, another bishop of Rome, Victor (d. 198), thought that the churches in Asia Minor were out of step with the rest of the Christian world and set out to persuade them to conform to the Roman practice (and also the custom in Jerusalem). He called together a gathering of bishops in Rome and urged his fellow bishops elsewhere, such as in Gaul, to oppose the Quartodecimans. Some who followed the Roman practice considered Victor headstrong and pleaded with him not to divide the churches over the issue. The ancient custom of the churches of Asia Minor should be respected.

The matter was not resolved at the time, but as the decades passed the Quartodeciman practice declined, and at the Council of Nicaea in 325, the first churchwide council (ecclesiastical convention) to draw bishops from most parts of the Christian world, it was decided that the Pasch should be celebrated on the Sunday after the first new moon after the vernal equinox. Special calendrical tables were constructed to compute the date of the new moon (14 Nisan by Jewish reckoning), and with minor modifications that custom is followed to this day.

The most obvious reason for adopting the practice of Rome and Alexandria was that Sunday was the Lord's Day, the day of resurrection, and hence the Christian holy day. The Asian practice seemed to make the Church dependent on the Jewish community for computing the date of its most solemn annual celebration. By the second century the Church wished to establish its collective identity independent of the Jews. Christians were no longer another "way" under the umbrella of Judaism. The churches had begun to see themselves as a corporate body whose way of life had its own distinctive pulse independent of the larger society. The Quartodeciman controversy marks an important stage in Christian history, the beginning of a Christian liturgical calendar—Sunday as the Christian holy day and the Pasch (preceded by a period of fasting) as the annual celebration of Christ's death and resurrection. In time, as other festivals and holy days were added, such as the Feast of the Nativity (Christmas) and days to commemorate the death of martyrs and saints, the Christian calendar would shape the civic as well as the religious life of a new civilization.

As the controversy over the dating of the Pasch revealed, there was no central authority within Christianity in the second century. The Church was composed of a constellation of local communities spanning the Mediterranean Sea and the Middle East. They had a strong sense of unity among themselves, but they were only loosely organized. This unity was to be severely tested by another controversy in the second century, the dispute over *gnosis*. Gnosis is the Greek word for knowledge, and gnosticism is a term coined by modern scholars to designate an amorphous grouping of schools of thought within Christianity (or on the edge of Christianity) led by gifted and controversial teachers with a distinctive understanding of Christian revelation.

The beginnings of gnosticism are obscure, but its spiritual home was Alexandria, the cosmopolitan Greek-speaking city in Egypt on the Mediterranean coast where a school of sacred learning had been established in the second century. The city attracted educated men and women eager to find a higher understanding of Christian belief. It must be remembered that many aspects of Christian teaching were as yet undefined—how to understand the person of Christ, for example, or how the world came to be. There was much room for debate about the interpretation of the gospels and the letters of Paul and the relation between the Jewish Scriptures, what became the Christian Old Testament, and the new revelation in Christ.

Among those who came to Alexandria was a young man named Valentinus from a city in the Nile Delta. After spending some time in the city he moved to Rome, which had begun to attract Christian teachers from around the world. Justin Martyr, a Christian philosopher from Palestine, arrived in Rome about the same time, as did Marcion, a shipbuilder from Asia Minor, who repudiated the Christian use of the Jewish Scriptures. Valentinus became active in the intellectual life of the church in Rome and swiftly established himself as a respected teacher. He remained in Rome for fifteen years, until the episcopacy of bishop Anicetus (155–166), then moved on to Cyprus, where he died sometime after A.D. 160.

Why he left for Cyprus is unknown, but it is likely that as his teaching became better known he met with opposition from Christian teachers in the city. Only fragments of his writings remain. The loss is unfortunate because he was a skilled writer, the author of poems and hymns as well as other religious writings, and even his critics called him brilliant. He attracted disciples, and from their writings we have a good idea of the teachings of the Valentinian school. What they considered central can be seen in the Gospel of Truth, a work that may have been written by Valentinus, and if not, certainly by one of his disciples.

The Gospel of Truth begins with these words: "The Gospel of Truth is a joy for those who have received from the Father of truth the gift of *knowing* him through the power of the Word that came from the fullness—the one who is addressed as the Savior, that being the name of the word he is to perform for the redemption of those who were *ignorant* of the Father, while the name of the gospel is the proclamation of hope, being *discovery* for those who search for him."

For the Valentinians the greatest evil was spiritual ignorance. They believed that the world was an alien place created by a capricious and malevolent deity, the god of the Jewish Scriptures, and held that human beings were in thrall to an impenetrable darkness. "Anguish grew solid like a fog so that no one was able to see," says the Gospel of Truth. Salvation was found in gnosis, illumination or secret knowledge. Christ, an emissary from a higher realm, had descended from the Father to reside for a time in the body of Jesus. He came not to effect something but to open the eyes of spiritual men and women to hidden mysteries and, through gnosis, deliver them from the sway of cosmic powers and disclose a glorious kingdom of light.

Gnostics drew widely on the writings that became part of the New Testament, and toward the end of the second century Heracleon, a gnostic thinker, wrote the first commentary on the Gospel of John. Their works display a deep spiritual yearning expressed at times with poetic beauty and religious imagination. Yet when one takes up a gnostic treatise—and many are now available to us—one senses a different spirit at work in them from other Christian writings. Their authors dismember the biblical narrative, and the words of the New Testament are scrambled in strange and confusing patterns, shrouded in clouds of abstractions and unchecked astral speculations. Though their ideas seem original, they are not profound, and their mysteries, often alluring, are merely recondite.

Yet gnosticism had wide appeal, and by the middle of the second century gnostic teachers had gained a hearing in many Christian communities. Even their critics admitted that they had "made an effort to understand the teachings of Christianity." To some, gnosis seemed compatible with the Christianity they had learned. This posed a vexing problem within the churches, and it was not long before Christian leaders began to mount a counteroffensive against gnostic teaching. One of these was a bishop in Lyons in Roman Gaul (France) named Irenaeus. The location of his city, Lyons, is significant, for it shows that by the middle of the second century Christianity was no longer confined to the lands bordering the Mediterranean. Even this early, Christians could be found beyond the Alps on the Rhone River.

Irenaeus was born in Smyrna (modern-day Izmir) in western Asia Minor on the Aegean Sea. The date of his birth is uncertain, but it was probably between A.D. 130 and 140. According to his own account, as a boy he had known the venerable bishop Polycarp (also of Smyrna), who had sat at the feet of the apostle John. "I remember," writes Irenaeus, "how he [Polycarp] spoke of his conversation with John and with others who had seen the Lord; how he repeated their words from memory." As a young man Irenaeus went to Rome to study and may have been in the city when Valentinus was there. His native language was Greek, and the church in Rome at that time spoke Greek. From there he moved to Lyons in southern Gaul, again to a Greek-speaking Christian community probably made up of merchants from Asia Minor, and was ordained a presbyter (priest). Shortly after his ordination, while on a mission to Rome, the bishop of Lyons died in a persecution fueled by anti-Christian feelings in the city. When Irenaeus returned to Lyons he was made bishop of the city.

As bishop he soon discovered that some in the city were confusing members of his congregation with strange teachings. Irenaeus was concerned that their language "resembled ours," and to some of his people their teaching had the ring of "plausibility." They also cited the "oracles of God," that is, the apostolic writings, to support their views and claimed to be in possession of a higher knowledge to which they alone had access. Irenaeus responded to the challenge by writing a large and detailed critique of gnosticism as it was taught by Valentinus and his disciples.

His book, titled *Against Heresies,* was composed when the Christian Bible was first taking shape. Until the latter part of the second century the only scriptural norm was the Jewish Scriptures, which Christians called simply "the books." They circulated in a Greek translation made by Jews in the second century B.C. According to a pious legend, the project to translate the Jewish sacred books was undertaken by the Egyptian king Ptolemy Philadelphus (285–246 B.C.), who wanted to have a Greek version of the Jewish Scriptures for his great library in Alexandria. He assigned the task to seventy scholars (hence the name Septuagint) and, working independently of one another, they produced word-for-word identical Greek translations. In truth the translation was the work of a smaller company of scholars working in different places over a long period of time. It was completed before the rise of Christianity, and it is this version, not the original Hebrew (and Aramaic) version, that was cited in the New Testament and in other early Christian writings. The Septuagint was the first Christian "Bible."

Within two decades of the death of Christ, Christians had begun to compose their own writings. The earliest were the letters of Paul (d. A.D. 65), and in the next generation and beyond other books were written, including the four gospels, the Acts of the Apostles, 1 Peter, Hebrews, the Didache (an early Christian manual), the letter of Clement to the Corinthians, the Epistle of Barnabas. But oral tradition was esteemed more highly than written documents. Although Ignatius seems to have known some of the letters of Paul and one or two of the gospels, he does not appeal to them as authorities. For Ignatius the only real "authority" was Jesus Christ, not a written scripture. "For me," he writes, "the archives are Jesus Christ, . . . his cross and death and his resurrection and faith through him."

Ignatius was not alone in preferring oral tradition over written books. A few years later a bishop from Asia Minor named Papias remarked that although the evangelist Mark had done nothing wrong in writing down the sayings of the Lord, he preferred what Andrew or Peter or Philip, the apostles, had said. "For I did not suppose that information from books would help me so much as the word of a living and surviving voice." But as the decades rolled by oral tradition became more diffuse and less reliable, and written texts began to gain acceptance. Already in the second century the letters of Paul were handed on not as individual works but as a corpus of writings.

Written texts were an integral part of early Christian worship. The first part of the Eucharist was centered on the reading and exposition of a passage from the gospels and also from the Jewish Scriptures, the Septuagint. In describing the Christian Eucharist in the middle of the second century Justin Martyr, the Christian philosopher, says that readings were taken from the "remembrances of the apostles," by which he meant the gospels, and the "writings of the prophets," by which he meant the Septuagint. This pairing of apostolic writings with the Septuagint accorded the early Christian writings an authority, if only implicitly, that was not unlike that of the sacred books of the Old Covenant. The public reading of the apostolic writings helped prepare the way for the formation of a Christian Scripture.

Many writings, however, were being circulated in the churches, and there was no agreed collection of authoritative Christian books. Besides those books that are today part of the New Testament, here is a partial list of others that circulated: the Didache, 1 Clement, the Gospel of Thomas, the Gospel of Truth, the Gospel of the Egyptians, the Gospel of the Hebrews, the Gospel of Judas, the Epistle of Barnabas, the Shepherd of Hermas, the Apocalypse of Peter, and others. In determining which books were apostolic no single criterion was used, but one factor weighed heavily: usage. Those books that had been known for a long time, received in Christian communities across the Christian world, and read in Christian worship were judged trustworthy witnesses to the faith handed on by the apostles.

The Christian Bible was not the work of a group of bishops sitting down with a stack of books before them, discussing the merits of each, and putting some in one pile and others in another. The process was gradual, a slow winnowing over several generations as the books commended themselves. There was of course some fuzziness around the edges. In certain circles there were questions about books such as 2 Peter or James, the Revelation of Saint John or the epistle to the Hebrews. Though Hebrews was thought to be written by Paul, its elegant Greek style suggested another author, and it was not known in the Latin-speaking regions in the first two centuries.

In Irenaeus's book against the gnostics, written at the end of the second century, the basic structure of the New Testament, the four gospels, the Acts of the Apostles, and epistles is visible for the first time. But as yet there was no general term to refer to the collection of writings as a whole. The term "New Testament" was first used a decade or so later by a Latin writer named Tertullian who lived in Carthage in North Africa. "Testament" is a Latin word used to translate the Greek term for covenant. In the New Testament the term is used in the account of the Last Supper, "This cup is the new covenant in my blood" (1 Corinthians 11:25; Luke 22:20), and Paul contrasts the "new covenant" introduced by Christ with the covenant made with Moses (2 Corinthians 3:6). But the term "covenant" was not used to refer to a collection of books. By the middle of the second century, however, the word came to signify "the books of the old covenant," though it was not used to refer to the Christian books. There seemed to be some reluctance to transfer its meaning to designate a collection of books. Origen of Alexandria (d. 254) refers to the "sacred scriptures of the so-called old and so-called new covenant [testament]," suggesting that the terminology was still novel in his day.

Although for Irenaeus the most authentic tradition was oral, what "the elders, the disciples of the apostles, have handed on to us," in his writings it is clear that Christian revelation had become definitively bound to written documents. In his view Christ's life and teachings were accessible in authoritative books that went back to the earliest period of Christian history. These writings, along with the Jewish Scriptures, the Septuagint, made up the Christian Bible. Accordingly, Irenaeus presents his case against the gnostics by appealing both to the apostolic Christian writings, what came to be called the New Testament, and to the Septuagint, the Jewish Scriptures—that is, the Old Testament.

A central feature of gnostic teaching was that there are two gods: the god of the Old Testament, a subordinate and inferior being who formed this world of matter and favored the Jewish people, and the God of all, an ineffable and transcendent being, a God of love and compassion revealed in Christ. Irenaeus showed that according to both the Jewish Scripture (Deuteronomy 5:8) and the Christian Scripture (1 Corinthians 8:4) there is one God, "maker of heaven and earth, who formed man . . . called Abraham, led the people [of Israel] from the land of Egypt, spoke with Moses, gave the law, sent the prophets," and is also the "Father of our Lord Jesus Christ." Christian faith did not begin with Christ—it had its beginnings with God the creator who had given the law to the Jewish people and sent the prophets.

Irenaeus's summary of the biblical narrative reflects what was called the "rule of faith." In the second century there were no creeds as such, but at baptism, catechumens—men and women who had been instructed in Christian teaching and were about to be received into the Church—were asked a set of three questions dealing with the Father, Son, and Holy Spirit. The "rule of faith" had a Trinitarian structure and identified God by events recorded in the Scriptures, the creation of the world, the call of Abraham, the coming of Christ in the flesh, and the sending of the Holy Spirit. We believe, wrote Irenaeus, in "one God almighty from whom are all things . . . and in the Son of God Jesus Christ our Lord . . . who became man, and in the Spirit of God."

For Irenaeus the "rule of faith" handed on orally was the key to the interpretation of the Bible. The written books were to be understood in light of what was found in a simple confession of faith, that is, in the Church's tradition. Here was the rub for the gnostics. They were disdainful of what had been received from tradition, from earlier teachers, and preferred their own private interpretation to the rule of faith. Irenaeus found their views willful and doctrinaire. For example, they took the phrase "god of this world" in 2 Corinthians (4:4) to be a reference to a lesser God, the creator of the world, who had "blinded the minds of unbelievers." In fact the phrase refers to Satan, the anti-God.

Irenaeus compared gnostic exegesis to the literary practice of selecting individual lines at random from Homer's *Iliad* to create a new narrative that disregarded the story as told by Homer. Without respect for the plot that held the books of the Bible together, the gnostics were able to bend and twist individual scriptural passages to fit their religious ideas. If, however, one does not know the pattern that gives meaning to the whole, a scheme set forth in the rule of faith, the Scriptures are as inscrutable as a mosaic in which the tiny colored stones have been arranged haphazardly without reference to the original design. In other words, the written Scriptures must be interpreted in light of tradition. Or, to put it more precisely, the tradition embodied in the apostolic writings, that is, the New Testament, needs to be complemented by the tradition, equally apostolic, that had been handed on orally (primarily in Christian worship) from one generation to another.

Gnosticism was an esoteric and elitist movement led by brilliant individual teachers without deep roots in the Christian past. As Irenaeus puts it sarcastically, "there were no Valentinians before Valentinus, nor Marcionites before Marcion." Christianity was not simply an affair of beliefs or ideas drawn from the Scriptures; the apostolic faith was known through the witness of persons and the teachings and practices of a community that extended back in time. One cannot ignore, said Irenaeus, the public and documented lineage of teachers who have handed on the faith from one generation to the next. So he names several prominent churches, Rome, Smyrna, Ephesus, where the teaching of the apostles was received through a succession of bishops. By the end of the second century the office that first came into view at the time of Ignatius had worked its way more deeply into the Church's life and self-understanding.

Irenaeus helps us understand why the Church's early history is taken up with so many controversies over doctrinal matters. Unlike the religion of the Greeks and the Romans, the Christian religion is not only a matter of ritual; Christians affirmed that certain things were true. They not only believed *in* God, they also believed *that* God was creator of the world, and that Christ had risen from the dead. Already in the New Testament one finds creed-like statements such as: "There is one God, the Father, from whom are all things, and for whom we exist, and one Lord, Jesus Christ, through whom are all things and through whom we exist" (1 Corinthians 8:5). It is a small step from this language to the rule of faith and to the Apostles' Creed that begins: "I believe in God the Father Almighty and in Jesus Christ his only son our Lord . . ."* Christian teaching does not lend itself to every possible

---

*The Apostles' Creed is a fourth-century statement of faith written in Latin, based on an earlier creed used in Rome that grew out of the threefold interrogatory confession or "rule of faith." It is used in the Western Church primarily as a baptismal creed. It reads:

> I believe in God the Father almighty, creator of heaven and earth;
>
> And in Jesus Christ, His only Son, our Lord, Who was conceived by the Holy Spirit, born from the Virgin Mary, suffered under Pontius Pilate, was crucified, dead and buried, descended to hell, on the third day rose again from the dead, ascended to heaven, sits at the right hand of God the Father almighty, then He will come to judge the living and the dead.
>
> I believe in the Holy Spirit, the holy Catholic Church, the communion of saints, the remission of sins, the resurrection of the flesh, and eternal life. Amen.

opinion; it imposes limits that cannot be formulated in advance, but become evident over time. The conflict over gnosis showed that some differences could not be tolerated.

Just as Ignatius allowed us a glimpse of Christianity as it was being formed at the end of the first century, Irenaeus gives us a picture—much more complete—of how things stood at the end of the second century. To be sure he is only one person and he lived far from the center of things. We cannot assume that what we find in Lyons in Gaul is replicated in all parts of the Church. By this time there were other organized Christian communities, the Montanists, an apocalyptic movement that believed the Holy Spirit had been poured out anew on its leaders, and the Marcionites, who taught that the God of the Old Testament, a God of law, had nothing to do with Jesus Christ. Yet Irenaeus represents the form of Christianity that would endure, spread to all corners of the known world, and transform ancient civilization.

5

Constructing a Catacomb

In the oft-cited passage from the Epistle to Diognetus, a second-century writing, it is said that Christians are distinguished from others neither by nationality (Egyptians or Scythians, for example), nor by language (such as Aramaic or Coptic), nor by customs. They call no country home, they do not live in their own cities, and they observe the mores of the people among whom they live. They are known to honor Christ as God, they shun the gods and goddesses of Greece and Rome, and they gather weekly for a ritual meal. Yet, there is little else that set them apart. When they worship they use the language of the city in which they dwell, they have no temples, in fact no buildings of any kind, nor a religious calendar. During the first two centuries Christianity as a body was largely invisible.

By contrast the Jews were known as an ancient people with a long and venerable history. In the cities of the Roman Empire they had their own buildings and neighborhoods, they refused to eat pork products (which the Romans found strange), their Scriptures were composed in an alien script written from right to left, they had a distinctive way of dressing (fringes on men's garments), and they were idle on Saturday. They ordered their lives by a distinctive calendar of festivals and holy days stretched out over the year. Even after the destruction of the city of Jerusalem and their holy temple, the Jewish communities in the empire and beyond still looked to the Land of Israel as their homeland. As a people they were granted a privileged status in Roman law, they were exempt from participating in the civic cult, and their religious customs marked them as a corporate body within society.

The first palpable sign that Christianity was beginning to occupy public space was the construction of a Christian cemetery in Rome. Early in the third century, the Christian community in the city took the bold step to build an underground burial chamber. The land was located on the Via Appia outside the city and is known today as the catacomb of Saint Callixtus, named after a Roman Christian who oversaw its planning and construction and became bishop of Rome (218–223). Christians were not the first to bury their dead in catacombs. A century earlier Jews had begun to inter underground. Like the Jews, Christians considered the Roman practice of cremation an offense against the sanctity of the body.

A catacomb included a series of corridors with horizontal niches the size of a small coffin cut into soft volcanic rock called tuff. Dark and dank, lit by oil lamps, permeated with the odor of decaying corpses, catacombs were uninviting places. Yet they became sacred to the early Christians. The catacombs were not places of hiding during persecution. They were simple tombs in the midst of which were carved out small chapels and rooms and more elaborate niches for the burial of martyrs and revered members of the community. Often they were built near the main roads and in proximity to pagan cemeteries. Their location was not secret, and when Christians laid their dead to rest or gathered in the catacombs to celebrate the Eucharist their comings and goings were known to their fellow citizens.

The catacomb of Callixtus is composed of ten burial chambers and chapels whose walls and ceilings were decorated with geometrical designs and paintings. Sometime in the latter part of the second century Christians in Rome had acquired a small burial plot to bury their dead in graves above ground. But when this area was exhausted they embarked on a more ambitious undertaking, the construction of a subterranean necropolis where the faithful could bury their dead and gather to pray for those who had gone before. The architecture of the space and construction required careful planning, organization, ample financial resources, and leadership. The catacomb was a communal not a private project.

Already in the second century the churches had begun to look after the burial expenses of poor Christians. The *Apostolic Tradition,* a collection of prayers and rules guiding church life, mentions that care of the cemetery was a responsibility of the bishop. A catacomb under the jurisdiction of the bishop provided a suitable burial place not only for the poor but also for those who had died as martyrs. In the mid third century, Cyprian, bishop of Carthage, instructed his presbyters to "give special care and solicitude" to the bodies of martyrs. They were to keep a record of the day a martyr died so that his or her "memory" could be celebrated when the "sacrifice" was offered. Accounts of the deaths of the martyrs were preserved in the archives of the churches to be read on the anniversary of each one's martyrdom. Already in the second century the death of Polycarp was celebrated annually.

Memory attaches itself to tangible things. Though the narrow tunnels where the dead slept were a domain of sadness and tears, in the tiny chapels the faithful could celebrate the Eucharist in the presence of the precious remains of loved ones and friends, martyrs and bishops. The dead remained very much alive for the early Christians. In the Eucharist prayers for the faithful departed were part of the great prayer of thanksgiving over the offerings of bread and wine. In constructing a catacomb with chapels and altars as well as tombs Christian leaders had more in mind than a place of burial. The dead created for the first time a Christian space that bound the community together over time, knitting the tremulous present to the grander past and forging solid and stable feelings through collective memory. And it is in this setting, where the irresistible ravages of time and mortality were most palpable, where hope was joined to memory, that the first Christian art is found. "Death," as Wallace Stevens wrote, "is the mother of beauty."

Before the early third century there is no evidence of Christian art. Some have argued that in the early years Christians were aniconic—opposed to religious pictures, hostile to artistic representation of biblical events and persons. But that view has been abandoned by scholars. Though there is no archaeological evidence of Christian art before the catacomb of Callixtus, from literary sources we know that by the end of the second century Christians had begun to find ways to give visible expression to their beliefs. Clement, a Christian scholar in Alexandria, said that Christians purchased objects engraved with symbols. "Let our seals [for example, a precious stone with a design engraved on it] be a dove or a fish or a ship running in a fair wind or a musical lyre such as the one Polycrates [ruler of the Greek island of Samos in the sixth century B.C.] used or a ship's anchor such as the one Seleucus [a Hellenistic king in Antioch in Syria who died in 281 B.C.] had engraved on his sealstone. And if someone is fishing he will call to mind the apostle [Peter].... We who are forbidden to attach ourselves to idols must not engrave the face of idols [on our rings], or the sword or the bow, since we follow the path of peace, or drinking cups, since we are sober. Many licentious people carry images of their lovers and favorite prostitutes on their rings."

Clement's point is this: If a Christian wished to have a ring that expressed his faith he should go to a craftsman whose stones were engraved with figures that could be given a Christian meaning. What he says about rings would apply equally to other objects, such as an oil lamp, or a bowl, or a pitcher. As yet there were no Christian artists or craftsmen who designed objects with distinctive Christian images. So Clement recommends that Christians buy rings that were in common use and readily available in workshops in the markets of the city. Though they may be stamped with symbols that bear one meaning to the maker and to most buyers, some of the engravings could be given a Christian sense. A dove could be taken to symbolize the Christian virtues of gentleness and peacefulness; a fish could be a symbol of Christ because the letters of the Greek word for fish (*ixthus*) could be taken to spell the first letters of the words JESUS CHRIST SON OF GOD SAVIOR; a ship could signify the Church carrying the faithful over the turbulent waters of life; a young man with a lyre could depict David singing the psalms; and an anchor could be a symbol of hope (Hebrews 6:18–19).

The early Christians had no objections to images. They were happy to employ symbols, even the figure of a human being, such as a fisherman, to signify Christian beliefs. But at this stage in Christian history they did not yet have their own artistic vocabulary; they had to adapt what was available in the wider culture. Still, in wearing certain kinds of rings or using lamps engraved with particular images they were making choices about what symbols were appropriate for Christian art. The list of images that Clement deemed acceptable offers the first repertory of Christian symbols, some of which are still in use today, including a fish or an anchor or a ship. In these early years what the symbols represented lay in the eyes of the beholder. As far as Roman society was concerned, the Christian meaning was hidden and known only to the faithful.

What Clement describes with respect to personal and household objects is replicated on a larger scale in the ceiling decorations of the catacomb of Callixtus. But first a few details on how the catacomb was constructed. After the plans were in order, diggers were employed to excavate under the earth, build staircases and passageways, cut out *loculi* (burial places), construct rooms and galleries. Then plasterers were brought in to cover the ceilings of the rooms to be decorated. The rooms were often square with a slightly domed ceiling, designed so that the center of the dome would be the central focus of the chamber. Painters divided the ceiling with colored lines to create a series of symmetrical frames that could hold pictures or other decorations, of birds, flowers, baskets, fruits, vases. The ceiling designs and pictures were integral to the whole project, the result of a well-executed plan, not casual drawings added as an afterthought. Just as Christians had to decide which symbols were appropriate on rings or lamps, so those who commissioned painters for the catacombs had to decide, with little precedent as guide, which images were fitting for a space consecrated for Christian use.

One of the most prominent figures in the catacomb is a young man carrying a lamb on his shoulders. To later Christian eyes this image represented the good shepherd of the Gospel of John (10:11). But the figure of a shepherd carrying a sheep was well known in Greek and Roman painting and sculpture long before the rise of Christianity and can be found centuries earlier in sculptures from the Fertile Crescent. Called the *kriophoros,* or lamb or ram bearer, to the Greeks and Romans it represented the virtue of philanthropy or care for others. On one ceiling in the catacomb there are two shepherds in subordinate positions. Were the figures a representation of Christ as the good shepherd one would expect there to be only one shepherd. In choosing to paint two shepherds on the ceiling of a chamber in the catacomb, it is possible Christians wished to show that they, like others in society, practiced *philanthropia,* or care for others, perhaps giving the virtue a Christian meaning by interpreting it as *agape,* love of neighbor.

On another ceiling in the catacomb of Callixtus, however, the figure of the shepherd is placed in the central medallion. This may suggest that it depicts Christ as the good shepherd. Tertullian, a Latin writer from Carthage in North Africa, says that in the Eucharist Christians used cups engraved with the figure of the shepherd. He interprets the shepherd as a representation of Christ the shepherd who leaves the ninety-nine sheep to seek out the one who was lost (Luke 15:3–7).

The figure of the shepherd carrying a sheep also appears on terra-cotta oil lamps, a large number of which were produced in central Italy in the years between 175 and 225, when the catacomb of Callixtus was being constructed. We cannot be certain that Christians purchased these lamps, but the rise in production of shepherd lamps at this time is intriguing and makes one wonder if Christians bought them for the same reason they bought rings with the image of a dove. They were beginning to experiment with different ways of giving visual form to their faith.

A particularly provocative example of such experimentation in the catacomb of Callixtus is a painting of the Greek singer Orpheus with a lyre, clothed in a short tunic, wearing a Phrygian cap and surrounded by wild beasts. In Greek myth Orpheus had a voice of such sweetness that no one could resist his melodies. He met and wooed the young maiden Eurydice, but their joy was brief. Shortly after they were married, she died from a serpent's bite. Determined to free her, Orpheus went down into Hades and so charmed the netherworld with his singing that he won her release—on the condition that on his return he would not look back at her. At the very end of their journey back to earth, however, he did look back to see if Eurydice was behind him, and he lost her forever. So he forsook the company of human beings and retired into the woods near his home in Thrace (northern Greece), where his mournful song enchanted the trees and rivers and tamed the wild animals.

Why Christians should be attracted to the myth of Orpheus is a mystery. Christian writers seldom drew on ancient myths to interpret the person of Christ. But Clement, that most learned Christian in Alexandria, thought the parallel between Orpheus and Christ was fitting. He knew the Greek myth well and calls Orpheus a skilled master of his art who pacified wild beasts by the power of his song. But, writes Clement, Christ's new song is able to tame "the most intractable of all animals—man." It is possible that Orpheus entered Christian iconography via Judaism, which pictured King David, the singer of the psalms, as Orpheus. What is certain is that the myth of this gentle man who could bring peace through song appealed to Christians. It is a particularly bold example of Christians adapting a common artistic image for their use.

Another figure that appears in the catacombs is the *orant*, a standing male or female figure with hands uplifted in a gesture of prayer. This is the same gesture one sees today in some churches when the Our Father is recited. In Roman art the orant was a symbol of piety or devotion to the gods. Again we cannot be sure what

Christians saw in the figure, or even whether it served as anything more than a form of decoration, but it is possible they adapted it because it signified devotion not to the gods but to the one God. An early charge against the Christians was that they were superstitious, and in the minds of the Romans the opposite of superstition was "piety." Justin Martyr, a second-century apologist (one who wrote in defense of Christianity), addressed a treatise to the emperor Antoninus Pius (A.D. 138–161) in which he argues that Christians, like the Romans, are pious and virtuous. The adoption of the orant may have carried a similar message, this time in a work of art rather than in words.

From these images, the lamb-bearer, the orant, and Orpheus, we learn that the first Christian art drew on familiar and conventional models drawn from Roman art. Yet they were turned to new ends by those who chose them to decorate a Christian burial place. Context is everything, and the meaning depended on associations made by those who planned them and prayed in rooms decorated with them. The catacomb was not a museum where people wandered about to gawk at unfamiliar figures. It was a sacred space that displayed images whose meaning was familiar. The Christians who came there did not have to be told what they meant.

Had we only the images of the shepherd, the orant, and Orpheus, the catacombs would tell us little more than what we learned from Clement's remark on what kinds of seals to purchase. But there was more to the art of the catacombs than these figures illustrate. Callixtus and his advisers also commissioned pictures that depicted persons and stories from the Bible. The prophet Jonah is represented four times in the catacomb of Callixtus, for example, and appears often in other catacombs. Most often the story of Jonah is told in a series of pictures. First there is an image of Jonah being cast overboard from a ship. To the left (the pictures run from right to left), Jonah is being eaten by a sea monster, and the final scene has him reclining under the broom tree.

With this painting we are moving into new artistic territory. For the artist is depicting an event that is recognizably Christian. Yet the visual vocabulary he employs is taken from Roman art. The painter, whether a Christian artist or a skilled pagan hired for the task, did not draw the pictures of Jonah with the text of the Bible before him. He exploited a repertory of stock models that were known in Roman art. The image of Jonah under the broom tree is modeled on the familiar figure of Endymion, a handsome young man with whom the goddess Selene had fallen in love. In Greek art Endymion was depicted sleeping in a cave where he would be visited periodically by his lover. Christians adopted the image of the sleeping Endymion and used it over and over in paintings in the catacombs and on Christian sarcophagi (stone coffins). In choosing what should appear on the walls or ceiling of the catacomb they had to decide which of the many stories from the Bible would be depicted and which models from Roman art served that end.

The figure of Daniel in the lion's den also appears in the catacomb of Callixtus. Here too, as in paintings of Jonah, the artist did not work directly from the text of the Scriptures. He drew on a familiar model of a heroic figure, a handsome young man, and added two lions to suggest the biblical account. The painting invokes the story of Daniel who flaunted the king's decree by praying to the God of Israel. For his insolence Daniel was cast into a den of lions but miraculously delivered by God's intervention. The Christian painting is not a portrait of a heroic individual but the depiction of a biblical story. Though Christians used symbols, they were subordinate to the representation of events and persons.

As those who planned the catacomb of Callixtus used images from the surrounding culture to create a distinctively Christian art, so other Christians were doing something similar with articles for use in the home. Early in the third century someone decided to take the popular shepherd lamp and make it into a distinctively Christian object. A good example is a terra-cotta lamp first discovered in the seventeenth century and today in the possession of the Bode Museum in Berlin. Like other lamps bearing the kriophoros it has a figure of a shepherd surrounded by sheep on either side. But to the left of the shepherd one clearly sees the figure of Jonah being cast out of the mouth of the great fish, and to the right he is resting under the broom tree in the familiar Endymion pose. Above the shepherd's right shoulder is a bird perched on a box that may symbolize Noah's ark and the dove (Genesis 8:8–9). The sun and moon, Helios and Selene, and seven stars sparkle in the background. Though the visual language is drawn from Roman art, the idea of placing the shepherd with Jonah and the ark and dove is the work of Christians. Whoever made the lamp was a Christian or someone following the instructions of a Christian patron.

Besides images of events from the Old Testament in the catacomb of Callixtus there are also some scenes from the New Testament. One painting depicts the baptism of Jesus, a young man in the middle of a river and another person standing on the bank with an outstretched hand. In the upper left-hand corner there is a bird. The bird is most likely the dove mentioned in the accounts of Jesus's baptism in the Jordan, and the person on the bank is John the Baptist. In other catacombs there are depictions of the multiplication of the loaves and fishes, the wedding at Cana, Jesus with the woman at the well, the raising of Lazarus. What is not found is any depiction of the crucifixion. It was apparently too degrading to be pictured in Roman society. The earliest known representation of the crucifixion is found on the wooden doors of the Church of Santa Sabina in Rome in the mid fifth century. Neither do we find facial portraits of Christ like those familiar from later Christian art, or images of the Virgin Mary and the child Jesus.

So we are very much at the beginnings of Christian art, and the significance of the catacomb of Callixtus lies as much in the project itself as in the paintings found on the walls and ceilings. A "cultural event of some importance was taking place," wrote the art historian Paul Corby Finney, for we see here a "transition from models of accommodation and adaptation that were materially invisible to a new level of Christian identity that was palpable and visible." For the first time Christians were beginning to create a "material culture," something that is tangible, occupies space, is public (though underground), and is recognizably Christian. Art was an essential part of this endeavor.

Few decisions were more momentous for the history of Christianity and Western civilization than the admission of religious images on the walls of the catacombs. In the fourth century, when Christians began to build churches, images assumed a prominent place in their decoration, and in the centuries that followed pictorial art would adorn church buildings in East and West. By depicting events and persons from the Bible, Christians introduced a fresh subject matter to ancient art that would displace the stories and the heroes that had dominated artistic work for centuries. One need only visit a modern museum and walk from a gallery displaying Greek and Roman art to rooms dedicated to early Christian art to see how radical and enduring this transformation was.

Christianity was beginning to intrude into the public life of the city, a development some found offensive. The Carthaginians resented that Christians had their own cemeteries. "No places here [in our city] for Christians," they said. The time was still far off when Christians could construct spacious buildings offering large panels for the display of Christian art. But the emergence of a Christian material culture in the early third century is a first step along that road.

Although the numbers of Christians were few in relation to the empire as a whole, the new movement was beginning to lay the foundations for a Christian culture. And by culture I do not mean primarily what we call high culture, but the "total harvest of thinking and feeling," to use T. S. Eliot's phrase—the manners, morals, customs, and arts; the pattern of inherited meanings and sensibilities embedded in rituals, rules, and language; the institutions, practices, persons, and stories that order and inspire the behavior, affections, and thoughts of a people.

6

A Learned Faith:
Origen of Alexandria

In the early centuries few Christians made an impact outside the Christian community. Although by the beginning of the third century they had already composed a considerable body of writings, including the letters of Paul and Ignatius, different kinds of gospels, colorful tales of the lives of the apostles, an account of the martyrdom of Polycarp, Irenaeus's book against the gnostics, these were read largely by Christians. Some wrote apologies, works that explained and defended Christianity to the outsider, but even these writings may have been aimed primarily at Christians. Few outsiders had detailed knowledge of Christian beliefs and practices, and Christianity appeared to be an alien and superstitious way of life. Some observers were impressed at the way Christians lived but thought their teachings incapable of reasonable explanation and defense. Christianity had not raised up a thinker whom its cultured despisers had to take seriously.

But in the 180s in the city of Alexandria a child was born of such uncommon gifts that when he grew to maturity all who knew him or read his writings, whether Christian or pagan, recognized his genius. According to one story, when he was a child his father was so in awe of his precocious son that he would steal into his room as he slept, uncover his breast and kiss it reverently as though it were the shrine of a divine spirit. When he began to write, even philosophers knew he was someone to be reckoned with. His name was Origen, and what he accomplished during his lifetime has reverberated down the centuries to this day. His work announced that Christianity would be not only a community of faith but also a tradition of learning. Under his tutelage the doctrines Christians confessed and the Scriptures they read in worship became the subject of rational and philosophical scrutiny within the Church.

The details of Origen's life are sparse. Christians had not yet begun to compose biographies of their heroes, so there is no ancient account of his life, and only two letters remain from his hand. The historian Eusebius gives a brief sketch of his life in his *Ecclesiastical History* and, magnanimously, includes a few passages from a biting critique of his thinking by the pagan philosopher Porphyry. "Though schooled in Greek thought," wrote Porphyry, "he [Origen] plunged headlong into barbarian [that is, Christian] recklessness." We also possess an admiring treatise by one of his students, a man named Gregory, praising Origen as teacher and mentor. His instruction, said Gregory, was personal and individual, an exercise in spiritual as well as intellectual formation. Origen "incited us more by what he did than by what he said." But the most extensive information on Origen's life and thinking come from Origen himself. He left a large body of writings: commentaries on books of the Bible, theological treatises, a major work in defense of Christianity, sermons and devotional writings, among which is the first Christian treatise on prayer.

Origen was raised in a Christian home, a biographical detail of some significance. What little we know about the lives of other Christian "intellectuals" in the early years shows that most were raised outside the Church and embraced Christianity as adults. The Christian philosopher Justin Martyr (d. 153), a native of Neapolis (modern Nablus) in Roman Palestine, became acquainted with the Christian Scriptures only after he had made the rounds of the regnant philosophical schools of his day. Clement, a Christian philosopher who taught in Alexandria the generation before Origen, was converted to Christianity only after he had studied at the feet of several philosophers. He first read the Scriptures as an adult. Origen, however, was introduced to the Bible as a youngster by his father, and the words and images of the Scriptures formed his imagination and tutored his affections while he was still young. By the time he was an adolescent he knew large sections of the Bible by heart.

In A.D. 199–200, when Origen was seventeen years old, the emperor Septimius Severus passed through Alexandria en route to join the Roman legions arrayed against the Parthians on the eastern frontier. At the instigation of local pagan priests he allowed the Roman governor in Alexandria to initiate a persecution against Christians. Origen's father, a catechist in the local church, was arrested and executed. No event penetrated more deeply into Origen's soul and none was remembered with greater gratitude. The experience of seeing his father martyred united Origen, as it were, by blood to the Church. His father's death haunted his memory and inspired his devotion, and thirty years later he recalled his witness with loving admiration in a sermon preached in Caesarea in Palestine. "It is of no advantage to me having a martyr as a father unless I live virtuously and honor the nobility of my birth, confirming his witness and the confession by which he shone in Christ." Later, when the Church was again threatened with persecution, Origen wrote a beautiful treatise, *Exhortation to Martyrdom,* on the dignity of the martyrs. Although he himself did not gain the crown of martyrdom, he acquitted himself honorably during a later persecution.

When his father was arrested the family's property was seized and handed over to the imperial treasury, and Origen's mother was left destitute with seven children. A wealthy Christian woman stepped in and took him into her home and offered to pay his educational expenses. So he was able to continue his studies in rhetoric and literature, the staple of education at the time. When he later turned to scholarly study of the Bible, what he learned during these years about reading and interpreting literary texts would prove invaluable.

His benefactress was a disciple of a popular Christian teacher from Antioch named Paul. The impressionable young Origen took to Paul and was fascinated by his ideas—most likely a form of gnosticism—but Eusebius, no doubt protecting his reputation, says that Origen would not pray with Paul and "loathed" his heretical views. Yet the encounter with Paul shows that he had first-hand contact with gnostics, and later when he wrote against their teaching he clearly knew what he was talking about. With his teeming intellect Origen was open to many ideas and different ways of thinking. Though he rejected gnosticism's central claims, for example, that the creator God and the father of Jesus Christ are two different deities, other aspects were integrated into his own thought.

By the time he was twenty Origen had begun to apply his gifts to the study of philosophy. There were no universities, and it was customary that a young person who wished to pursue advanced study would hire on as the disciple of a single teacher. Origen had the good fortune as well as the prescience to approach one of the most accomplished philosophers of the time, Ammonius Saccas. Plotinus, the bold and imaginative interpreter of Plato in antiquity and a powerful influence on the young Augustine, was also Ammonius's student. So was the philosopher Longinus, whose famous essay on the "sublime" remains a classic of Western thought. When Origen is added to this company it is an illustrious trio indeed. Christianity was standing on the threshold of a new stage in its young life.

From Ammonius, Origen gained first-hand knowledge of the Greek philosophical tradition, especially Plato, but also Aristotle and the Stoics. Ammonius also introduced him to philosophers of his own time, and the careful reader can discern traces of ideas and arguments of contemporaries or near contemporaries in his treatises. Of course Origen did not need to be taught the virtues of an inquiring mind—that was a gift from birth—but his philosophical training taught him to use language precisely and make distinctions with teeth. Though his writings pour forth a torrent of words, his prose is always fresh and invigorating, displaying the unmistakable clarity of a great mind.

His teachers were also Jews. Christians shared a common Scripture with the Jews, and in Alexandria Jewish thinkers had long dealt with the challenge of translating the ancient Jewish tradition into the Greek cultural milieu. The Septuagint, the Greek translation of the Jewish Scriptures, was produced in Alexandria. The most famous of these thinkers was an Alexandrian Jew named Philo (d. A.D. 50), whom Origen, encouraged by his fellow Alexandrian Clement, read avidly. From Philo he learned how a Jewish philosopher thought through major biblical themes, for example that God is beyond human knowing, in language that was intelligible to a Greek-speaking public.

But Origen came to know Jewish thinking in its Hebrew dress as well. And in some ways this aspect of his learning is more consequential. So scrupulous was Origen in his examination of the Scriptures, says Eusebius, that he studied the Hebrew language and "secured for himself a copy, in the actual Hebrew script, of the original documents circulating among the Jews." He was the first Christian to take a scholarly interest in the Hebrew version of the Old Testament, the Jewish Scriptures read in the synagogue. A century and a half later an admirer (and copier) of Origen, Jerome, would translate parts of the Old Testament from Hebrew into Latin. Origen's teacher, a Jew from Palestine who had converted to Christianity, not only taught Origen Hebrew, he also introduced him to Jewish biblical exegesis. At the very beginning of the scholarly study of the Old Testament, Christians had access to an alternate exegetical tradition, not as something to be refuted—though of course there was argument—but as a different way of interpreting the biblical text.

By the time he was twenty years old Origen had begun to take on students. He had been making his living as a teacher of grammar, but now he gave himself wholly to the study of the Bible and Christian doctrine. When the Christians of Alexandria were again visited by persecution, Origen stood with several of his students whom the authorities had singled out as converts from paganism to Christianity. He also began to live a more austere and ascetic life, fasting for long periods, abstaining from wine, restricting his hours of sleep, sleeping on the floor, and even going about barefoot. Eusebius reports that Origen, in his zeal to give himself wholly to Christ, took the admonition of Jesus in Matthew (19:12), to make oneself a "eunuch for the sake of the kingdom of heaven," literally. About which Edward Gibbon, the Enlightenment historian of the Roman Empire, quipped in a witty and mordant footnote: "As it was his general practice to allegorize Scripture, it seems unfortunate that in this instance only he should have adopted the literal sense."

Initially Origen's bishop, Demetrius, was forgiving, and took his rash act as a sign of the vigor of his faith, but as Origen's stature grew he became less indulgent. Origen's lectures in Alexandria were popular, drawing women as well as men, and Demetrius felt his own authority threatened. Though Origen was a faithful son of the Church, committed to the rule of faith, Demetrius was uneasy having a brilliant —and independent—lay scholar holding forth in the city and attracting crowds. So Origen decided to leave for a spell, "desiring," he said, "to see the most ancient

Church of the Romans." While in Rome he had personal contact with other Christian teachers from around the empire.

He returned to Alexandria in 217, now in his early thirties, to resume his biblical studies. Again fortune came his way. He was approached by another wealthy patron named Ambrose who offered to provide him with secretaries to take shorthand (in antiquity books were often dictated rather than written by hand), copyists, and the tools needed to write his books. He employed seven shorthand writers as well as female scribes skilled in penmanship. Later, he viewed Ambrose as a "slave-driver" because of his persistent requests. But had it not been for Ambrose's high aspirations for Origen, it is unlikely we would have had so many writings from his pen. Two of his important works, the *Commentary on the Gospel of John* and his great apology in defense of Christianity, *Against Celsus,* were dedicated to Ambrose.

The first project undertaken with Ambrose's support was as unique as it was ambitious. Origen began to prepare an edition of the Old Testament with the text of several Greek versions (including the Septuagint) alongside the original Hebrew version written in Hebrew characters and in Greek letters (so a Greek speaker would know how the Hebrew words were to be sounded), copied out in six parallel columns, hence its name, *Hexapla*. Christians had little knowledge of the Hebrew version of the Bible, and few realized that many passages in the Septuagint, the Greek version, differed from the original.

For example, the Hebrew version of Genesis 2:4 reads: "These are the generations of the heavens and the earth when they were created." In the Septuagint the verse reads: "This is the *book* of the generation of heaven and earth when they were made." The Septuagint adds the word "book," perhaps in imitation of Genesis 5:1 where the same phrase, "book of the generations" occurs. Because of what he read in Genesis 5 a scribe could have mistakenly inserted the word "book" in 2:4. For this reason Origen wanted to have access to the Hebrew original.

Of course the Septuagint reading of Genesis 2:4 is a minor variant, but Origen believed that every word of the Bible, every nuance, every turn of phrase was precious. Even seemingly insignificant differences had to be noted. Not all were, however, minor. Aquila, for example, a Jewish translator, rendered Isaiah 7:14, "a young woman shall conceive," whereas the Septuagint had "a virgin shall conceive." Without a knowledge of the Hebrew text Christians could not discuss the meaning of this verse intelligently with Jews. The Hexapla ensured that a Christian scholar of the "divine words," as Origen called the Scriptures, would have a firm textual basis for interpreting the Bible.

The Hexapla was an innovative attempt to deal with a major literary challenge, a sacred book written in a language few adherents could read or understand. No other ancient Greek or Latin text had this character. Because the several versions were set side by side in columns, the layout of the book was quite different from other books, and it influenced the form of other writings. In the fourth century Eusebius, bishop of Caesarea and the first church historian, compiled a large historical work, the *Chronicle,* in which events in various ancient kingdoms under different rulers were set down side by side in parallel columns. He noted key synchronisms between Greek, Roman, and Jewish history, marking off the tables by decades so the reader would be able to locate a person or event and see it in relation to others. Eusebius also composed a book called "Gospel Canons" that divided the gospels into numbered sections. He drew up ten tables listing parallel passages, first in all four gospels, then in three, then in two, and finally passages that appeared in only one of the gospels. He gave the sections numbers so the reader was able to move easily from a passage in one gospel to a parallel in others. The modern division into chapters and verses was not created until the thirteenth century.

All this scholarly work in Caesarea over the course of a hundred years led to the formation of the first Christian library. Begun during Origen's day, it was expanded after his death by a wealthy patron who wished to preserve Origen's writings. Over time it became a large collection of pagan, Jewish, and Christian writings, and a scholarly center for the copying of books was established. One of the beneficiaries of the library in Caesarea was Jerome, who lived in Palestine at the end of the fourth century. Jerome was unusual in that he knew Latin, Greek, and Hebrew, and by drawing on the books collected in Caesarea he bequeathed to later generations an ideal of "trilingual scholarship" (Hebrew, Greek, Latin) that lives on to this day among learned Christians.

If the Hexapla required the skills of a philologist and a text critic, another early work of Origen's, *On First Principles,* could have been written only by someone who was a theologian and philosopher. This book, Origen's first venture into theology, deals with the chief points of Christian doctrine. Here is how he explains his reasons for writing the book: "Many of those who profess to believe in Christ hold conflicting opinions not only on small and trivial questions but also on matters of the greatest importance; that is about God or the Lord Jesus Christ himself or about the Holy Spirit." In contrast to Irenaeus's treatise against the gnostics, a robust defense of Christian teaching addressed to truculent opponents, Origen's *First Principles* was a patient and probing inquiry for orthodox Christians. His aim was to provide warrants for Christian faith—to offer rational and scriptural support for the "rule of faith"—and to weigh different opinions on matters that were disputed.

For Origen tradition was not a genteel legacy to be protected but a living thing to be contested as well as defended. He realized that there were many topics not addressed in the rule of faith, matters, he explained, on which the apostles had been silent. For example: whether the Holy Spirit was "begotten" like the Son (who is called the "only-begotten" in the New Testament [John 1:14]); whether the soul comes into existence at conception; how devils come to be; how and when angels were created (they are not mentioned in the account of creation in Genesis); whether God is corporeal. Though Origen believed firmly in the truth of the Scriptures, he knew that simply citing scriptural texts fostered neither understanding nor conviction. Interpreting the Scriptures required the work of reason no less than did philosophy. His aim was to make the "knowledge that leads to a good and happy life" a matter not only of faith but also of persuasion.

But his reasoning sometimes led to provocative and speculative conclusions, especially in dealing with the beginning and ending of things. For example, he thought it was contrary to the purposes of God that some would be condemned to eternal damnation. Had not Saint Paul written that "nothing can separate us from the love of God"? (Romans 8:39) If so, it is reasonable to believe that in the end God's love will draw all things to himself and bring all persons into his life. As further support for this view he cited Paul's words in the chapter on resurrection in 1 Corinthians: "When all things are subjected to him [God]," then "God will be all in all" (1 Corinthians 15:28). If God is all in all, nothing will be beyond his sway, and even the most heinous sinners will be restored and enjoy God's presence.

For Origen, human life, in this world and in the next, was a continuous process of moral purification whose end was to "behold God" with purity of heart. Though purgation may be long, arduous, and painful, at the end no creatures will be left out. One can detect here the seeds of the later doctrine of purgatory. Although most found Origen's teaching on the "last things" unsound, some, notably Gregory of Nyssa in the fourth century, thought he penetrated deeply into the mystery of God and was quite right to assert that the ultimate restoration of all things (*apokatastasis*) was a biblical doctrine. In the sixth century, however, Origen's writings were condemned; but that did not stop people from reading and learning from them.

On a visit to Palestine in A.D. 215, Origen was received warmly by Theoctistus, the bishop of Caesarea, even though he was a layman. His own bishop Demetrius considered this a breach of ecclesiastical discipline and asked Origen to return to Alexandria. A decade later Origen made another visit to Caesarea, and this time Theoctistus ordained him to the priesthood. Demetrius was incensed. Theoctistus had no authority to ordain someone who was not under his jurisdiction, and Origen's mutilation made him unfit for an office in the Church. Obediently Origen returned to Alexandria for a time, but in 234 he settled permanently in Caesarea, ironically after Demetrius had died.

Caesarea was a large port city (called Caesarea Maritima) located on the Mediterranean coast (north of Tel Aviv) some forty miles west of Jerusalem. It was rebuilt on a lavish scale by Herod in the first century B.C. and made the civil and military capital of Judea. According to the book of Acts, Philip and Peter preached there and Paul was taken into custody from Jerusalem to Caesarea to stand trial. It was one of the first cities to have a Christian community, and it quickly became the most important center of Christianity in Palestine, exceeding Jerusalem, which had become a Roman colony named Aelia Capitolina. Caesarea was also the home of a large Greek-speaking Jewish community. Because of its close proximity to Galilee, the center of Judaism in Palestine where the Mishnah, the first codification of Jewish law, was made in the early third century, Origen had contact with Palestinian Jewish thought and scholarship.

Origen was to spend the rest of his life in Caesarea, and his most mature works were written there, including many of his biblical commentaries. He was the first Christian to write scholarly commentaries on books of the Old Testament, such as Genesis and Psalms, as well as on the New Testament, including the Gospel of John and the epistles of Paul. Two features stand out in his commentaries: a deep respect, even reverence, for the words of the text, and the conviction that a spiritual meaning could be drawn from every passage of the Bible.

Consider his interpretation of the following passage from the book of Deuteronomy, for example. "If you walk in my statutes and observe my commandments and do them, then I will give you your rains in their season, and the land shall yield its increase, and the trees of the field shall yield their fruit" (Deuteronomy 11:13–17). Origen begins by putting questions to the text. If "rain" is given as a reward for those who keep the commandments, how does one explain that this same rain is given to those who do not keep the commandments, and the "whole world profits from the common rains given by God"? This leads him to propose that the term "rain" can have another sense than water from the heavens, because in this passage it seems to refer to something that is given only to those who walk in God's statutes and observe the divine law. It signifies something given "only to the saints."

With the puzzling use of the term "rain" in the passage as a starting point, Origen proceeds to examine the word "rain" elsewhere in the Scriptures and discovers that it is sometimes used in a metaphorical sense. Moses, for example, said, "May my teaching drop as the rain, my speech distil as the dew" (Deuteronomy 32:1–2). In this passage rain is a metaphor for Moses's words, and hence of the Word of God. That is to say, in the Scriptures "rain" can have another meaning than the plain sense. This way of interpreting the Old Testament is called allegory, which means giving a word or image "another sense" than the obvious meaning. Allegory had been used by Greek literary scholars to interpret the *Iliad* and the *Odyssey* of Homer, and by Jewish thinkers such as Philo on the Jewish Scriptures. But Origen is self-consciously following the example of Saint Paul, who had allegorized the story of Hagar and Sarah in Genesis (Galatians 4:21–31) and had written that what had happened among the ancient Israelites was to be understood "figuratively" (1 Corinthians 10:11). This did not mean that Old Testament history had no significance in its own right, but that it carried another, deeper meaning as well. Origen taught Christians to read the entire Bible as the living Word of God, a book that is always fresh, always new, always contemporary, always more profound than it appears on the surface.

Origen also addressed the world outside the Church and in particular the critics of Christianity. Since the early part of the second century Christian thinkers had written treatises in defense of Christian teaching and practices. They were called apologists, from the Greek term for "defense," and their task was to present Christian beliefs and practices to a society that knew little of this new religion. By the time Origen was writing there was a small body of apologies written in Greek by such figures as Justin in Rome, Athenagoras in Athens, Melito in Sardis in Asia Minor, Theophilus in Antioch, and Clement, Origen's predecessor, in Alexandria, and in Latin by Tertullian of Carthage. But Origen towers over all earlier writers, not only for the brilliance of his arguments, but also for the strategy he adopted in responding to critics of Christianity.

In the latter half of the second century a Greek philosopher by the name of Celsus had written a large work attacking Christianity. Celsus knew Christianity at first hand and had read Christian writings, including books that would become part of the New Testament. He called his work *True Word,* or *True Doctrine,* and his argument, reduced to a formula, is this: "what is old is true." The truth of religious practices and beliefs is judged by their antiquity.

Because Celsus's book was still being read in the middle of the third century, Origen decided to write not a general defense of Christianity as others had done, but a detailed refutation of Celsus's work. It was a fortuitous decision that has had unintended and happy consequences. For in his book Origen cited Celsus's actual words, paragraph by paragraph, before offering his rebuttal. Though Celsus's book has been lost, it is possible on the basis of Origen's citations to reconstruct not only his arguments but the actual words he used. And his excerpts from Celsus's book give us a very good idea of how the ancient Romans viewed Christianity at an early stage in its history.

Thanks to his tutelage by the philosopher Ammonius, Origen was able to meet Celsus on his own ground. He knew the authors Celsus marshals in support of his critique of Christianity and was able to respond argument for argument, text for text. In contrast to *First Principles,* where Origen drew on the Scriptures, here he appealed to what he calls "common notions" that are shared by all thoughtful men and women. At the same time he knew that Christianity was not the fruit of philosophical insight or deduction from presumed first principles. Its truth rested ultimately on the person of Christ, his life and character, and the community of men and women whose lives had been changed by him. Though his book is filled with arguments, in the end it is an invitation to the critics of Christianity to open their eyes to the new thing that is happening in their world.

* * *

Christianity brought into being a new kind of community, defined not by nation or people or language, but by its worship of the one God as known through Jesus Christ. Though it had similarities with Judaism, Christianity had no ties to a people or a land. By severing the bonds that fastened religion to people and place—a characteristic feature of religion in the ancient world—Christianity created a community whose practices, beliefs, and self-understanding set it apart. As the Church grew in numbers and influence, its independence would be severely tested, and at times the line between Church and "state" was so fine as to appear invisible. Yet the early experience of the Church as a society in its own right was never forgotten, and the struggle for the "freedom" of the Church in relation to political authority is a recurring theme in Christian history.

In the Decian persecution in 249 (discussed in the next chapter), Origen was imprisoned, bound in chains, stretched on the rack, and consigned to a dark, dank cell. He described his sufferings as "full of help to those who need encouragement." When the persecution ended he was released. What he had desired all his life, to die a martyr like his father, was not granted him. But his health was ruined, and he died shortly thereafter, probably at Tyre in 253, from the treatment he had received in prison.

7

Persecution:
Cyprian of Carthage

The first general persecution of Christians began in January 250. The date is noteworthy. Christianity had been around for more than two hundred years, yet this was the first systematic effort on the part of imperial authorities to force Christians to give up their beliefs and worship the Roman gods.

In popular imagination the early Church is portrayed as undergoing repeated and ruthless persecution. In truth, suppression of Christianity in the Roman Empire was spasmodic and infrequent, usually prompted by local circumstances. We know about some of these incidents: the execution of bishop Polycarp by fire early in the second century, the beheading of Justin Martyr and his companions in Rome in mid second century, the cruel mistreatment of a group of martyrs in Lyons in Gaul several decades later, the "passion" (suffering) of two women—Perpetua, a young mother, and her pregnant slave Felicity—in Carthage early in the third century. But looking over the empire as a whole, and observing the slow but steady growth of Christianity during the first two centuries, one can only conclude that in most cities Christians were free to go about their lives without fear or harassment. Christianity had the good fortune to come on the scene at a time of peace, stability, and prosperity in the empire, and by the beginning of the third century the new religion was vibrant and growing.

At the end of the first century there were fewer than ten thousand Christians in the Roman Empire. The population at the time numbered some sixty million, which meant that Christians made up one hundredth of one percent, or 0.0017 percent according to the figures of a contemporary sociologist. By the year 200, the number may have increased to a little more than two hundred thousand, still a tiny minority, under one percent (0.36). By the year 250, however, the number had risen to more than a million, almost two percent of the population. The most

65

striking figure, however, comes two generations later. By the year 300 Christians made up 10 percent of the population, approximately six million.

All of these figures are estimates. Because there are no hard demographic data, they can be used only with other evidence. They show that in absolute numbers Christianity grew slowly at first, but the pace picked up in the third century, and if one were to draw a graph for the fourth century the line would mount in a steep upward curve. Christians could be found in all the major cities of the empire and in many smaller cities, and it was becoming apparent that Christianity was not a passing phenomenon. What is more, the Church attracted people from all walks of life and from all social classes, and its leaders were well educated, cultured, resourceful, and articulate.

The third century, however, was a time of testing for the young churches—and in different ways for the empire itself. For the society the problems were many, defeats in war, incursions of peoples living on the borders, monetary collapse, floods, famine, plague. "The whole period was one uninterrupted series of confusion and calamity," wrote Edward Gibbon, the historian of the decline of the Roman Empire. In the second century the reigns of four emperors spanned eighty years, but in the third only a few ruled for more than ten years, and some only for months. The first emperor in the new century, Septimius Severus, was a strong and vigorous leader, who was emperor for two decades, but from his death in 211 until the accession of Decius in 249 there was a succession of a dozen rulers. Still, for the average provincial, life changed little from generation to generation. And at midcentury, in 248, the founding of the city of Rome was celebrated with a grand and extravagant festival marked by sacrifices of animals, hunting of exotic beasts in the Circus Maximus, theatrical presentations, and three nights of pageants. A new beginning seemed at hand.

At the time of the celebration the emperor was Julius Philippus, a native of Syria, hence known as Philip the Arab, but four years into his reign he was challenged by Decius, a military commander appointed to restore order on the Danube. After being proclaimed emperor by his troops in 249, Decius defeated Philip in a battle at Verona in northern Italy. Although he ruled for only two years—he was killed in a battle with the Goths in Dacia in the Balkans in 251—his reign was eventful, if not for Rome then certainly for Christianity. In Christian memory his name became a symbol of persecution.

Decius was born in Pannonia in the Balkans, on the northeastern frontier of the empire, early in the third century. Within the same decade, at the other end of the empire, in the province of Africa, near Carthage, the great city in North Africa, second only to Rome in the western Mediterranean, a wealthy landholding Roman family celebrated the birth of a son. His name was Thascius Caecilianus Cyprianus. Cyprian and Decius would never meet, but Decius's reign as emperor would be the fateful turning point in Cyprian's life.

Like other boys from his social class, Cyprian received a thorough grounding in Latin grammar and rhetoric, and after completing his studies he embarked on a career as an orator and teacher of rhetoric in Carthage. A polished Latin stylist and a gifted speaker, well-born and self-assured, Cyprian quickly gained fame as an orator and respect as an advocate. But he found himself, in his own words, "tossed about on the foam of this boastful age, uncertain of my wandering steps, knowing nothing of my real life." He was being drawn to Christianity, but based on his own experience he could not understand how a person could be "quickened to new life" by washing in water, cast off like a garment what he had been previously, and be changed in "heart and soul." How could habits that had become "inveterate by long accustomed use" be given up?

After Cyprian came under the influence of an aged priest named Caecilianus (hence the surname Caecilian), he embraced Christianity. As a sign of his new life he bestowed his fortune on the poor. Within two years of being received into the Church, in the mid 240s, he was ordained a priest and shortly afterward elected bishop, probably at the beginning of 249.

At the end of the same year, Decius made his entrance into Rome as the new emperor. One of his first official acts on claiming the imperial purple was to issue a series of coins honoring the divinized emperors of the past. He took the name of Trajan, a revered emperor in the second century. And to ensure a public display of the religious devotion for which the Romans were renowned, at the beginning of 250 he ordered that all citizens of the empire were to offer sacrifice to the gods. He intended this to be a public gesture of gratitude for past beneficence and a pious prayer for future help. The decree called for a formal act of religious observance: offer a libation, participate in a sacrifice by eating of the sacrificial victim, or in some cases, sprinkle a pinch of incense on an altar. Those who performed the required rite were issued a *libellus,* a certificate, that testified that the bearer had fulfilled his civic obligation.

Religion was part of the fabric of Rome's civic life, and the gods demanded worship through concrete, publicly visible gestures of piety. Centuries earlier Cicero, the Roman statesmen, had written: "Disappearance of piety toward the gods will entail the disappearance of loyalty and social union among men . . . and of justice, the queen of all the virtues." For Decius, those who observed religious rites devoted to new or strange gods tore the fabric of society, threatening the peace on which the welfare of the empire depended. Jews had long been exempted from having to venerate the Roman gods, and this exemption remained in effect in the third century. Christians, however, enjoyed no exemption, yet they shunned the civic ceremonies that included veneration of the gods. As the number of Christians mounted, their absence became more conspicuous and more offensive. Decius's project was a well-crafted policy, no casual undertaking.

Sacrifices for the emperor's health and longevity were traditionally offered on

January 3, and it is likely Decius's decree was issued in anticipation of this festival at the beginning of 250. The first person to be arrested was the bishop of Rome, Fabian, and he died a few weeks later in prison from harsh and brutal mistreatment. It was understandable that imperial authorities acted first in Rome. By the middle of the third century the Church in Rome was large and well known. According to Eusebius, besides the bishop there were forty-six presybters, seven deacons, seven subdeacons, forty-two acolytes, fifty-two exorcists, readers, and doorkeepers, and over fifteen hundred widows and needy persons. In other cities authorities also moved swiftly against the leaders of the churches. In the first month, Alexander, bishop of Jerusalem, was arrested and died in prison, Fabian bishop of Antioch was martyred, Dionysius, bishop of Alexandria, was apprehended and imprisoned. And, as we have seen, Origen, the Church's most prominent thinker, living in Caesarea in Palestine, was cruelly tortured on the rack.

To carry out the imperial order, commissions were set up in cities and towns all over the empire. In Carthage the commission was composed of five prominent citizens. They had no authority to punish, nor were they ordered to seek people out. The populace took care of that. Their sole responsibility was to confirm that a person had sacrificed to the gods. The certificate gave the name of the person, the town and the date, and the names of the members of the commission who witnessed the sacrifice. Two copies were made, one for the person and another for the archives. When someone refused to offer sacrifice, the matter was referred to higher authorities.

Copies of certificates of sacrifice were found in the parched dry sands of Egypt early in the twentieth century, and they give us a good idea of how the legal process was carried out (see box). A person had to come before the members of the commission and offer a libation or eat sacrificial meat. The act of sacrifice was personal and public, and there was no way one could hide. One made the sacrifice or refused. In either case what a Christian did was known to others in the city or town and to fellow Christians.

The immediate impact of the commission's work on the Christian community of Carthage was devastating. Many Christians complied, some coming forth voluntarily to sacrifice. Some even brought their own wine or other offerings. In one city a bishop showed up with a lamb under his arms for sacrifice! Cyprian laments that only a tiny band stood firm. This is not surprising. As the number of Christians increased, the boundaries between the Christian community and the larger society were becoming porous. Some Christian parents, for example, gave their daughters in marriage to pagan men. Some saw no contradiction between participating in the civic cult one day and presenting themselves for the Eucharist on Sunday. And of course the price for refusing to sacrifice was high: confiscation of property, imprisonment, torture, or death. Some bribed officials to secure a libellus, others went

---

LIBELLUS FROM A VILLAGE IN EGYPT, DATED SUMMER 250

[1st hand]. To those appointed to oversee the sacrifices. From Aurelia Charis
   of the village of Theadelphia. I have always been constant in sacrificing
   and shown piety to the gods, and now too, in your presence, in
   accordance with the orders I have poured a libation, and I have offered
   sacrifice, and I have eaten of the sacrificial offerings. May you prosper.
[2nd hand]. We, Aurelius Serenus and Aurelius Hermas, saw you sacrificing.
[3rd hand]. I, Hermas, certify it.
[1st hand]. The year one of the Emperor Caesar Gaius Messius Quintus
   Traianus Decius Pius Felix Augustus, Pauni 22 [June 16, 250].

---

into hiding, and yet others fled. In some cases the authorities finessed the matter, allowing a father to sacrifice for his family. The aim was not execution, but to weaken and thin out the Christian community.

Fearing that the Church would fragment, Cyprian decided that the only way to hold things together was to go into hiding. So he fled the city and kept in touch with his clergy through letters and messengers. Understandably he was roundly criticized for his action, and his authority weakened. But his decision was calculated. He knew that in other cities the bishop was first to be apprehended, and that if he were arrested and executed the local community would be leaderless and in disarray. He was well known to the authorities and would be a precious trophy if imprisoned. He also judged (correctly) that he could not count on his presbyters.

His decision to flee proved prescient. On his return the Church was faced with an unprecedented problem that called for firm and resolute leadership. Persecution had divided the community between those who had stood firm and those who had, in Cyprian's words, "broken their oath to Christ" by offering sacrifice. Idolatry, venerating false gods, transgressed Christianity's most fundamental belief in one God. Dubbed the "lapsed" because they had either sacrificed or obtained certificates (by whatever means) stating that they had sacrificed, by Church law they were excluded from participation in the Eucharist. The other group was made up of those who had courageously confessed their faith, been imprisoned, flogged, twisted on the rack, starved in dark damp dungeons, and in some cases executed. Their steadfastness not only brought honor, it conferred on them unique spiritual prerogatives. And there was the rub.

The lapsed began to turn to the "confessors," those who had confessed their faith in Christ yet lived through the persecution, to ease their return to full fellowship. The confessors complied by issuing letters of reconciliation stating that the bearer of the letter should be received into communion on the strength of the intercession of the confessor. At first the letters were given to specific individuals, but soon the confessors were issuing generic letters, "vague and indefinite certificates," says Cyprian, that could be used by anyone. In effect the confessors were usurping the authority of the bishop, who alone had the right to forgive sins and impose penance. When some presbyters (who had not supported Cyprian's election as bishop) took the side of the confessors a showdown was inevitable.

From his place of exile Cyprian pleaded for patience. He urged that nothing be done about the lapsed until the persecution had ended. No matter what promises the confessors made, the lapsed must undergo penance and be reconciled to the Church as a whole, not granted pardon by individual confessors. By acting independently of the bishop the confessors threatened the unity of the Church at a time when everyone needed to hold together. They also invited laxity. So in a letter to his clergy Cyprian ruled that anyone who admits the lapsed back into fellowship before the clergy could meet would be banned from communion with the Church. In the meantime he sought to build support among the clergy in North Africa.

The persecution ended as abruptly as it began. By spring 251, Cyprian was back in Carthage. Summoning all his rhetorical skills, he addressed the community in a memorable oration "on the lapsed," a work at once wise, generous, biting, and resolute. He praises the courage and faith of the confessors, he grieves for the "wounded," meaning those who had sacrificed, and even counts himself among the "fallen" because of his flight. The long years of peace had "undermined the practice of the faith," and all must share the blame. Nevertheless Cyprian was unbending on the key point: no one except the bishop can forgive a sin committed against God through worshiping false gods, by practicing idolatry.

For Cyprian, in a matter of such gravity the intercession of the confessors and martyrs cannot displace the Church's system of penance. Though their efforts are noble and compassionate, their time has not yet come. They will have their say when Christ returns. Appealing to the example of the saints in the book of Revelation, he notes that when those who "had been slain for the Word of God" cried out to God to "avenge our blood on them that dwell on earth" (Revelation 6:9–10), they were told to be patient. Judgment will be rendered only at the end of time.

A few weeks later bishops from all over North Africa met to reach a judgment on the matter. The debate turned on how to balance the need for compassion and forgiveness of sins with the uncompromising statements in the Scriptures against idolatry. For example, Jesus had said, "whoever denies me before men I also will deny before my Father who is in heaven" (Matthew 10:32–33). In an impassioned debate, scriptural texts were cited on both sides of the issue, and in the end a moderating position was adopted. Each case must be considered individually on its merits. Those who had received certificates of sacrifice (but had not actually sacrificed) were to be readmitted after a time of penance (depending on the circumstances in which the certificate had been received). Those who had sacrificed would undergo "prolonged penance" and be reconciled to the Church on their deathbeds.

The council was a victory for Cyprian and for episcopal authority. Though the confessors were honored, their claim to possess unique spiritual authority was overruled. The issue turned on the nature of the Church, on its unity, its order and hierarchy. By blurring the lines between the Church and society the confessors compromised the Church's holiness as a unique community set apart from the society at large.

For Cyprian the controversy was not simply a matter of theological ideas; it also had to do with fidelity to the dead. The martyrs defined the true nature of the Church. One tiny detail makes this clear. He instructed his presbyters to give special care to the bodies of the martyrs in Carthage. He wished them not only to see to their proper burial, but also to keep a record of the day on which each martyr died. If we know the date of their martyrdom, said Cyprian, "we will be able to include the celebration of their memories in our commemoration of the martyrs." It was to this community, the company of the martyrs, that the lapsed must be reconciled. The faithful dead created a vivid memory that the living belonged to a unique fellowship.

The conflict over how to deal with dissension in Carthage led Cyprian to write the first Christian treatise on the nature of the Church, titled *On the Unity of the Church*. In it, Cyprian argued that there is only one Church and that unity is of its very essence. The unity of the Church throughout the world must be mirrored in the local church. He had a keen sense that the Church in Carthage was part of a network of communities stretching from one end of the Roman Empire to the other. In a memorable phrase he spoke of "this holy mystery of unity" (*hoc unitatis sacramentum*) symbolized in the seamless cloak of Christ (John 19:23). And in perhaps his most often quoted line he wrote: "You cannot have God for your Father if you do not have the Church for your mother."

This unity would soon be severely tested by another controversy that pitted Cyprian and the Church at Carthage against the Church in Rome. As we have seen, baptism was a solemn ritual administered once in a lifetime. But because of divisions within the Church, the question arose as to what the bishop should do when someone who had been baptized in one of the "sects," such as the Montanists or the Marcionites, asked to be received into the Catholic Church. In Africa it had been the practice to receive such a person through the laying on of hands by the bishop. At a council in Carthage in 230, however, it was decided that those who had been baptized in a separate communion should be rebaptized when joined to the Catholic Church. With the emergence of schismatic groups in the wake of the persecution—some rigorist and others lax on the matter of penitential discipline—the issue of baptism took on new urgency.

As the issue heated up, Cyprian defended rebaptism and wrote letters to bishops in Africa outlining the reasons for his position. In baptism a person "put on Christ." One could not be more or less Christian, as though the gifts of Christ could be separated and parceled out in bits and pieces. For Cyprian, Christian baptism was a complete break with the world.

Carthage had long had a close relation to Rome. The coast of North Africa was not far from Sicily, and travel to Rome by sea was relatively easy. All through the conflict over the lapsed, Cyprian had been in communication with the Church in Rome. But when news reached Rome of the decision about rebaptism, Stephen, the bishop of Rome, rejected the views of the Africans as contrary to ancient and apostolic practice. The Africans sent an embassy to Rome to try and resolve the conflict, but Stephen refused to receive the bishops and insulted Cyprian, calling him a "false Christ and false apostle." In turn Cyprian, skilled in the art of invective, responded with his own litany of insults, calling Stephen "arrogant, inconsistent, self-contradictory, ill-considered, and inept" and dismissing his views as "erroneous."

Neither side would bend, and in early September 256 Cyprian called an extraordinary synod of bishops and sent letters to key bishops in Africa accompanied by a packet of letters that laid out, from his point of view, the course of the dispute. Later in the same year, at a council in Carthage, the bishops of Africa gave their support to Cyprian, although some acknowledged that there might be legitimate differences of opinion on the matter. No doubt Cyprian heard their objections. In the introduction to the minutes of the council written in Cyprian's hand one can detect a moderation of his earlier views. He was chary of breaking communion with Rome. In this matter, he wrote, we judge no one nor do we reject communion with anyone "if he thinks differently from us." And for good measure he adds: "None of us has set himself up as bishop of bishops."

In 257 the historical record goes silent, as the Church was again visited by persecution at the instigation of another emperor, Valerian. This time Cyprian was arrested at once and brought before the Roman proconsul. The "acts" of Cyprian, a chronicle of his trial and death based on official court records and the testimony of eyewitnesses, gives us a vivid, and largely unembroidered, account of his appearance before the authorities.

> The proconsul said to Cyprian the bishop: "The most sacred Emperors Valerian and Gallienus have thought fit to send me a letter, in which they have commanded that those who do not observe the Roman religion must recognize the Roman rites. I have therefore made inquiries concerning yourself. What answer do you give me?"
>
> Cyprian the bishop said: "I am a Christian and a bishop. I know no other God but the one true God who 'made heaven and earth, the sea, and all that is in them' [Acts 4:24]. This God we Christians serve, to Him we pray day and night for ourselves, and for all men, and for the safety of the emperors themselves."

The proconsul said: "Do you persist in this decision?"

Cyprian responds: "A right decision taken before God cannot be changed."

He was then banished to exile in Curubis, a city on the coast some thirty miles east of Carthage. A year later, in July 258, he was recalled from exile to face trial again. Cyprian was advised to flee, and even though he knew his death was certain he refused. He did, however, hide for a spell because the new proconsul, Galerius, was in Utica at the time, not in Carthage, and he wanted, in his words, to "confess his faith in that city where he has been placed in charge over the Lord's flock." He wished to die among his own people. In his final letter to the faithful, he wrote that "it is in your midst that I ought to be making my confession, it is there I ought to suffer, it is from there I ought to go forth to the Lord."

When Galerius returned to Carthage he summoned Cyprian, who set out at once for the city. On arrival he retired to his "gardens," until he was called to appear in court. Several days later, on September 13, two high officials came with a carriage to take him to the proconsul.

The next morning, on September 14, he was brought before Galerius, who asked: "Are you Thascius Cyprianus?" Cyprian responded, "I am."

Proconsul: "The most reverend emperors have ordered you to perform the religious rites."

Cyprian answers: "I will not." Then Galerius tries reasoning with him. "Consider your own interest." To which Cyprian responds: "Do as you have been ordered. In so clear a case there is no need for deliberation."

Then Galerius said:

> You have long persisted in your sacrilegious views, and have joined to yourself many other abominable persons in a conspiracy. You have set yourself up as an enemy of the gods of Rome and of our religious practices; and the pious and venerable emperors Valerian and Gallienus, Augusti, and Valerian the most noble of Caesars have not been able to bring you back to the observance of their sacred rites.
>
> Since you have been convicted as the instigator and leader of a most atrocious crime, you will be an example for all those whom in your wickedness you have gathered to yourself. Our laws will be vindicated by your blood.

Finally he read his decision from a tablet: "Thascius Cyprian is sentenced to die by the sword." Cyprian responded: "Thanks be to God."

Cyprian was taken to the place of execution, where "he removed his outer cloak, spread it on the ground so that he could kneel on it. Next he removed his dalmatic [inner garment] and gave it to his deacons; then he stood erect and began waiting for the executioner. When the executioner came, Cyprian told his friends to give the man twenty-five gold pieces. His brothers spread cloths and napkins in front of him." They wished to soak up his blood so they could become holy objects to be venerated after his death.

Cyprian tried to bind his eyes with his own hands but was unable to do so. A presbyter and subdeacon fastened the cloth on him. And so, writes the Christian editor of the "acts," "the blessed Cyprian went to his death, and his body was laid out near by to satisfy the curiosity of the pagans. At nightfall, however, the Christians removed the body, and accompanied by a cortège bearing tapers and torches, it was carried in a solemn procession to the cemetery of Macrobius Candidianus the procurator, which lies on the Mappalian Way near the fishponds and was buried there. A few days later the proconsul Galerius Maximus died." To which the narrator adds, the day was sunny and cloudless as though "rejoicing in the thought of its martyr."

Cyprian's time as bishop of the church in Carthage in the mid third century is a good vantage point from which to look back on the first two hundred years of Christian history and to cast an eye toward the future. In the early centuries Christianity was made up of small, tightly knit communities distinct from society, an "enclosed garden," to use Cyprian's metaphor. To become a Christian meant a break with family and friends, neighbors, colleagues, and business associates. The norms of behavior were set very high, and the churches had an elaborate and rigorous system of penance to deal with grave offenses. The Church had a keen sense of its otherness, a society within society with its own standards of admission and moral expectations, organization, and rituals.

But things were changing. The growth in numbers in the first half of the third century brought about a weakening of the bonds that held the community together. When faced with the prospect of torture, imprisonment, or death, some Christians returned to their former way of life. Others tried to have it both ways. Cyprian, however, held to an older view of the Church as the community of the elect; he believed that persecution winnowed the chaff from the wheat. Christians were to keep free of civic rituals, refuse to eat meat sacrificed to idols sold in the markets, and even turn their eyes when passing pagan statues. The bishop and the magistrate lived in different worlds, and the emperor was a distant figure.

But the time was not far off when the growing number of Christians would reshape the Church's self-understanding. Christian leaders began to realize they had responsibilities to the larger society, and with the conversion of an emperor to Christianity at the beginning of the fourth century, Christians would be thrust into positions of leadership. Slowly but inexorably the lines between the Church and society would be blurred, and the Church would begin to take on the marks of a civic and public institution.

8

A Christian Emperor:
Constantine

Although Christianity became linked to the fortunes of the Roman Empire, the role Rome was to play in the Church's history was not apparent in the early centuries. Some Christians thought it providential that Christ was born during the reign of Augustus, the first Roman emperor, but most saw no convergence between the hopes of the Church and the aspirations of earthly rulers. In the early centuries the life of the Christian communities went on largely independent of the political affairs of the society around them. There were of course sporadic persecutions, social and cultural influences on Christians (on the earliest art, for example, as the catacombs show) and on Christian thinking (as the writings of Origen attest), but in large measure the early history of Christianity is a story that unfolds within the Christian communities.

That would change dramatically in the fourth century. With the conversion of Constantine, a Roman emperor, to the new religion early in the century, the Church began to assume a prominent role in society. Later in the century, under Emperor Theodosius, Christianity was declared the official religion of the Roman Empire. In some form Christianity held this place in the countries of Europe, and in some of the American colonies, until the nineteenth century. A visible sign of the change was the construction of imposing church buildings that displaced the ancient temples and changed the urban landscape. In most cities of Europe to this day a stately church or cathedral sits on the central public square.

At the end of the third century, however, the old world was still very much in place, and in the first decade of the fourth century the Church endured a time of persecution unprecedented in severity and scope. In the decades since the death of Cyprian in the mid third century the advance of Christianity had quickened. In some regions Christians made up a significant minority of the populace, and across the empire Christians were growing in number and influence. By the beginning of the fourth century there were more than two hundred bishops in Latin-speaking North Africa, and in Egypt Christianity had put down roots not only in the Greek-speaking city of Alexandria on the Mediterranean coast but up the Nile River among the native Coptic-speaking people.

The new religion was no longer a novelty, an alien and little known sect—it had become a powerful social and intellectual force. The churches owned property and Christianity had many sympathizers in the cities and towns. In Nicomedia, where the Eastern emperor often resided, a Christian church building could be seen from the palace. Yet to many Romans, including some of society's most influential citizens, Christians practiced an impious religion whose way of life was seditious and subversive of the commonweal.

In the fall of 284 a high-ranking military officer from Dalmatia in the Balkans named Diocles was acclaimed emperor by the army. On his elevation to the purple he added a few letters to his name, and he is known to history as Diocletian. For the Romans he would become one of the most enterprising rulers in their long history and for Christians one of the most despised. A man of great energy and determination, he first eliminated his rivals. Then he embarked on an ambitious program to reorganize the imperial administration, impose price controls across the empire, raise taxes, and fortify the frontiers. To magnify the dignity of the imperial office he introduced elaborate court ceremonial and etiquette borrowed from Eastern potentates.

His most original contribution was the novel idea of dividing the empire into two geographical regions with two senior emperors, called *augusti,* one for the East and one for the West, and two junior emperors, called *caesars,* one for each *augustus.* The empire was too large and far-flung for one emperor to be in all the places where he was needed, especially since he had to lead armies onto the field of battle. Diocletian also hoped to rectify the failures of the dynastic system by providing for an orderly succession; when the augustus died, authority was passed on to his caesar.

In theory it was a reasonable system, but the dispersal of authority increased rather than diminished rivalry among contenders for the empire's highest office. And by decentralizing the empire it led to a de facto division between East and West, roughly between Italy, North Africa, Gaul, and Spain, in the west, and Greece, the Balkans, Syria, and Egypt in the east. The tetrarchy, as the new administrative system was called, also introduced into historical accounts a bewildering medley of names of emperors that make it difficult to follow the course of events in the early fourth century. So let the reader be warned: in the pages that follow emperors seem to spring up like mushrooms after a soaking rain.

Here then is the cast of characters at the time the tetrarchy was established. The senior augustus was Diocletian, who had his palace in Nicomedia in northwestern

Asia Minor; the augustus of the West, Maximian, was located in Milan in northern Italy. The Western caesar, Constantius Chlorus, the father of Constantine, was based in Trier, across the Alps in Gaul, and the Eastern caesar, Galerius, had his headquarters in Sirmium in present-day Serbia. Significantly, the city of Rome was no longer the administrative center of the empire, and within a few decades a new capital, Constantinople, would be built on the European side of the Bosporus, the strait that divides the Asian from the European parts of Turkey today and connects the Black Sea to the Aegean. The division of the empire portended the division between Western and Eastern Christianity.

Although Diocletian showed no particular interest in Christianity during the early years of his reign, he wished to restore ancient Roman ways by grounding public morality in traditional religious practice. In an edict on marriage in 295, he said: "The Roman empire has attained its present greatness by the favor of all deities only because it has protected all its laws with wise religious observance and concern for morality." In 297 Diocletian proscribed the practice of Manichaeism, an Eastern religion imported from Persia, whose missionaries were active in the empire. And he welcomed the advice of leading philosophers who offered, in the name of the traditional religion, arguments against Christianity.

Several incidents during his reign confirmed his suspicion that Christianity was resistant to full integration into society. A Roman proconsul, on a routine visit to the city of Tebessa in Numidia (Algeria) to recruit soldiers for the third Augustan legion stationed there, interviewed a young Christian man, Maximilian, twenty-one years old. The young man refused induction (though he was reminded that other Christians served in the military) on the grounds that he could not wear the lead seal around his neck marking his legion since he had been marked by the "seal" of Christ. For his refusal and his disloyalty he was sentenced to death and summarily executed. A few years later a Christian centurion publicly renounced his military oath.

During a religious sacrifice at which the emperor Diocletian and Galerius, his caesar, were present, something went awry. The auguries, inspection of the entrails of the animal to be sacrificed, did not yield the proper signs. After the priests tried again and again without success to achieve the desired result, one declared that there were "profane persons present who obstruct the rites." Several Christian attendants on the emperor had made the sign of the cross at the ritual. Enraged, Diocletian ordered that everyone who lived in the palace must offer sacrifice to the Roman gods or be scourged. He also instructed military commanders that soldiers who "impiously" refuse to sacrifice should be discharged from the army. Yet he resisted the efforts of his caesar, Galerius, to inaugurate a general persecution.

But in February 303, after a visit to the oracle of Apollo at Didyma in western Asia Minor, Diocletian relented. He insisted, however, that the goal was not to kill

Christians but to put pressure on them to give up their religion and return to the worship of the ancient gods and goddesses of Rome. In a dawn raid imperial soldiers plundered the Christian church in Nicomedia, burned the Scriptures, and razed the building. The next day an edict was published ordering that churches across the empire were to be destroyed, Christians forbidden to assemble, the Scriptures handed over to authorities to be cast into the flames, and Christians of rank deprived of their privileges (acting as plaintiffs in cases of injury, for instance). A few months later another edict enjoined the arrest of the higher clergy (bishops and priests).

Across the empire Diocletian's directives were differently enforced. In the West, where Constantius Chlorus, Constantine's father, was caesar there were no martyrs, only the burning of a few churches. In the East and in North Africa, however, the edicts were strictly and rigorously carried out. In the city of Cirta in present-day Tunisia, for example, authorities demanded that the bishop hand over the Scriptures. When he explained that they were in the possession of the lectors (readers), the local authorities emptied the church of all its valuables, including sacramental vessels and provisions set aside for the poor. Christians who had refused to divulge the names of the lectors or tell where they lived were arrested (see box).

Across the empire, however, the actual number of martyrs was few. In the West the persecution had effectively come to an end at the close of 306, but in the East it lasted for the better part of a decade. Contemporary accounts tell a doleful tale of destruction and suffering. Eusebius wrote a book recounting the stories of the martyrs of Palestine, the province in which his city of Caesarea was located. Many churches were destroyed, the Scriptures and liturgical books burned, and Christians imprisoned, maimed, or horribly burned (from a gridiron). And, as in earlier persecutions, there were some who capitulated by handing over the Scriptures, offering sacrifice, or managing through guile to get around the laws. A Christian businessman in Egypt, for example, on seeing an altar in a law court on which he would be asked to offer sacrifice before bringing his case, arranged power of attorney for a pagan friend to act on his behalf.

But the persecution could not be sustained. Christians were too numerous, their communities too cohesive and organized, and their leaders too adroit to be done in by the sword. By forcing a choice between Rome and Christianity, the emperors badly misjudged the strength and resiliency of the Church. There was little popular support for the policy, and some citizens actually shielded Christians. Diocletian and Galerius represented a narrow and hard paganism that was divorced from the social fact that Christians were not outsiders but neighbors, friends, members of one's family, shopkeepers from whom one bought bread or vegetables or fish.

In the midst of the first wave of persecution Diocletian took sick and lost the will to rule. In spring 305 he summoned the imperial court, his leading generals, and a

[*The mayor arrived at the house where the Christians used to meet, and he spoke to Paul the bishop.*]

Mayor: "Bring out the writings of the law and anything else you have here, according to the order, so that you may obey the command."
Bishop: "The readers have the scriptures, but we will give what we have here."
Mayor: "Point out the readers or send for them."
Bishop: "You all know them."
Mayor: "We do not know them."
Bishop: "Edusius and Junius in the municipal office know them."
Mayor: "Never mind the business about the readers. The municipal office will point them out. Produce what you have."

[*There follows an inventory of the church plate and other property, including large stores of male and female clothes and shoes, that are brought out along with three priests, two deacons, and four subdeacons, all named, and some gravediggers.*]

Mayor: "Bring out what you have."
Subdeacons Silvanus and Carosus: "We have thrown out everything that was there."
Mayor: "Your answer is entered in the record."

[*After some empty cupboards had been found in the library, Silvanus brought out a silver box and lamp, which he said he had discovered behind a barrel.*]

Mayor's clerk Victor: "You would have been a dead man if you had not found them."
Mayor: "Look more carefully, in case there is anything else here."
Silvanus: "There is nothing left. We have thrown everything out."

[*When the dining room was opened there were found four bins and six barrels.*]

Mayor: "Bring out the scriptures that you have so that we can obey the orders and command of the emperors."

[*The subdeacon Catullinus produced one very large volume.*]

Mayor: "Why have you handed over only one volume? Produce the scriptures that you have."
Subdeacons Marcuclius and Catullinus: "We have no more because we are subdeacons, the readers have the books."

Mayor: "Show me the readers."

Marcuclius and Catullinus: "We do not know where they live."

Mayor: "If you do not know where they live, tell me their names."

Marcuclius and Catullinus: "We are not traitors. Here we are: order us to be
    killed."

Mayor: "Put them under arrest."

[*The subdeacons nevertheless divulged the name of one reader, Eugenius, and when the mayor
arrived at his residence Eugenius surrendered four books. The mayor then turned to the other
two subdeacons, Silvanus and Carosus.*]

Mayor: "Show me the other readers."

Silvanus and Carosus: "The bishop has already said that Edusius and Junius
    the clerks know them all. They will show you the way to their
    houses."

Edusius and Junius: "We will show them, sir."

[*The mayor proceeded to visit the six remaining readers. Four of them produced their books
as ordered: five volumes from the first, eight from the second, five large codices and two small
ones from the third, two codices and four fascicules from the fourth. The fifth declared that he
had no books. The last reader was not at home, but his wife produced six books that were in
his possession, after which the mayor had the house searched. When no other books were
found, he again addressed the subdeacons.*]

Mayor: If there has been any omission, the responsibility is yours.

company of troops to the palace near Nicomedia where he had been proclaimed
emperor two decades earlier. In a tearful address he announced that he was abdicat-
ing and turning over his authority to his caesar, Galerius. The assembly, waiting to
hear whom he would name to replace Galerius, turned its eyes to Constantine the
son of Constantius Chlorus, the caesar of the West. But Diocletian surprised the
crowd by naming two close friends, coarse and hardened soldiers, Severus and
Maximin, as caesars. About the same time Maximian, the augustus in the West, also
stepped down. This meant that Constantius Chlorus became the augustus of the
West. His son Constantine, disappointed that he had not been elevated to the rank
of caesar, set out at once from Nicomedia in Asia Minor to join his father in
the West.

When Constantine arrived in Gaul, Constantius was about to cross the English
Channel to Britain to meet the Picts, a troublesome federation of tribes living in the
north of the island. Soon after his arrival Constantine led the army beyond Hadrian's Wall to defeat the Picts. Less than a year later, in July 306 at York in Britain, as

Constantius lay dying, he designated his son Constantine to succeed him as augustus of the West, and Constantine was acclaimed emperor by the army. When Galerius, the senior augustus in the East, heard that Constantine had been proclaimed augustus by his army, he responded by sending him a purple robe. This was a signal to Constantine that only Galerius could bestow imperial authority on him, and he proclaimed him caesar, not augustus, as his father and the army had wished. Constantine shrewdly accepted the lesser honor, thereby securing the legitimacy of his rule in the West and his place in the college of emperors. His first action on assuming imperial power was to proclaim a formal end to the persecutions in the regions under his rule, Britain, Gaul, and Spain. By restoring the right of Christians to worship God according to their rituals Constantine set himself apart from his imperial colleagues and put himself on record as a friend of Christianity.

In 311 the senior augustus Galerius, close to death, issued a proclamation ending the persecution. The aim, he declared, had been for the Christians to return to the "institutions of the ancients," the religion of the Romans, but he acknowledged that the result had been only hardship, suffering, and dissension. He ruled that citizens should "be Christians"—that is, live openly, and meet together in their places of worship. He also released those who had been imprisoned, though there is no evidence of his restoring property that had been confiscated. What he granted to the Christian communities in the East was not new. In Italy and Africa they had already been granted the right to practice their form of worship, and in Constantine's realm their property and buildings had been restored. What was new was that he asks Christians to pray "to their God" for "our safety and that of the state [*res publica*]" so that "from every side the res publica may be kept unharmed." Prayer, not sacrifice, was now the mark of piety. Even though Galerius had no liking for Christians and found them willful and refractory, his decree recognized Christianity as a legitimate form of worship that could contribute to the well-being of the empire. A few months later, he died.

When Galerius died, Maxentius, Maximian's son, who had married Galerius's daughter and, like Constantine, been passed over as caesar, claimed for himself the title of augustus, with hegemony over Italy and North Africa. This meant that if Constantine was to assert his rule over the West he would have to defeat Maxentius. So he gathered his army, crossed the Alps, and marched purposefully and deliberately toward Rome, where Maxentius and his army were waiting. What happened next is a matter of great dispute. A Christian account written shortly after the battle reports that in a dream Constantine was instructed to "mark the heavenly sign of God" on the shields of his soldiers before taking the field. The sign was the letter X with a vertical stroke through it. Armed with this sign, Constantine's soldiers gained the victory.

But a later account by Eusebius based on Constantine's own report to him says that the sign appeared in the heavens during the day, in fact in the afternoon when the sun was beginning to wane, and that it was also seen by the army. All were astounded at the sight, and Constantine was at a loss as to what it meant. According to Eusebius's account this unusual spectacle in the sky did not take place at the Milvian Bridge up the Tiber River from Rome, but when Constantine was on the march with his troops elsewhere, probably in Gaul. A third account in a panegyric of Constantine written by a Roman orator, dated two years earlier in 310, also says the event took place on a march and what Constantine saw was the sun God Apollo surrounded by a circle or wreath of light.

It seems there were two key moments, one a strange marvel in the sky in A.D. 310, and the second a dream before the battle with Maxentius outside the city of Rome in 312. Most likely what happened is that on a march with his army in Gaul in 310 Constantine and his troops saw a "halo-phenomenon" surrounding the sun, which sometimes appears on a winter afternoon. The sun is surrounded by a circle of light that has two lesser suns on a horizontal axis to the right and left, called *parhelia,* or colloquially, sun dogs, and another point of light above the sun, called the upper tangent arc. When all three are visible the points of light extending out from the center form an image that resembles a cross in a circle. Such displays of light happen infrequently, but one did occur in our time in northern New Mexico on February 25, 1988, and there are reports from antiquity of similar phenomena.

From what we know of Constantine's religious inclinations prior to his embrace of Christ, he took the vision of light in the heavens as a sign of the sun god Apollo, the Sol Invictus, the "unconquerable Sun." Coins minted under Constantine's rule from 310 suddenly began to be stamped with the legend SOLI INVICTO, "to the unconquerable Sun," and when he declared Sunday a legal holiday, he said it was the "day of the revered Sun." But the sun had long been a symbol of the one God and had been used as a metaphor of Christ, the "sun of righteousness" (Malachi 4:2). The image of Christ-Helios (sun) appears in a Christian tomb where Jesus rides a solar chariot with the rays of his cross radiating from a solar disk. As Constantine became more inclined to the God of the Christians one can understand that the strange spectacle in the sky resembled a light-filled cross associated with Christ.

As Constantine marched down through Italy without serious opposition he became convinced that his campaign had divine protection. In a dream before the decisive battle he discerned that the light he had seen in the heavens was a manifestation of the Christian God and the circle around the cross represented a crown, the symbol of victory. According to Lactantius, a contemporary Christian writer, Constantine took the vision to mean, "in this sign you will be victor." So he instructed his soldiers to prepare a new military standard bearing an X with a line running down through the middle in a circle. Viewed from one perspective it looked like the familiar Chi-Rho symbol, the first two letters of "Christ" in Greek (equivalent to "Ch" and "R") superimposed on each other. In identifying and interpreting the sign with Christ, Constantine was no doubt aided by the bishops who accompanied him. The new standard was called "labarum," a word whose origin is unclear, but it is probably Celtic, not Latin, and may have something to do with a heavenly prodigy.

Although there will always be questions about the spiritual depth of Constantine's experience, the point to remember is that we are dealing with the conversion of the emperor at a time when Roman authorities were uncertain how best to deal with a powerful religious minority. As emperor, any decision he took on religious matters could not be solely personal; it also affected how the affairs of the empire would be administered. For the Romans, religion and public policy were interwoven. Constantine was seeking a way to reconcile the role of religion in public life with the refusal of a significant segment of the citizenry to venerate any other god than the one God. As the historian Harold Drake has observed, Constantine was casting about "not only for a god in whom to believe but a policy he could adopt." His conversion signaled the emergence of a new political as well as religious program. Realizing the bankruptcy of the policies of his predecessors and the growing strength of the Church, Constantine believed that Christians could do more to further his goals than could the adherents of the traditional religion.

Constantine's rival Maxentius made his stand at the Milvian Bridge that carried the great northern highway of Italy across the Tiber into the city of Rome. Things went badly from the beginning for Maxentius, and his army was no match for Constantine's might and determination. The battle ended swiftly and decisively, and Maxentius, in full armor astride his horse, died ignominiously when the pontoons of the bridge across the river collapsed and he drowned. The date was October 28, 312. The next day, convinced that his victory had come through Christ, Constantine entered Rome in triumph as the sole ruler of the West, to the acclamation of the populace.

The city Constantine entered was the ancient capital of the Roman Empire, with its venerable public buildings encircled by great walls for a length of twelve miles. On the Capitoline Hill, the present-day Campidoglio, stood the ancient temple to Jupiter, Juno, and Minerva; on the Palatine Hill were found the residences of the imperial family; below was the Roman Forum with temples, triumphal arches, statues, and the Colosseum. Breaking with ancient tradition, at the culmination of his triumphal procession through the city, Constantine refused to ascend the Capitol to offer the customary sacrifices to the gods. The symbolism of his gesture was not lost on the citizenry, and in the weeks that followed Constantine had to tread cautiously. Though there were many Christians in the city, the members of the Senate, the great families, and many of the rank and file still venerated the ancient gods.

But Constantine was determined to give the Christian God a public face, and as early as the winter of that year he began the construction of a church in Rome. In the past emperors had built temples to the gods, but Constantine erected a basilica to the one God in which a new sacrifice, the sacrifice of the Eucharist, would be offered. Prudently, however, he did not locate the church in the sacred center of the city among ancient and revered monuments. He chose a site in the southeastern part of the city near the Celian Hill, just inside the walls, in an area of private homes and military barracks—a relatively remote location. There was no reason to offend the sensibilities of the populace by thrusting a new god in their faces and giving the appearance that he was dismantling the old order. He arranged for the building to be constructed with funds donated to the Church as a private corporation.

The barracks on the site were razed and by spring work had begun on the construction of the first church building in the ancient capital of the empire, a cathedral for the bishop of Rome, on the site of what is today Saint John Lateran. For the Romans the traditional religious building was a temple, but Constantine's architects realized that the form of the temple was ill-suited to the needs of Christian worship, so they adopted the form of the Roman basilica, a multipurpose rectangular building used as an audience hall for law courts, business dealings, bazaars, even military drills. Most basilicas were modest in size and decoration, but this first church in Rome was built on a grand scale, seventy-five meters long and fifty-five meters wide, with two rows of columns on either side of the central nave forming four aisles. The inner columns were taller than the outer columns, which allowed for a clerestory in the central nave. The nave terminated in an apse with an altar, semicircular benches for the clergy against the rear wall, and a ceremonial seat (*cathedra*) for the bishop.

The Lateran basilica was an opulent building with colored marble columns and marble walls and floor. It could accommodate three thousand people and was part of a complex that included an octagonal baptistery and a residence for the bishop and staff. Ostensibly the church was the work of a private religious group, but by its size and splendor it was in fact a new kind of public building and a symbol of the triumph of Christianity, as the Dome of the Rock in Jerusalem built after the Islamic conquest would become a symbol of the triumph of Islam.

When the church was begun Constantine was ruler of the West, not of the empire as a whole. There were two other "emperors" in the East, Licinius and Maximin Daia, and each was determined to eliminate the other. They met in battle at Adrianople (modern Edirne in European Turkey, west of Istanbul) in the spring of 313. Maximin was hostile toward Christianity and made a vow to Jupiter that if he was victorious he would "utterly destroy the Christian name." Licinius, on the other hand, was sympathetic to Christianity—at least for a time—and ordered that a prayer addressed to the "great God, the holy God," be copied and distributed to his lieutenants so they could teach it to those in their command. Before his final battle with Maximin in Adrianople in the spring of 313, when the armies were in sight of each other, his soldiers put down their shields and removed their helmets. Stretching their hands to heaven they joined the emperor in reciting the prayer three times. Whether by piety or military valor, Licinius carried the day.

In winter of that same year, 313, before the battle with Maximin, Licinius and Constantine had met in Milan. The occasion was the marriage of Licinius to Constantine's half sister, Constantia. But the two emperors used the occasion to discuss matters of state and agreed on a policy concerning the practice of religion. During the summer of 313 Licinius sent letters to provincial governors in the territories formerly ruled by Maximin in the East, in Asia Minor and Syria, granting Christians the rights they had already acquired in the West and restoring their property. This letter has often been called the "Edict of Milan," but the term is a misnomer. It was not an edict, but a letter posted by Licinius from several cities in the East, such as Nicomedia, the residence of the emperor. Like other official correspondence, however, it was written in the name of both emperors and its content reflects the hand of Constantine.

The letter is noteworthy in several respects. For one thing it deals not only with Christianity but with all forms of religious worship practiced in the empire. To assure "reverence for the divinity," Licinius wrote, "we grant both to Christians and to *all men* the freedom to follow whatever religion each one wished." Second, it goes beyond toleration and adumbrates in a few phrases a new understanding of religious freedom. Each person should be granted the freedom "to give his mind to the religion which he felt was most fitting to himself." Because the supreme divinity is to be served with a "free mind," the worship of God cannot be coerced; it must be an act of the will and arise out of genuine devotion and piety.

The philosophical underpinnings of this decree can be found in a Christian author by the name of Lactantius. In his defense of Christianity he had argued that Christianity should be tolerated not because there are many ways to God, the conventional defense of religious toleration. Rather Lactantius believed that coercion is inimical to the nature of religion. He offered a theological rationale for religious freedom rooted in the nature of God. Religion has to do with love of God and purity of mind, neither of which can be imposed or coerced. "Why should a god love a person who does not feel love in return?" he asks. Religion must be "voluntary." "Nothing," he writes, "requires freedom of the will as religion." This understanding came to shape later Western ideas of religious freedom.

Finally, the letter treats the Church as a corporate body with the right to own property, including church buildings. "Since . . . Christians are known to have possessed not only the places in which they were accustomed to assemble but other property which belongs by right to their body [*corpus*]—that is, to the churches not to individuals—you will order all this property, in accordance with the law which we have explained above, to be given back without any equivocation or dispute at all to those same Christians." Though we know from other sources that churches had owned property, such as the catacomb of Callixtus, this letter makes clear that the Church was to be viewed as a legal corporation with distinct rights and privileges.

Although Constantine and Licinius agreed on how to deal with Christians and other religious communities, they nevertheless had different religious views. Constantine had embraced Christianity and begun to favor the religion in his realm, giving it a privileged status. Licinius, on the other hand, was a traditional pagan who believed that there were many gods ranked in a hierarchy, with one god at the pinnacle. For him the first god, the *summus deus,* was Jupiter, the king of the gods, not the God of Abraham, Isaac, and Jacob. Although he joined Constantine in granting Christians the right to practice their religion in his territory in the Eastern empire and restored building and property to the churches, he soon turned against Christians, purging them from the civil service and the military, and forbidding assemblies of bishops.

A showdown was inevitable, and the uneasy peace between the two emperors was broken when Constantine met Licinius in battle at Adrianople and drove him back to Byzantium (the future Constantinople). In September 324 the two armies again met at Chrysopolis outside Chalcedon, across the Bosporus in Asia Minor, and Constantine was victorious. After the battle Licinius offered his imperial purple cloak to Constantine as an act of homage, and his life was spared, but a year later he would lose his head. Constantine entered Nicomedia, the imperial capital in the East, twenty years after he had fled in disappointment to the West. He was now the sole ruler of the empire.

Constantine celebrated his victory over Licinius by founding a new city in the east. He had never felt at home in Rome, and he began to envision a new capital, a metropolis that would be free of the monuments and memories of pagan Rome, a city built from the ground up as a fitting embodiment of the new religion and a throne for himself.

He chose a place where a small Greek city, Byzantium, had existed for centuries. It was a promontory on the northern shore of the Sea of Marmara, on the European side near the entrance to the Bosporus, surrounded to the east by a deep inlet known as the Golden Horn, facing Nicomedia across the sea, the residence of the Eastern emperor. Constantine wasted no time getting things moving. The tracing of the city wall, a kind of consecration of the spot, took place in November 324, only six weeks after his victory over Licinius. Constantine may himself have laid out the area with spear in hand. The official dedication of the new city took place six years later in the new hippodrome, and from that time until his death Constantine spent a few months each year in the new capital. By 334 many of the requisites of the new city were in place, the walls, aqueduct, palace for the emperor, and layout of the streets, but the actual building of the city would take decades. It was destined to become the new Rome and the center of a Christian empire, which did not come to an end until the fifteenth century, when the Ottoman Turks captured Constantinople.

9

The Council of Nicaea and
the Christian Creed

In any telling of the story of Constantine's rise to power, his triumph over rivals, his embrace of Christianity, and the building of a city bearing his name in the East, Constantine is the protagonist. But in giving allegiance to the God of the Christians he had taken on a new constituency as well as a new creed and one that was quite unlike any he had known previously. To become a Christian was one thing; to deal as emperor with Christianity as a corporate body was another matter. For the Church was an independent society with intelligent leaders accustomed to running their own affairs and, unlike pagan priests, they were not functionaries of the state.

So it was with surprise and some dismay that Constantine learned that Christians did not agree on certain things, even on matters of great import. In the decade after Constantine became emperor, controversy broke out in the Christian East on a teaching of such consequence that it divided the Christian world for the next several generations. Not only was there division among leaders and faithful, wrote Eusebius, "sacred matters" were "subject to disgraceful public mockery in the theaters by unbelievers." What is more, the dispute dealt with a highly complex theological and philosophical matter, the likes of which had no precedent in Roman religion, and which Constantine, a man who had spent more time in the field leading armies than reading books in a library, was ill-equipped to grasp. Even though the emperor was *pontifex maximus,* the highest priest in the empire, the initiative in religious matters had passed from him to leading bishops of the Church. Or so it seemed.

The chief problem was this. The central Christian affirmation is that God is one. The first Christians were Jews who recited the Shema each morning: "Hear O Israel the Lord your God is one God." Saint Paul had written, "For us there is one God, the Father, from whom are all things" (1 Corinthians 8:6), and his words are echoed in the early rules of faith: "one God, the maker of heaven and earth, and of all that are in them." But Paul had also written that Christ is "designated Son of God in power according to the Spirit" (Romans 1:3), and the evangelist John began his gospel with the memorable words: "In the beginning was the Word [*Logos,* a Greek word meaning reason or word, and also used for Christ], and the Word was with God and the Word was God." As early as the beginning of the second century outsiders had observed that when Christians gathered together they sang hymns to Christ "as to a god."

So the question arose: did worshiping Christ as God mean that Christians believed in two gods? If the answer was yes, how could they claim to confess one God and urge the faithful to spurn the gods of the Romans? Of course Christians answered no. Still this did not put an end to the matter, for it was unclear precisely what it meant to call Christ God. Was he God in the same sense that God the creator was God, or was he a divine being ranked below the creator?

By the fourth century the relation of Christ to God the Father, the creator of the world, had vexed Christian thinkers for generations. Persons as different as Origen in Greek-speaking Alexandria on the coast of Egypt and Tertullian in Latin-speaking Carthage in North Africa had addressed the topic in their books. But the matter was brought to a head early in the fourth century by the sermons of a presbyter (priest) in Alexandria named Arius who hailed from Libya, the Roman province directly west of Egypt. Even though what we know about him comes largely from his critics, he was described as a learned and cultivated man, serious and even austere in demeanor and eloquent in speech.

In sermons that were popular among the people of Alexandria, Arius taught that God was wholly singular, unlike any other being, beyond human comprehension and thought, unique. So rigorously did Arius stress the utter transcendence of God that he seemed to be suggesting that Christ, the Son of God, was less than God the Father, subordinate, and hence not fully divine. Christ, for example, had a beginning; he was not eternal like the Father. In the words of Arius, "there was a time when he was not." And if Christ came into existence at a certain time, it was reasonable to call him a "creature": a being like other beings that had been made, such as angels. Of course Arius believed that Christ was an exceptional, godlike creature, but he taught that only the Father was truly God. Arius was trying to preserve the central Christian belief that God was one, and at the same time give due veneration to Christ.

For several years Arius was able to teach in Alexandria without drawing attention to himself. But when he became involved in another dispute, his bishop, Alexander, became alarmed as he heard reports of his preaching. For if Christ was not truly God, as Arius claimed, Alexander reasoned, how could he be creator of all that exists or redeem humankind from sin, as the Scriptures clearly teach? Arius's ideas seemed to challenge central articles of faith. So Alexander convoked a meeting of bishops, what in ecclesiastical language is called a council, in 318. There Arius was condemned of heresy: of choosing to preach things that were contrary to Christian teaching.

Had Arius been simply a solitary presbyter with unorthodox views, the matter might have ended there. But his incautious language had exposed a sensitive nerve. Many bishops, especially in the East, were sympathetic to his arguments. It soon became evident that there was a wide range of opinion in the Church, even distinct schools of thought, on Christ's relation to the Father, and the differences could not be easily reconciled. In truth, the controversy was not primarily about Arius's teaching; it was the beginning of a sustained project to define and express a profound mystery, that in the person of Jesus of Nazareth, God had become a human being. Arius ignited a tiny spark that kindled a mighty fire.

Almost immediately after the condemnation of Arius, bishops in the Greek-speaking cities of the eastern Mediterranean began to take sides, some coming to Arius's defense, others championing Alexander or staking out another position. Some wrote letters to other bishops to muster support for their views. And so began one of the most historic epochs in Christianity, a time when leading bishops of the Church disagreed profoundly on central matters of Christian teaching. Ecclesiastical councils publicly debated deep theological issues, with the aim of reaching consensus on language to express central Christian beliefs in formal statements of faith. The disagreements ran deep, and the disputes were often bitter and sometimes violent. From the beginning of the fourth century to the middle of the sixth century, more than 250 councils dealt with a wide range of topics.

As the theological storm was gathering strength, the emperor Constantine had his mind on other things. For a decade Constantine and Licinius, the other augustus, had been vying with each other for control of the empire. In 322, to repel Gothic invaders, Constantine had crossed into Licinius's territory. By 324 the two men were at war, and on September 24 of that year Constantine's army, led by his son Crispus, vanquished Licinius, a victory hailed throughout the Christian world. In the final book of his *Ecclesiastical History,* written soon after the battle, Eusebius, with customary hyperbole, was exultant. "Licinius was cast down prostrate. But Constantine the most mighty victor, resplendent with every virtue that godliness bestows, together with his son Crispus, an emperor most dear to God and in all respects like his father, recovered the east that belonged to them, and formed the Roman Empire, as in days of old, into a single united whole."

In the midst of celebrating his triumph, Constantine learned of the uproar in Alexandria. His first response was to send a delegation, headed by Hosius, bishop of Cordoba in Spain, to Alexandria carrying a letter to bishop Alexander urging him to negotiate peace between the parties. It is clear from this letter that Constantine's sole concern was political, yet he recognized, however dimly, that there was a theological matter at issue, namely how to reconcile "diverse opinions concerning the deity." Understandably he found the matter "small and trivial," and the dispute an "idle question." Impatient with intransigent bishops, he pushed for a swift resolution of the matter so he could enjoy "quiet days and untroubled nights." Little did he sense that he would die decades before the dispute was resolved.

Even though the controversy involved complex matters of Christian theology—properly the responsibility of bishops—Constantine decided to step in to adjudicate the matter. His decision, "to look after our affairs," as a Christian historian observed somewhat innocently in a later century, set a precedent: later emperors would make it their business to intervene in ecclesiastical matters. The Church's internal life was becoming a matter of state. So Constantine proposed a council of bishops, a political decision without precedent. In the past, councils had been called by bishops in the region; this council was convoked not by the bishop of Alexandria, where the dispute had begun, or by bishops of other apostolic cities, such as Antioch or Rome, but by the head of state, the Roman emperor. Church councils would quickly become instruments of imperial policy.

The bishops had been planning to meet at a council in Ancyra (modern Ankara, Turkey) in central Asia Minor in spring 325. Their purpose was twofold: to celebrate Constantine's victory over Licinius and to come to an agreement on the date of Easter. But at the emperor's order the council was transferred to Nicaea, a city that was more accessible by sea and not far from the imperial palace in Nicomedia. Constantine planned to take part in the proceedings.

Invitations to the council were sent out to bishops all over the Christian world. For this reason Nicaea came to be considered the first "ecumenical" council, or worldwide gathering of bishops. Though most of the bishops came from Greek-speaking cities of the eastern Mediterranean, some came from the West, for example from Gaul and Calabria in southern Italy, and others from Syriac-speaking areas to the east, yet others from Armenia and even Persia. The bishop of Rome, Sylvester, did not attend, but he sent two representatives. And the president of the council, Hosius, hailed from Cordoba in Spain.

Tradition has it that 318 bishops attended, but the number was probably a little over 200. Many had lived through the terrible years of persecution two decades earlier and bore on their bodies the marks of their suffering. It was reported that when Constantine greeted Paphnutios, a bishop from the Thebaid in the Nile Valley whose eye had been gouged out during the persecution, he reverently kissed the empty socket. The bishops traveled at the emperor's expense, and his guests were treated sumptuously while in attendance at the council. Bishops were becoming civic and political figures, and within the space of a few decades they were even players in the affairs of state. As the vast resources of the emperor were made available to the churches, the inevitable corruption of money and power made its way into the highest offices of the Church. The pagan historian Ammianus Marcellinus observed that some bishops received "gifts from ladies of high station, ride in carriages, dress splendidly and surpass kings in their lavish tables."

The council convened in June 325. Unfortunately, there are no minutes of its proceedings. From reports, however, we know that the bishops convened in the central assembly room in the palace and were seated in rows parallel to the walls awaiting the emperor's arrival in silence. When the emperor entered, without his customary military guard, "resplendent as one of God's angels in heaven," in the words of Eusebius, all rose. He stepped to a golden armchair, but took his seat only after the bishops beckoned him to do so. Constantine then addressed the bishops in Latin, and his words were translated into Greek. He expressed an ardent desire that they would put dissension behind them and bring about a spirit of peace and concord pleasing to God as well as to himself.

At once the issues were joined, and charges were met with countercharges. Constantine allowed each bishop to have his say, but he had difficulty following the arguments. Not only did they deal with sophisticated points of theology, the bishops spoke in Greek and his language was Latin. As the debate proceeded some bishops submitted statements of faith—local creeds used in their dioceses. But all were simple confessions of faith used to instruct converts when they were baptized and received into the Church. None addressed the issues raised by Arius. A fuller theological statement was required.

For the ancient Greeks and Romans, religion was an affair of rituals and practices, not doctrine. Christians, however, not only believed *in* God, they also believed *that* God had created the world, that human beings were made in the image of God, that Christ, the divine Son, had become man, suffered, died, and rose from the dead, that at the end of time there would be a general resurrection. In other words, they claimed that certain things were true, and these truths required precise language to state clearly and unambiguously what was meant. Already in the New Testament one can find formulaic language to speak about God. As I have already noted, Paul, drawing on the Jewish Shema, wrote: "There is one God, the Father, from whom are all things, and for whom we exist, and one Lord, Jesus Christ, through whom are all things and through whom we exist" (1 Corinthians 8:5).

The bishops had hoped they would be able to resolve the conflicts and agree on a statement of faith using scriptural language. But they discovered at once that biblical expressions ("from God," "true Power and Image of the Father") were ambiguous and could be bent to accommodate differing views. Still, they did not wish to depart too radically from the language of the Bible. So the formulations they finally agreed on used familiar biblical words ("Son of God," "begotten," "light") and included a brief narrative of Christ's birth, suffering, death, and resurrection. But they also introduced two terms that are not found in the Scriptures, "substance" or "being" (in Greek, *ousia*), and "of one substance [or being]" (*homoousion* in Greek). These terms, however, were closely linked to key biblical texts (such as 1 Corinthians 8:4–6) and were employed to clarify and interpret what was found in the Scriptures.

A key point of dispute was the relation of Christ, the Son, to the Father. Arius had said that the Son is "from nothing." But such language was contrary to the clear testimony of the Scripture, as in the opening words of the Gospel of John, "In the beginning was the Word and the Word was *from God*" (John 1:1), and the Epistle to the Hebrews that says Christ is "the exact stamp of [God's] substance" (Hebrews 1:3). To secure this teaching the bishops at Nicaea introduced the expression "from the substance" of the Father. That is, the Son, who is begotten of the Father, derives his existence from the essence of the Father. Everything in the world comes into existence by an act of divine will, meaning it was "created"—but Christ was from the Father's very being, or ousia.

The second term, *homoousion,* is a refinement of the expression "of the Father's being [ousia]." It is constructed from the word *ousia* and *homo,* which means "same" or "like." Hence it is translated "of like substance" (or being) or "of the same substance" (or being). With this term the council fathers wished to say not only that the Son comes from the "being" of the Father but also that he is in every respect the same substance or being as the Father.

Finally, the bishops appended a series of "anathemas," or condemnations, to the creed stating that certain expressions can no longer be used in Christian preaching or teaching. When it appeared that a consensus had emerged, the statement of faith was solemnly read out loud to the assembly in Greek:

> We believe in one God, the Father Almighty, maker of all things visible and invisible.
>
> And in one Lord Jesus Christ, the Son of God, begotten from the Father, only begotten, that is from the substance of the Father, God from God, Light from Light, true God from true God, begotten not made, of one substance with the Father, through whom all things were made in heaven and on earth; who for us men and for our salvation came down and became incarnate, becoming man, suffered and rose again on the third day, ascended to the heavens, and will come to judge the living and the dead.
>
> And in the Holy Spirit.
>
> Those who say there was a time when he was not, or before he was begotten he was not and that he came from non-being, or from another substance or being, or that he was created, or is capable of moral change or mutable—these the catholic and apostolic Church anathematizes.

When it came time to vote on what had been read, most of the bishops were in agreement, although seventeen sided with Arius. Others, with some consternation, realized that views they held were now excluded. Yet others complained that the creed represented a dangerous innovation in Christian teaching without support from the Scriptures or earlier Christian tradition. And of course some who had supported Arius before the council now had to join in his condemnation. Arius himself was given the choice of signing or being sent into exile, and he honorably chose exile.

The statement of faith of the bishops at the Council of Nicaea marks a significant development in the history of Christianity. For it is the first declaratory creed—a confession of faith that takes the form of a statement beginning with the words "we believe." The term "creed" comes from the Latin, *credo,* I believe. Further, this creed was not a personal confession of faith of a bishop or of a local Christian community; it was a formal statement of Christian teaching adopted by bishops from all over the Christian world under the auspices of a Christian emperor. Its purpose was to clarify fundamental matters of faith and to exclude certain opinions as heretical: deviant and unacceptable. Hence the creed appends anathemas at the end.

The bishops at the council also issued a series of "canons" dealing with liturgical, disciplinary, and jurisdictional matters. In these regulations one can discern the outlines of an embryonic body of Christian law. Canon 6, for example, rules that the bishops of three major cities shall have jurisdiction over the regions in which they are located, Alexandria in Egypt, Antioch in Syria, and Rome in Italy. Canon 20 forbade kneeling for worship on Sunday and during the weeks after Easter and Pentecost.

The most consequential canon had to do with the date of Easter. As we have seen, the question of the date of Easter had not been resolved in the second century. By the early fourth century, practice was more uniform, but there were still differences in reckoning the date. To put an end to the scandal of churches celebrating the central Christian festival on different days, and of having to depend on the synagogue for setting the date, the bishops issued an encyclical letter, which was sent around to the churches, ruling that the practice in Rome and Alexandria is to be followed, namely that Easter be celebrated on the first Sunday after the full moon after the vernal equinox.

Nicaea, alas, did not put an end to the dispute of the relation of Christ to God the creator. In fact the council added fuel to the debate by exposing differences among the bishops, generating further controversy that would occupy the minds and consume the energy of leading bishops of the Church until the end of the century. The controversy would draw the emperors more deeply into ecclesiastical affairs. The fourth century would go down in Christian history as a time of learned and sophisticated theological debate joined with low, dirty, partisan politics, of councils opposing or contradicting other councils, of disputes over the election of bishops, and of the exile of controversial bishops. Even the man in the street was drawn into the dispute. "If you ask anyone for change," one observer wrote, "he will discuss with you whether the Son is begotten or unbegotten. If you ask about the quality of bread, you will receive the answer, that 'the Father is greater, the Son is less.' If you say you would like a bath, you will be told that 'there was nothing before the Son was created.'"

The Nicene controversy brought onto the stage several of the most forceful personalities and deepest thinkers in the Church's history. One was Athanasius, who became bishop of Alexandria in 328, when he was only twenty-nine years old. Of all the protagonists in the great debate over the Trinity, he was the first to mount a full-scale defense of the teaching of the Council of Nicaea. But he was also headstrong, uncompromising, calculating in dealing with opponents, and he was condemned by a council in 335 and exiled to Trier in Gaul. Later he was deposed from his see, where he was allowed to return only toward the end of his life. But he had a profound understanding of the mystery of Christ, and in a series of essays dealing with biblical texts that were under dispute, he showed that the biblical language about Christ made sense only if Christ were fully God and had a unique relation to God the Father.

It was, however, left to another generation to provide the theological rationale and technical language to resolve the dispute. Of these the most notable figures were three bishops in Asia Minor, two brothers, Basil of Caesarea and Gregory of Nyssa, and Basil's close friend, Gregory Nazianzen. They worked out the implications of what had been decided at Nicaea and took up a new issue, whether the Holy Spirit, like the Son, was fully God. Basil wrote the first treatise in the history of Christianity on the Holy Spirit to show that if the Holy Spirit is not fully God there is no reason to baptize "in the name of the Father, and of the Son, and of the Holy Spirit." The Spirit must be given the same glory, honor, and worship as the Father and the Son.

In 379 Flavius Theodosius Augustus became Roman emperor. He had served as *magister militum,* the chief military officer in the Balkans, and after the death of the emperor Valens at the humiliating defeat of the Roman forces at the battle of Adrianople by the Goths in 378, he was made augustus of the East by the senior augustus Gratian. In 384 he became sole emperor. Theodosius was a pious Christian raised in Spain by parents who confessed the faith of Nicaea. On assuming the purple he refused the traditional title of Roman emperors, pontifex maximus, high priest. When he first arrived in Constantinople, the capital of the empire, he summoned the Arian bishop of the city, Demophilus, to an audience. Because of the divisions spawned by Nicaea in some cities there were two bishops, one Nicene and the other Arian or Homoean: those who believed that Christ was of "like substance" (homo*i*ousion) with the Father, not of "one substance" (homoousion) with the Father. Though the difference between the two terms was only an iota in Greek, they represented profoundly different understandings of the relation of the Son to the Father. For forty years the church in Constantinople had been in the hands of the Homoeans, and Theodosius informed Demophilus that he had to make a choice: either subscribe to the creed of Nicaea or resign as bishop of the city. Demophilus chose to resign, and Theodosius handed over the churches in the city to the Nicene community. Demophilus was forced to meet with his followers at a church outside of the city.

The Nicene bishops knew that Theodosius was sympathetic to their views, and at a council in Antioch in 379 a group of bishops, led by the bishop of Antioch, signaled to the emperor that the time was ripe to unite the warring factions and bring the Eastern bishops in line with the West, the Latin-speaking regions, which were staunchly Nicene. So in spring 381 Theodosius summoned the bishops to a council in the capital, Constantinople, with Meletius, bishop of Antioch, as the president. There were no bishops from the West and no legates from Rome. It was assumed by those in attendance that the aim of the council was to reaffirm Nicaea. But so much had happened in the previous fifty years that the Nicene wording had to be revisited and a new topic had to be debated: the status of the Holy Spirit in relation to the Father and the Son.

Unfortunately we have no minutes of the proceedings and, surprisingly, the text of the creed adopted at Constantinople is not mentioned in our sources until it appears in the decree of another council, Chalcedon, in the middle of the next century, some seventy years later. But most scholars believe that the text cited at Chalcedon was indeed produced at Constantinople in 381. It reads as follows:

> We believe in one God the Father almighty, maker of heaven and earth, of all things visible and invisible.
>
> And in one Lord Jesus Christ, the only begotten Son of God, begotten from the Father before all ages, light from light, true God from true God, begotten not made, of one substance with the Father, through Whom all things came into existence, Who because of us men and because of our salvation came down from heaven, and was incarnate from the Holy Spirit and the Virgin Mary and became man, and was crucified for us under Pontius Pilate, and suffered and was buried, and rose again on the third day according to the Scriptures and ascended to heaven, and sits on the right hand of the Father, and will come again with glory to judge living and dead, of whose kingdom there will be no end.
>
> And in the Holy Spirit, the Lord and life-giver, Who proceeds from the Father, who with the Father and the Son is together worshiped and together

glorified, Who spoke through the prophets; in one holy catholic and apostolic Church. We confess one baptism to the remission of sins; we look forward to the resurrection of the dead and the life of the world to come.

This creed differs from that of Nicaea in three respects: it has a new section on the Holy Spirit; it drops the phrase "of the being [ousia] of the Father," though it keeps the term *homoousion;* and it eliminates the anathemas against Arius.

The elimination of the anathemas is understandable. The teaching of Arius was no longer an issue. But excising the phrase "of the substance of the Father" is surprising, and its omission has puzzled historians and theologians. The simple explanation is that the actual words of the creed of Nicaea were not sacrosanct. What was important was its central theological idea, that the Son is God in the same way that the Father is God, and the term *homoousion* (of one substance with the Father) expressed this theological idea. The bishops had no intention to diverge from Nicaea, and eventually the creed of Constantinople was called the Nicene Creed. No doubt few could pronounce its full title: the Nicaeano-Constantinopolitan Creed.

What is decidedly new is the third section on the Holy Spirit. At Nicaea the creed only included the phrase "and in the Holy Spirit." Now it has a full article, a whole section, on the Holy Spirit. The intention was to affirm that the Holy Spirit, like the Son, is fully God. This is expressed in the initial descriptions of the Spirit as "Lord and Giver of Life." These terms are taken from scriptural texts where the Spirit is called "Lord" (2 Corinthians 3:17) and the one who "gives life" (John 6:63 and 2 Corinthians 3:6). Only God, it was assumed, can give life.

In the earlier stages of the controversy the debate centered on whether the Son was fully God, and in this sense it was primarily about the relation of the Son to the Father. The creed of Constantinople shows that between the Council of Nicaea and the Council of Constantinople, Christian thinkers had decided on precise terminology to express their understanding of God in a distinctly Trinitarian way. This is evident in the use of the term "proceeds" with respect to the Spirit. Taken from the Gospel of John (15:26), the word signified that the relation between the Spirit and the Father is different from that of the Son. The Spirit "proceeds from the Father," whereas the Son is "begotten of the Father."

Note too that the term *homoousios* was not used of the Holy Spirit. Apparently not everyone was ready to affirm the full divinity of the Spirit. No fewer than thirty-six bishops at the council held that the Spirit should not be worshiped as Christ is worshiped. Nevertheless the creed is quite explicit in saying that the Spirit is to be worshiped and glorified *with the Father and the Son.* In Greek the terms are "co-worshiped" and "co-glorified." If the Spirit is given equal worship to the Father and to the Son, then he is equal in status to the Father and Son: that is, he is fully God.

Although the issues that gave rise to the Council of Nicaea and the debates that followed seem abstruse, the controversy stemmed from a matter of central importance to Christian life: how the Church expresses its core beliefs and what language should be used in Christian worship and prayer, Nicaea became the definitive Christian confession of faith, and in little more than a century the revised form of the creed adopted at Constantinople became a constituent part of the Church's central act of worship, the Eucharist. It was sung at the end of the first part of the Eucharist when the Scriptures were read and expounded, and to this day orthodox Christians—those who uphold the faith of Nicaea (the majority of Christians in the world)—recite the Nicene Creed at each Sunday celebration of the Eucharist and on festivals.

The Councils of Nicaea and Constantinople ensured that Christianity's distinctive understanding of God would become a permanent and enduring part of Christian tradition. Although Christians were unreservedly and unequivocally monotheistic and believed, along with Jews, and later with Muslims, that there is one God, they understood that God was not a "solitary God," as one church father put it. This affirmation, that God's inner life was triune, was a great impetus to Christian thinking and to spiritual life, for it affirmed that the deepest reality is communal.

Monasticism

In the year the controversy over Arius erupted in Alexandria a farmer in the village of Karanis in lower Egypt, fifty miles south of present-day Cairo, filed a legal petition alleging that a neighbor's cow had trampled and destroyed the plantings in his fields. By happy fortune this petition was discovered some decades ago on a papyrus preserved in the sands of Egypt. In it the plaintiff, Aurelius Isidorus, complained that the cow had done this more than once. So he caught the cow and as he was leading it back to the village he was met on the road by its owner and his friends carrying clubs. They began to beat him and threw him to the ground. He would have been killed, so read the petition, had the "deacon" Antonius and a "monk" named Isaac not happened along the road and come to his defense.

The papyrus is written in Greek, and the term used for the monk, *monachos,* means "solitary." From it the English term "monasticism" is derived. This petition is the oldest surviving document to use the term *monachos,* and because of its association with "deacon" this monachos seems to have been someone holding a religious office.

It has often been said that monasticism had its beginnings in the deserts of Egypt. But the casual use of the term "monk" for someone familiar to people in a small Egyptian town indicates that before there were monks in the desert there were *monachoi,* solitaries, living in the towns and villages of Egypt. That is not surprising, since Christianity had an ascetic strain from the beginning. According to the Gospel of Luke, Jesus had taught his disciples: "The sons of this age marry and are given in marriage; but those who are counted worthy to attain to that age and to the resurrection from the dead neither marry nor are given in marriage, for they cannot die any more, because they are equal to angels and are sons of God, being sons of the resurrection" (Luke 20:34–36). And Saint Paul had written: "The time is growing short; from now on, let those who have wives live as though they had none" (1 Corinthians 7:29).

Already in the second century the Greek physician and philosopher Galen observed that the Christian community included "not only men but women who refrain from cohabiting through their lives" and practice self-control in matters of food and drink. Christian writers also report that certain members of the Church had made themselves "eunuchs" for the sake of the kingdom of God by refraining from marriage and abstaining from wine and meat. At an early date in Christian history men and women withdrew from the fixed patterns of society to devote themselves to prayer and service to God. By creating an alternate social structure within the Church they laid the foundations for one of the most enduring Christian institutions: monasticism.

It was not until the fourth century, however, that monasticism comes clearly into view, and when it does it seems to have sprung up spontaneously in different, though similar, forms in various parts of the Christian world. The time was ripe. The Church was growing rapidly, and inevitably earlier ideals were lowered or compromised. The new movement renewed the radical demands of the gospel and put new models of a holy life before the faithful.

In any account of the early history of monasticism the figure that stands out is a charismatic Egyptian named Antony, who had the good fortune to have his "life" written by one of the most powerful and influential bishops in the fourth century, Athanasius of Alexandria. Due to the popularity of Athanasius's *Life,* Antony has gone down in history as the founder of monasticism. It is, however, more accurate to call him a renewer rather than a founder, and it may be that his iconic status in church history is as much due to Athanasius's literary gifts as to his own extraordinary life. Athanasius's biography of Antony offered a compelling vision of the solitary life and an irresistible model for others.

As Athanasius tells the story, Antony was raised in a prosperous family in a Coptic-speaking village in lower Egypt along the Nile. His parents died when he was in his late teens, leaving him a large family farm to care for and a younger sister. One day, about six months after the death of his parents, while walking to church he remembered that in the book of the Acts of the Apostles some had sold all their possessions and placed them at the feet of the apostles to be used to care for the poor. As he was pondering these things in church it happened that the gospel for that day included the words: "If you would be perfect, go, sell what you possess and give it to the poor, and you will have treasure in heaven" (Matthew 19:21). Jesus seemed to be addressing him directly, and at once Antony gave away his land and possessions, keeping only a few things to provide for his little sister.

At the time, in the late third century, there was an old man in a neighboring village who had practiced the "solitary life" from his youth. That is, there were already "monks" in the village where Antony lived, and he took one of these solitaries as a model for his life. At first he followed his example in the vicinity of the village. In Egypt the desert begins a few hundred feet from the Nile and one can stand on a small hill and gaze across the green strip that hugs the river where the lush fields end abruptly and the mauve sand begins. One could live in the desert yet be close to a village. After some years Antony decided to go deeper into the desert and cut himself off, as far as possible, from all human community. The decision to seek a more severe solitude in the "great desert" was his innovation, and the image of a monk alone in a cave deep in the desert inspired many men and women to follow his example.

How did he spend his time? According to Athanasius he worked with his hands, most likely weaving baskets to earn a little money to pay for his meager diet. He lived on bread seasoned with salt and water, ate no meat and drank no wine, and ate only once a day, devoting himself to prayer by reciting passages he had memorized from the Scriptures. He had no books. And he girded himself like an "athlete" (a term used for the martyrs) to do battle against the devil, who "could not bear seeing such purpose in a youth."

Satan's strategy was to awaken in Antony memories of the things he once cherished: the bonds of kinship, such as those with his sister, or the satisfactions of food and life's other pleasures. With only his thoughts for companionship Antony discovered the truth of the words of Jesus (Mark 7:20), that the most lethal temptations arise not from without but from within the human breast. "We have acquired a dark house full of war," Antony once said. By separating himself from others Antony wished to combat temptation armed only with the weapons of the Spirit. But he learned that detachment only magnified one's sins and doubts. As another wise monk said, in the world the demons fight through people and things, in the desert they assault us through our thoughts. Hence solitude offered an optimal arena to meet the devil in combat.

Though this strange and reclusive man of the desert broke with all the conventions of society, he did not leave his humanity behind. Like those who lived in the world, he suffered dejection and listlessness, knew grief and the terrors of the soul, feared death, and was troubled by confused and disordered thoughts. Yet through a slow and exacting regime he achieved tranquillity of soul. And it was this that set him apart.

After twenty years in the desert by himself (save for visits of friends who brought him bread), he came forth, says Athanasius, "as though from some shrine." Though he had eaten little during those years, his body was strong and he had reached a state of "utter equilibrium." Now that he had learned to conquer his body and care for his soul he was ready to teach others what he had learned. So through "regular conversation" he strengthened the resolve of those who had already taken up the monastic life and inspired others.

Antony lived to be a very old man, 105 years. At his death, his disciples, following his instructions, wrapped his body in cloth, buried it in the earth, and disclosed the place to no one. All that remained was a sheepskin cloak and his shining example. "It was," wrote Athanasius, "as if he were a physician given to Egypt by God." The date was in the mid fourth century (A.D. 356), and Athanasius's *Life of Antony,* written shortly after his death, became a literary sensation. It was quickly translated into Latin and read in Italy and Gaul and North Africa and also translated into Syriac, the language of the Christian East. The little book made a deep impression on many, including Augustine.

Although Antony was the most famous monachos, he was not without company. About the time he retreated deep into the desert, another Egyptian by the name of Amoun had begun to live a solitary life in the same desert, and a certain Macarius settled in the remote desert of Scete between modern day Cairo and Alexandria. But the most enterprising contemporary of Antony was a man named Pachomius (d. 346), who had converted to Christianity after being discharged from the army. Three years later he became the disciple of a local monk and remained with him for seven years. Nothing happens quickly in the lives of these monks. There is a story of a young monk who was distraught that he had not found peace. An older brother asked him how many years he had worn the monastic garb. The young man responded: eight. To which the old man replied, "Believe me I have been in this habit seventy years, and not for one day could I find peace; and you would have peace in eight?"

Pachomius was one of several leaders who set about the task of organizing the monks into communities. He was not the first to do so, but he was the most successful. As Antony would go down in Christian history as the most heralded model of solitary, or anchoretic monasticism, Pachomius would be remembered as the most enterprising symbol of communal, or coenobitic, monasticism. (The term *anchoretic* comes from the Greek word *anachoresis,* which means retiring or retreating. Another term for the solitary form of monasticism is *eremitic,* from the Greek word for desert. *Coenobitic* comes from the Greek terms *koinos* [common] and *bios* [life]. The term *ascetic* comes from the Greek word for training or exercise and originally referred to training oneself for athletic competition. In monastic literature it refers to the disciplining of body and spirit to foster contemplation of God.)

At first Pachomius brought solitaries who lived in the same vicinity together. But as the numbers grew he established new foundations in other places and organized them into close-knit communities under a single head. The monks followed a regime of regular times of prayer, work, and meals, and Pachomius composed the first monastic "rule," a collection of directives and precepts, to govern their common life. They lived not in caves or huts but in a complex of buildings that would eventually include a kitchen, bakery, dining hall, infirmary, assembly hall, and church. The community was divided into "houses" with space for forty monks, each with his own cell where he slept and prayed. They wore a distinctive garb (called a habit), a sleeveless tunic belted at the waist with a hood and a goatskin cloak.

In the early morning the community gathered while it was still dark for communal prayer, each monk in his assigned place. The reader stood at an ambo, or reading desk. At the completion of each reading from the Scriptures he clapped his hands, and the monks stood to make the sign of the cross and recite the Lord's prayer. A second clap signaled that they were to be seated. Surprisingly in the Pachomian monasteries the monks plaited reeds into baskets during the reading of the Scripture. The rest of the day was spent in manual labor, baking, gardening, tanning, sandal making, and so on. In the evening they gathered again for communal prayer. The Eucharist was celebrated twice in the week, on Wednesday and on Sunday.

The meals were simple, but not austere. In contrast to Antony and other anchorites who ate only bread seasoned with salt and water, cooked vegetables were served in the Pachomian monasteries, and on some occasions they enjoyed cheese, olives, and fruit. The main meal was taken at midday, a lighter repast in the evening. Wednesdays and Fridays were fast days.

Although the deep stillness of the vast deserts of Egypt was first to draw men and women to embrace a new way of life, the solitary life had begun to take root in other parts of the Christian world, especially in greater Syria. By the end of the fourth century the deserts of Syria were filled with devout Christians eagerly "hunting after God," as a Syrian chronicler put it. Like the monks of Egypt, they were often uneducated, suspicious of book learning, speaking only the language native to their region. These spirited and energetic men and women were untouched by the literary culture and refinement that formed the outlook of the bishops. Monasticism was a lay movement. By the simplicity of their lives and their winsome homespun wisdom they delighted and provoked the faithful and stirred them to new heights of virtue.

Syria produced one of the most bizarre and unforgettable figures in early Christian history, Symeon the Stylite (d. 459). After living in a monastery northeast of Antioch for ten years, Symeon asked permission to go out on his own to live in the open on the crest of a hill. Later he mounted a small pillar and perched himself at its top, suspended as it were between heaven and earth, with his hands outstretched in prayer. Over the year the pillar grew taller and taller until at his death it was reported to be more than twenty feet high. As his fame spread people came from all over the world to marvel at his devotion and to seek healing from his hands.

Though monasticism was a way of life that thrived on solitude and seclusion, the monks were never really cut off from the Christian communities. Wherever they went they attracted the devout and the curious. The more eccentric their behavior, the more they were admired and loved. But there was another reason. In Syria the line between the desert and settled and cultivated land was never clean, and the holy man found himself drawn into the affairs of the neighboring village or town. When people found themselves at enmity—at the time of a communal harvest, for example —or had a grievance, they would often turn to a holy man for counsel and help in settling disputes. The practice has lived on for centuries. In his great novel *The Brothers Karamazov,* Fyodor Dostoevsky has a memorable scene of the visit of the quarrelsome Karamazov family with the gentle monk Father Zosima to resolve family differences.

Early on monasticism also set down roots in Armenia, that ancient land surrounding Lake Van between the Black Sea and the Caspian Sea where the biblical Mount Ararat is located. In the middle of the fourth century a man named Eustathius organized ascetical communities that were also devoted to serving the poor and needy. From Armenia the movement spread westward, and Basil of Caesarea, who later was a leading figure in defense of the Council of Nicaea, came under his influence. When the young Basil returned from studies in Constantinople he decided to form a small community of prayer with a group of friends. Unlike the monks of Egypt and Syria, Basil was a sophisticated and gifted writer, and in his writings he offered a theological rationale for the ascetic life, what he called the "philosophical life."

Because human beings are made in the image and likeness of God, wrote Basil, when the soul turns to itself it is drawn by the light that comes from God. "This is a thing that everyone ought to know—that we have eyes within, deeper than these eyes; and a hearing deeper than this hearing. As the eyes of sense behold and recognize the face of a friend or a lover, so the eyes of the true and faithful soul, spiritually illuminated with the light of God, behold and recognize the true friend. . . . The soul is smitten with passionate love for God, and . . . it possesses an unbounded, unfailing love for the Lord for whom it longs." The aim of withdrawal from society was to "draw close to God," and prayer allows one to "hold God always in memory."

Basil's use of the term "philosophical life" for the solitary life shows that Christian monasticism drew not only on the sayings of Jesus and Christian teaching but also on ideas and practices that were well established in the Roman world. By the time Christianity came on the scene, philosophy was understood not as a theoretical undertaking but as conversion to a "way of life" that formed character and trained people to practice the virtues. The truth had to be lived to make it one's own. The moral exercises of the philosophers became the spiritual exercises of the monks.

Basil belonged to a large Christian family with deep roots in the Christian community in Cappadocia in central Asia Minor. His grandmother had been a disciple of the famous teacher Gregory Thaumaturgus, who had founded the church in a neighboring city, and his mother Emelia was the daughter of a martyr. Of the ten children in the family, two of his brothers became bishops, Peter of Sebaste and Gregory of Nyssa. But the person who had the greatest influence on Basil besides his parents was his older sister Macrina, who had pioneered a kind of household asceticism consisting of prayer, simple diet, and household work. From her efforts a new kind of monasticism took shape that served the community, including such activities as caring for orphan girls.

Due to Macrina's influence Basil's views about the "solitary" life gradually became more oriented toward society. Human beings, he said, are social creatures and nothing is more characteristic of human nature than "to associate with one another." For this reason the Lord said, "A new commandment I give to you that you love one another" (John 13:34). Basil became critical of self-absorbed hermits. And when he was made bishop he sought ways to adapt the monastic vision of radical devotion to God to life in the city. The solitary life of prayer would be complemented by the active life. Contemplation and service were to go hand in hand, and one of Basil's most enduring achievements was to establish hospitals for the sick and hospices to serve pilgrims.

Macrina emerges as a key figure in the history of asceticism. Although we hear more about the male founders of monasticism, Macrina is a sterling reminder that from the beginning women were not simply followers, but leaders, and made their own distinctive contribution to the new Christian society. This is all the more remarkable because the Romans did not easily give up their women to a life of virginity without childbearing. From the beginning there was a solid contingent of female ascetics among the monks. Virgins and widows set up houses of their own within a village or town to practice abstinence, prayer, and service to others. In the early fourth century a woman named Didyme gathered a group of ascetic women who were not only diligent in prayer but also active in crafts and mercantile affairs, making sandals or baking and selling cakes.

Monasticism allowed women to step free of inherited roles and expectations and opened up new vocations in the church and society. For the first time in Western history women became public figures who were admired for their virtue, piety, learning, and wisdom. There were, of course, female models in the Scriptures— Sarah, Rahab, Naomi, Judith, Susanna, Mary—and in the tales of the martyrs— Felicity and Perpetua—but as monasticism won favor, the spiritual power of women acquired new visibility and influence. The great women writers of the medieval world, Catherine of Siena, Hildegard of Bingen, Julian of Norwich, Brigitte of Sweden, follow in the train of these early female solitaries.

The exploits of women were as admirable, and in some cases as histrionic, as those of their male counterparts. A certain Susan was once visited by a "blessed and god-fearing monk." Each observed the other in combat with demons. Susan, however, proved stronger and more resilient. Not only did she get the best of the demons, she had no fear of them. She was unmovable, and the demons cried out: "This is a woman, but she is stone, and instead of flesh she is iron." Another woman, Melania, was erudite and scholarly. She had read three million lines of Origen, two and a half million of Gregory and Basil, transforming herself into a "spiritual bird to make the journey to Christ."

By adopting the ascetic life women became participants with men in the pursuit of holiness. So remarkable were their examples that ancient authors insist that they were the equal of men. Speaking of a certain Domnina, Theodoret of Cyrus, the author of a book on the lives of solitaries in Syria, said: "Virtue cannot be separated into male and female . . . For the difference is one of bodies not of souls. . . . There is neither male nor female (Galatians 3:28). . . . Women too may be models of the virtuous life."

Although these women and men embarked on a very private and individual quest, their sayings and stories, and the stirring example of their lives, were celebrated and remembered by the Christian people. As the age of the martyrs faded into the past the faithful craved tales of extraordinary feats of holiness, and these plucky and spirited men and women became living icons signaling a more exacting vision of the Christian life. Though the solitary life was a radical choice, the monks were neither idealists nor romantics. They knew the life they chose was hard, but they made it rewarding, and by their homespun wisdom, wry humor, and lively stories they enlarged the moral and spiritual horizon of those who lived in the world.

Some of their sayings remind one of advice columns in the daily newspaper. John, a monk in Gaza, was once asked: "If someone is not actually criticizing another person but is gladly listening to criticism, is he also condemned for that?" To which John responds: "Even listening gladly to criticism is criticism and receives the same condemnation." Others take the form of spiritual counsel. Once Barsanuphius, also from Gaza, was asked: "When I recite the psalms, my mind wanders or is distracted, what should I do?" Barsanuphius answers: "If you are distracted, then take up the same psalm from the last word you remember. And if this happens once, or twice, or three times, and you cannot remember which point or find any word that you remember in the part you have just recited, then take up the psalm from the beginning." And if that does not work, he adds, go on to the next psalm.

In all their sayings the persistent refrain is: "Attend to oneself." Only by looking within could the mind be set free to love God and serve others. "Be vigilant in attending to oneself," said Barsanuphius, "that you may set God before you at all times. Then the words of the prophet will be fulfilled: 'I foresaw the Lord before my face continually, for the Lord is on my right hand so that I may not be moved.'" The monks knew that purity of heart and singleness of will spring from within. "The mind that does not have a place to turn or any stable base will undergo change from hour to hour and from minute to minute due to the variety of distractions," wrote John Cassian (d. 435), a Latin-speaking monk living in Gaul. "The things that come from the outside continually transform it into whatever occurs to it at any given moment." To which he added: "Everything lies in the soul's inner sanctuary."

It is often said that the marks of monasticism are poverty, chastity, and obedience. And there is certainly truth in that. But reading through the lives of these men of the desert and contemplating their wise and pungent aphorisms, I am inclined to think that one should also emphasize prayer and love, and perhaps work. Prayer comes first, because without regular and disciplined prayer there is no genuine spiritual life. And prayer for the monk meant something very specific, reciting the strophes of the psalms. Left to our own thoughts and words prayer moves on the surface. The psalms loosened their tongues and gave them a language to read the book of the heart and to enter more deeply into conversation with God.

For every story or saying that praises self-restraint, control of the passions, or inner discipline one will find others that make love, compassion, and gentleness the highest virtues. Here, for example, is a story about a visit of two monks. Marcianos, the older host, invites Avitos to dinner. "Come, my dear friend, let us have fellowship together at the table." But Avitos declined: "I don't think I have ever eaten before evening. I often pass two or three days in succession without taking anything." To which Marcianos responds: "On my account, change your custom today, for my body is weak and I am not able to wait until evening." Still Avitos refused, and Marcianos says: "I am disheartened and my soul is stung because you have expended much effort to come and look at a true ascetic; but instead you are disappointed and behold a tavern keeper and profligate instead of an ascetic." Finally Avitos relented, and Marcianos, realizing that now the younger man is open to what he has to teach, says: "My dear friend. We both share the same existence and embrace the same way of life, we prefer work to rest, fasting to nourishment, and it is only in the evening that we eat, but we know that love is a much more precious possession than fasting. For the one is the work of divine law, the other of our own power. And it is proper to consider the divine law much more precious than our own."

Monasticism sprang up independently of the bishops and the clergy, and the monks had to support themselves through a simple craft. Hence the importance of work in monastic writings. Over time useful labor came to acquire a spiritual character. Not only was work purposeful because it produced something; the monks learned that it focused the mind in a way that was not unlike prayer.

The monks had their critics both within the Church and without. Pagans considered the monastic life a vile and disgraceful profession, heaping abuse on the monks for their coarseness, lack of learning, and misanthropy. They considered them rustics, vapid men who were anti-city and anti-culture, who packed themselves into caves to avoid life in society. Christian clergy were often suspicious of the monks and saw them as a threat to episcopal authority. And parents were resentful of the challenge to their comfortable way of life. John Chrysostom, the famous Christian preacher, wrote an entire book titled *Against Those Who Oppose the Monastic Life*. In it he cites the comment of an upstanding citizen of Antioch: "Incomprehensible! How could the son of respectable middle-class parents with a good education and excellent prospects for a steady comfortable life leave his home to go off and join a company of dirty vagrants!"

Yet once monasticism took hold in society there was no stopping its growth. In the fourth, fifth, and sixth centuries, and in medieval Christianity both East and West, nothing was more vital to Christian life than monasticism. It is among the oldest and most durable Christian institutions and must be reckoned as a distinctive mark of classical Christianity along with the Eucharist and baptism, bishops, creeds, and the canon of Scripture. It proved to be versatile, resilient, and adaptable. In the early Middle Ages, as Christianity began to move out beyond the Roman Empire into northern Europe, monks spearheaded the missionary effort, and in the East, after the rise of Islam, it was the monasteries that made it possible for the churches to make the transition from Syriac to Arabic by translating the Scriptures, the liturgy, and other religious texts into the holy language of the Muslims.

A Christian Jerusalem

In the year 409 a monk named Euthymius made the long journey from his homeland in Armenia to Palestine to behold with his own eyes the places where the great events of biblical history had taken place, to touch the rock of Golgotha where Christ had been crucified, and to kiss his sacred tomb. He was the first of a large company of monks from all over the Christian world to leave their native lands and settle in the desert of Judea east of Jerusalem, the "desert of the holy city" or the "dear desert," as the monks called it, never to return home.

Although the city of Jerusalem has always kindled the Christian imagination, in the early years Christian affection was fastened on the heavenly city. Saint Paul drew a contrast between the "Jerusalem above" and the "present Jerusalem" (Galatians 4:25–26), and the last book of the Bible, Revelation, concludes with a vision of "the holy city, the new Jerusalem, prepared as a bride adorned for her husband" coming down from the heavens (Revelation 21:2). In the mid second century, Melito, a bishop in Asia Minor, wrote: "The Jerusalem below was precious, but it is worthless now because of the Jerusalem above."

Yet among the major cities that were the stage for early Christian history— Alexandria, Caesarea, Antioch, Carthage, Rome—only Jerusalem could claim a tangible link to Jesus of Nazareth and to Christian beginnings. This singular fact was seductive and gradually worked its way into Christian consciousness. Already in the third century pilgrims had begun to visit Jerusalem to pray at the sites of biblical history, and in the fourth century Christians claimed the earthly city, the city of bricks and stones, as their own. The arrival of monks from Armenia at the beginning of the fifth century is a small sign of Jerusalem's transformation into the "holy city" of the Christians.

After the defeat of Bar Kochba, the leader of the final Jewish revolt against Rome in A.D. 135, the Jewish city was plowed under by the Romans. Emperor Hadrian founded a new city in its place and named it Aelia Capitolina after the emperor's family, Aelius, and Jupiter the god of the capitol mount in Rome. So thoroughly had the Romans expunged Jerusalem from memory that in the early fourth century a Roman magistrate in Caesarea did not recognize the name Jerusalem when a Christian identified it as his home.

During the war with the Romans in A.D. 70, Christians, like other Jews, suffered the cataclysm of burning and destruction. In the aftermath of the war some fled to Pella, a city across the Jordan River, to rebuild their lives, but a small community remained in the city and, according to our earliest records, at the time of the emperor Hadrian (d. 138) the church in Jerusalem was made up of "believing Hebrews"—that is, Jewish Christians. The church that comes to light toward the end of the second century was not a new foundation but a continuation of the first church in Jerusalem. The strength of Christianity in the region, however, lay in the coastal cities, Caesarea, the great port on the Mediterranean and administrative capital of the region, and cities such as Ascalon, Diosopolis, Tyre, and also Gaza.

By the beginning of the fourth century, however, Jerusalem began a swift rise in eminence and authority. Already at the Council of Nicaea in 325 it was declared that though second to Caesarea in the ecclesiastical order, Jerusalem should be held first in honor. But the key mover was Constantine the Christian emperor and, according to later Christian tradition, his mother Helena, who envisioned the building of a Christian Jerusalem. He had already initiated ambitious building projects else-where. Soon after his triumph at the Milvian Bridge the emperor built the huge church of Saint John Lateran in Rome and later commissioned churches in other parts of the Christian world, in Gaul, North Africa, and Tyre in southern Lebanon. He also set his architects to work on plans for a new Christian capital in the East, Constantinople, to be adorned with monumental churches and memorials to martyrs on a grand scale.

But Constantinople was a city without history whose stones bore no memories. Jerusalem was the city of David, the Jewish king who had transferred the Ark of the Covenant from Shiloh to Jerusalem, the new capital of Israel. Most important it was the place of Jesus's death and resurrection. Jerusalem displayed the grainy texture of the biblical past. So in 325 Constantine turned his attention to Palestine, where he wished not simply to rebuild the city but to construct a "memorial" of what God had done there.

According to Eusebius, Constantine's biographer, the emperor wanted the central monument in the city to be constructed at the very place where Christ had been buried. There was a local tradition among Christians that kept alive a memory of where the tomb had been located, but a pagan temple had been built over the site. To make way for the new building this temple was razed, and as the digging proceeded, says Eusebius, the workmen uncovered the rock of Golgotha not far from the tomb of Christ. There Constantine instructed his architects to design a "house of prayer worthy of God."

It is clear from Eusebius's account that this was no common place. His report of the discovery of the rock of the crucifixion bristles with a sacral vocabulary that is unusual in early Christian writings. The term "place" has become incandescent, afire with energy and potency. Constantine's greatest concern, he writes, was how he might adorn "this *holy place* . . . which from the beginning was *holy* . . . and now appears more *holy* because it has brought to light proof of the suffering of the Savior." Formerly Christians had spoken of virtuous men and women as "holy," of the "holy" Church or of "holy" Scripture. Now holiness is attributed to a place, the "most blessed place," the "saving cave," the "most marvelous place in the world."

From some passages in the New Testament it seems that Christianity dethroned place as the locus of God's presence. The most famous text is the saying of Jesus in the Gospel of John: "Woman, believe me, the hour is coming when neither on this mountain nor in Jerusalem will you worship the Father . . . God is spirit and those who worship him must worship in spirit and in truth" (John 4:21–24). Early Christian writers reproached pagans for associating the divine with particular places. We have no need to go to a shrine to "seek God," wrote Origen. Yet from early times Christians gathered for worship at the tombs of holy men and women. In the second century Christians in Rome built a small shrine at the resting place of the apostle Peter, and in the early third century they constructed a catacomb where they could bury their dead and celebrate the Eucharist in close proximity to the remains of those who had gone before.

The shrine at the tomb of Christ, however, differed from those of the apostles and martyrs in one notable particular. It did not hold any human remains. In John Chrysostom's memorable words, "The whole world runs to see the tomb which has no body." What was being marked was not the resting place of a martyr, but the place where something had happened, this historical event, Jesus's death, burial, and resurrection. Because a place, unlike bones, is stationary and immovable, the church had to be built at the very spot where the sacred events had occurred. This intimate bond between event and place would spawn within Christianity a new form of piety: worship at the holy places where the saving events had taken place.

But before looking at the form this new devotion would take, a few words on the building itself. The site presented a challenge to Constantine's architects, for they not only had to design a shrine to adorn the holiest "place" in Christianity, they also had to construct a building large enough to serve the growing Christian community in the city and the pilgrims who would gather there on festival days, particularly for the great Paschal celebration in spring. To this end the architects created a large, sophisticated architectural complex consisting of four parts: an outer atrium, a large basilica, an inner atrium, and a rotunda, a circle of large columns surrounding the tomb separated from the basilica by a second, inner courtyard. The hill of Golgotha was across the courtyard to the east, immediately contiguous to the church.

The typical early Christian basilica had two rows of columns marking off a central nave and two side aisles, but the basilica in Jerusalem had four rows of columns, with two aisles on either side of a central nave. The ceremonial entrance had three large portals, and immediately to the east was a spacious atrium surrounded by porticoes on three sides. The atrium had three gateways that opened on to the chief north–south street of the city, the Cardo Maximus, a street that even today is the main north–south street in the old city of Jerusalem. Though only a remnant of the original complex remains, the visitor to Jerusalem can sense the grandeur and magnitude of the original church by walking almost three hundred feet from the present entrance of the Church of the Holy Sepulcher to the souk, a commercial quarter, that now occupies the ancient Cardo Maximus.

The church and shrine in Jerusalem, like the churches in Rome and elsewhere, were public buildings. With the construction of the catacomb of Callixtus in Rome in the third century, Christians had begun to create a material culture that gave Christianity a visible presence in society. But the catacombs were outside the city walls and underground. With the conversion of the emperor to Christianity and the rapid growth in numbers, the Church was now able to construct its own buildings within the city, altering the urban landscape. The fourth century gave birth to a distinctive style of Christian architecture that was public in character, spacious in design, and monumental in appearance. When the complex at the tomb in Jerusalem was completed, it was the grandest and most prominent building in the city.

But the complex at Calvary and the tomb was not primarily a monument, it was a place of worship. Unlike the Roman temple that was designed to house the statue of a god or goddess, the Christian church, in the form of a basilica, a large meeting hall, was designed to accommodate congregational worship. And as the Church began to occupy civic space with its buildings, Christian liturgy and rituals began to take on a public character. Christian worship was no longer the gathering of a private religious association, it was becoming a solemn civic ritual that drew large numbers of the populace into a shared public ceremony. When the bishop entered the church in procession with his presbyters he was an imposing figure clothed in the garments of a high magistrate and accompanied by the book of the gospels.

Toward the end of the fourth century a devout woman named Egeria from the west, most likely Gaul, made a long pilgrimage to the Christian holy places in the East and to Jerusalem. On returning, she wrote an account of her journey to her friends (or religious sisters, as she may have been a nun) and in it gave us a vivid picture of the uniqueness of Jerusalem in Christian piety and the mysterious link between Christian faith and the land of biblical history. Egeria wanted to see with her own eyes the places where the saving events of the Bible had taken place.

By the time she visited Jerusalem the city was a bustling Christian metropolis filled with pilgrims, monks and nuns, clerics, a growing Christian population, and a bishop who stood in a succession that went back to the apostle James, who first governed the Church. Within a few decades Jerusalem would be elevated to the status of patriarchate and would rank with the principal Christian capitals of the East, Alexandria, Antioch, and Constantinople. Its new monuments at the holy places dazzled pilgrims from all over the world, and the elaborate liturgies celebrated in the several churches thrilled the faithful.

By far the longest section of Egeria's narrative is devoted to the city of Jerusalem and the holy places in the vicinity of the city. When she reaches Jerusalem her interest shifts away from seeing places to describing the rituals that took place in the churches and at the holy sites. "I am sure it will interest you to know," she writes, "about the daily services they have in the holy places, and I must tell you about them." By the time she arrived in Jerusalem, Christian worship during Holy Week had settled into a distinctive pattern dictated by the holy places. That Christians could gather for worship at the very spot where the saving events had taken place made a deep impression on the local Christians as well as pilgrims. "What I admire and value most is that all the hymns and antiphons and readings and all the prayers the bishops say, are always relevant to the day which is being observed *and to the place* in which they are used."

On Thursday of the "great week" (Holy Week), after services in the Martyrium (the great basilica) the congregation would return home for a short meal and then gather at the shrine on the Mount of Olives. After psalms and readings and prayers they would proceed to the hillock of the Ascension. Early in the morning they moved to the place where Jesus had been arrested in the Garden of Gethsemane and then returned to the atrium of the chapel next to the rock of Golgotha. On Friday the faithful came to the same chapel to venerate the wood of the cross and to listen to the accounts of the passion of Christ in the gospels. This was followed by services of prayer in the Martyrium and the Anastasis (the tomb), where the bishop said a prayer from inside the tomb. Then they returned to the great church to continue the vigil.

Besides giving information on Christian worship in fourth-century Jerusalem, Egeria sheds light on the languages spoken in the city. Though the liturgical language in Jerusalem was Greek, many people spoke Syriac (Aramaic), and some spoke Latin. Jerusalem was located on the western edge of the Syriac-speaking world. Here is her description of the languages used in worship: "In this province there are some people who know both Greek and Syriac, but others know only one or the other. The bishop may know Syriac, but he never uses it. He always speaks

Greek, and has a presbyter [priest] beside him who translates the Greek into Syriac, so that everyone can understand what he means. Similarly the lessons read in the church have to be read in Greek, but there is always someone in attendance to translate into Syriac so that the people understand. Of course there are also people here who speak neither Greek nor Syriac, but Latin. But there is no need for them to be discouraged, since some of the brothers or sisters who speak Latin as well as Greek will explain things to them."

The form of worship practiced in Jerusalem, prayer at the place where the event took place, is called "stational" liturgy: a ritual that halts or stations itself at a particular place. Memory is linked inescapably to something tangible, and in Jerusalem the Eucharist could be celebrated at the places that were invoked in the prayers offered by the bishop. The narrative in the gospels (recording Jesus's life from birth through death) indelibly imprinted on the minds of Christians the sanctity of time. In Jerusalem the holy places made possible a sanctification of space.

Stational liturgies are by their very nature public occasions, and in Jerusalem the clergy and faithful flung open the doors of the churches and poured into the streets. Because the events celebrated had taken place in different parts of the city, the congregation walked from one place to another, sometimes on the same day, and solemn ritual processions became a distinctive feature of Christian worship. A Christian calendar was being filled out, and on the principal festival days (the Pasch, Epiphany, Pentecost) the faithful could be seen making their way through the streets of the city singing hymns and chanting psalms. Christianity was moving from a private mode of worship to one that took over the streets and made them a theater for Christian ceremony and parade.

The implications were far reaching. Christians were becoming more self-conscious about building a new culture that stamped its face on the society. Space is never ideologically neutral. Jerusalem was becoming a Christian city, the city of the Christian God, a city of uncommon symbolic power for the Christian empire. As it became the Christian city par excellence, it acquired political as well as religious significance. There was a peril in this new assertiveness. Should a hostile army invade Jerusalem (as in fact happened twice in the seventh century), that would not only disrupt the public worship of the triune God, it would also threaten the stability of the Roman Empire.

Egeria also visited other places in the region. She traveled across the Jordan, for example, where Moses had blessed the children of Israel before his death. "When we reached this plain," she writes, "we went on to the very spot, and there we had a prayer, and read from Deuteronomy not only the song, but also the blessings he pronounced over the children of Israel (Deuteronomy 32–34). At the end of the reading we had another prayer, and set off again with thanksgiving to God." She then explains the simple ritual that she and her companions followed when they arrived at a holy place: "It was always our practice when we managed to reach one of the places we wanted to see to have first a prayer, then a reading from the book [the book of the Bible that recorded the event], then to recite an appropriate psalm and then another prayer. By God's grace we always followed this practice whenever we were able to reach a place we wanted to see."

To this day Christian pilgrims from all over the world practice the same simple ritual that Egeria and others observed in antiquity. They read the account in the Scriptures of the biblical event that took place at the site, sing a hymn, recite a psalm, and offer a prayer (and in some cases celebrate the Eucharist). The events of the past live on not only in memory, but in material things like stones and dust, and praying at the place where something sacred took place releases uncommon and untutored affections.

Without the images and impressions of touch and sight, memory is formless and vacuous. This elementary truth was understood by pilgrims such as Egeria and by learned theologians who had never seen Jerusalem. No one expressed it more clearly in this period than Paulinus, a bishop from the city of Nola, in Campania, southern Italy: "No other sentiment draws people to Jerusalem than the desire to *see* and *touch* the places where Christ was physically present, and to be able to say from their own experience, 'We have gone into his tabernacle, and have worshiped in the places where his feet stood' [Psalms 132:7]."

Paulinus's sentiments were echoed by Christians living all over the Mediterranean world, and not only in reference to the holy places in Jerusalem. By the end of the fourth century the tombs of martyrs and saints had become places of pilgrimage, drawing Christians to see and touch the relics (remains) of holy men and women. Veneration of the holy places in Palestine did not stand apart from other forms of devotion that were taking root at this time. A new tactile piety that attached itself to things, to bones and other relics, to places and shrines, to sacred books, even to liturgical implements like chalices and veils, was evident all over the Christian world. Some pilgrims journeyed from Jerusalem down through the Judean desert to the Jordan River to bathe at the place where Christ was baptized.

For the pilgrim the holy places were not simply historical sites that invoked a memory of the past. Seeing was more than seeing, it was a metaphor for participation. There is a story of a man named Peter who went to Jerusalem "in order that by seeing the places where the saving sufferings had taken place might worship *in them* the God who saved us." It was not enough that the eye of the soul enjoy God through faith. Peter's delight in the holy places was like the pleasure a lover receives from gazing on the clothing of the beloved. Wounded with love for God and longing to see God's "shadow," Peter "took himself to those saving places where he could see the founts that gushed forth."

Jerusalem and Palestine were not only places of pilgrimage. During the fourth, fifth, and sixth centuries the population of Roman Palestine grew rapidly. New buildings were constructed at a dizzying pace, trade increased, the economy flourished, jobs were plentiful (especially for skilled craftsmen and artists), and agriculture and viticulture were extended to previously uncultivated areas. It is estimated that the number of inhabitants of Jerusalem rose to over fifty thousand from a previous high of ten to fifteen thousand. On the basis of archaeological surveys of the region, it has been estimated that there were four times as many people living in the country during the Christian period than in biblical times. The most potent factor for the growth of population was the influx of people and money as a result of the discovery of the holy places. Pilgrims, like tourists, were good for business.

During this period Christians first began to use the term "holy land" to designate the city of Jerusalem and the land surrounding the holy city. In 1884 a mosaic map of the Holy Land was discovered on the floor of a Christian church at Madaba, a village east of the Jordan River not too far from present-day Amman. This is no ordinary map. Though it includes cities, rivers, deserts, and so forth, it also includes biblical sites and monuments commemorating events in the history of Israel, places mentioned in the gospels or church history, pilgrimage centers, and monasteries. Egypt has a place on it, because Egypt had been graced by the physical presence of Christ. According to the Gospel of Matthew, Joseph, Mary, and the child Jesus fled to Egypt to escape the wrath of King Herod and remained there until Herod's death (Matthew 2:13–23).

Jerusalem sits at the center of the map with a legend in Greek, THE HOLY CITY. So detailed is the depiction of Jerusalem that scholars are able to identify its principal buildings and streets, its gates and towers, and even its public baths. The most prominent building is, of course, the rotunda surrounding Christ's tomb and the great basilica the Martyrium with its three doors facing east. Other monasteries and churches in the city such as the basilica on Mount Zion and the New Church of the Theotokos (the Virgin Mary, mother of God) built by Justinian (d. 565) also appear. The mosaicist also included the remains of the wall supporting the massive platform on which the Jewish temple stood, what is known as the Western Wall, an object of veneration by Jews then and now. More than one Christian writer observed that the new city of the Christians was built "facing that old and deserted city [of the Jews]."

The Madaba mosaic is a map both of the past and of the region as it existed when the map was set in the floor of the church in the sixth century. Not all the sites are holy places. It marks, for example, a place where one could change horses and find an inn and cities that did not exist in biblical times, such as two cities in the Negev desert to the south, Mapsis and Elusa. At the height of the Christian epoch there were six cities located within a few miles of each other deep in the desert. Each city had at least two churches and several had three or four. Palestine had become for Christians a homeland as well as a Holy Land. One has the sense of a vibrant and flourishing society that gave architectural form to its faith in the building of churches. More than five hundred churches were built in the Holy Land during the Christian era.

Although the ancient Land of Israel had become a Christian country, there were still Jews living in the land, particularly in Galilee in the north and in Caesarea. Understandably the Christianization of the Land of Israel was not welcomed by the Jewish population that considered Jerusalem and the territory surrounding it a unique inheritance of the Jewish people. *Eretz Israel* (Land of Israel) remained a center of Jewish learning, and several of the most important bodies of Jewish writings were compiled there, including the Jerusalem (or Palestinian) Talmud, a collection of expositions and debates on matters of Jewish law, and a number of *midrashim*, commentaries on the books of the Torah. From archaeological evidence we know that with few exceptions Jews were able to go about their affairs and practice their way of life without interference. New synagogues were constructed and older buildings remodeled. They also shared in the prosperity and economic growth that was diffused through the country as a whole.

But the gradual Christianization of the land was deeply troubling to the Jews, and Jewish writings from the period indicate that Jews had not given up the hope of restoring Jewish rule in Jerusalem and rebuilding the temple. A Jewish poet could write: "Establish your throne in the city of the kingdom [Jerusalem]." The Jews realized that Christians, unlike the earlier Romans who had no interest in Jerusalem as such, had a spiritual investment in the city. Christians now claimed Jerusalem as their own, and in the city of David they had built a magnificent temple to the God of David and Solomon. In this temple, which took the place of the Jewish temple, Christians worshiped the God of Israel, prayed the psalms, and read the Jewish Scriptures (the Old Testament) as their own book. For the earlier Romans, Jerusalem was the city of a conquered people on the edge of the empire; for Christians it had become *the* holy city.

And it was this new fact, that the Temple Mount stood in ruins, and the splendor of Jerusalem had been transferred to the Anastasis, the Church of the Resurrection at the site of Christ's death and resurrection, that would give rise to an assault on Christianity from an unexpected quarter, the imperial throne.

Emperor Julian, the Jews, and Christians

Emperor Constantine died in 337, and after some months of political maneuvering, along with the execution of several members of his family by other family members, he was succeeded by his three sons, Constantine II, who became caesar in the West, Constantius II, who ruled in the East, and Constans, who had responsibility for Italy and North Africa. Politics was bloody business in those days, and it was hardly an arrangement that could last. In 340 Constantine II was killed. For the next ten years there was relative peace between the brothers, but Constans was killed by a usurper in 350, and Constantius II became sole ruler until his death in 361.

Even though Constantine's sons were Christians, they parted company on the issues that divided the churches after the Council of Nicaea. Constans supported the Nicenes, but Constantius sided with the council's critics and sent into exile pro-Nicene bishops, including Athanasius, the most resolute and articulate defender of the council. Only after the death of Constantius was the Nicene party able to gain the upper hand. But Constantius's most fateful legacy was to arrange the marriage of a "cousin," the son of a half-brother of Constantine, named Julian, to his sister Helena and to appoint him caesar with charge of Gaul and Britain. When Constantius died, Julian became sole emperor.

Few figures in early Christian history hold as much fascination as Julian. He reigned for only nineteen short months in 361–363, but his ideas as well his actions shook the foundations Christians had been patiently building for several generations. To some he was a noble and tragic figure, an ensign of classical culture, cut down by cruel fate at the age of thirty-one; to Christians he came to be known as Julian the Apostate. For Julian committed the unpardonable sin of abandoning the faith in which he had been raised to embrace paganism with an enthusiasm bordering on fanaticism. As a young man he studied with a philosopher named Aedesius who emphasized the religious and ritualistic elements of Neo-Platonic philosophy. Julian was fascinated by rituals that could alter one's state of consciousness and was initiated into the cult of Cybele, an Anatolian goddess, whose worship involved the sacrifice of a bull. The experience changed his life, and he resolved to cast off Christianity and worship the gods of Greece and Rome. He could not, however, announce openly that he had turned away from his childhood formation; his cousin, the emperor Constantius, was a Christian, and it was assumed that all members of the imperial family were Christians. For ten years Julian kept his beliefs to himself and went through the motions of Christian ritual. Only when he became emperor was he able to announce publicly his "conversion."

By the time Julian became emperor the imperial throne had been occupied by Christians for almost half a century. Looking back on this period with the long view of history it seems that the triumph of Christianity was inevitable; it was only a matter of time before the old ways would be displaced. But for those Christians born in the early decades of the fourth century, who had heard first-hand accounts of the persecutions under Diocletian, the new status of the Church seemed fragile. A Christian future was not assured. Policies could change, and as one bishop observed late in the century, unbelievers could again be our rulers. Traditional religious practices were woven into the institutions of society and stamped on the fabric of communal life: in the civic calendar, for example, in the educational system, and in marriage customs. Still, it came as a shock to Christians that a member of the family of Constantine, who had served as a lector in the Church, could spurn the Church's faith and turn passionately and ostentatiously to the gods of Greece and Rome. On returning from military triumphs in Gaul and Germany, he wrote to a former teacher: "We worship the gods openly. And most of the troops who are returning with me worship the gods. We sacrifice oxen in public. We have offered the gods many hecatombs as thank-offerings. The gods command me to purify everything as far as possible, and I obey them enthusiastically."

Julian wished not only to restore the traditional forms of worship, most notably animal sacrifice; his aim was to subvert the influence of Christianity and eventually purge the society of the new religion. To do this he devised two ingenious projects. The first had to do with the schools, and the other was a bold and improbable building project in Jerusalem.

Six months after he became emperor, Julian issued an edict that "schoolmasters and teachers" should excel in "morality" and "eloquence," and city councils across the empire were to evaluate the qualifications of teachers in light of these criteria. On first reading, the decree sounds innocuous, but the body of traditional writings (such as the poems of Homer) studied in school were chosen not only on literary or aesthetic grounds: literature carried the moral and spiritual values of the society. Since those values were suffused with religion, even the teaching of grammar and rhetoric, the foundation of the educational system, instilled belief in the traditional gods, Zeus, Hera, Apollo, Artemis, Aphrodite, Heracles, and the others.

The publication of this edict alarmed Christian leaders and angered Christian parents whose children, they believed, would be deprived of a proper education. Training in rhetoric was the gateway to a successful career in law or the civil service. Their fears were well grounded. The emperor said that Christian teachers had to make a choice: either they must give up their Christian beliefs or resign their positions in the schools; teachers should not "teach what they disapprove. If they are genuine interpreters of the ancient classics, let them first imitate the ancients' piety toward the gods. If they think the classics wrong in this respect, then let them go and teach Matthew and Luke in the Church."

Julian's school law was an astute and calculated attack on the leadership of the churches. He knew that Christians had not yet developed their own educational system and were wholly dependent on the pagan schools for the education of their children. Without the benefit of a solid grounding in grammar and rhetoric, the Church would soon lose one of its most potent resources, men who could speak Greek or Latin correctly and write refined and elegant prose.

Julian followed up the decree on the schools with a frontal literary attack on Christianity, a book with the derisive title *Against the Galilaeans*. For the first time Christians were faced with a critic who had arisen within, someone who knew the Scriptures well and was able, according to one writer, to "heap up testimonies" from the Bible against the faith. Several generations later, in the mid fifth century, *Against the Galilaeans* was still being read avidly by pagan critics to provide ammunition for attacks on Christian teaching and to ridicule Christian practice, for example veneration of the remains of the dead.

Julian believed that animal sacrifice was the highest form of worship, and he was dismayed that with the rise of Christianity the practice had declined. As emperor he promoted the renewal of sacrifices at the temples across the empire. He knew that the Jews had once practiced animal sacrifice, but no longer did. In an effort to gain support from the Jews for his religious reforms, Julian asked them to restore their ancient cult. He reasoned that if the Jews would restore Jewish sacrificial worship, the Christians would be the only people who did not offer sacrifice, isolating them from the rest of the society as deviants. However, Jewish leaders informed Julian that it was not possible according to Jewish law to offer sacrifices except in the city of Jerusalem. If he wished to have the Jews resume sacrifices he would have to give them back their city and restore their temple.

The Jewish temple in Jerusalem had been destroyed by the Roman armies when Emperor Titus captured the city in A.D. 70. The temple had been razed in earlier times, as well, and the Jews driven into exile. But, according to the Scriptures, each time God had restored the city to his people and the temple was rebuilt. This time, so Christians believed, things were different. As Origen remarked, never before "had the Jews been ejected for so long a time from their ritual and worship." Because the Jewish law could not be observed fully without the temple, it seemed to Christians that the loss of the city proved that Judaism was a thing of the past.

Julian knew that Jesus had predicted the destruction of the temple. According to the gospels, Jesus once looked over at the temple adorned with noble stones and said: "You see all these, do you not? Truly, I say to you, there will not be left here one stone upon another, that will not be thrown down" (Matthew 24:2). If the temple were rebuilt, Jesus would be shown to have been a false prophet. Indeed, to underscore the truth of Jesus's prophecy, Christians had deliberately left the Temple Mount in ruins when they constructed a new Christian city centered on the Church of the Resurrection. Christian pilgrims made a point of climbing the Mount of Olives to see the desolation with their own eyes and exult that the Jews had been deprived of their "famous house." As long as the temple was in ruins—and it was presumed that it would remain so—Christianity seemed triumphant.

Julian's plan would have been futile had there not been flourishing Jewish communities in the Roman Empire. So deeply has the historical memory of the West been shaped by Christianity that it often seems the Jews exit the stage after the rise of the Church and do not return until the nineteenth and twentieth centuries. In much writing on the history of Western civilization, the Jews appear only intermittently at times of persecution or displacement. Little is said about the continuous history of Jewish life in western Europe or Byzantium. The Judaism that is most familiar is the religion of ancient Israel, not the Judaism that emerged after the coming of Christianity.

But the Jews did not disappear, nor did they go underground. To be sure, the decades after the destruction of Jerusalem were a time of testing for the Jewish people: they had to learn to live without traditional institutions, such as the priesthood, and their holy city. But there was no significant decline in the Jewish population, and scholars estimate that they numbered five or six million in the early centuries of the Roman Empire. By all measures Jewish life not only continued, it flourished and entered on a time of intense spiritual activity and renewal. During the early Christian centuries resourceful Jewish leaders laid the foundations of rabbinical Judaism, the Judaism that we know today. Early in the third century the Mishnah, the primary collection of post-biblical Jewish law, was edited, and in the centuries that followed the Jerusalem (Palestinian) and Babylonian Talmuds, which contained debate and discussion of Jewish scholars over the interpretation of the law, were compiled. It was a time of religious vitality, material prosperity, and intellectual creativity within the Jewish communities.

In most cities, especially in the eastern Mediterranean, Christians lived alongside vibrant and confident Jewish communities. Even Christian leaders were impressed at the strength and resiliency of Jewish life and the attraction of Judaism to others. Some Christians went into the synagogues on festival days, to hear the blowing of the shofar on Rosh Hashanah, for instance, and others adopted Jewish customs. Much to the frustration of Christian teachers who had no Hebrew, the Jews had the original versions of the Old Testament. In debates with Jews, Christians were put at a disadvantage because the Jews knew the Hebrew text while Christians could cite only translations. As Augustine ruefully observed: the Jew is the "bearer of the books from which the Christians believe."

Julian was not the first to use Judaism to reproach the Christians, but unlike earlier critics, he was not a solitary philosopher. He was emperor of the Roman world and was able to buttress his criticism with a conspicuous historical gesture only he could carry out: rebuild the Jewish temple in Jerusalem. More than anything, a new temple in the historic Jewish city would put the lie to Christian claims and prove that Jesus was a false prophet.

Julian moved swiftly and reconstruction began in the spring of 363. But the work was cut short almost at once by a fire or some other catastrophe at the site. Christians of course took this as a sign of divine vengeance. Then a few weeks later, on a military campaign on the Persian frontier, Julian was struck down by a spear from an unknown assailant. Before his project in Jerusalem had truly begun it was aborted, and the Church's bitter foe was dead. But that did not put an end to the threat. Even though his efforts were unsuccessful, he had committed money, men, and materials to rebuild the Jewish temple, and the work had actually begun, and this continued to alarm Christians. As one bishop put it: he "had put the power of Christ on trial."

Julian's reign illuminates an aspect of early Christian history that is often ignored: Jews were a continuous challenge to Christianity in the early centuries. In the fourth century, even though Christianity had been around for three hundred years, Christians had difficulty coming to terms with the social and religious fact that the "old" Israel, as Christians thought of the Jews, had not given way to the "new" Israel, the Church. Christian leaders marveled at the Jewish observance of the law. John Chrysostom, a Christian presbyter in Antioch in Syria, acknowledged, albeit reluctantly, that the fervor of Jewish piety confounded the Christians. "You Christians should be ashamed and embarrassed at the Jews who observe the Sabbath with such devotion and refrain from all commerce beginning with the evening of the Sabbath. When they see the sun hurrying to set in the west on Friday they call a halt to their business affairs and interrupt their selling. If a customer haggles with them over a purchase in the late afternoon, and offers a price after evening has come, the Jews refuse the offer because they are unwilling to accept any money."

John Chrysostom is particularly famous in the history of Christian relations with Jews, because he preached a series of eight sermons on Jews and Judaizing Christians in the fall of 386. John had been preoccupied with "Arian" sympathizers in the city, but as the Jewish "holy days" approached he interrupted his sermons against the Arians to turn to what he considered a more pressing problem. At this time of the year, he says, the "Jewish festivals follow one after another in succession."

The aim of the sermons was to dissuade Christian Judaizers from participating in Jewish rites and to demonstrate the truth of the Christian religion. "If the Jewish rites are holy and venerable," he says, "our way of life must be false." In the mind of the early Christians there was no middle ground between Judaism and Christianity. Only one could be true.

John was a well-trained and gifted speaker, and in these sermons he marshals all the techniques of ancient rhetoric to vilify the Jews. Here, for example, is how he introduces the topic of the first sermon: "Today I wanted to return to the same contest [with the Arians]. . . . But what can I do? Another more terrible sickness beckons and our tongue must be turned to heal a disease which is flourishing in the body of the Church. . . . What is this sickness? The festivals of the wretched and miserable Jews that follow one after another in succession—Trumpets [the New Year, or Rosh Hashanah], Booths [the Feast of Tabernacles], the Fasts [days of penitence between New Year and the Day of Atonement]—are about to take place. And many who belong to us and say that they believe in our teaching attend their festivals, and even share in their celebrations and join in their fasts. It is this evil practice I now wish to drive from the Church."

With these words the ears of the audience pricked up and the chatter subsided, for the people knew they were in for a show. The young presbyter, who had already made a reputation for his eloquence, was going to display his gifts in a blistering attack, what the rhetors called an "invective," on the Judaizers, most of whom were well known to the members of his congregation, and some of whom may have been present. They would not be disappointed:

> But if those who are sick with Judaism are not healed now when the Jewish festivals are "near, at the very door" (Matthew 24:33), I am afraid that some, out of misguided habit and gross ignorance, will share in their transgressions, and sermons about such matters would be pointless. If the offenders are not present to hear what we say today, afterwards medicine would be applied in vain because they have already committed the sin. This is the reason I am in a hurry to take up this matter before the festivals.

The ancients were not embarrassed by name-calling and obloquy. Yet the asperity of these homilies gives us pause. Still, there is no evidence that John's homilies led to violence against the Jews. His goal was to win back refractory members of the Church by shaming them, not to do physical harm to the Jews.

Alongside the stereotyped insults drawn from the repertoire of classical invective,

John's sermons on the Judaizers also employ a distinctly Christian theological vocabulary drawn from the Scriptures and earlier Christian writings. For example, Christian writers claimed the Jews did not understand their own Scriptures. Among all the ancient peoples they alone had been given the prophets who spoke of Christ, yet when he appeared they hardened their hearts and refused to acknowledge what was plainly set forth in their ancient books. "Do not be surprised if I have called the Jews wretched. They are truly wretched and miserable for they have received many good things from God yet they have spurned them and violently cast them away."

Often John draws on images from the Scriptures to make his point. "The 'sun of righteousness' [Malachi 4:2] rose on them first, but they turned their back on its beams and sat in darkness. But we, who were nurtured in darkness, welcomed the light and were freed from the yoke of error. The Jews were branches of the holy root, but they were 'lopped off' [Romans 10:19]. . . . They read the prophets from ancient times, yet they crucified the one spoken of by the prophets."

There is more to these sermons, then, than the conventional opprobrium of the rhetorical tradition. Christian theological convictions color the choice of words. This is particularly evident in John's use of the phrase "Christ-killers." The term had come into the Christian vocabulary in the fourth century to refer to the Jews who lived in Jesus's time. But by John's time the historical reference is transmuted to refer to the Jews of his own day. In one telling passage he relates the death of Christ to the destruction of the temple. "You Jews crucified him. But after he died on the cross, he then destroyed your city; it was then that he dispersed your people; it was then that he scattered your nation over the face of the earth."

In the thinking of early Christians there was a link between the death of Jesus and the destruction of the temple. Of course the two events took place forty years apart, but as the generations passed they seemed to be related as cause to effect. As Origen put it: "The city where Jesus suffered these indignities had to be utterly destroyed. The Jewish nation had to be overthrown, and God's invitation to blessedness transferred to others, I mean the Christians." In other words, the destruction of the city of Jerusalem was taken as evidence that Christianity had displaced or "superseded" Judaism.

Though John's sermons are concerned primarily with the attraction of Judaism to Christians in the city of Antioch, Julian's plan to rebuild the temple was very much on his mind. Because Jerusalem had become the "holy city" for Christians, what happened there bore directly on the truth of Christianity. One of the proofs that Christ is truly God, says John, is that he "predicted the temple would be destroyed, that Jerusalem would be captured, and that the city would no longer be the city of the Jews as it had been in the past." And to confirm this he adds: if one visits Jerusalem today "you will see only the bare foundation."

The future of the city of Jerusalem comes up in other Christian writings in this period. Rumors that the temple might still be rebuilt were circulating in northern Syria several generations after Julian's death. For example, the last verse in the prophet Ezekiel reads, "The Lord is there." When this was translated into Greek it came out "The Lord is its name." Christian interpreters took this to mean that Jerusalem was the city of the Lord—that is, of Christ. Jews, however, who based their views on the Hebrew version, took it to mean that the glory of the Lord, the *Shekinah,* would return to the city of Jerusalem: to the temple.

In commenting on this verse of Ezekiel, Theodoret, bishop of the city of Cyrrhus in Syria, explained to his readers that the city of Jerusalem had been built and rebuilt several times in the past, but in his time some believed that "another building of Jerusalem has been promised and worship according to the Law of the Jews will be established there." This possibility terrified Christians in the region, and to allay their fears Theodoret reminded them of what the city had become under Christian rule. "Today in Jerusalem there is the church of the Cross [the chapel at Golgotha], the church of the Resurrection, the church on Mount Zion, the church in Holy Bethlehem, and many other churches." But then he goes on to say: "If the temple of the Jews were rebuilt, would these be destroyed, or would they continue to be held in honor?" The answer, he opines, is that the Christian buildings would no longer be esteemed and greater honor would be shown to the Jewish temple. Were this to happen the Christian mysteries and the Jewish rites, that is animal sacrifices, would be celebrated side by side, making conflict and strife inevitable.

Although Christianity began as a movement of Jews for Jews, its greatest growth came not among Jews, but among gentiles. Because Christians claimed to be the rightful inheritors of the tradition of ancient Israel and believed on the basis of the Hebrew prophets that Jesus of Nazareth was the Messiah (Christ), conflict with Jews who did not become Christian—the majority of Jews—was inevitable. As the new movement constituted itself and established new practices, such as baptism in place of circumcision, the Christian communities were marked off as distinct from the synagogue. Though Christians and Jews shared a common tradition, the Jewish Scriptures, the Christian Old Testament, and belief in the one God, Christians viewed the Jews as rivals. What is more, the Jewish observance of the law made Christians an easy target to pagans who knew the books of Moses. Why, asks Julian, do you Christians not circumcise your male children when it is clearly commanded in the law of Moses?

The reign of Julian brought the conflict between Christians and Jews into sharp focus. Julian's abortive attempt to rebuild the Jewish temple allows us to see with uncommon clarity that the presence of law-observant Jewish communities was a spiritual challenge to Christianity. Christian thinkers had no difficulty fitting biblical Judaism, meaning pre-Christian Judaism, into their understanding of history. Israel's hopes came to fulfillment in the person of Christ, and the Church is the "new" Israel. But coming to terms with the Jewish communities of the present was another matter.

John Chrysostom's homilies on the Judaizers were often copied by later Christian scribes, and they appear frequently in manuscripts of John's works. Because of his popularity as a preacher, the purity of his Greek style, and his exemplary life, his writings have had a role in shaping Christian attitudes toward the Jews in times and places far removed from fourth-century Antioch. Already in the sixth century a Byzantine writer during the time of Justinian (d. 565) composed a series of works in which he drew freely on John's homilies on the Jews, lifting whole passages verbatim. But the ideas John sets forth are not his own; they are to be found in many other Christian writings, in sermons, in biblical commentaries, in polemical works, in theological treatises. We are dealing here with a legacy that has had a profound impact on the long history of Christian relations to the Jews.

But the Roman Empire in the fourth century was not the world of Byzantium or medieval Europe. Christianity was still in the process of finding its place in society and was torn by internal strife, mercurial loyalties, and strident critics such as Julian. Without an appreciation of this setting, and the challenge Jewish observance of the laws of Moses presented to Christians, we cannot understand why John responded to the Judaizers with such passion and fervor.

Bishop and Emperor:
Ambrose and Theodosius

Although Julian's brief reign as emperor disquieted Christians, he was a man of the past. The Church was growing in numbers and influence, and with each new generation the imprint of Christian beliefs on the mores of society became more visible. City life had begun to move to the rhythms of Christian time. Sunday had become a religious holiday, and festivals such as the Pasch (Easter) and Pentecost in spring and the Nativity (Christmas) in the dead of winter began to displace the Roman calendar. As churches rose from the ground in the center of cities the urban landscape had a new orientation, and in sermons and letters the growing self-confidence of Christian leaders is palpable. Nowhere is this more evident than in the career of Ambrose, who became bishop of Milan, the great city in northern Italy, a decade after Julian's death.

Ambrose was born in A.D. 339 in Trier, where his father, Aurelius Ambrosius, was the praetorian prefect—the chief imperial official—in Gaul (France) during the reign of emperor Constantius II, the son of Constantine the Great. His father died while Ambrose was an infant, and his mother moved the family, including his older brother, Satyrus, and sister, Marcellina, to Rome, where he had his schooling. The family was well placed in ecclesiastical circles, and Ambrose's sister received the veil from Pope Liberius at an elaborate ceremony in the recently constructed Basilica of Saint Peter in Rome. Like other youths from well-to-do families, Ambrose received a traditional education in Latin grammar and rhetoric, but he also learned Greek, making him part of a small company among Latin Christian writers—Jerome was another—who could read Origen and other Greek Christian writers and the Alexandrian Jew Philo without translations into Latin. After he had completed his education he began to practice law, but was soon pressed into service on the staff of the praetorian prefect of Italy. From there he was appointed governor of the provinces of Liguria and Emelia in north central Italy, with his seat at Milan.

When Auxentius, the bishop of Milan, died in 373, partisan crowds began to gather in the cathedral. The city was deeply divided between the supporters of Nicaea and its critics, the Homoeans, who confessed Christ to be "like" the Father, not "of one substance" with the Father as the Nicene Creed had it. Auxentius believed with the Homoeans (Arians), and Ambrose, though only a layman, was known to favor the Nicenes, or Catholics. As soon as he heard that crowds were milling about the cathedral quarreling over the successor to Auxentius, he came to the church to quell the unrest. According to his ancient biographer, when Ambrose entered the great basilica, he proceeded at once to the front of the church to address the crowd. Suddenly the voice of a small child far to the rear cried out: "Ambrose for bishop!" At once the mood of the crowd changed and the people took up the cry, "Ambrose for bishop. Ambrose for bishop." Whatever Ambrose himself thought of the proposal, he did not respond to the acclamation, but left immediately to attend to his duties as judge. Later he would write that he had been "snatched from the magistrate's tribunal and my robes of office into the priesthood," and then adds, "I began to teach what I had myself not yet learned."

Ambrose seems to have made a half-hearted attempt to flee the city, but the next morning, in the revealing phrase of his ancient biographer, he "found himself" at the chief ceremonial entrance to the city, the so-called Roman gate. Soon a petition was addressed to the Christian emperor Valentinian to rule on the circumstances of the "election." In the meantime Ambrose went into hiding in the home of a friend.

No doubt the emperor saw in Ambrose a proven civil servant and a man of sound judgment, and he soon sent word that he was satisfied and pleased with his election. In rapid succession Ambrose was baptized, marched through the several ecclesiastical offices, including deacon and presbyter, and consecrated bishop. His baptism took place on one Sunday, his ordination as priest during the week, and his consecration as bishop the following Sunday. Everything, according to his ancient biographer, was carried out with "the utmost grace and rejoicing" among the faithful, though his opponents (of which there were many) said the whole affair was irregular and ill-considered, a scheme worked by his influential friends. The date was December 7, 374. It was an auspicious time and place to become bishop.

Sitting astride the great east–west highway from the Balkans to Gaul and the north–south highway from southern Italy to the Alpine passes leading to the Rhineland, Milan was centrally located, with good communications to all parts of the empire. Up until the end of the third century it was a respectable provincial capital, the commercial and administrative hub of the region. But in 300 the Western emperor Maximian moved his residence to Milan, and with him came the imperial court. The city quickly became the empire's political center, as its power and influence eclipsed even that of the ancient capital of Rome. By then the city was largely Christian, and as head of the Christian community Ambrose was, next to the emperor, the most important public figure in the city. It was a new role for a Christian bishop.

A comparison with Cyprian (d. 258), who was bishop of Carthage, the chief city in North Africa, a century earlier is instructive. Like Ambrose, Cyprian had come from an upper-class family of means (he sold much of his property on election), had received a thorough education, was a gifted speaker and skilled Latin stylist, and seems also to have studied law. Unlike Ambrose he was a convert to Christianity. In his day the church in Carthage was a small closely knit community—we might call it a private association, a city within the city—whose life went on largely independent of the society at large, and featured regular worship, caring for the poor, widows, orphans, and the sick, burying the dead, visiting prisoners, welcoming Christian visitors. Christians may have owned some buildings, but there were no conspicuous Christian structures.

It is estimated that in the year 200, out of a population of 60 million people in the Roman Empire, there were only about 200,000 Christians, less than one percent of the population. By the middle of the century, when Cyprian was bishop, this number had increased to a little more than a million, perhaps two percent of the citizenry. Carthage was a large city of some 350,000 to 400,000 inhabitants, which meant that Cyprian was head of a community that numbered well under 10,000, perhaps closer to 5,000.

As bishop Cyprian was certainly known outside the Church, but he was not a public figure. The emperor was an august and distant personage across the sea in Rome, and as bishop Cyprian's charge lay with his clergy (numbering fewer than ten) and the affairs of Christians under his care. Of his many letters that are extant most were addressed to presbyters, deacons, confessors, and other Christians. Political authority, whether in Rome or in Carthage, was "other," in some cases a benign other, and in some cases a menacing and repressive other. Persecution was not only a possibility, it became a bitter fact of life. The great crisis of Cyprian's episcopacy was an aggressive and systematic effort, led by the emperor, to weaken if not destroy Christianity, beginning with the bishops.

Ambrose came to the office of bishop several generations after the last great persecution of Christians in the first decade of the fourth century. Since the accession of Constantine to the imperial throne all the emperors, save Julian, were Christian. In the city and suburb of Milan there were five church buildings. The cathedral, above which the present cathedral of Milan is built, was an imposing structure measuring some eighty by forty-five meters. It was nearly as large as Saint John Lateran, the huge church in Rome built by Constantine. Its grandeur and solidity not only changed the look of the city, it also conferred authority and dignity on the bishop who spoke from its *cathedra,* a chair in the apse set aside for his use alone. A community that was previously scorned now had a very prominent podium on a majestic stage, especially when the bishop was a gifted public speaker like Ambrose.

Political developments also favored the Christians. In 378, after the disastrous defeat of the Roman armies at Adrianople, the emperor Gratian appointed Theodosius, a pious Christian, to the chief military office in the Balkans to fight the Goths, and in 379 made him augustus with responsibility for the eastern provinces of the empire. A year later Theodosius issued from his headquarters in Thessalonica an edict to the inhabitants of the capital, Constantinople. It is known by its opening words, *cunctos populos,* "all peoples." Theodosius ruled that henceforth Catholic Christianity as confessed by Damasus, the bishop of Rome, and Peter, the bishop of Alexandria, would be recognized as the official form of Christianity in the empire. "According to the apostolic teaching and the doctrine of the gospel, let us believe the one deity of the Father, the Son, and the Holy Spirit, in equal majesty and in a holy Trinity."

This decree was a first but momentous step in the establishment of Christianity as the official religion of the Roman world. Significantly, it was issued by the emperor without consultation with bishops. It was less an effort on the part of the Church to impose its beliefs on the society than a political gesture on the part of the emperor to bring about religious unity in a fractured empire. The consequences were far reaching, for the decree cemented the alliance between the Church and political power that had emerged since the years of Constantine's rule, and shaped Western civilization for the next fifteen hundred years.

By the time Ambrose became bishop, Milan was a Christian city. A dramatic demonstration of the hold of Christianity on the affections of its citizens can be seen in the discovery of the remains of two Christian martyrs, Gervasius and Protasius, during Ambrose's episcopacy.

Christians revered the bones of the martyrs, and from the earliest period of the Church's history the faithful built shrines and gathered at their tombs to offer the Eucharist and remember the heroes of the faith. By the fourth century church buildings had begun to be sanctified by depositing relics of the martyrs in them. In the summer of 386 Ambrose planned to dedicate a new church with a celebration of the Eucharist, a sermon, and special prayers for the occasion; but the people demanded more. They wanted relics and implored him: "Consecrate this building in the same way you consecrated the Roman Basilica." In that church relics of Saints Peter and Paul had been placed. Ambrose replied that he would "if he could find relics of martyrs."

A search was undertaken, and Ambrose instructed the diggers to probe beneath the floor of another Church built above an ancient Christian cemetery. Ambrose's premonition turned out to be sound, and soon bodies were uncovered with bones intact except for the heads—a sign that they might indeed have been martyrs. On the testimony of several elderly men it was determined that the remains belonged to the martyrs Gervasius and Protasius, who were thought to have suffered martyr-dom during the reign of Emperor Nero, though more likely at the end of the second century. Two days later the relics were carried in procession to the new church and a blind man, formerly a butcher, touched the fringe of the bier with a handkerchief, applied it to his eyes, and his sight was restored—certain proof that the relics were genuine.

When the procession reached the church Ambrose was so overcome with emo-tion that he was at first unable to speak (according to his account). But during the reading of the lessons he gained his composure. Taking his place between the biers, "holy relics on my right hand and on my left hand," he gave thanks to God for the discovery of the tombs of the martyrs. This was a gift beyond telling, he said, for the church of Milan had been "barren of martyrs" for too long. Now it had become a "joyful mother of children." In the words of a hymn composed for the occasion: "We were not able to be martyrs, but we have found martyrs."

This whole affair seems staged, and what we know about the discovery of the relics comes primarily from a letter Ambrose wrote to his sister, Marcellina. Au-gustine, however, was in Milan at the time and describes the event in similar terms in his *Confessions*. What is significant is not so much what Ambrose did, but what the people of the city demanded of him. As Neil McLynn, a recent biographer, has observed, the fourth-century cult of the martyrs "was not a pantomime staged for the vulgar but a channeling of powerful energies too intractable for the bishop to have controlled at will, and too pervasive for him to have thought to try." There is no more telling mark of the new society being constructed in the wake of Con-stantine than this liaison between city, people, and religious devotion embodied in the veneration of martyrs and saints. The new order sprang from the ground; it was not imposed from above.

During his first years as bishop Ambrose gave himself to pastoral and catecheti-cal matters. He wrote a treatise on virginity to his sister Marcellina and other essays promoting the religious life. He led the faithful in common prayer, preached reg-ularly, and encouraged the veneration of the relics of the saints. But these halcyon months were not to last. In November 375, the Western emperor Valentinian died and was replaced by his teenage son Gratian; in the East, Gratian's half brother, Valentinian II, a five-year-old boy, became emperor, effectively giving power to his mother Justina, an aggressive Homoean, or Arian.

Although most of the citizens of Milan were Nicene Christians, there was a company of Gothic troops quartered in the city, and these soldiers were Homoeans with no church of their own. According to old Roman law religious buildings were under the authority of the emperor. In an earlier dispute between Catholics and Arians the emperor Gratian had sequestrated, or taken into his own custody, a church building without any protest from the Catholics.

At the beginning of Lent in 385, Ambrose was summoned to the imperial palace and told that he had to give up the Basilica of Portius, a church in the possession of Catholics outside the walls of the city. He refused. A few weeks later Justina tried another ploy. There were two principal churches in the city, the Old Basilica and the New Basilica, and she requested that one of these churches be given to the Homo-eans. On Friday before Palm Sunday the order came down to relinquish the build-ing. Ambrose replied: "A bishop cannot give up the temple of God."

On Saturday the praetorian prefect of Italy showed up in the church where Ambrose was presiding with a modest request that he hand over the Portian Basil-ica (outside the walls of the city, hence a less important church). Ambrose stood firm. On Tuesday a delegation from the emperor again met with him, reminding him that disposal of religious buildings was within the rights of the emperor. To which he responded: if the emperor asked of me anything of my own, "my estates, my money, everything that is mine" he would not refuse him, but "the things of God are not subject to the authority of the emperor."

The next morning, before daybreak he went to the Portian Basilica to celebrate the liturgy and found the church surrounded by soldiers. When Ambrose finished his sermon, an imperial secretary approached him and in the name of the emperor said: "What is your aim in acting contrary to my wishes?" To which Ambrose responded: "I cannot surrender the basilica, but I cannot use arms [to defend it]." Ambrose spent the night in the Portian Basilica reciting psalms with his clergy. The next morning, Holy Thursday, as Ambrose was preaching on repentance (the text was from the prophet Jonah), word arrived that the emperor had relented and given orders that the soldiers leave the church. He had not only misread the mood of the populace, he misjudged Ambrose's strength and resolve.

Ambrose could not afford to be moderate. Beneath his studied poise was an indomitable will driven by the resolute conviction that the emperor was not the arbiter in religious matters. In his language: "In a matter of faith it is the practice for bishops to judge Christian emperors, not emperors bishops." The initial Christian portrayal of Constantine, as reflected in the writings of Eusebius of Caesarea, depicted him as a priestly figure, but Ambrose effectively desacralized the office by insisting that the emperor was a layman who had to reckon with an alternate authority. The establishment of Christianity took place as much against political power as in collusion with it. This is evident in a more famous and quite different confrontation that had taken place a year earlier.

Since the days of Emperor Augustus, a statue to the goddess Victoria had stood in the senate house in Rome, and as senators entered the chamber they made an offer-ing of incense at her altar. As the number of Christian senators increased, the altar became an embarrassment, if not an offense to Christian sensibilities. In 357 Em-peror Constantius had removed the altar, but a few years later it was restored. In 382, however, against the protests of conservative pagans in the senate, Emperor Gratian again ordered its removal and cut off subsidies of the state cult, effectively severing one of the last ligaments that bound the Roman state to ancient religious practices.

Gratian, however, died a year later, and with the accession of the youthful Valentinian as emperor of the West a group of pagan senators seized the opportunity to stage a public procession on the occasion of a traditional festival. In the summer of 384, Symmachus, a distinguished senator and prefect of the city of Rome, at the request of members of the senate (some may have been Christian), penned a memorable plea to the emperor, a famous *Memorial* (*Relatio* in Latin) calling for a return to "the religious conditions that for so long have benefitted the commonweal."

The *Memorial* is an elegant plea, and even Ambrose acknowledged the "glittering eloquence" and "golden tongue" of Symmachus. It appealed not only to a sense of fairness and justice but also to the affections of citizens of the empire: "Grant us, we beseech you," he writes, "that what we received as boys we may as old men leave to those who come after us." But its theology of a benign universal deity rendered every particular religious belief otiose. "We gaze upon the same stars," wrote Symmachus, "the sky is common to all, the same world envelops us. What difference does it make by what wisdom a person seeks the truth? We cannot attain to so great a mystery by one path." Unlike modern readers who are attracted to the apparent sweet reasonableness of Symmachus, in Ambrose's day most realized that the *Memorial* was a frontal attack on the God of the Bible. Prudentius, the Christian Latin poet, praised the "unfading golden sheen" of his speech, but wickedly added that when one considers the content it is as though a man had set out to till "muddy ground with a golden fork."

Ambrose's response is forceful, direct, and uncompromising. Again his argument turns on his authority as bishop. If this were a "civil matter" it would be one thing, but since it is a "matter of religion I appeal to you as bishop." Ambrose addressed Valentinian as a fellow Christian and member of the Church. The issue, as he saw it, turned not on toleration but on idolatry, specifically whether a Christian emperor can lend his support to the worship of a false god, Victoria. Ambrose rejected the notion that there is a neutral place to stand. Even in the senate chamber one must choose between paganism or worship of the one God.

Ambrose's next move was as audacious as it was unexpected. If Symmachus's request were granted and the altar restored, he writes the emperor, do not think for a moment that the bishops will turn the other way and allow the matter to pass unnoticed. Then he adds: "You may come to the church if you wish, but you will not find a bishop there, or if so, it will be one who will resist you." It was a bold and risky act. No one had ever challenged the emperor so directly on a matter that traditionally fell within his authority. Though the Church may be complicit with political power, that does not give the emperor a license to promote idolatry.

In the summer of 388 Ambrose was caught off guard by an unexpected challenge from a different quarter that led to another standoff with the emperor. In Callinicum, a border military town on the Euphrates River, a group of Christians set fire to a Jewish synagogue. The Roman governor of the provinces of the East referred the matter to the emperor of the East, Theodosius, who ordered the bishop to rebuild the synagogue out of his own funds. When Ambrose heard of the incident and the emperor's response, he wrote Theodosius at once to protest. The emperor had no business ordering a bishop to rebuild a synagogue with Christian funds.

Understandably, Ambrose's action has provoked vigorous critical commentary among modern scholars. He is said to be "plainly wrong," a "bully" and a "bigot," a religious zealot acting out of "unbalanced zeal" and "fanaticism." To be sure, his action was legally tenuous and morally dubious and rested on the ignoble assumptions of his age. Yet his reasoning had a certain logic to it in the ancient world. The issue of the synagogue at Callinicum, as Ambrose saw it, was not whether the Jews have a right to their own building and freedom to worship according to their traditions, but whether a Christian bishop can in good conscience contribute to the reconstruction of a house of worship of a rival religion. In Ambrose's melodramatic language, the emperor's order would force the bishop to become either an "apostate," if he acceded to the order, or a "martyr" if he refused. Reluctantly, and no doubt with a troubled conscience, Theodosius gave in to Ambrose's demands.

The most dramatic event during Ambrose's tenure in office was his confrontation with the emperor Theodosius over a bloody incident in the city of Thessalonica. One evening in a tavern a popular charioteer had made sexual advances to an attendant of Butheric, the commander of troops quartered in the city. The charioteer was arrested. When the people clamored for his release, Butheric refused, whereupon the mob savagely murdered him and dragged his body through the streets. Theodosius was outraged, and he ordered the people of Thessalonica to be invited to a spectacle in the circus, a Roman arena for chariot racing. In the midst of the race, soldiers rushed in and for three hours massacred several thousand citizens, mowing them down "like corn at harvest time," according to an ancient historian. Ambrose received news of the massacre while attending a council of bishops. He realized that the eyes of the other bishops were on him and firmly took the position that mass murder was a grave sin and the emperor must do penance for his deed before he could receive Communion.

In a famous painting by Peter Paul Rubens, *Emperor Theodosius Refused Entry into Milan Cathedral,* two figures stand at the door of a church, Theodosius in the garb of a Roman soldier, Ambrose in brocaded cope and miter, his outstretched left hand blocking the emperor from the door. The scene as depicted is the work of Rubens's imagination; the standoff never reached that point. Nor was it a showdown between ecclesiastical authority and political might. The issue, as Ambrose presents it, was how as bishop he could persuade the emperor, a faithful member of the Church, to submit to penance. My aim, he wrote to Theodosius, is "not to put you to shame . . . but to put this sin away from your kingdom." The letter to the emperor was written in his own hand for the emperor alone to read. Significantly, Ambrose did not include this letter in his official correspondence to be published after his death. He wished neither to humiliate Theodosius nor to diminish his authority.

In the early Church there was no "private" confession. According to church law the emperor could not present himself quietly before the bishop, confess his sin, and receive absolution. The penitential discipline of the early Church was unremittingly harsh and carried out in front of the Christian people. The penitents were segregated from the rest of the community, assigned a special section in the church, and forbidden to receive the Eucharist. As Ambrose reminded Theodosius: "I dare not offer the Sacrifice if you intend to be present."

Although Theodosius was a mature and self-assured leader, Ambrose insisted that he submit to the discipline of the Church and join the company of penitents. The emperor was "within not above the Church." Ambrose was not laying down a principle about the relationship of Church and state; he was invoking the ancient discipline that had long governed the way the Church dealt with grave sin. What is new in the confrontation with Theodosius is not what Ambrose says, but that he says it to an emperor, the august and lordly potentate. At a time when the Christian cult could have become a department of the imperial administration, Ambrose drew clear boundaries around the Church. This is all the more impressive because as the Christian community grew the lines separating the Church and "the world" were blurred if not erased. When the social fabric seemed to have no seam, Ambrose stitched in a well-defined border.

In the long history of the Church the failings of the bishops have been many, but the office has proven remarkably resilient. When the Church was young and innocent Ignatius said that the bishop is the sign of the Church. This was no less true in Ambrose's day, as the Church was adapting to the new age ushered in by Constantine. Only as bishop could Ambrose have urged a Roman emperor to make the words of David the king of Israel his own: "I have sinned greatly in that I have done this deed; and now, O Lord, take away the iniquity of your servant, for I have failed miserably."

Architecture and Art

Architecture is the most conspicuous of the arts. Unlike poetry or painting, it occupies and shapes public space as a tangible and inescapable object whose impact is felt by all who make their way about the city. This was particularly true in the Mediterranean world, where life was lived outside. Such quotidian activities as cutting hair, repairing a sandal, or teaching children their ABCs took place out of doors. In the fourth century the face of the cities was changing as Christian churches were constructed across the Mediterranean world, altering, for example, the location of streets and alleys and opening up space for religious processions as well as markets.

One of Constantine's first gestures as emperor was to build a large church in the city of Rome, Saint John Lateran. In the decades that followed he commissioned churches in other cities, most notably in Jerusalem and Bethlehem, and of course he built a new Christian city on the European side of the Bosporus at the site of the ancient city of Byzantium, naming it after himself, Constantinople, the city of Constantine. His reign began an intensive period of church building that lasted up to the Muslim conquest in the seventh century. The energy and exuberance displayed in the planning and construction of churches in these centuries is remarkable.

Some of these buildings are still standing and in use, and from the remains of others we can imagine their architecture and design. On occasion, ancient authors will give us a first-hand description of buildings they had seen. Eusebius celebrated the "dazzling beauty" of a new church in Tyre (Lebanon), "its unimaginable grandeur, its brilliant workmanship, its towering walls that reach to the sky and the costly Lebanese cedars that form the ceiling." The church was "utterly breathtaking, a marvel of beauty. The evidence of our eyes makes instruction through the ears unnecessary."

The principal religious building in the ancient world was the temple—the house of the god or goddess whose image it contained. It was usually a rectangular structure with a relatively modest interior space, or *cella,* fronted with a porch and a row of columns. The Roman temple stood on a raised platform and was reached by stairs leading up to the entrance at the rear of the porch. The statue was placed facing the door so that the god could see the sacrifice, which was roasted at a stone altar in front of the temple. The temple was not a place for people to assemble; the worshipers gathered outside in front in the open air where they could share in the meat of victims that had been sacrificed.

Because the Roman temple was designed to house an image of the god, not to accommodate a large group of people, it was ill-suited for Christian worship. The Christian liturgy included the reading of the Scripture and an exposition of what was read (sermon), processions, including carrying the book of the gospel into the midst of the Church, responses to the prayers, the singing of psalms and hymns, and the eating and drinking of bread and wine that had been blessed. From an architectural perspective, Christian worship required a large interior space where people could gather, a podium, called an ambo, at which the Scriptures could be read, a table or altar, where the vessels holding the bread and wine could be placed, and ample space for movement of the clergy and people. There were no seats in the early churches, and people stood during worship.

The building that best suited the needs of Christian worship was the basilica, a spacious multipurpose hall, often without interior columns or aisles, with a raised platform at one end. A basilica normally included a clerestory, large windows set up high on the side walls to provide light. Unlike the temple, which had a single purpose, the basilica could be used for different kinds of activities: legal affairs, buying and selling, a reception hall for civic gatherings. It was a place to transact business, hear the latest news, display objects for sale, change money, to see and be seen.

In the fourth century, when Christians began to build churches, they took the basilica rather than the temple as their model. The Christian basilica usually had two rows of columns that created a large central area, the nave, and two side aisles, a slightly raised platform for the altar and a seat for the bishop (presbytery or chancel), a semicircular apse at the east end, and a timber roof, in some churches exposed, in others concealed by a flat ceiling. Most churches had a simple brick exterior without ornament. The people entered through a forecourt open to the sky, and in some cases it included a fountain for washing one's feet. It is likely that the early Christians worshiped unshod. The altar was a stone table set out from the wall, and the reading desk or ambo stood in the midst of the nave. Some churches were oriented so that the apse was on the east end and the congregation and priest faced east during the Eucharistic offering.

Of course the actual plan of a Christian basilica varied from place to place depending on the physical constraints of the location, the resources of the local community, and the imagination of the architects and skill of the builders. But initially the basic outline was remarkably uniform, with differences in the kind of material used, the interior decorations, and the dimensions. In large cities, such as Rome or Milan, and at popular pilgrimage sites like the tomb of Christ in Jerusalem or the cave of the nativity in Bethlehem, churches had four rows of columns and four aisles instead of the more conventional two rows of columns and two aisles.

A good example of a classical Christian basilica, still standing without radical alterations, is the church of Santa Sabina on the Aventine Hill in Rome, constructed between A.D. 422 and 432. The building has a broad central nave flanked with two rows of columns and a semicircular apse. The columns, twenty-four in all, fluted and crowned with Corinthian capitals, were taken from an earlier building, but they were carefully chosen to complement one another and to enhance the finely proportioned interior. The columns support arches with marble inlay in the spandrels displaying chalices and patens, or liturgical vessels. The walls above the arches may at one time have held mosaics. The only mosaic that remains, however, is a dedicatory inscription in Latin on the rear wall. On either wall above the columns there are large windows that flood the interior with light. Unlike most other Christian basilicas, there are also three windows that open on the apse.

Because it created a new kind of interior space that invited decoration, the Christian basilica offered new possibilities for artistic expression. Previously Christian art was confined to relatively private buildings, but in these new structures pictures could be displayed in large very public spaces. The focal point in the church was the apse, a deep semicircular space at the end of the building with a wide half dome beneath the arch where the altar was located. It gave the artist a large unified area in which to work, and the medium used most often was colored tesserae (cubes of stone or glass). Mosaics had been used for floor decorations, but Christian artists put them in the apse and on the walls, often using gold as a predominant color, especially for background. When the church was lit with oil lamps the tiles bathed everything in soft light.

The earliest surviving decorated basilical apse is found in the church of Santa Pudenziana in Rome, built at the end of the fourth century. In the center of the mosaic sits Christ dressed in common Roman garb, a pallium, or cloak, over a tunic with a pair of light blue stripes, and wearing sandals. In his hand is an open book bearing an inscription, *Dominus conservator ecclesiae Pudentianae* (I am the Lord, the preserver of the church of Pudenziana). On either side sit the apostles, with two women standing behind them about to place a crown on the heads of Paul and Peter, who sit closest to Jesus. Above Christ is a large cross studded with precious stones, and below the cross are the stately buildings of the new Christian Jerusalem.

Another example of an early apse mosaic can be found in the Basilica Euphrasiana in the city of Porec in Croatia. The arch above the apse pictures Christ holding an open book with the text, *Ego sum lux vera* (I am the true Light), flanked by the twelve apostles, six on either side. In the vault of the apse is the Virgin Mary sitting on a throne with the child Jesus under a wreath held by the hand of God. Next to her are angels, Bishop Euphrasius holding a model of the church and local saints, including Saint Maurus, the first bishop of Porec. All are surrounded by a meadow of flowers.

Although the apse mosaic was the central focus in the new Christian basilicas, artists realized that the area on the walls immediately above the columns offered another spacious area suitable for decoration. A stunning early example of mosaic wall decoration can be found in another building in Rome, the church of Santa Maria Maggiore, Saint Mary Major, constructed shortly after Santa Sabina during the time of Pope Sixtus (432–440) to honor the Blessed Virgin Mary. The date is significant. At the Council of Ephesus in 431, the third ecumenical council, the bishops had solemnly affirmed that the title *theotokos,* God-bearer, was appropriate for the Virgin Mary.

The floor plan of Saint Mary Major is similar to that of Santa Sabina, a large central nave with two rows of Ionic columns, and a semicircular apse at the east end. But the entablature sits directly on the columns, and this gives the interior an austerity and majesty that is quite different from the feeling one has on entering Santa Sabina. Above the nave walls are pilasters that form an upper order, each flanked by a tier of colonettes (small columns) and a stucco frieze with large semicircular windows at the top.

Above the columns and below the clerestory are twenty-seven mosaic panels (out of an original forty-two) depicting scenes from the Old Testament, including the offering of Melchizedek, Abraham and the three mysterious visitors, the blessing of Jacob by Isaac, the passage of the Israelites through the Red Sea, the fall of Jericho. The triumphal arch, the wall that divides the basilica from the apse, has New Testament scenes of the birth and infancy of Christ and the Virgin Mary, although these images were created much later. As the architecture directs the eye of the worshiper toward the altar in the apse, so the mosaic panels direct the mind to the fulfillment of biblical history in the birth of Christ by the Virgin Mary.

The mosaics at Santa Maria Maggiore represent a considerable expansion of biblical subjects beyond those found in earlier Christian art. In the catacombs and on sarcophagi, for example, the images are heavily weighted toward miracles of deliverance and healing: Daniel in the lion's den, the three men in the fiery furnace, the raising of Lazarus, the healing of the paralytic, Jesus putting clay on the eyelids of the man born blind, the woman with an issue of blood who touches the hem of Christ's garment. To many of the faithful, Christ's primary significance was as a miracle worker, and, remarkably, in some cases he is pictured with a magician's wand as he performs a miracle!

Over time, however, the repertoire of images was expanded to include the adoration of the magi, the entry into Jerusalem, events from Christ's passion, and most notably, the Crucifixion. The first representation of the crucifixion in the history of Christian art appears on a door of cypress wood at Santa Sabina. The door includes eighteen panels (out of an original twenty-eight) depicting scenes from the Bible. One of the panels depicts Christ hanging on a cross flanked by the two malefactors on smaller crosses on either side. Five panels have scenes from the Old Testament: Moses receiving the tablets of the law, the Exodus from Egypt, the wanderings in the desert, the abduction of Habakkuk by the angel (Bel and the Dragon 33–39), the Ascension of Elijah (2 Kings 2). Among the New Testament scenes, several portray miracles of Christ (healing of the blind man, the multiplication of loaves and fishes, the wedding at Cana), but there are also panels featuring the adoration of the magi, the trial of Christ, the denial of Peter (with the cock sitting on a pillar), Pilate washing his hands, two women and an angel at the tomb, the resurrected Christ appearing to two women, and the ascension of Christ.

Because some of the scenes are missing and the original order has been changed, one cannot be certain how the panels originally fitted together, but there does seem to be symmetry between stories from the Old Testament and events in the New Testament. The miracles of Moses in the desert, sweetening the bitter waters of Marah, provision of quails and manna, the striking of water from the rock, for example, are complemented by miracles of Christ, the healing of the blind man, the multiplication of the loaves and fishes, turning water into wine during the wedding at Cana. Like the mosaics at Santa Maria Maggiore, the artist saw events in the life of Christ as the fulfillment of what had happened in ancient Israel. Artistic convention, in other words, reflected the Christian understanding of the relation between the history of Israel recorded in the Old Testament and the events of Christ's life in the New. The full meaning of what happened in ancient times was only revealed in Christ.

As these two churches illustrate, Christian art tends toward narrative, the telling of a story, the depiction of events from biblical history. Even if the artist pictured only a single event, such as the denial of Peter, the event was understood as part of a larger story. On occasion Christian artists used symbols, for example, a lamb or a cross, but these are exceptions, and as we shall see later in discussing the controversy over icons, there came a time when symbols were discouraged, even prohibited. Further, unlike later Islamic art with its love of calligraphy, Christian art seldom includes scriptural texts. Though the Scriptures include the poetry of the Psalms, the moral precepts of Proverbs and Sirach, and the letters of Saint Paul, the Bible is first and foremost a book of history, the history of the people of Israel and of Jesus Christ and the first Christian communities. So it was to this history, and the persons and events who appear in the biblical stories, that Christians turned when they wished to decorate their churches.

The pattern of prophecy and fulfillment is vividly displayed in a building from the sixth century, the church of San Vitale in Ravenna in northeastern Italy. After the decline of the city of Rome and the fall of the Western Roman empire in 476, Ravenna became the most important city in Italy. Located on the Adriatic Sea with a good port (now silted in), it was easily accessible by sea to the capital in Constantinople. During the reign of the Ostrogothic king Theodoric, and then the emperor Justinian, several remarkable ecclesiastical buildings were constructed. The most spectacular is the church of San Vitale, a building that combines architectural daring, sophisticated technical skill, and beauty of ornamentation.

San Vitale is central in plan and octagonal in form, with eight large piers that support a circular drum crowned with a dome and covered with a conical roof. Behind the piers is an ambulatory, and the domed area, well lit by high windows on the eight sides, creates a large central space for movement. The eucharistic liturgy was an affair of seeing as much as hearing, and the plan of San Vitale, as well as other like buildings, most notably Holy Wisdom in Constantinople, was designed to allow full participation of the faithful in the liturgical action. In the liturgy there were two solemn processions, the first entrance, or "little entrance," at the beginning when clergy carried the book of the gospel into the church, and the "great entrance" when the bread and wine were brought to the altar. The octagonal plan allowed the people to gather between the pillars and in the ambulatory, leaving the center of the church free for the procession of the clergy led by the book of the gospel or the bringing forward of the eucharistic gifts. As one writer put it, when the patriarch entered the church a great crowd gathered, "because they especially liked to see him make his entrance in his patriarchal vestments."

The octagonal plan did not allow for an apse. So the architects at San Vitale designed a presbytery (chancel) that protruded out from one of the bays between two of the piers and placed an apse at its end with a cathedra (seat) for the bishop. On the walls of the presbytery they executed an elaborate series of mosaics according to a plan that integrated biblical history and the Church's worship. At the opening of the chancel there is a high arch whose underside is decorated with a series of medallions: at the top is Christ, next to him one either side are Peter and Paul, and down the sides of the arch are the other apostles, and finally two saints, Gervasius and Protasius.

On either side of the chancel there are two columns between the pier and the exterior wall (cutting off the ambulatory that runs around the rest of the building) to create three arches, above which there is a large lunette covered with mosaics. Each lunette has two scenes taken from the book of Genesis.

On the left as one faces the altar stands Abraham offering a lamb on a large platter to the three mysterious visitors (Genesis 18:1–16), who sit at a table on which are three loaves marked with crosses in the fashion of eucharistic bread. Behind Abraham his wife Sarah, standing at the entrance to a small hut, looks over at Abraham and the visitors. On the right is the sacrifice of Isaac (Genesis 22:1–19). Abraham stands with his right arm extended holding a sword about to fall on Isaac, pictured as a boy with his hands bound and his head bowed awaiting the blow from the sword. Next to Abraham is a lamb with its head turned toward Isaac, and out of the heavens reaches a hand to restrain Abraham. The entire composition is beautifully balanced and adapted to the curve of the lunette.

In the lunette on the other side one finds Abel, the brother of Cain, lifting up a lamb, the "firstlings from his flock," to be offered as a sacrifice. Abel's name is spelled out directly above him. From the account in Genesis, the faithful would know that the Lord "had regard for Abel and his offering," but "for Cain and his offering He had no regard" (Genesis 4:4–5). To the right stands Melchizedek (with the name spelled out above him), the mysterious king of Salem (Genesis 14:17–23), dressed in ceremonial robes (behind him is a temple), making an offering of bread. Between them is an altar covered with a veil embroidered with gold and on the altar sits a large chalice and two loaves of bread. Both Abel and Melchizedek are looking at the hand of God reaching down from the heavens. In some ancient liturgies Abel, Abraham, and Melchizedek are mentioned in the prayer of thanksgiving over the gifts of bread and wine.

Above the lunettes are two flying angels holding a wreath surrounding a jeweled cross. On the side with the scene of Abraham and the mysterious visitors, the figure of Jeremiah (the name written out) unrolling a scroll is on the left, and on the right are Moses receiving the law and below him the Israelites at Mount Sinai. Above these scenes one finds the evangelists Matthew and Mark, each holding his gospel, which is identified (*secundum Marcum*, for example). On the other side, there are two angels with a cross in a circle above the lunette. To the left is Moses taking off his shoes before the burning bush, and Moses feeding the sheep of the flock of Jethro, his father-in-law. To the right is the prophet Isaiah holding a scroll unrolled. Above are the evangelists Luke and John.

In the space created by the groined vaults covering the area between the two walls of the chancel there are four angels in white robes with hands uplifted as if supporting the central medallion. At the apex is the Lamb of God framed within a large wreath against a dark blue sky dotted with gold and silver stars. The apse mosaic pictures a young, beardless Christ enthroned on a dark blue globe holding a scroll with seven seals. On either side stand two heavenly escorts flanked by Saint Vitalis and Bishop Ecclesius, during whose reign the church was built.

On the walls to either side of the apse mosaic are two other mosaics depicting the emperor, Justinian, and the empress, Theodora, taking part in a procession into the church. On the left the scene pictures the emperor preceded by the bishop, Maximius, who holds a jeweled cross, the deacon who holds the gospel book, and another deacon with a thurible smoking with incense. In other words, what is being depicted is the eucharistic liturgy. Behind the emperor is the donor and attendants and soldiers. On the right the empress, holding a large golden bowl, leads a procession of women. It is clear that the procession began outside in the atrium and proceeded from there into the church, because an attendant has pulled aside a curtain and one can see the fountain in the atrium.

Besides the splendor of the design, the brilliance of the colors, and the intricacy of the workmanship, it is evident that the mosaics in the sanctuary of San Vitale were conceived with a definite plan in mind. Like Santa Maria Maggiore, a series of scenes from the Old Testament, the sacrifice of Isaac, the offering of Melchizedek, are a prominent part of the overall scheme. But unlike Saint Mary Major and other churches in which Old Testament scenes are complemented by scenes from the New Testament, San Vitale has no images from the New Testament. What one has instead is an image of the seated Christ and the figure of the Lamb in the medallion on the ceiling. The omission of scenes of fulfillment from the New Testament is significant.

The four scenes from the Old Testament depict the offering of food, a lamb to the mysterious visitors, the offering of Isaac as sacrifice, the offering of Abel, and the offering of Melchizedek. The Old Testament images flank the altar in the presbytery, where the sacrifice of Christ is offered in the Eucharist, and the medallion of the Lamb on the groin vault is located directly over the altar. Instead of illustrating the fulfillment of Old Testament events by scenes from the New Testament, at San Vitale the offerings in the Old Testament find fulfillment in the actual sacrifice of Christ in the liturgy that took place at the altar directly below.

The decoration of early Christian churches was in service of the Church's worship; the setting determined what subjects were chosen to adorn the apse and the walls. The churches were not museums where pretty pictures were on display. The viewer had to have eyes to see and a heart that believed. Those who looked at the mosaics were participants in the events they depicted. In San Vitale, art has a ritual character.

Few things were more momentous than the inclusion of religious images in the decoration of churches. The artistic conventions of the ancient world did not go underground; they were adapted to new ends. Christianity, unlike Islam, welcomed the depiction of exemplary figures and auspicious events. By introducing a plenitude of subjects drawn from the Bible, Christian artists set the history of art on a new course. The "dimensions of this revolution are staggering," wrote the art historian Thomas F. Mathews. A visual language that had been developed over the course of a thousand years was displaced, and a "new language of images was laboriously composed, selected, assembled, rehearsed, and refined." The first intimations are visible in the decoration of the catacombs, but the depth and breadth of the transformation became apparent only in the churches built in the fourth, fifth, and sixth centuries. As the later history of Christian art shows, the achievements of these centuries was no passing phenomenon. An artistic tradition was created that would dominate Western art for the next thousand years.

Music and Worship

At the beginning of the twentieth century a papyrus was found in Egypt with a fragment of an early Christian hymn in praise of the holy Trinity. The papyrus is quite unusual, for it gives not only the Greek text of the hymn but musical notations as well, letters signifying the melody to which it was sung. The notations have been deciphered by musicologists, and a rendition of the hymn can be heard on a CD. As the stones of ancient buildings help us imagine how people lived long ago, so this precious document allows us to hear the sounds used by Christians from ancient Egypt as they raised their voices in praise of the Father, Son, and Holy Spirit. Here is their song:

> Let there be silence.
> Let the luminous stars not shine,
> Let the winds and all the noisy rivers die down;
> And as we hymn the Father, the Son, and the Holy Spirit,
> Let all the powers add "Amen Amen"
> Dominion, praise always, and glory to God,
> The sole giver of good things, Amen Amen.

Like all genuine religious music, this ancient hymn is timeless. As its simple words and pious sentiments were sung by Christians in the third century, it could be sung still by Christians in the twenty-first century. It is, however, more than a testimony to Christian devotion. Its explicitly Trinitarian vocabulary displays the intimate relation between what was confessed in Christian creeds and what was sung in Christian worship. Music was at the service of text and ritual, and any consideration of the formation of musical traditions within Christianity inevitably must focus on the ancient texts as well as on the music and the act of singing.

Singing was an integral part of worship in the Jewish temple in Jerusalem, as the many references to singing in the Old Testament attest. "Make a joyful noise to the Lord, all the lands. Serve the Lord with gladness. Come into his presence with singing!" (Psalm 100). Temple worship included musical instruments as well as the human voice: "Praise the Lord. . . . Praise him with trumpet sound; praise him with lute and harp! Praise him with timbrel and dance; praise him with strings and pipe! Praise him with sounding cymbals; praise him with loud clashing cymbals" (Psalm 150).

Instruments, however, seem to have been used in the Jewish synagogues only on special occasions, such as the celebration of the new year, Rosh Hashanah, when a ram's horn was blown. The earliest Christians may have followed the practice of singing without instrumental accompaniment. Clement of Alexandria, however, writing in the early third century, said that it is not "blameworthy" to sing praise to God "to the music of the cithara or lyre." For in doing so one is "imitating the righteous king of the Hebrews [David] who was well-pleasing to God." Whether his comment is simply an allusion to the Bible or a reflection of practice in Alexandria we cannot say.

Saint Paul says that Christians sang "psalms, hymns, and spiritual songs," and in the first decades they may have sung psalms and canticles from the Old Testament, such as the Song of Moses (Exodus 15:1–8) or the Song of Hannah (1 Samuel 2:1–10). But early on they began to compose hymns of their own modeled on Old Testament canticles. The most notable are the several canticles in the Gospel of Luke, the song of Mary (Luke 1:46–55), the Song of Zachariah the father of John the Baptist (Luke 1:68–79), and the Song of Simeon (Luke 2:29–35). Whether these "canticles" were originally sung—they may simply have been literary compositions—in time they became part of the Church's daily prayer as the Benedictus (Song of Zachariah), the Magnificat (Song of Mary), and the Nunc Dimittis (Song of Simeon). To this day these canticles are sung (or recited) at morning prayer, evening prayer, and prayer before retiring.

All the evidence from the first three centuries suggests that singing had a place in Christian worship from the beginning. In a letter to the emperor about the activities of Christians in a city in Asia Minor on the southern coast of the Black Sea, Pliny the Roman governor of the province observed that when they gathered together they sang a "hymn" (*carmen*) to Christ as to a god. And in the middle of the century Justin Martyr mentions offering up "prayers and hymns" to God for creation. But it is only in the fourth century that the makings of distinctive musical traditions within Christianity are evident. And the accent must be on traditions, plural not singular, because each geographical and cultural area had its own musical style. There is no single line of development. What came to be standard in the West, Latin plainchant, was quite different from what one found in Greek- or Syriac-speaking churches.

In Egypt the Copts had their own musical traditions, in which blind cantors played a prominent role in the liturgy, handing on melodies by memory. In Ethiopia there was a minor order of priests whose singing was essential for services. Legend has it that Saint Yared, who lived in Aksum in the sixth century, was inspired by the song of birds to create three methods of chanting for the Ethiopian liturgy. Ethiopian worship also included a kind of ritual dancing.

The differences in the musical traditions of the several linguistic and cultural regions can be seen by considering three hymn writers who flourished in the early centuries: Ephrem, who wrote in Syriac, Ambrose, who wrote in Latin, and Romanos, who wrote in Greek.

Ephrem, known in Christian tradition as the "lyre of the Holy Spirit," was born in the fourth century in the city of Nisibis on the Roman border with Persia in southeastern Asia Minor. His genius was recognized early, and his bishop gave him an official position in the Church as deacon with responsibilities for interpreting the Scriptures.

Ephrem's hymns follow a fixed pattern: verses or stanzas sung by a soloist interspersed with a refrain sung by a choir or by the congregation. The soloists' part consisted of four to ten half-verses, often in a pattern of 7+7 syllables, and the refrain was a brief verse repeated after each stanza. Each hymn had its own melody. Many of his hymns were written for specific liturgical celebrations, such as the nativity of Christ, and are based on the stories in the gospels. Like the paintings and mosaics of early Christian artists, Ephrem's poetry has a strong narrative element. Ephrem is, however, quite free adding details to the biblical narrative.

Here is the beginning of a hymn to be sung for the Nativity of Christ:

> At the birth of the Son a great clamor
> took place in Bethlehem, for watchers descended
> to give praise there, a great thunder
> were their voices [Luke 2:13]. With this voice of praise
> the silent ones [the animals] came to give praise to the Son.
> Refrain: *Blessed is the Babe by whom Adam and Eve grew young again.*
> Shepherds, too, came carrying
> The good things of the flock; sweet milk,
> Fresh meat, fitting praise.
> They divided [the gifts] and gave to Joseph the meat,
> To Mary the milk, to the Son praise.

In another Christmas hymn Ephrem dwells on Joseph's love for the new child. Note how he puts words into Joseph's mouth that are not found in the biblical account:

Joseph caressed the Son
As a babe. He served Him
As God. He rejoiced in Him
As in a blessing, and he was attentive to Him
As to the Just One—a great paradox!
Refrain: Praise to You, fair Child of the Virgin.
"Who has given me the Son of the Most High
to be a son to me? I was jealous of your mother
and wanted to divorce her. I did not know
that in her womb was a great treasure
that would suddenly enrich my poverty."

One fact about Ephrem's work as hymn writer and choral director is particularly noteworthy: he composed hymns especially for women to sing. According to Jacob of Sarug, another Syriac writer, as Moses encouraged the women to praise God after the Israelites had passed through the Sea of Reeds (he is thinking of Miriam leading the women in song, in Exodus 15:20–21), "so too Ephrem proved a second Moses for women folk and taught them to sing praise with the sweetest of songs." He continues:

> The blessed Ephrem saw that the women were silent from praise, and in his wisdom he decided it was right that they should sing out; as Moses gave timbrels to the young girls, so did this discerning man compose hymns for virgins. As he stood among the sisters it was his delight to stir these chaste women into songs of praise. He was like an eagle perched among the doves as he taught them to sing new songs of praise with pure utterance. Flocks of meek partridge surrounded him, learning how to sing a sweet song in purity of voice; He taught the swallows to warble. And the church resounded with the lovely sound of chaste women's voices.

A generation after Ephrem was writing in Syriac, Ambrose, bishop of Milan, had begun to write a different kind of hymn in Latin. During holy week in 386, led by the mother of the young emperor Valentinian, the Homoeans (Arians) had taken over one of the churches in the city. The Catholics, however, were able to gain possession of the church, and, according to Augustine who was living in Milan at the time, as the faithful kept vigil Ambrose composed a number of hymns to encourage them and prevent them from "succumbing to depression and exhaustion."

In contrast to the hymns of Ephrem, Ambrose's hymns are made up of short stanzas of four lines, in iambic dimeter (lines divided into two iambs). Each line had eight syllables, each stanza had four lines, and all the hymns include eight stanzas. A good example is his hymn "Creator of all things," one that gave Au-

gustine great comfort when his mother died. Here are two stanzas of the hymn as
Ambrose wrote it in Latin:

> Deus creator omnium
> Polique rector vestiens
> Diem decoro lumine
> Noctem sopora gratia
>
> Artus solutos ut quies
> Reddat laboris usui
> Mentesque fessas allevet
> Luctusque solvat anxios

And in a rhymed English version:

> Maker of all things, God most high
> Great Ruler of the starry sky.
> Who robed the day in beauteous light,
> In sweet repose the quiet night.
>
> That sleep may wearied limbs restore,
> And fit for toil and use once more.
> May gently sooth the careworn breast,
> And lull our anxious griefs to rest.

Ambrose's genius was to devise a form for hymns whose rhythm and vocabulary
were uncomplicated and could be easily memorized. There were of course no
hymnbooks. Ambrose drew on the language and images of the Bible, but unlike
biblical canticles these hymns were written in poetry, not prose, and employed
traditional Latin meter. It also seems that the hymns were sung antiphonally, that is
half the congregation singing one stanza, and the other half responding with the
next stanza, a practice that arose in Syria.

Among Greek-speaking Christians the outstanding figure was the poet and
hymn writer Romanos the Melodist. Romanos was born in Syria at the end of the
fifth century, but as a young man he settled in Constantinople. He is known as the
creator of the *kontakion,* a kind of sermon in verse presenting in more elevated
language what had been read in the gospel. Earlier, Greek-speaking bishops had
developed a distinctive style of preaching on high festival occasions that was closer
to poetry than prose, and Romanos built on this tradition. But he was also influenced by Syrian practice.

Like the Syriac hymns, Romanos's hymns called for a soloist who sang a highly
elaborate melody for the stanzas, and a chorus responded with a simpler refrain.
Here is the beginning of Romanos's Hymn on the Nativity of Christ:

> Today the Virgin gives birth to the Heavenly One
> And today the earth shelters the Unapproachable One.
> Angels and shepherds sing His praise;
> Led by the star, wise men make their way.
> For unto us is born
> A newborn boy, from before all time God.

Ephrem and Romanos wrote original hymns inspired by the Scriptures. But in the fourth century we begin to get evidence of the liturgical singing of scriptural texts, in particular the psalms. The reading of the Scriptures was a solemn moment in the liturgy. Cyprian says that there is no task "more befitting a voice that has confessed God" than "to resound with the formal reading of the Holy Scriptures." The lector (reader) would ascend a small raised platform, called *pulpitum* or *ambo,* in the center of the church, and proclaim the biblical reading for all to hear. Between the readings a cantor would ascend the ambo and sing the verses of a psalm, and the people would respond with a refrain, a single verse interspersed within the other verses. Apparently the cantor sometimes went on too long. Basil complains that people are "distracted, yawning, turning around unceasingly waiting for the cantor to finish the psalms so they will be dismissed from church."

Music also accompanied certain ritual actions in Christian worship. When the book of the gospels was brought forth to be read it was held aloft and carried in procession by the clergy. After the gospel was read there was a procession to return the book to its resting place. During the procession it became customary to chant the hymn known as the Trisagion, from the Greek words meaning "thrice holy." It reads: "Holy God, Holy Mighty, Holy Immortal. Have Mercy on Us." In the Latin-speaking churches the Trisagion was sung in Greek as well as in Latin.

Another Trinitarian hymn that came into the liturgy early was the Holy, Holy, Holy, known in the West from its first word, *Sanctus,* "holy." Based on the chant of the seraphim in Isaiah 6, the text of the hymn reads as follows:

> Holy, Holy, Holy, Lord God of Hosts
> Heaven and Earth are Full of your Glory.
> Hosanna in the highest.

The text of the Sanctus is found—with slightly different wording—in two ancient liturgical papyri from upper Egypt discovered in the twentieth century. In each case the Sanctus occurs at the beginning of the central prayer in the liturgy, the Anaphora, the blessing over the bread and wine. At a later date the Sanctus was expanded to include the words used by the crowd when they greeted Christ at his triumphal entry into Jerusalem: "Blessed is He who comes in the name of the Lord. Hosanna in the highest." In this form, which became standard in the West, the

Sanctus serves not only as a hymn of praise but also as an anticipation of the Christ who will become present in the consecrated bread and wine.

Another early hymn is the Gloria in Excelsis, based on the song of the heavenly host at Christ's birth according to the Gospel of Luke.

> Glory to God in the highest,
> And on earth peace good will toward men. (Luke 2:14)

The biblical verse was expanded with the addition of words of praise. One version from the fourth century reads as follows:

> Glory to God in the highest,
> and on earth peace, good will toward men.
> We praise you, we sing hymns to you,
> we bless you, we glorify you,
> we worship you by your great High Priest.
> You who are the true God,
> Who are the one Unbegotten,
> The only inaccessible being.
> For your great glory, O Lord and heavenly King,
> O God the Father Almighty,
> O Lord God, the Father of Christ the Immaculate Lamb,
> Who takes way the sin of the world,
> Receive our prayer,
> You who sit upon the cherubim.
> For you only are holy,
> You only are the Lord Jesus
> The Christ of the God of all created nature and our King
> through whom glory, honor and worship be to you.

This hymn, unlike the metrical hymns of Ambrose, is modeled on biblical canticles written in stichic form, that is verses in prose. Like the psalms, it employs a parallelism, "you are the one unbegotten, [you are] the only accessible one." Originally it may have been used at the celebration of Christ's nativity, but in the West it eventually became part of the Eucharistic liturgy and was sung at the beginning of the service before the opening prayer and the reading of the first lesson. In the Eastern Church it is sung at Morning Prayer.

In certain geographical regions, at the most solemn point in the liturgy there was no music or singing. According to several ancient authors, at the offertory procession, when the bread and wine were carried to the altar, the cantors and congregation watched in silence. "These things take place while all are silent," wrote a bishop in Asia Minor in the fifth century, for the worshipers are meant to think of Christ being led to his Passion. "When we see the offering placed on the table great silence falls on those present." The practice, however, was not universal. In North Africa, Augustine says that as the offering was being made it was the custom to sing hymns at the altar taken from the book of psalms. The practice was, however, an innovation.

By the fifth and sixth centuries churches in different parts of the Christian world had developed fixed orders of sung elements in the liturgy. The texts, largely from the psalms and other passages from the Scriptures, could be written down, but the melodies were handed on orally. This required trained singers who were able not only to read and pronounce the words of the texts, but also to sing melodies from memory. In the large cities the cantors formed a *schola cantorum*, a guild of singers who were able to train new singers and pass on to them the melodies they had learned.

For the history of Christian music in the West, the most significant developments took place in the eighth and ninth centuries. When the Carolingian kings, Pippin and Charlemagne, made an alliance between their expanding kingdom in northern Europe, principally in France and Germany, and the pope in Rome, they began to introduce the Roman style of chant in the cathedrals of the north. As Roman chant was appropriated by Frankish musicians a common repertory of Latin plainchant took shape that was eventually adopted by other regions in western Europe.

In the early centuries, transmission of melodies required face-to-face communication between a trained singer and novices. But in the ninth century Frankish musicians began to put their minds to the task of creating a system of notation to write down the melodies. Initially they devised a pattern of dots and squiggles placed above the text in different colored ink. Called neumes, from the Greek *pneuma* (breath), they sketched the general contour of the melody, up or down, without, however, measuring the intervals. They provided the novice with a visible trace of how the words were to be sung, but they served only as an aid for melodies that were already known by heart.

But over the next few generations Frankish musicians began to experiment with a system of lines that could indicate pitch. The most significant theoreticians were two Benedictine monks, Hucbald, a Frankish musician and composer (d. 930), and Guido of Arezzo (d. 1050), who brought things brilliantly into focus with the invention of the staff (or stave), parallel lines running across the page with the spaces between the lines as well as the lines indicating pitch. This was a revolution of the first order, and it made a profound impression on contemporaries.

When Pope John XIX (d. 1032) heard of Guido's work on musical notation he invited him to Rome to see for himself what Guido had done. In a letter to a fellow monk Guido tells what happened when he met with the pope: "John, of the highest apostolic seat, who now governs the Roman church, hearing the fame of our school and greatly marveling how, by means of our antiphoner [the book with the text and notations], boys might learn chants they had never heard, invited me with three emissaries. . . . The pope . . . frequently turning the pages of our antiphoner as if it were a marvel and studying the prefatory rules, did not leave that place or move from where he sat until he had learned one versicle he had never heard, fulfilling his wish, so that he might as soon as possible discover himself what he scarcely believed in others."

Another writer gives a similar testimony to the wonder of the new system of notation. A musician named Rudolf instructed a group of novices "in the art of music according to Guido and was the first to introduce that art into our cloister. To the amazement of the senior monks he made them sing straight away, only by looking, with art and yet with a silent master, what they had never learned by hearing."

The staff for singing Latin plainchant was an invention of Christian monks in northern Europe. Like the Latin language, plainchant helped to unify the European civilization that soon reached from the British Isles to east-central Europe, from Scandinavia to the Mediterranean Sea. And it set music in the West on a course that would make possible the achievements of not only the great church composers of the Renaissance, Giovanni Pierluigi da Palestrina or Victoria, but also Johann Sebastian Bach and Ludwig van Beethoven.

16

The Sick, the Aged, and the Poor:
The Birth of Hospitals

Cappadocia is a mountainous region set high on the plateau of central Anatolia, or Asia Minor. The major road between Constantinople and Syria traversed the province, and soldiers, merchants, and adventurers passed through repeatedly. Its large conical-shaped rocks give the landscape a moonlike appearance, and the area was irresistible to early Christian monks who carved monastic cells and churches in its soft rock. The area is known best in Christian history as the home of three of the most illustrious thinkers in the early Church, Basil of Caesarea, called the Great, his gifted younger brother, Gregory of Nyssa, and Gregory of Nazianzus, known to later generations as "the theologian." The "Cappadocians," as these three are known, were key players in the defense of the creed of Nicaea and forged the language to express the Christian doctrine of the Trinity. What is less known is that Cappadocia gave birth to the first hospital during the years that Basil was bishop of Caesarea, the chief city of the province, in the 370s.

Basil was born into a large and prosperous Christian family in Neocaesarea, some 150 miles northeast of Caesarea, in A.D. 330. His parents could trace their history back to the third century, and his grandmother had known disciples of the heroic "apostle" of the region, Gregory the Wonderworker. Legend has it that when Gregory became bishop of Neocaesarea there were only seventeen Christians, and when he died only seventeen people were still pagans. Basil's maternal grandfather had been martyred early in the century before the end of persecution. Besides Basil, two brothers became bishops, another brother was a monk, and his learned and saintly older sister Macrina—sometimes called the fourth Cappadocian —was a powerful influence on his life. To his grandmother, also named Macrina, Basil attributed his initial formation in Christian faith. He recalled that she taught the children "sayings" (verses from the Psalms and Proverbs) that she knew by heart and "molded and formed us in the teachings that lead to a godly life." Family and kinship, Basil once wrote, are an "unbreakable bond that gives continuity to life."

After receiving his childhood education in grammar and rhetoric from his father, an accomplished rhetor, Basil went to Athens, the great center of Hellenistic learning. For six years he immersed himself in the advanced study of Greek literature under the guidance of the most celebrated teachers of his day. Later in life, looking back on his education in Athens he said, citing Homer (*Odyssey* 1.3), that for one's education it is good "to have seen the cities of many men and to know their minds." But even as a young man his interests were turning toward the study of the Scriptures and the religious life. On leaving Athens, instead of taking a position as a teacher of rhetoric, he made a grand tour in the East to observe at first hand the new monastic culture being built in the desert.

It was quite a journey. In the first of his surviving letters Basil gives a brief account of his travels after leaving Athens. "I quickly made my way past the city on the Hellespont" (Constantinople), as "no Odysseus ever avoided the Sirens' songs" (*Odyssey* 12.158). Once past Constantinople he was tempted to linger as he made his way across Asia Minor, but he headed directly to Syria, where he could see with his own eyes the way of life of the monks in that region; from there he headed south to Egypt, the great center of monasticism. In another letter he says that he also visited monks in Palestine and as far east as Mesopotamia. In all his travels he marveled at "their steadfastness in their spiritual struggles," "their vigor in prayer," and their ability to endure cold and hunger and thirst. After seeing the lives of these "blessed men," says Basil, "I prayed that I myself, in so far as I am capable, might imitate them."

When he returned to his home he was baptized and decided to take up the solitary life on family land near the river Iris, not far from Neocaesarea. There, wrote Basil, he found "tranquility" far removed from the "turmoil of the city." But he was ill-suited for solitude. He invited his friend Gregory Nazianzen to join him, and soon they were at work preparing a selection of the writings of Origen of Alexandria for publication. But his bishop, Eusebius, recognizing Basil's talents, persuaded him to be ordained priest, and from 365, first as priest and then as bishop, he had the principal responsibility for overseeing the church in Caesarea.

In the year 368 Cappadocia suffered a terrible famine brought about by a very dry winter, when the skies offered neither rain nor snow. Because the region was inland, without access to the sea, and isolated, it was particularly vulnerable to food shortages. Hungry men and women roamed the roads looking like cadavers, and parents exposed or sold their infants. The suffering of the people, said Basil's friend Gregory, was intensified by the "insensitivity and greed" of the wealthy. When food ran out, the rich thought only of their own welfare and began to hoard what they had gathered in their barns. Seeing an opportunity to take a profit, they turned the distress of others into a boon for themselves.

In a homily on the parable in the Gospel of Luke about the rich man who laid up treasure for himself (Luke 12:16–21), Basil speaks with great feeling about the lot of the poor:

> How can I bring before your eyes the suffering of the poor man? He considers his finances; he has no gold and never will. He has some clothes and the sort of possessions the poor have, all worth only a few coins. What can he do? He turns his glance at length on his children; by selling them he might put off death. Imagine the struggle between the desperation of hunger and the bonds of parenthood. The former threatens him with horrible death; nature pulls him back, persuading him to die with his children. Often he starts to do it; each time he stops himself. Finally he is overcome, conquered by necessity and inexorable need. What then are his thoughts? Which one shall I sell first? Which one will the grain auctioneer favor the most? Should I start with the oldest? But I am reluctant to do so because of his age. The youngest? I pity his youth and inexperience of life. That one is the spitting image of his parents. This one is so quick to learn. What horrible misery.

In response to the crisis Basil organized a relief effort, calling on magistrates and wealthy families of the city to help their stricken neighbors, and he used his own family's wealth to make food available for the poor. He even set up a soup kitchen where he could gather the hungry together in one place and set before them "cauldrons of soup and salted meat." With the help of his own servants, he waited on the hungry himself.

From earliest times Christian leaders had taken to heart the exhortations in the Scriptures to care for the poor. In the words of the first letter of John: "If anyone has the world's goods and sees his brother in need, yet closes his heart against him, how does God's love abide in him?" (1 John 3:17). For centuries the churches had used their resources, even when the communities were small, to provide for the needs of the indigent. Already in the second century some churches purchased land for cemeteries where the poor could be buried. Bishops urged their clergy to be zealous in caring for the needy. In Carthage in the mid third century, Cyprian wrote to his presbyters and deacons: "You should take earnest care that the poor are provided with the means of alleviating their poverty," and "Be unsparing also in the care and attention you give to the poor."

The historian Peter Brown goes so far as to say that Christian bishops "invented" the poor. For the notion that the "poor" made a claim on the community as a whole was unknown in the ancient world. In Greece and Rome there was a long tradition of public giving by prominent citizens, and cities relied on the benefactions of the wealthy to construct civic building and adorn streets and places of assembly. The ostentatious munificence of benefactors was displayed in the architectural and artistic beauty of their city, bringing honor on themselves and renown among neighboring cities. The poor were invisible, and a civic screen shielded citizens from the destitute lives of the impoverished living in their midst. Lepers were excluded from society and kept at a safe distance from the city.

In the Scriptures, however, the poor stand out as a distinct category of persons to whom justice is due, a kind of divinely constituted holy order. Whether one reads the psalms or the prophets, the sayings of Jesus or the words of the apostles, the poor are held in honor. "Blessed is he who considers the poor," wrote the psalmist (Psalms 41:1). Again and again the prophets denounce those who exploit the poor and praise those who befriend the indigent. "Defend the poor and fatherless; do justice to the afflicted and needy" (Psalms 82:3). In the "sermon on the plain" in Luke's gospel, Jesus singles out the poor with these words: "Blessed are you poor, for yours is the kingdom of God. Blessed are you that hunger now, for you shall be satisfied" (Luke 6:20–21).

As these and other biblical passages were expounded in sermons, they worked themselves deep into the minds and hearts of Christians. In one sermon preached at the arrival of winter, Augustine told his congregation: "Now it is winter. Think of the poor. Think of how the naked Christ can be clothed. Pay attention to him as he lies in the portico, as he suffers hunger, as he endures the cold."

There was more to these sermons than pious exhortation. The admonitions of the Scriptures were translated into concrete deeds and instruments to serve the needy. Care for the poor was not left to the casual generosity of wealthy Christians; it became the responsibility of the community as a whole. Tertullian, writing in the early third century, says that the offerings of the church were used to bury poor people, supply the needs of indigent boys and girls, and to care for the elderly who are confined to their homes.

Over time, caring for the poor and needy came to be seen as a primary responsibility of the bishop. In a mid-third-century letter to the bishop of Antioch in Syria, the bishop of Rome casually remarked that his church supported fifteen hundred widows and persons in need. In another part of the Christian world, a city in North Africa, the church had in its storehouse shirts for men and veils for women, dresses and shoes for women, as well as containers of oil and wine for the hungry.

Papyri from Egypt give tangible evidence of the administrative structures that had been set up to distribute aid to the needy. In the city of Oxyrhynchus, twenty-five miles south of present-day Cairo, four memos were issued on one day ordering that the widows of three churches were to receive one diploun (three to four liters) of wine, and widows of another church were to receive five diploun. On another day the "holy church" of Oxyrhynchus instructed Peter, the steward of the church, to provide a widow named Sophia with a coat. Churches kept lists of widows who needed assistance. These provisions were not random acts of charity; they were part of an organized and regular system for providing food and clothing. In these cities the responsibility for overseeing the care of widows was taken over by a group of laywomen known as the "women of the widows." Significantly, the most common commercial property owned by churches was a bakery.

By the fourth century Christians had begun to construct buildings to care for the poor and needy, called by various names, *xenodocheion,* hostel or hospice, or *ptocho-tropheion,* poorhouse. In some cases these foundations served needy travelers and pilgrims, at a hostel on the road from Jerusalem to Jericho, for instance, and in other cases they provided a place where lepers could live; in yet others they served the indigent men and women living in the community. Even outsiders took notice of these new Christian institutions. The emperor Julian chided his fellow pagans that the Galilaeans (Christians) supported not only their own poor but those of others as well.

Basil also took an interest in the sick and infirm. When he was a student at Athens, he had shown particular attentiveness in the study of medicine, not only in its practical side, but also in its theory and principles. He had gained enough experience to know, as he put it in one of his letters, that incompetent physicians often make people's illnesses worse. In one of his writings on the monastic life, *The Longer Rule,* he addressed the question as to whether relying on the "art of medicine" is in keeping with Christian piety. Medicine, he wrote, like the know-how of a farmer or the skill of a weaver, is a gift of God. Because the body is susceptible to illness, God has given human beings the skills to heal illness. "Just as we would have no need of the labor and toil of the farmer if we were living among the delights of paradise, so we would not require the art of medicine for healing if we were immune to disease." The work of the physician who heals bodies redounds to the glory of God no less than the work of those who care for the soul. As the Lord used clay for healing (John 9:6), so also it is good that physicians use the things of the earth for the cure of bodily ills.

The early Christians were ambivalent about the practice of medicine. Though the book of Sirach praises the work of doctors ("Honor the physician with the honor due him," Sirach 38:1), many thought the sick should rely only on God for healing. Turning to a physician for cure was a sign of lack of faith in God's power. Medicine was an art practiced by pagans, and Christians should shun their herbs and unguents.

Not everyone, however, shared these views. With characteristic clarity of mind, Origen of Alexandria made a vigorous defense of medicine. "God, creator of human bodies, knew that such was the fragility of the human body that it could be subject to different kinds of maladies and injuries. That is why foreseeing the sufferings to come, he also created from the earth the means to heal [such as herbs and plants], so that if the body is assailed by sickness, there would be cures."

By the fourth century, Christian opinion had swung in Origen's direction. Basil's younger brother, Gregory of Nyssa, praised the skill of medical practitioners who by ingenuity and experiment had learned over the course of centuries which herbs were harmful and which beneficial. This knowledge was passed on in the "science of medicine," and physicians were able to draw on the experience of others in treating disease.

Gregory highlighted the theoretical advances in medical science; another fourth-century bishop, John Chrysostom, spoke from experience of the work of physicians. When he was in exile in a tiny town on the Black Sea, he said that he missed the medical facilities and doctors in the great city of Constantinople where he had been bishop. And he noted that empathy and compassion were as necessary for a physician as technical skill.

During the fourth century a rudimentary system of health care had arisen in the monastic communities. Isolated from the city, the monks had to care for their own. From random comments in the lives and tales of these men and women of the desert, we learn of their efforts to care for the sick in their midst. In some cases care was informal: a monk would make the rounds of the cells to see if anyone was sick or in need of food. In other cases the monasteries built an infirmary that provided inpatient care under the supervision of physicians and nurses. The main remedies for illness were rest, diet, and the application of herbs and salves, but there is some evidence of the use of surgery. In one instance a surgeon had successfully inserted a catheter in a monk who was unable to pass water.

One of the significant by-products of the growth of medical care among the monks was the destigmatizing of illness. A leader among the monks in the monasteries of Pachomius, Theodore, chided his fellow monks for claiming that sin was the cause of illness. The Coptic monastic leader Shenoute once said that if anyone laughing or mocking calls someone blind, lame, dumb, cripple, maimed, or other names he shall be punished.

Basil was familiar with the health care system that had arisen among the monastic communities. But when he became bishop he undertook a more ambitious project: to build a freestanding institution that would care for the sick as well as the needy. The new foundation, located on the outskirts of Caesarea, was a large complex that included medical facilities for the sick staffed with nurses and physicians, living space for the elderly and infirm, a hostel for travelers, a hospice for lepers who had been driven from the city because of disfigurement, a church and a monastery. According to Gregory, Basil cared for the lepers "not only in word, but also in deed." To support those who worked in the complex there were kitchens, refectories, baths, storehouses, and stables. So numerous were the buildings that Gregory Nazianzen called it a "new city" in which "disease" is treated by monks, "misfortune" is a blessing, and "compassion" is honored.

Basil's institution was much more than a hospice or poorhouse. One writer says that it served those who are "seriously ill" and "especially in need of medical care." Basil's friend Gregory Nazianzen says that it was designed to provide a place where the sick would be cared for by trained physicians schooled in the arts of medicine. It differed from poorhouses and other forms of medical care in several ways. First, it included facilities where patients could stay during the course of their treatment. Second, it engaged trained medical professionals, doctors and nurses, to diagnose and provide treatment for the patients. Finally, its services were provided free of charge.

The temples of the Greek god Asclepius were a distant precedent for Basil's foundation. In the early empire the *asclepeia,* as they were called, had facilities to care for the sick and places for them to stay. But the primary form of care was incubation: sleeping in the temple in the hope that proximity to the god would bring healing. There is no evidence that the temples had trained physicians on the staff or offered medical care.

Of course an institution of this sort was expensive and stretched the resources of the Church. Basil's family was wealthy, well-connected, and respected in imperial and provincial circles, and the land the new foundation was built on was given to the Church by the emperor Valens. In a revealing passage in his history of the time, the fifth-century bishop Theodoret of Cyrrhus says that the emperor was so pleased with Basil's project that "he gave him fine lands to care for the poor," and adds "because they suffered serious bodily ailments and were particularly in need of care and *cure* [emphasis added]." But there remained a question as to whether the complex should be subject to taxation. Since the time of Constantine the churches had been granted exemptions from taxes, not only on the personal income of the clergy but also on land the churches owned. Yet the state expected something in return, and one way of justifying the exemption was to point to the church's social services, in particular caring for the poor.

To make a case for government support of his new foundation, Basil wrote to the provincial governor Elias to remind him what his new institution provided to society and the scale of its activities. Not only did it employ physicians and nurses and their assistants, funds were needed for the upkeep of buildings for the staff and patients and stables to keep horses for travelers. Among the things he requested an exemption for, Basil mentions a "house of prayer," a residence for the bishop and clergy. The Church was no longer a private institution; its affairs were now interwoven with the life of the society.

The new foundation came to be known as the *Basileias,* after its founder, Basil. In a ninth-century manuscript it is pictured as a large oblong building surrounded by arched stoa, or covered walkways. Through the arches one can see Basil and Gregory Nazianzen ministering to the sick. The Basileias became the model for other hospital-like institutions in the Byzantine world. One of the most famous was the imperial monastery of Christ Pantokrator (ruler of all), built in the early twelfth century by the emperor John II Komnenos. The complex included a three-part church dedicated to Christ, to the archangel Michael, and to the Virgin Mary, a monastery, a hospital, home for the aged, and a sanatorium for lepers. The Typicon of the monastery, the founding document, gives an extensive and detailed account of the buildings, the routine of life, the religious ceremonies, and the hospital.

The hospital included fifty beds, with mattress, pillow, sheets, and cover. An additional blanket of goat's hair was provided in winter. Six beds were set aside for the extremely sick or incapacitated. There were three hearths, one in the main hall, a smaller one in the surgical area, and another in the women's quarters, as well as two latrines, one for men and one for women, which were to be cleaned regularly and illuminated at night. Bathing facilities were provided, and the patients were given 850 grams of bread daily, two vegetables dressed with olive oil, two onion heads, and wine.

The staff was made up of two physicians in each of the five sections of the hospital, five medical assistants, and two servants. In the women's ward there was a female physician, four female medical assistants, and servants. Others had responsibility for surgery, for internal medicine, and for teaching. The physicians made rounds once a day in winter and twice in summer. The staff also included pharmacists, laundresses, porters, grooms, priests, bakers, latrine cleaners, millers. The Divine Liturgy was celebrated on Wednesday, Friday, Saturday, Sunday, and feast days. The hospital also included a library, a lecture hall, and an office for records.

Of course the hospital at the monastery of the Pantokrator in Constantinople was many centuries removed from the institution established by Basil. But Basil had set the direction. The Basileias had facilities where the sick could be cared for under the eyes of a trained physician. Patients were given shelter and a bed to sleep in, their personal needs and nourishment were provided for, and they were able to stay in the facility as long as treatment was needed. In effect, a new kind of public institution was created under the supervision of the Church, but supported in part by public funds. These hospital-like complexes founded in the Christian East more closely resemble modern hospitals than anything in pagan antiquity or in the Latin West. In the early Middle Ages in the West, when a monastic institution included medical facilities it was said that it was built according to the "customs of the orientals."

With the emergence of institutions specifically devoted to care of the sick and the cultivation of the medical arts, the status of physicians in society rose, and illness came to be viewed with greater understanding. Basil's friend Gregory Nazianzen said that he took the lead in urging others to treat the ill with dignity. In the fourth century the grand new churches that were being built in cities across the Roman Empire were the most visible signs of the burgeoning Christian culture, but Basil's "new city" and the medical establishments it inspired made their own imprint on society.

17

The Bishop of Rome as Pope

Far beneath the ornate baroque interior of the Basilica of Saint Peter in Rome lie the remains of an ancient cemetery. Nothing gives evidence that Christians were buried in the tombs, but close by there was a vacant field where people of modest means were laid to rest under terra-cotta slabs placed over their bodies. Sometime in the middle of the second century A.D. a brick wall was constructed to set off a new burial ground from the older cemetery. When the site was excavated in the 1940s, archaeologists found a small niche in the wall with a slab at the base, a column on either side, and another slab resting on the two columns. It was a religious shrine, and inside the wall sat a small marble chest.

The chest was empty, but it may once have held the bones of Peter, the leader among the disciples of Jesus. Already in the second century his tomb had become a place of devotion, and in the fourth century a Christian church was built on the site. From the location of the basilica, it seems certain its architects had been instructed to build directly above the place of Peter's burial, and today the altar of the present church of Saint Peter, reconstructed in the sixteenth century, stands over his tomb.

A capital fact of the early history of the papacy is that Peter, the leader among the disciples, spent his last years in Rome and was martyred there, most likely during the reign of Emperor Nero, in A.D. 64. Paul also was martyred in Rome, and the association of these two apostles with the city gave Rome a unique place in Christian memory, endowing it with singular authority. Only of Rome could it be said that it was the city "where the [two] apostles to this day have their seats and where their blood without ceasing witnesses to the glory of God." Those words were written in the fifth century, and today in the piazza before the Basilica of Saint Peter in Rome stand two monumental statues, one of Saint Peter holding the key to the kingdom and the other of Saint Paul holding the sword of the Spirit.

From the New Testament we know that Peter stood out among the followers of Jesus. He was called to be a disciple at the beginning of Christ's ministry (Mark 1:16), his name appears first in the several lists of the disciples (Mark 3:16, for example), and he is singled out as their spokesman. He was present at key moments in Jesus's life, most notably at the Transfiguration (Mark 9:2–8) and at his crucifixion. At the same time he was rash and impetuous, and at one point, according to the Gospel of Matthew, he was rebuked by Jesus (Matthew 26:40); on the night before Jesus's death Peter denied three times that he knew Jesus. Yet at the end of the Gospel of John, after asking Peter three times whether he loves him (to which Peter responds, "Yes, Lord, you know that I love you"), Jesus says to him, "Tend my sheep," indicating that Peter would have responsibility for shepherding the fledgling community. His name appears first in the list of witnesses to Christ's resurrection (1 Corinthians 15:5), and when Paul went up to Jerusalem after his conversion he met with Peter and James, the leaders of the Church in Jerusalem.

The most memorable passage in the New Testament about Peter is found in the Gospel of Matthew, where Jesus says to Peter: "And I tell you, you are Peter, and on this rock [*petra*] I will build my church, and the powers of death shall not prevail against it. I will give you the keys of the kingdom of heaven, and whatever you bind on earth shall be bound in heaven, and whatever you loose on earth shall be loosed in heaven" (Matthew 16:18). These words are written in Latin at the base of the dome of the Basilica of Saint Peter in Rome in gold letters six feet high: *Tu es Petrus et super hanc petram aedificabo ecclesiam meam et tibi dabo claves regni caelorum.* Few passages from the Bible have been more controversial than this one, especially since the Reformation, yet it comes into play in the early Church only gradually. It is first cited in the third century by Stephen, bishop of Rome, in his dispute with Cyprian over rebaptism.

Though Peter figures large during the lifetime of Jesus and in the years immediately after Jesus's death, the sources are silent about his years in Rome and the early history of the church there. The first leader to come into view in Rome is Clement, who lived at the end of the first century and wrote, in the name of the church in Rome, a fraternal letter of exhortation and encouragement to the church in Corinth. Another was Telesphorus, who was martyred during the reign of Emperor Hadrian (ca. 138).

The best known and most forceful bishop of Rome in the early years was Victor (189–198), the first Latin-speaking leader of the Christians in the city. Before that time the church in Rome had been largely made up of Greek-speaking immigrants. As we saw in an earlier chapter, Victor believed that the Paschal Festival (Easter) should be celebrated on the Sunday after Passover, not on the fourteenth of Nisan, the day of Passover in the Jewish calendar, as was the practice of the churches in Asia Minor. The dispute over the date of the Pasch was rancorous, and Victor broke off fellowship with those who followed a different custom.

The Easter controversy is the first instance of an attempt on the part of the bishop of Rome to intervene in the affairs of churches outside Rome. To some his actions seemed imperious, but his gesture was a portent of the future. Rome, more than any other church, took an interest in what was happening in other parts of the Christian world, and was invoked by others as a guardian of authentic Christian tradition. Already in the second century, in defending the apostolic faith against the gnostics, Irenaeus, bishop of Lyons in Gaul, appealed to the "preeminent authority" of the Church of Rome where, in his words, the apostolic tradition has been "preserved continuously."

By the end of the second century, pilgrims to the city were shown the "trophies" of the apostles: the tombs of Peter on Vatican Hill and of Paul on the Via Ostiensis, outside the walls on the road to the coast. And from the middle of the third century a feast honoring the memory of Peter and Paul was celebrated in the city on June 29—as it is today. In the fourth century Prudentius, the early Christian poet, commemorated the day in a famous poem. "The marshland of the Tiber," he writes, "knows that its turf was hallowed by two victories, for it bore witness to both the cross [Peter] and the sword [Paul], from which blood flowed over the same grass soaking it twice."

In the controversy over rebaptism in the third century, Stephen, bishop of Rome, and Cyprian, bishop of Carthage, faced off against each other. Cyprian believed Christians baptized by bishops not in communion with the Catholic Church should be rebaptized if they wished to be received into fellowship. Stephen, however, resisted Cyprian's stern approach and responded that if a person was baptized in the name of the Father, Son, and Holy Spirit, even though the priest who performed the baptism was schismatic, the baptism could stand. The wayward soul could be received again into the Church by the laying on of hands.

As in the case of the Easter controversy, Rome's position was eventually vindicated and accepted by the Church at large. Over time the idea began to take root that Rome possessed the gift of discernment and the wisdom to set forth the apostolic faith clearly and faithfully. During this controversy, for the first time a bishop of Rome, Stephen, invoked the words of Jesus from Matthew in defense of his actions. "You are Peter and upon this rock I will build my church." Cyprian, however, felt Stephen had exceeded his authority and rebuked him, rewriting his treatise *On the Unity of the Catholic Church* to edit out passages that gave Rome a unique role in the Church as a whole. But he did not break off fellowship, and even though he was a sharp critic of Stephen he believed that Rome had a singular vocation to embody the unity of the Church.

By the middle of the third century the bishop of Rome had begun to acquire an unparalleled authority in the West—in Italy, North Africa, Gaul, and Spain. Not, however, in the East. There the churches looked to the bishops in the major cities, Alexandria in Egypt or Antioch in Syria. This geographical fact, that Rome was the principal city in the West, whereas in the East there were several, would lead to a quite different understanding of how the Church was to be governed at the highest level. With the building of the city of Constantinople as the capital of the empire and the rise in prominence of the city of Jerusalem in the fifth century, the East would have four major cities whose bishops would bear the title "patriarch." In the West there was only Rome.

With the conversion of Constantine in the fourth century, Rome was the recipient of his benefaction. One of his first acts as emperor was to build the monumental church of Saint John Lateran, the cathedral of the bishop of Rome. But that was only the beginning. He commissioned other churches in the city, including Santa Croce in Gerusalemme and San Sebastiano; he gave grants of property and built baptisteries; he decorated these buildings lavishly, furnishing them with gold and silver liturgical vessels, works of art, and endowments to maintain the properties. For the Church in Rome, Constantine's conversion, the historian of the papacy Eamon Duffy writes, "was a bonanza beyond their wildest imaginings."

Although the grandeur of its churches and the pageantry of its rites dazzled visitors, it was Rome's role in the fractious debates and ecclesiastical disarray after Nicaea that enhanced its ecclesiastical authority. As regional councils condemned the decrees of other councils, and emperors went wobbly, the churches sought a stable point of reference. Most of the big names in fourth-century theology—Athanasius, Basil, Gregory Nazianzen, Gregory of Nyssa—came from the East, and the debates took place largely among Greek-speaking bishops. In the debates the bishops of Rome stood on the sidelines, but their sympathies were with the defenders of the Council of Nicaea, and they used their influence to advance its teaching. When Athanasius, bishop of Alexandria, a prominent defender of the council, was banished from his see by Emperor Constantius, he was warmly received by Pope Julius (337–352).

To mediate between the warring parties, Julius requested that the emperors call together bishops on both sides of the dispute at a council in Sardica (modern-day Sofia in Bulgaria). But feelings were running high, and the council ended in chaos and confusion. When bishops from the East refused to participate if Athanasius was allowed to sit after being deposed by Emperor Constantius, the Western bishops convened independently. They restored Athanasius and issued a statement of belief affirming the unity of the Father and the Son, though in somewhat ambiguous language. It took several decades before the theological issues were resolved, but Rome was again on the side that eventually proved victorious.

The Council of Sardica ended in schism, with each side excommunicating the other, but its significance in the history of the papacy far outstrips the ecclesiastical wars of the fourth century. For the bishops gathered there adopted a set of canons affirming that the bishop of Rome would have the privilege of serving as a court of appeal. That is, Rome acquired what has been called "appellate jurisdiction": the right to adjudicate disputes among other bishops. The term "appellate" is significant; Rome was called upon to act as judge, not as teacher. Only in the fifth century did Rome begin to see itself charged with responsibility to instruct the church at large. So important were the canons of Sardica that in the records of the Church in Rome—and Rome kept careful records—this council was ranked second only to Nicaea. In fact, in the fifth century its canons were cited as Nicene.

By the end of the fourth century the task of constructing a Christian Rome was taken over by its bishops. None was more energetic in this regard than Damasus, a native of Rome who was elected bishop of the city in 366. A man of learning and culture, a poet and a lover of the arts, he erected churches (including San Lorenzo) and shrines to the Roman martyrs, and became famous for adorning them with "gleaming gold" and "precious marbles." Damasus moved about comfortably among the noble old families of the city and set out to create a distinctive Latin Christian culture. Over the next few centuries the papacy became the West's most concrete link with the Roman past. Damasus strove to redirect the hereditary piety of the noble senatorial families, the old pagan *Romanitas,* or Romanness, toward the new Christian Rome. He commissioned the scholar Jerome to translate the Bible into graceful and elegant Latin, for example, to replace the crude Latin versions made earlier. This translation, known as the Vulgate, was to become the Bible of Western civilization.

In the late fourth century Milan in the north of Italy and Constantinople in the east had become major political centers. The rise of Constantinople as an ecclesiastical as well as political center threatened to upstage Rome's ancient authority. At the Council of Constantinople in 381, the bishops declared that because Constantinople was the "new Rome" it should have a preeminence of honor after the old Rome. To many this seemed reasonable, but Damasus observed that the authority of Constantinople and that of Rome rested on quite different foundations. For Constantinople had been founded only in the fourth century, and its standing in the Church was derived from its political importance. Rome's authority was based neither on the decisions of a council nor on its estimable past as the capital of the empire, but because its bishop was the successor of Peter, the chief of the apostles.

Damasus's immediate successor, Siricius (384–399), inaugurated a practice that would in yet another way set the bishop of Rome apart from other bishops. Whereas his predecessors had acted primarily as a court of appeal, Siricius took the initiative to issue official letters in response to problems elsewhere in the Church and send out directives he considered binding on the churches. The first, dated 385, was written in response to a list of questions sent to him by Himerius, bishop of Tarragona in Spain, dealing with matters such as when baptisms were to be administered, qualifications for ordination, clerical celibacy, and the like. In its formal style, the letter was similar to decrees issued by the emperor.

Siricius began the letter by observing that, as a successor of Peter, a graver responsibility was laid on him (he uses the formal "we") than on other bishops, for Rome was the "apostolic rock on which Christ built his universal Church." After detailing the specific questions addressed to him, he said it was proper for the "apostolic see"—the "seat" of the bishop of Rome—to be consulted in such matters. Then he ruled on each question, setting down in a few sentences how the matter should be dealt with. He also asked Himerius to communicate what he had written to the other bishops in the region. One can understand why this letter is sometimes called the first papal decretal, for it set a precedent that would be followed by later bishops of Rome. Because these decretals were preserved and collected, they provided a body of "case law" on which later bishops could draw.

These early papal letters dealt largely with moral, disciplinary, and liturgical matters. In the fifth century, however, bishops of Rome were drawn into theological disputes, and some of their letters dealt with doctrinal matters. Early in the century, for example, Augustine of Hippo sent Innocent I (401–417) a treatise called *On Nature,* written by a British monk named Pelagius, and Innocent responded with three letters condemning the theological views expressed there. Augustine and his fellow North African bishops were looking for an affirmation of what they had already decided (that the teachings of Pelagius were in error), but Innocent interpreted their sending the work to him as a request for an authoritative decision by Rome. In his words: "Nothing should be taken as finally settled unless it came to the notice of this see so that other churches might learn from this what they should teach." The office of judge was imperceptibly becoming that of teacher.

As Rome's political power declined, paradoxically, the authority of its bishop mounted. In 410 the city was sacked by an army of Visigoths led by Alaric. In the decades following, North Africa was overrun by the Vandals, and in midcentury Attila the Hun invaded northern Italy. In these dark and desolate times the Church of Rome raised up one of its most illustrious and beloved leaders, Leo, who served as bishop for twenty years, from 440 to 461. He has gone down in history as Leo the Great, the first "pope" to be honored with that epithet. The only other pope to be called "the great" was Gregory, who was bishop 150 years later.

The term "pope" was not, however, used widely in Leo's day. The title comes from the Latin "papa," which is derived from the Greek "pappas," meaning father. In the early Church it was used for bishops and sometimes for presbyters. It first came into general usage as a title for the bishop of Alexandria in the third century, and by the end of the fourth century it was used occasionally for the bishop of Rome. By the early Middle Ages in the West it came to be used exclusively for the bishop of Rome, but in the East "papa" continued to be used for the bishop of Alexandria. Today the Coptic patriarch of Alexandria is called Papa.

In the history of Rome and Italy, Leo is remembered as a courageous defender of the city. According to tradition, when the armies of Attila the Hun were preparing to march on the city, Leo went out to meet the ferocious warrior face to face and persuaded him not to attack. In the sixteenth century the great Italian painter Rafael commemorated the meeting of Leo and Attila with a painting in the Vatican. But it is as pastor and teacher that Leo is revered in the Church's history. He is the first bishop of Rome from whom we have a sizable body of writings, letters as well as sermons.

During the course of his pontificate Leo preached a sermon annually on the anniversary of his consecration as bishop of Rome, what he called his "nativity." In these sermons Leo displays an almost mystical identification with the person of Peter. This is quite new. The bishop of Rome, says Leo, should be received not simply as the successor of Peter, but "as Peter," and when he speaks it is Peter who speaks and governs through him. "Regard him as present in the lowliness of my person," for "blessed Peter does not relinquish his government of the Church." Because Peter was first among the disciples, "ordained before the rest," in Leo's words, and the "rock" on which Christ built his Church, the bishop of Rome has supreme and universal authority in the Church. As Christ gave greater responsibility to Peter than to the other apostles, so the bishop of Rome was charged with oversight of the Church at large.

Leo was vigorous in his solicitude for the churches of the East. This can be seen most clearly in the controversy over the person of Christ that divided the Eastern churches in the fifth century. The controversy will be taken up in a later chapter; here I only wish to observe that Leo prepared a long doctrinal letter to Flavian, the bishop of Constantinople, setting forth his theological views on the disputed question of the divine and human nature of Christ. The letter (known as the Tome) is a remarkable document, without precedent in the early history of the papacy. For Leo writes to explain a fundamental matter of Christian doctrine in the hope that his exposition will be acceptable to all parties.

The emperor, however, had already called a council to meet at Ephesus to adjudicate the issues. Leo dutifully sent his legates at the emperor's bidding, but the council, dominated by Dioscorus, bishop of Alexandria, was one of the most contentious, even violent gatherings in the early Church, featuring bishops fighting with fists rather than arguments. In the tumult, Leo's letter to Flavian was ignored. Outraged, Leo branded the council "non judicium, sed latrocinium": not a judicial gathering, but a council of thieves. His letter, however, received a hearing two years later, at the Council of Chalcedon in 451, where it was read in its entirety (translated from Latin into Greek) and accepted enthusiastically. Though he did not address the technical theological questions raised in the debate, his Tome was a balanced and judicious summary of Christian teaching on the person of Christ. In the following decades its simple language and imprecise terminology—in the minds of some theologians from the East—came to invite misunderstanding.

It is clear from the minutes of the Council of Chalcedon that the bishops, most of whom were from the East, did not view Rome's authority as Leo did. Following the Council of Constantinople in 381, they affirmed that Constantinople, the "new Rome," was to be honored second after Rome. In itself this was unobjectionable to Rome. But then the council fathers added that the "prerogatives" granted to the "older Rome" had been derived from its status as an "imperial city." That is, the authority of Rome, like that of Constantinople, rests on its historic place in the empire, not on the apostolic origins of its bishop. Understandably, Leo, and the bishops that succeeded him, rejected this canon outright. Rome's authority rested on Christ's words to Peter.

As the controversy over the person of Christ intensified in the years after the Council of Chalcedon, the emperors were drawn more deeply into ecclesiastical affairs. For Rome this was an unwelcome development that blurred the line between ecclesiastical and political matters. The issue came to a head during the reign of Emperor Anastasius (491–518), who actively supported the critics of the Council of Chalcedon. From Rome's perspective, the emperor had no business taking sides in the dispute. One wonders, though, whether Rome would have protested so loudly had the emperor agreed with the pope. In any case, Pope Gelasius (492–496), a forceful and dynamic figure, took the bold step of writing a letter to Emperor Anastasius instructing him on the limits of his authority in religious matters. This letter would shape papal thinking on the relation of church and state throughout the Middle Ages.

Here is what Gelasius wrote:

> There are two powers, august Emperor, by which this world is chiefly ruled, namely, the sacred authority of the priests and the royal power. Of these that of the priests is the more weighty, since they have to render an account in the divine judgment even for the kings of men. You are also aware, dear son, that while you are permitted honorably to rule over human kind, yet in things divine you bow your head humbly before the leaders of the clergy and await from their hands the means of your salvation. In the reception and proper disposition of the heavenly mysteries you recognize that you should be subordinate rather than superior to the religious order, and that in these matters you depend on their judgment rather than wish to force them to follow your will.

The issue here is not the relation of church and state. At the time that Gelasius was pope the empire was ruled by a Christian emperor, and he assumed that the empire was a Christian kingdom. What prompted the letter was that the emperor (who was sympathetic to the critics of Chalcedon) had presumed to judge a theological matter, how the Church formulated its teaching about the person of Christ. So Gelasius drew a sharp line between the authority of the bishops, centered on the pope, and royal or imperial authority invested in the emperor in Constantinople. Each had received his authority from God, and each was sovereign in his own sphere, but the spiritual authority was superior to the temporal because the bishops had to answer to God for the spiritual health of the faithful, including the soul of the emperor. Gelasius's elevation of the ecclesiastical order over the political echoes the language of Ambrose to Emperor Theodosius in the fourth century.

The emperor did not see things that way, and a few years later Anastasius told another pope, Hormisdas (514–523), who put pressure on him to uphold the decree of Chalcedon: "You may thwart me, reverend sir, you may insult me; but you may not command me." That, however, was precisely what the popes were doing, for in a matter of Christian teaching the emperor was subject to the bishops. Eastern bishops, including the patriarch of Constantinople, were much readier to submit to the authority of the emperor, and Gelasius's strong language reflects the independence and self-confidence of the popes in dealing with political authority, a characteristic of the papacy that shaped the course of medieval history.

The last major figure to serve as bishop of Rome in the formative years of the Church's history was Gregory the Great (590–604). He was a gifted spiritual writer and an accomplished administrator; his compassion for the poor and practical good sense, administrative skill and tireless energy, and above all his humanity and pastoral wisdom have endeared him to later generations.

Gregory is sometimes considered the first medieval pope, but he was most assuredly a man of the ancient world who looked back as well as forward. Born into an old Roman family in 540, he received a traditional grammatical and rhetorical education. He had a fine mastery of Latin and good knowledge of earlier Latin Christian writers, particularly Augustine. But by the end of the sixth century, the world Augustine had lived in was a distant memory. The empire that had once been centered on the Mediterranean was disintegrating, and a new world was being born north of the Alps. Gregory was a contemporary of Muhammad, and although Islam had not yet begun its rapid expansion, the time was fast approaching when the Mediterranean would become a wide and deep Muslim moat stretching from Egypt to Morocco, cutting off Christians on its northern shores from the formerly Christian lands in North Africa.

Although Emperor Justinian (527–565) regained much of the territory that had been part of the empire before the invasions of the fifth century, in Italy the Lombards, a Germanic people who were Arians rather than Catholics, had occupied the northern part of the peninsula. Ravenna, a city in northern Italy (south of Venice) on the Adriatic Sea, the residence of the imperial viceroy and the headquarters of the imperial troops, was cut off from Rome. Without military support from Constantinople, the bishop of Rome had to assume responsibility for defending the city against the Lombards. Slowly and ineluctably the pope was becoming a political as well as spiritual leader of the Catholic people.

By the sixth century the Church of Rome had become a major landowner. Under Constantine the Church was granted the right to own property, and as the population declined and wealthy families died out, their estates were often deeded to the Church. In Gregory's day the Church of Rome held lands in Gaul, the Balkans, North Africa, Sardinia, and central and southern Italy, especially in Sicily. It fell to the pope to administer these lands, and Gregory's letters are filled with detailed instructions about the price of corn, the sale of cows or horses, wages for workers. The revenue from these estates was used for the upkeep of churches, feeding the poor, charitable foundations, and schools.

These lands would become the basis for the pope's political power and an integral part of the medieval papacy. Because Rome was no longer the capital, or even a major political center, neighboring rulers acknowledged the pope as its temporal ruler with political sovereignty. The regions he ruled over came to be called the "patrimony of Peter," or, at a later date, "states of the Church"—commonly known as the Papal States. The pope was no longer simply a bishop; he was on the way to becoming a medieval prince. Even in modern times the pope continued to be a temporal ruler, and large sections of Italy were administered by bishops and priests. Only in the nineteenth century, when the modern state of Italy was formed, did the territory that formed the Papal States come under Italian rule. The pope was granted a tiny enclave adjacent to the Basilica of Saint Peter, and to this day the bishop of Rome, unlike other religious leaders, is the sovereign of a small area of land, the Vatican City.

Gregory had an active interest in the affairs of the Church in Italy, Spain, and Gaul, but his imagination reached beyond the lands that had long been part of the Catholic fold. He was the first pope to mount a self-conscious effort to evangelize a people that was largely pagan. After a chance encounter with several English boys at a slave auction in Rome, he commissioned Augustine, the prior of a monastery in Rome, to organize a mission to the English people. In 597, Augustine and a group of monks landed in England. At first they were greeted with suspicion, but soon the king, Ethelbert, granted them permission to stay. Ethelbert's queen, Bertha, had been a Christian before her marriage, and through her efforts the king was baptized; at Christmas of that year many of the people were brought into the Church in a mass baptism. Augustine became the first bishop of the city of Canterbury.

Gregory stands at the beginning of a great period of expansion of Christianity into Europe. During his pontificate were laid the foundations of the papacy's later potent influence in the West. In the period that followed his death, the popes would turn decisively to the lands north of the Alps—France, Germany, Scandinavia, Croatia, Poland—as northern Europe was evangelized by monks in communion with Rome. Over time the pope came to be the de facto head of the Latin Church, which remained the principal form of Christianity in Europe up to the Reformation in the sixteenth century. As if anticipating what was to come, Leo the Great had written: "Rome has become a priestly and royal city, the head of the world through the holy see of Peter."

18

An Ordered Christian Society:
Canon Law

From its beginning, the Christian Church was a rule-making community. Even when the churches were very small, Saint Paul laid down guidelines for the ordering of their common life. In his letters he has things to say about marriage and divorce (1 Corinthians 7), membership in the church (1 Corinthians 6), celebrating the "Lord's supper" (1 Corinthians 10), and meat as part of a public sacrifice to idols (1 Corinthians 8). The Gospel of Matthew includes sayings of Jesus on marriage and divorce (Matthew 19:3–9) and gives language to be used in baptizing someone who has responded to the preaching of the gospel. "Go therefore and make disciples of all nations, baptizing them in the name of the Father and of the Son and of the Holy Spirit" (Matthew 28:19).

In the early decades decisions had to be made about matters of discipline, leadership, liturgical practice, and ethical standards, and the churches began to set down rules to govern practice and behavior as well as fashion norms for what was taught. According to the Acts of the Apostles, a gathering of Christian leaders at Antioch adopted guidelines concerning food offered to idols, marriage, and other matters (Acts 15:19–20). From the pastoral letters (1 and 2 Timothy, Titus) we learn that the churches had adopted criteria to evaluate someone who was to serve as bishop, the overseer of the local community (1 Timothy 3:1–7). Those who were chosen were invested into their office by "the laying on of hands" (1 Timothy 4:14).

The earliest Christian writing to organize rules for governing the affairs of a local church is known as the Didache, or Teaching of the Twelve Apostles. It is a kind of manual on church order, most likely written in Syria at the beginning of the second century. The first part of the Didache draws on the Ten Commandments and edifying sayings from the gospels, psalms, and Proverbs to present a moral code for the Christian life. "Do not be double-minded or double-tongued, for a double tongue is 'a deadly snare'" (Proverbs 12:6). Or: "Be humble since 'the humble will inherit the earth'" (Psalms 37:11; Matt 5:5). "Be patient, merciful, harmless, quiet, and good; and always 'have respect for the teaching' [Isaiah 66:2] you have been given."

Next the work turns to baptism and the Eucharist, how to deal with itinerant prophets, the election of bishops and deacons, and related matters. Concerning baptism, the Didache says that after being instructed in the faith a candidate for membership would be baptized in "running water" with the words, "in the name of the Father and of the Son and of the Holy Spirit." If running water is not available, one should baptize in some other water. If neither is at hand, "pour water on the head three times" while repeating the words, "in the name of the Father and of the Son and of the Holy Spirit." Pouring water over the head was an exception: baptism was by immersion.

Only those who had been baptized could share in the eucharistic meal. "You must not let anyone eat or drink of your Eucharist except those baptized in the Lord's name. For in reference to this the Lord said, 'Do not give what is sacred to dogs.'" The Eucharist was to be celebrated "every Lord's Day," and before taking part in the Eucharist the faithful were to confess their sins so that their "sacrifice" may be pure. If members are at enmity with others they should make peace before participating in the Eucharist.

In the early years the Church was plagued by traveling prophets who claimed to speak in the name of the Lord. So the Didache includes firm directives on how to judge whether a prophet speaks truly and is faithful to Christ. When a wandering prophet arrives in the community he is to be welcomed warmly, but "he must not stay beyond one day." If he asks for money for his travels, "he is a false prophet." Though a prophet is expected to speak in ecstatic utterances (that is, in tongues), the truth of what he says is to be judged by his actions. "It is by their conduct that the false prophet and the true prophet can be distinguished."

The Didache was written at a very early date in the Church's history, and its rulings are not presented systematically; yet it set a pattern for later church manuals, or church orders, as they came to be called. For example, an unknown writer in Syria produced a work known as *Didascalia,* the teaching of the twelve apostles, that deals with the duties of the clergy, worship, penance for grievous sins, the role of deaconesses, even how to deal with disputes within the congregation. In Syria in the fourth century the Didache and the *Didascalia* were incorporated into a much fuller church order known as the *Apostolic Constitutions,* or "Ordinances of the Holy Apostles through Clement."

In the West the earliest church order we possess is called *The Apostolic Tradition,* compiled in the third century. Where it was written is uncertain, but it reflects the practices of the Church in Rome. Like the Didache it deals with the election and consecration of bishops, baptism and Eucharist, daily prayer, fasting, who can be admitted into the community, and discipline, and presumes a developed ecclesiastical structure including presbyters (priests), deacons, readers, and subdeacons.

In the early years how to deal with newcomers was a persistent problem. According to the *Apostolic Tradition,* when someone new was presented for baptism, the leaders of the community inquired about his occupation. Pimps and prostitutes were excluded. So were sculptors or painters who trafficked in idols, actors (ancient plays were filled with allusions to the gods and goddesses), charioteers, gladiators, pagan priests, magicians. A soldier was told he must not kill people, nor take an oath (in the name of a pagan god or goddess). Other writings testify that persons with these occupations always received strict scrutiny.

After a long period of instruction and moral formation, those who had been accepted for baptism were to bathe, fast, and present themselves to the bishop. Then in a rite of exorcism the bishop would drive out every foreign spirit: he would blow on their faces and touch the eyes and nostrils with spittle. The night before baptism they would hold vigil, listening to readings and receiving further instruction. Baptism took place at daybreak. A tank or pool would be filled with water, and the catechumens (those who had been instructed) would take off their clothes to prepare for immersion.

At this period in Christian history most people who were baptized were adults. But in the midst of the description of baptism the *Apostolic Tradition* inserts the surprising sentence: "You are to baptize the little ones first." Apparently infant baptism was permissible—though not conventional—and parents or guardians would speak for the children. Then came the men, followed by women, who were to let down their hair and take off any jewelry. Nothing could be taken down into the pool. First the bishop would anoint each person with oil, "hand over" the trinitarian rule of faith, immerse the catechumen three times, and anoint him or her with oil a second time. Then the newly baptized were clothed, and the celebration of the Eucharist followed.

The Didache, the *Didascalia,* and the *Apostolic Tradition* were composed to serve the needs of specific local churches. In the early centuries there was no ecclesiastical structure beyond the local bishop, who was responsible for the oversight of the church in his city. Each local church dealt with its disciplinary and organization problems in its own way. Cyprian wrote: "We are not forcing anyone in this matter; we are laying down no law. For every appointed leader has in his government of the Church the freedom to exercise his own will and judgment, and one day will have to render an account of his conduct to the Lord." Nevertheless there was an implicit recognition in these early writings that the local church is part of a larger spiritual fellowship, and what is done in one place was in harmony with what was believed, confessed, and practiced elsewhere.

In the first two centuries, the primary source of authority was the bishop in consultation with presbyters and people, but as the Christian population expanded and the number of bishops increased, new forms of governing emerged. The most significant new institution was a gathering of bishops—a council, in the Church's vocabulary—in a certain region to deal with matters of common concern. The aim of the council was to discuss problems brought before the assembly and to reach a consensus so that the churches would act in concert.

The first councils in the West of which we have knowledge took place in Carthage early in the third century and then during the episcopacy of Cyprian in the middle of the century. These were formal gatherings in which the bishops sat near the altar and the presbyters alongside. The people and lower clergy stood. That the council gathered in a church (or a large room) around an altar indicates that this was not simply a meeting, but a solemn ecclesiastical gathering in which the Eucharist was celebrated and prayers were offered that the Holy Spirit be present in the deliberations. Nevertheless the council was a quasi-legislative body, and that meant resolutions were presented, issues were debated, the roll was called, and a vote was taken.

By good fortune we have a detailed record of a council held in Elvira (Granada) in southern Spain early in the fourth century to deal with disciplinary matters. Nineteen bishops and twenty-six priests were in attendance, representing thirty-seven different communities. There was no fixed agenda, but it is clear that similar problems had arisen in different places within the churches in Spain. The council adopted eighty-one canons, brief rulings on what was decided, and happily the texts of the canons were preserved. They make for lively reading.

The most pressing concern was the relation of Christians to the pagan institutions and culture in which they lived. It must be remembered that for many Christians the line between paganism and Christianity was porous. The traditional religion of the cities, unlike Christianity, was inclusive, and there were no obstacles to participation in different cults. It was natural that after becoming a Christian some continued to participate in pagan rites while sharing in the Christian Eucharist. The first canon deals precisely with this kind of situation. "It is decided that anyone of a mature age, who, after the faith of saving baptism, approaches a temple as an idolater and commits this major crime [idolatry], because it is an enormity of the highest order, is not to receive Communion even at the end [that is, at death]."

The council gave special attention to persons who had been pagan priests before being baptized and had reverted to paganism. So the second canon deals with *flamines* (a particular group among pagan priests) who, after being baptized, participated in a pagan sacrifice. That was of course a most serious offense. Other flamines did not go so far as to sacrifice, but continued to perform their functions as priests. These could be readmitted to Communion, but only after a long period of penance.

Besides reversion to paganism, sexual offenses appear often in the canons: adultery, incest, divorce, fornication, prostitution, homosexuality, pederasty, and the like. Any notion that the early Church was made up of the pure and innocent vanishes quickly on reading these ancient canons. One canon rules against clergy who do not stay put but "run around the provinces seeking after profitable business. . . . If they want to pursue business, let them do it within their own province." Apparently some churches were unable to support a bishop, and clergy had to seek income elsewhere—as long as their business dealings did not compete with those of neighboring bishops!

With the accession of a Christian to the imperial throne in the early fourth century, the convocation of bishops in council took on new importance. When the affair of Arius came to the attention of Constantine, he decided to summon bishops from all over the Christian world to a churchwide council. More than three hundred bishops attended, far more than at any regional council, and the chief matter on the agenda was the dispute over the teaching of Arius. But the bishops at Nicaea also approved twenty canons dealing with administrative, disciplinary, and liturgical matters.

Like the canons of the Council of Elvira, some of the canons of Nicaea deal with problems that arose in relation to paganism. For example, one canon rules against ordaining men who only recently had converted from paganism. Others deal with matters of church order. Though the ordination of a bishop by a single bishop was permissible, it was decided that at least three bishops should be present at an ordination, a canon that still holds. On liturgical matters the council issued a canon against kneeling on Sunday and during the season of Pentecost. Kneeling was a sign of penance; hence "one should offer one's prayers to the Lord standing."

One canon dealt with the status of three of the most ancient churches, Antioch, Alexandria, and Rome. The question had arisen about the jurisdiction of the bishop of these cities over neighboring cities. The bishops ruled that the see of Alexandria had jurisdiction over Egypt, Libya, and the Pentapolis (modern Benghazi), Rome over the churches in Italy, and Antioch over those in Syria. Significantly, Jerusalem is not included in this list. In Palestine the principal see was Caesarea on the coast, but it did not possess the ancient "prerogatives" of Antioch, Alexandria, and Rome. However, at Nicaea the bishops did address the status of Jerusalem—which is called Aelia, the name Romans gave to the new city built after the destruction of Jerusalem. The bishop of Aelia is to be "honored," though not granted the "dignity proper to a metropolitan." Jerusalem was not raised to the status of metropolitan (or patriarch) until the fifth century, at the Council of Chalcedon.

Besides adopting twenty canons, the bishops at Nicaea also addressed a letter to "the church of the Alexandrians informing them of the decisions of the council." In it they informed the Egyptians that a decision had been taken on the date of the celebration of the Pasch. The practice of celebrating the Pasch on 14 Nisan, the date of the Jewish Passover, would no longer be allowed, and the custom of the church at Alexandria and Rome—celebrating on a Sunday—would now be observed so that all the churches would keep the chief Christian festival on the same date.

As a gathering of bishops from around the Christian world, the bishops at Nicaea understood themselves to be acting in the name of all the churches. Although a Christian bishop such as Ignatius in the early second century had a sense of being part of a universal communion, it was only in the fourth century that the "catholic," or universal, dimension of the Church took institutional form. Shortly afterward the term "ecumenical" (worldwide) began to be used by bishops such as Eusebius and Athanasius to designate a council whose authority included all the churches. In a significant phrase, the bishops say explicitly that what they have decided should be observed in "every community of Christians." There was a growing consciousness of the Church as a universal body with authority to govern its interior life through rules and directives issued on the authority of the bishops in council.

In the fourth century, bishops in leading cities began to write general letters to fellow clergy to deal with pressing problems. Among Eastern writers, the most extensive body of letters comes from Basil the Great, bishop of Caesarea in Cappadocia (370–379). Basil came from a venerable Christian family, and he was a man of great personal holiness, a gifted administrator, and a prominent Christian teacher. As the leading bishop in central Anatolia, his advice was sought by other bishops on disciplinary matters.

Among his letters several respond to inquiries by Amphilocius, a younger bishop of Iconium, a city in a neighboring province. The list of problems is quite extensive, and Basil deals with them one by one: adultery, fornication, abortion, abduction, consanguinity, heresy, monastic abuses, homicide, polygamy, and so on. In responding to Amphilocius, Basil sometimes appeals to earlier canons, sometimes to Christian practice, and in some cases he cites apt biblical texts. Basil is not legislating; he is drawing on tradition and experience to advise a fellow bishop. But in time his letters dealing with disciplinary matters acquired a canonical status and were acknowledged to carry authority for churches in the East.

As we saw in the previous chapter, Pope Siricius (d. 399) wrote a letter in response to a list of questions sent to him by a bishop in Spain. Its formal style is similar to a decree issued by the emperor. Before the letter was sent it was read aloud before him and other clergy, implying that he had consulted with his clergy before writing. The authority of his letter derived from the authority of the Church of Rome. He wished, as bishop of Rome, to establish norms governing the Church's life in regions outside Rome's immediate jurisdiction. As this letter, and the letters of other popes and bishops, such as those written by Basil, were preserved and collected, they provided a body of "case law" on which later bishops could draw.

By the end of the fourth century, as the number of canons and letters of prominent bishops mounted, canons from earlier councils and letters of the fathers were gathered into collections to guide the work of future councils. The earliest collection, the *Apostolic Canons,* includes eighty-five canons attributed to the apostles. They are not, however, apostolic, but rather come from fourth-century councils. They deal with disciplinary matters, ordination of the clergy, the Christian life, liturgical practices. The collection of canons from earlier councils gradually created the idea of an ecclesiastical code that could be passed on from generation to generation.

In later centuries the canons came to be seen more as a body of law for the Christian society than directives to deal with immediate problems. The term "canon" comes from the Greek word *kanon,* which means rule or norm. It had been used to signify the "canon" of Scripture, meaning those books that are recognized as authoritative and serve as a norm for Christian teaching and life. The word appears in the record of the Council of Nicaea to refer to the twenty canons that are appended to the solemn proclamation of the creed, the theological statement of the bishops on Arius. In the strict sense the canons were not "law." They were intended to educate, exhort, and chastise, seldom to punish, but in time the term "canon law" came to be used to designate the Church's body of rules and regulations.

The collectors of the canons of early councils are largely anonymous, but in the fifth century one person stands out: Dionysius Exiguus, Dionysius the Short, a monk who lived in Rome at the turn of the fifth to the sixth century. Dionysius was a native Greek speaker who also spoke Latin, and he worked tirelessly to make the writings of Greek-speaking theologians available to Latin readers. He also had an interest in chronology and came up with the idea of fixing the year of the birth of Christ, in his language, the date of the "incarnation of our Lord Jesus Christ." It was a momentous decision, for it meant that in the new Christian civilization time would be reckoned from the birth of Christ, *anno Domini,* in the year of our Lord. Dionysius's reckoning was off by a few years—Christ's birth actually took place between 7 and 4 B.C.—but the new scheme caught on and was approved by the Synod of Whitby in England in 664. It would, however, take centuries for the idea of Christian reckoning of time to be adopted across the Christian world.

Dionysius's other major contribution was a collection of canons of Eastern and Western councils that influenced the development of a body of canon law. He included canon 6 of Nicaea, which gave Alexandria and Antioch primacy among the churches in the East and Rome in the West, and also the third canon of the first Council of Constantinople, which proclaimed Constantinople the "new Rome," and awarded it the "privileges of honor after the bishop of Rome." Although Dionysius wrote from a Roman perspective, he was scrupulous in giving the Eastern patriarchates their due. Nevertheless, he did not translate canon 28 of the Council of Chalcedon, a canon Rome did not accept, which gave Constantinople second place after Rome. He also compiled a collection of papal letters that began with the letter of Siricius.

A half century after Dionysius had made his collection, John Scholasticus, a priest in Antioch and a trained lawyer, made a collection of canons. The canons were drawn from general councils—Nicaea, Constantinople I, and Chalcedon—as well as regional synods in the East. His collection also included encyclical letters of Eastern bishops, most notably Basil the Great, and he arranged the material according to subject matter so that it could be readily consulted.

In 565, the year Emperor Justinian died, John Scholasticus became patriarch of Constantinople. Since the fifth century, ecclesiastical matters had become part of the Roman civil code, and in his corpus of civil law Justinian had included legislation dealing with church institutions. Drawing on this material, John made another collection of canons under fifty headings that was to play a role in the development of canon law in the East similar to that of Dionysius's collection in the West. Several centuries later, when the Christian mission in the East had reached into the Slavic world, Methodius, the missionary to the Slavs, translated Scholasticus's collection into the Slavic language, and it became the basis for the canon law of Slavic-speaking Christendom.

Justinian's grandson, Justinian II, became emperor of the Byzantine Empire in 585. Though the empire was trying to regain territory in the Balkans that had been taken by the Slavs, and was besieged by Arab armies in eastern Anatolia, Justinian thought that the Church's law needed to be brought up to date. The previous two ecumenical councils, Constantinople II (553) and Constantinople III (680–681), had dealt only with theological matters, neglecting matters of discipline and morals. In calling a council, known as Quinisext (Fifth–Sixth) in 692, Justinian's primary aim was to formulate a body of new canons to deal with pressing problems.

A primary topic before the bishops was clerical discipline, not only in matters of morals but also in caring for the faithful entrusted to them. In areas that had been overrun by the Slavs, clergy had fled their churches and were loath to return; they preferred spending their time in the safety of Constantinople. The perennial issue of itinerant monks under no discipline was on the agenda, and the bishops ruled that they had to affiliate with a monastery under the discipline of the abbot. Gambling, horse racing, theatrical dances, consulting soothsayers, and use of incantations were prohibited, and abortion was condemned as murder.

Rome had refused to accept canon 28 of the Council of Chalcedon, which gave Constantinople equal privileges with those of Rome, though it was second in honor. At the Council Quinisext the bishops reaffirmed the ruling of Chalcedon: "The see of Constantinople shall have equal privileges with the see of Old Rome, and shall be highly regarded in ecclesiastical matters as that is, and shall be second after it."

Because the Quinisext was a completion of the two previous ecumenical councils, Justinian thought that the pope would confirm its decisions. But Pope Sergius (687–701) refused. In the course of the next two decades efforts were made to bring about a reconciliation between Rome and Constantinople, and in 710 Pope Constantine I made a journey to Constantinople at the request of the emperor. The pope was received with great pomp and ceremony and apparently gave his verbal assent to the canons of the Quinisext Council.

As with other aspects of Christian life, each cultural and linguistic region developed its own forms of church law. Only in the medieval period were sustained efforts made to prune and order what had been received from the early centuries. In the West, for example, there were more than sixty collections of canon law before the eighth century.

The development of ecclesiastical law is significant not only for the legislation itself, but also for what it tells us about the self-understanding of the Church. Christians thought of themselves as part of a visible society, a parallel sovereignty, a corporate body in its own right with a distinctive way of life, rituals, institutions, norms of behavior, and the like. As the churches developed their own style of architecture and art, worship and music, they also forged their own bodies of law.

Kriophoros (lamb bearer), marble, a Roman copy from the second or third century A.D. of a Greek original from the fifth century B.C. (Wikimedia Commons)

Ceiling from the catacomb of Callixtus, Rome, with two kriophoroi (standing figures carrying a lamb, at lower left and upper right corners) and two orantes (standing with arms raised in a prayer gesture, at upper left and lower right corners), third century (Photo, Pontifical Commission for Sacred Archaeology)

Kriophoros, fresco from the crypt of Lucina in the catacomb of Callixtus, third century
(Scala/Art Resource, New York)

Jonah cast into the ocean, a mural from the catacomb of Callixtus, mid fourth century (Photo, akg-images / André Held)

Clay oil lamp with kriophoros, third century (bpl, Berlin / Staatliche Museum / Art Resource, New York)

Temple of Augustus, Pula, Croatia, first century A.D. (© iStockphoto.com/Sergiy Palamarchuk)

Church of Santa Sabina, Rome, fifth century (Wikimedia Commons)

Church of Santa Sabina, interior view (Wikimedia Commons)

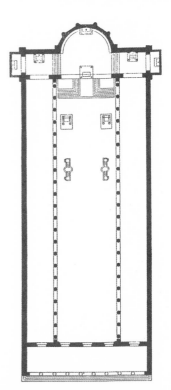

Church of Santa Maria Maggiore, Rome, floor
plan, fifth century (Wikimedia Commons)

Crucifixion scene, from a door of Santa Sabina,
Rome, fifth century (Alinari / The Bridgeman Art
Library International)

Abraham and three visitors, mosaic panel from Santa Maria Maggiore, fifth century
(Scala/Art Resource, New York)

Church of San Vitale, Ravenna, interior, sixth century (Scala / Art Resource, New York)

A mosaic lunette in the presbytery of San Vitale, depicting the sacrifice of Abel and Melchizedek (Alfred Dagli Orti / The Art Archive at Art Resource, New York)

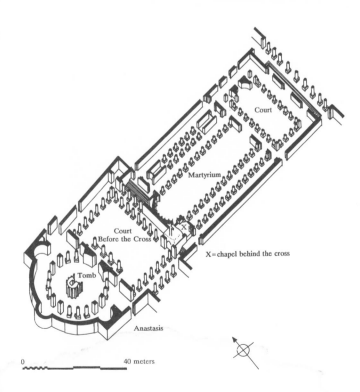

Abraham and the three visitors, and the sacrifice of Isaac, mosaic lunette, San Vitale, Ravenna (Gianni Dagli Orti/The Art Archive at Art Resource, New York)

Floor plan of the basilica and shrine at Golgotha, Jerusalem, fourth century

Court

Martyrium

Court
Before the Cross

X = chapel behind the cross

Tomb

Anastasis

0   40 meters

A Coptic painting of Christ and Saint
Menas, sixth century (Clio20/Wikimedia
Commons)

Egyptian painting on funeral cloth,
showing Osiris leading the deceased to
Anubis, second century (bpk, Berlin/
Staatliche Museen/Sandra Steiss/Art
Resource, New York)

Church of Hagia Sophia (Holy Wisdom), Constantinople, seventh century
(© iStockphoto.com/Steven Allan)

Church of Hagia Sophia, interior view (Dean Strelau/Wikimedia Commons)

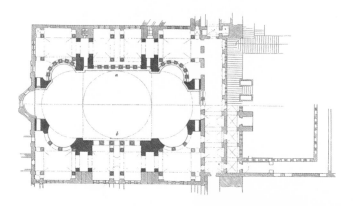

Church of Hagia Sophia, floor plan (Wikimedia Commons)

Christ Pantokrator, encaustic from Saint Catherine's Monastery, Mount Sinai, sixth century (Wikimedia Commons)

Gold plate with scenes from the gospels, Sogdiana, eighth or ninth century (The State Hermitage Museum, Saint Petersburg; photograph © The State Hermitage Museum / photo by Vladimir Terebenin, Leonard Kheifets, Yuri Molodkovets)

Apse mosaic depicting Christ, the apostles, and the city of Jerusalem; from the Church of Santa Pudenziana, Rome, fourth century (Wikimedia Commons)

Saint Catherine's Monastery, Mount Sinai, exterior view, sixth century (© iStockphoto.com/Branko Vidmar)

Icon of the Virgin and child with two saints, Saint Catherine's Monastery, sixth century (Erich Lessing/Art Resource, New York)

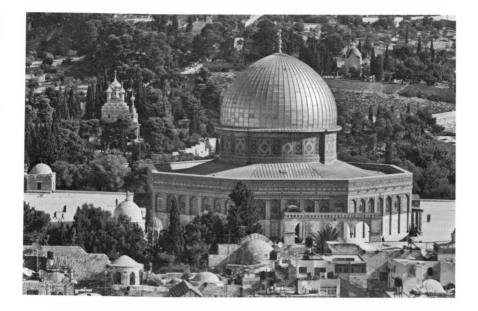

Dome of the Rock, Jerusalem, eighth century (© iStockphoto.com/ Vladimir Khirman)

Wall painting of Mary, Jesus, and a Nubian queen, from a monastery in Faras, Nubia, eleventh or twelfth century (© John Warburton-Lee Photography/Alamy)

Wall painting of Saint Peter and a Nubian bishop, from Faras, Nubia, tenth century (© Hickey & Robinson, Houston/The Menil Foundation)

Ambrose preventing Emperor Theodosius from entering the cathedral in Milan, by Peter Paul Rubens, ca. 1615 (Kunsthistorisches Museum, Vienna; photo, Erich Lessing/A Resource, New York)

Augustine of Hippo

It is a conspicuous, if seldom noted, historical detail that during the first millennium of Christian history the Church attracted many of the most gifted thinkers in the ancient world. The parade of luminaries is impressive: Clement and Origen of Alexandria, Eusebius of Caesarea, Athanasius of Alexandria, Hilary of Poitiers, Gregory of Nyssa, Basil of Caesarea, Gregory Nazianzen, Maximus the Confessor, John of Damascus, and of course the four Latin *doctores ecclesiae* (teachers of the Church), Jerome, Ambrose, Augustine, Gregory the Great. Yet Augustine towers above all. It is not hyperbolic to say that during his lifetime he was the most intelligent man in the Mediterranean world. From the time of Plato and Aristotle, the great philosophers of ancient Greece, across more than fifteen centuries until Thomas Aquinas in the High Middle Ages, he has no equal.

Augustine surpasses measurement. More than any other Christian author in the early centuries, he is a world. He lived very long, seventy-six years, and wrote more profusely and thought more profoundly than any other early Christian, and his vigorous intelligence and fertile imagination moved across a much larger canvas. The steady flow of his thought passed through all the great questions pondered by thoughtful men and women in antiquity: freedom and determinism, how does one know, what is the highest good (*summum bonum*), what makes human beings unique, what kind of a being is God, how did the world come to be, how does one account for evil, what is the place of the affections in the virtuous life. He pondered two of the most mysterious and elusive aspects of human experience, memory and time.

Augustine also dealt with new questions prompted by the coming of Christ and the emergence of a new kind of community, the Church: the reliability of the biblical writings, the nature of biblical language, allegory and the interpretation of the Scriptures, history and faith, revelation and reason, sin and grace, predestination, God as triune, love, the sacraments, the Church and political power.

He penned one of the most quoted lines of all times: *Fecisti nos ad te et inquietum est cor nostrum, donec requiescat in te.* "You have made us for yourself, Oh Lord, and our heart is restless until it rests in you." He wrote expositions of the Bible and sermons (on all 150 psalms), a massive work in defense of Christianity (*The City of God*), philosophical essays (on free will, the immortality of the soul), catechetical and educational treatises (*Christian Teaching*), doctrinal expositions and polemical tracts, an introspective account of his own conversion written as a prayer to God (the *Confessions*), hundreds of letters (plus some found only two decades ago).

In his last years Augustine even wrote a book called *Retractationes,* or second thoughts, a reassessment of his writings, book by book. Unlike conventional philosophers, artists, and politicians today who write self-serving autobiographies, Augustine knew that he was a great man, a towering figure whose many writings would be quarried to support all sorts of opinion. In writing the *Reconsiderations* he wanted future readers to know why he had written each book and to ward off the inevitable misunderstandings that would follow.

His writings reveal a person with deep empathy for the suffering of his fellow human beings. "The attitudes and movements of the body, when they are graceful and harmonious, are reckoned among the primary gifts of nature. But what if some illness makes the limbs shake and tremble? What if a man's spine is so curved as to bring his hands to the ground, turning the man into a virtual quadruped? Will not this destroy all beauty and grace of body whether in repose or in motion?"

Although he is revered as a saint of the Church, Augustine was a man made of flesh, not of marble. His letters and books, many of which speak vividly of his feelings, give us a sharper picture of Augustine as a human being than anyone from antiquity. Chastened by experience, his thinking has a hard-won clarity. He wrote knowingly of the unpredictable and ungovernable desires that break through the order and conventions of human life.

He was a practiced, seductive Latin stylist. Every word fits flush, and even in English his sentences captivate and beguile the reader, as in this passage from the *Confessions*.

Late have I loved you, beauty so old and so new; late have I loved you. And see, you were within and I was in the external world and sought you there, and in my unlovely state I plunged into those lovely created things which you made. You were with me and I was not with you . . . You called and cried out and shattered my deafness. You were radiant and resplendent, you put to flight my blindness. You were fragrant, and I drew in my breath and now pant after you. I tasted you, and I feel but hunger and thirst for you. You touched me, and I am set on fire to attain the peace which is yours.

In reading Augustine it is hard to keep one's distance. His words soar off the page to sink into the soul of the reader, moving the affections as well as stirring the intellect.

Augustine was born in 354 in the small city of Thagaste, sixty miles from the Mediterranean in the Roman province of Numidia (Algeria), in North Africa. His mother, Monica, was a devout Christian, but his father Patricius had interest only in his son's education and advancement. Though his parents were not wealthy, thanks to the generosity of a local dignitary, a friend of his father, Augustine received a solid grounding in Latin grammar and rhetoric, one of the few paths that led to a better life for a young man from a small provincial town.

When he was seventeen he continued his education in the bustling city of Carthage (near present-day Tunis in Tunisia) on the Mediterranean coast. During his years there he took a common-law wife and had a son by her, Adeodatus (given by God). At nineteen he became a "hearer" of the Manichaeans, a dualistic sect that attracted clever, intelligent young men. Over time he grew weary of their intellectualism and disillusioned with the kind of disciples they attracted. Still, during his twenties he remained a hearer for nine years.

From Carthage Augustine moved to Rome, where he taught rhetoric. But then in 384, when he was thirty years old, he was offered a position in Milan, at the time a more important city than Rome and the residence of the emperor in the West. At Milan he came to know the bishop, Ambrose, whose dazzling command of Latin rhetoric made a deep impression on him. He also learned from Ambrose how to read the Bible. Through Ambrose and the examples of others, notably the philosopher Victorinus, and the prayers and entreaties of his mother, Augustine became a catechumen and was baptized by Ambrose at Easter, 387.

While preparing to sail back to North Africa, his mother Monica died in Ostia, the seaport of Rome. One of the most affecting passages in his *Confessions* is the account of her death. At first Augustine held back his tears, because he did not think it right to pour out "tearful dirges and lamentations" for a devout Christian woman whose faith was "unfeigned" (1 Timothy 1:5). But after a restful night he wrote that he was "glad to weep before you [God] about her and for her, about myself and for myself. Now I let flow the tears which I had held back so that they ran as freely as they wished. My heart rested upon them, and it reclined upon them because it was your ears that were there, not those of some human critic. . . . And now, Lord, I make my confession to you in writing. Let anyone who wishes read and interpret as he pleased. If he finds fault that I wept for my mother for a fraction of an hour, the mother who had died before my eyes who had wept for me that I might live before your eyes, let him not mock me but rather, if a person of much charity, let him weep himself before you for my sins."

In returning to Thagaste, Augustine intended to found a monastery with his friends. But a few months later on a trip to Hippo Regius, a city on the Mediterranean coast, he was abruptly ordained a priest by popular acclaim and the not so subtle manipulation of the bishop Valerius. After spending some time studying the Scriptures, he was allowed to preach, and within two years he was expounding the creed to bishops. Four years later, in 395 when he was forty-one years old, he was made bishop of Hippo, and for the next thirty-five years (he died in 430) he was bishop of a provincial city on the Mediterranean in North Africa.

Before his ordination Augustine had spent his time in literary and philosophical pursuits with friends of like mind. Now he had become a figure of authority, a very public person whose life was shaped by the persistent duties thrust upon him. As bishop his tasks were not only pastoral, preparing candidates for baptism, presiding at the celebration of the Eucharist, burying the dead; he was also called upon to act as a local arbitrator, hearing petty disputes among farmers or settling inheritance claims of quarreling family members. He preached regularly, and as he grew more familiar with the Scriptures his thinking moved in new directions. He carried on extensive correspondence with other bishops and public officials, and he was drawn into ecclesiastical disputes in his own region and across the empire.

In the course of his years as bishop, three major controversies occupied his attention: with the Manichees, who were harsh critics of Catholic Christianity; with the Donatists, a large community of Christians with its own bishops who had brought about a schism among the churches of North Africa; and with a British monk named Pelagius and his followers over sin and grace.

The Manichees taught that humans are spiritual beings bound to material bodies created by an evil god. In reply Augustine showed that evil was rooted in the human will, not in matter like flesh, and defended the goodness of God and of the created order. His thinking can be summed up in an aphorism: "Whatever *is* is good," meaning that whatever has been made by the good God is by the very fact that it exists good.

The dispute with the Manichees dealt with central issues concerning the interpretation of the Bible, particularly the Old Testament, and the nature of good and evil. Augustine's writings against them are important for understanding the development of his thinking, but for the history of Christian doctrine Augustine's treatises and letters on the Donatists and the Pelagians are more consequential.

Donatism had its beginning early in the fourth century in the wake of the last persecutions of the Church. In 311, when a new bishop of Carthage, named Caecilian, was appointed, one of the bishops who consecrated him was accused by a group of rigorist bishops of handing over copies of the Scripture to the Roman authorities during the persecution. His ordination was declared invalid. After Caecilian refused to appear before a council of hard-line bishops, they elected a new bishop, Majorinus, and led a group of churches in North Africa into formal schism. The people of Carthage supported Caecilian, and Rome stayed in communion with him. A few years later Majorinus was succeeded by Donatus, and hence his followers came to be called Donatists by the Catholics. There were now two "churches" in Africa, that of the Catholics and that of the Donatists.

During the fourth century, efforts were made to reconcile the two groups, but the Donatists were fiercely loyal to their bishops, and the schism persisted until Augustine's day. The Donatists saw themselves as the true church, the community of the pure without spot or wrinkle, an enclosed garden set apart from the world. Because they thought the Catholic Church had become contaminated, they rejected its sacraments and broke off communion.

Donatism raised in acute form questions about the nature of the Church: is the Church the community of the righteous or is it a body made up of pure and impure, true Christians and nominal Christians? As the number of Christians mounted in the fourth century, and the churches were made up of people of all sorts and from every level of society, including high government officials and emperors, could it demand the same fervency of commitment that had prevailed in earlier generations? The conventional good person of society had become the conventional good Christian in the Church. How was one to reconcile biblical language describing the Church as the "bride of Christ" or the "body of Christ" with a community made up of the good, the bad, and the indifferent, the imperfect as well as the virtuous?

Because there was a large Donatist community in Hippo when Augustine became bishop, these questions were urgent. Drawing on the work of an earlier bishop in North Africa named Optatus, Augustine argued that the Church included sinners as well as saints, chaff among the wheat, men and women who were manifestly not holy but who as members of the Church were in the process of being healed. In his words, the form of the Church is "not those who are now just, but those who are being made just." The line between devout believers and those who went through the motions of believing was so faint as to be invisible. Only at the end of time would the wheat and the chaff be separated.

The Donatists, however, believed that the boundaries between Church and world were sharp and distinct. They saw themselves as successors of the church of the martyrs. For Augustine the Church was a mixed body that penetrated society as a whole and, perforce, reflected different levels of commitment. Nevertheless all Christians were bound together by their participation in the sacraments and shared in holiness because they were united to Christ. Baptism derived its validity not from the moral or spiritual health of the priest who administers it but from Christ. It is Christ who baptizes, not the minister. The sacraments are endowed with a mysterious objective power drawn from Christ independent of the disposition of the priest. As Augustine famously wrote: "The Word [of Christ] comes to the element [the water] and it becomes the sacrament."

Because the Church is the body of Christ there can be only one Church. Here was the rub. The Donatists were an exclusive community and said to the Catholics:

"You have your sheep. I have mine. Don't trouble mine and I won't trouble yours." For Augustine, however, unity was of the essence of the Church and schism was spiritual estrangement. The one Church is universal and the Christians of North Africa were part of a fellowship that could be found all over the empire and beyond. By resisting efforts to find a common bond with the local Catholics, the Donatists cut themselves off from Christians in other parts of the world. "There is no other Catholic Church," wrote Augustine, "than that which according to the promise [Psalms 61:2–3] is spread abroad throughout the whole world."

This desire for unity helps explain Augustine's actions. When words failed, he sought other ways to end the schism. It must be remembered that this was not merely a polite debate among gentleman bishops. The Donatists had support among the Berbers, a people who lived in the countryside and spoke languages other than Latin. Sometimes members of the Donatist churches committed acts of violence against Catholic leaders. In one incident a band of Donatists attacked the bishop of Bagai in his church at the altar, beat him with a machete, and dragged his body to the edge of town and left him for dead. Shortly afterward, in June 405, an imperial edict was posted in Carthage branding the Donatists as "heretics," and the churches of the Donatists were declared illegal.

A few years later, in June 411, a conference of Donatist and Catholic bishops (284 Catholics, 284 Donatists) met in Carthage under the presidency of an imperial commissioner. When the Donatists arrived, they refused to sit with the ungodly Catholics, so all had to stand in the summer heat. The history of the schism was rehearsed, each side stated its views, and after three sessions the commissioner ruled that the Donatists had not proved their case. So harsher legal remedies were introduced.

Augustine had reluctantly concluded that in dealing with the Donatists coercion was necessary, and he welcomed government intervention. In a letter to a Donatist bishop, he wrote: "Originally my opinion was that no one should be forced to the unity of Christ, but that we should act with words, fight with arguments, and conquer by reason." Two things led him to change his opinion. He was appalled by the violence of the Donatists, and he also discovered that legal actions against them were working. In Hippo and in other cities Donatists had began to return to the Catholic Church. Characteristically, Augustine has a scriptural text to explain what was happening: "Give a wise man a chance, and he will become wiser" (Proverbs 9:9).

Augustine saw the new laws as a way of buttressing a pastoral strategy of correcting the excesses of sinful men with firmness. The Donatists were fellow Christians, as were the imperial officials, and Christ was the shepherd of the whole Church. What he was urging was not so much that the state suppress heresy but that the Church discipline its own members. As bishop, Augustine was the pastor, the shepherd, of all the Christians in Hippo. In answer to the objection of a Donatist bishop that one cannot be forced into "righteousness," Augustine appealed to the parable of the wedding feast in the gospels. When the friends who had been invited gave excuses as to why they could not come, the master said to his servant: "Whomever you find, *force* them to come in" (Luke 14:23).

In the end, Augustine offered a biblical and pastoral justification for government intervention in an ecclesiastical controversy. What was new was not that the state took an interest in the affairs of the churches. That had been going on since the time of Constantine. What was new was that a prominent bishop would provide a theological rationale for repressive measures against a schismatic group. One should not, however, conclude from this that Augustine had envisioned a merging of ecclesiastical and political authority. At the same time that he was engaged in the controversy with the Donatists, he began writing a large book on the relation between the Church and society.

The *City of God*, Augustine's most ambitious work, was begun a few years after A.D. 410, when a Gothic army under the leadership of Alaric entered Rome, sacked the city, and terrorized the inhabitants. Rome, the symbol of security and permanence, the emblem of an entire way of life, a city that had stood for a thousand years, was humbled. "If Rome can perish," wrote Jerome, "what can be safe?"

Augustine reacted as a Roman and a Christian. He felt that the world he lived in could no longer be taken for granted. The language he loved, the writers he admired, the history he remembered—all were threatened. The sack of Rome also heightened tensions between Christians and pagans, who seized the moment to renew attacks on the Church. Rome, they claimed, had stood for centuries because it served the traditional gods. With the advent of Christianity, the gods had removed their protecting hand and the eternal city was overrun by barbarians.

Although the *City of God* was occasioned by the sack of Rome, it is much more than a response to the catastrophe. Like the writings of earlier apologists, it is a defense of Christianity addressed to those who do not worship the one God. But because Augustine was living in a Christian empire, his task was different from that of earlier apologists. With the accession of Constantine to the purple, some Christians, most notably Eusebius, bishop of Caesarea, saw the destiny of Rome and of the Church converging. Rome was a blessing to Christ and Christ to Rome. In Eusebius's view, the Church and the empire formed a single polity: one God, one Christ, one emperor, one empire, and one Church. By the time Augustine became bishop it seemed that the whole world had become a chorus praising Christ. Like his contemporaries, Augustine believed that Rome had placed itself under Christ's rule.

But as his thinking matured Augustine began to have doubts about this sanguine view of history, and in the *City of God* he divests the Roman Empire of religious significance. Whereas Eusebius had envisioned one "city," that is, one polity, Augustine detaches the Christian community from the state and speaks of two cities, the earthly city and the city of God. The phrase "city of God" comes from the psalms: "There is a river whose streams make glad the city of God, the holy habitation of the most High" (Psalms 46:4). The Romans, writes Augustine, had "no other city to praise" than the earthly city, the institutions they had built over centuries, but for Christians there is another city made up of those who worship the one God. The city of God is more than the Church, because it includes the angels and the saints who have gone before, but wherever the Church is found, says Augustine, there will be "God's beloved city."

Augustine's great insight was to treat the two cities in tandem, for in this life the two are intertwined. Citizens of the city of God are also citizens of the earthly city, and many of the citizens of the earthly city belong to the city of God. Accordingly, the city of God must join hands with the earthly city "about things pertaining to mortal life." Nevertheless their ends, their ultimate purposes, are different. Both seek peace, but the earthly city strives for peace between peoples and kingdoms and peace within society. For the heavenly city, however, peace is a "perfectly ordered and harmonious fellowship in the enjoyment of God." The city of God yearns for a fulfillment that will only be brought to perfection by God at the end of time. Though the citizens of the city of God share in the life of the earthly city, they have no ultimate stake in it. "She takes no account," he writes, "of any difference in customs, laws, and institutions by which earthly peace is achieved and preserved." When measured against the city of God, political authority is always provisional.

The *City of God* is a book about the community whose founder is Christ, not a treatise on political life. Augustine's theme is the justice due God and the community that serves and worships the one God. The city of God is not, however, an ideal; the Church is an actual community with its own history and memory, beliefs and language, calendar and rituals, institutions and practices. Christianity is inescapably social, and for Augustine the great metaphor for becoming a Christian was not an individual being born again, but becoming part of a city.

Augustine called the *City of God* a "great and arduous work." It was not a tract for the times. Yet as he was composing it he was drawn into yet another controversy that would occupy his attention for the rest of his life.

Pelagius was a monk from Britain who arrived in Rome in the 380s. A leader in the burgeoning ascetic movement that had swept across the Christian world in the fourth century, he was shocked by the undisciplined lives and moral laxity of many Christians in the city. In his writings he set out a program of moral reformation based on the God-given ability of human beings to carry out the divine commandments. In a well-known letter to Demetrias, the granddaughter of a prominent Roman family who had decided to become a nun, Pelagius wrote: "Whenever I have to speak on the subject of moral instruction and the conduct of a holy life, it is my practice first to demonstrate the power and quality of human nature and to show what it is capable of achieving." God does not require the impossible, for Jesus had taught: "Be ye perfect as your Father in heaven is perfect" (Matthew 5:48).

Pelagius was well received in Rome and became a spiritual adviser to wealthy Roman families. His views of human capability and freedom were conventional, and no one sensed any deviation from orthodox Christian teaching. But one of his disciples, a man named Caelestius, was more outspoken. He drew the conclusion that if human beings are endowed with natural goodness because they are made in the image of God, then they begin their lives unencumbered by sin. Sin was a learned trait and human corruption the work of habit. In his words: "the sin of Adam harmed him alone and not the human race and at their birth infants are in that state which Adam was before his transgression." His views did not go down well with many bishops in the West, because infant baptism—practiced in the fifth century—implied that infants were in need of forgiveness. When Caelestius applied for ordination in Carthage he was rejected, and his teachings were condemned by a council of bishops in 411.

Augustine was not present at the council, but he had begun to have doubts about Pelagius's teaching on sin and grace, and his first writings on him come shortly after the council. After the sack of Rome in 410, Pelagius had fled to North Africa, and Augustine mentions that he saw him from a distance several times in Carthage.

In an early work, Augustine centered his critique on Pelagius's understanding of grace. For Pelagius the first grace was the freedom of the will that gave men the ability to choose the good. In addition, God showed his goodness to human beings by giving the Ten Commandments, raising up holy men and women as models of a holy life, and sending Christ, who by his example and teachings taught human beings how to live. And through his death God grants forgiveness of sins.

For Augustine, Pelagius had much too confident a view of human nature. In saying it was "possible" not to sin, he minimized the ungovernable desires that disrupt the order and discipline of life. Evil does not have to be introduced into the human heart—it is always lurking there. Sin is not primarily an affair of discrete transgressions, individual acts of the will; it is a condition that infects everything one thinks and does. "Sin dwells in me," wrote Saint Paul. Against our best intentions we find that we often do the very thing we do not want to do, as though we are not free to resist (Romans 7). Pelagius had little feel for the complexity of human motivation and action. Augustine once said that anyone who thinks he can overcome his drives and desires and hold fast to the good without wavering knows "neither what he seeks, nor who he is who seeks it." Here as elsewhere, Augustine writes with the authority of experience.

For Augustine, grace was a mysterious divine presence in the lives of human beings. Whereas Pelagius spoke about the external gifts of the law and the teachings of Christ that instructed the intellect and guided the will, Augustine spoke of a transformation that took place in one's innermost being. The inner life was the most important thing about being human. The goal was not simply to live a virtuous life; it was to enter into a new relation with God through love. Although Augustine acknowledged the gift of free will and the commandments, the primary agent of divine grace was the pouring of the Holy Spirit in the hearts of believers (Romans 5:5). Through the "gift" of the Spirit, he wrote, "there arises in one's soul the delight and the love of God." Only if one's heart is ablaze with love "can it cleave to the creator" (Psalms 73:28). And to let the reader know unmistakably what he means, he adds: "free choice is good only for sin."

Augustine also argued that human beings are bound together by the natural ties of procreation. Even before the outbreak of the controversy, he had used the term "original sin" to explain Paul's words "that nothing good dwells within me" (Romans 7:18). Citing the letter to the Romans, "sin came into the world through one man" (Romans 5:12–21), he argued that there was a solidarity of all human beings in Adam's sin. Sin was not simply a matter of bad choices, something grafted on to a good person, but a wound on humanity, a disease that was passed down from generation to generation. Its marks were pride, distorted desire, and misdirected love. Augustine had observed that even infants were self-centered and acquisitive. "I have personally watched and studied a jealous baby. He could not yet speak, yet pale with jealousy . . . he glared at his brother sharing his mother's milk." Even though made in the image of God, human beings were afflicted with a debilitating weakness, and without God's grace they were unable to turn to God.

In responding to Pelagius, Augustine's thinking on sin and grace was moving into territory that had not been explored by earlier writers. After spending some time in North Africa, Pelagius settled in Palestine, where he was asked to explain himself before a council of Eastern bishops at Diosopolis in Palestine in 415. After hearing his explanation of his teaching (which some may not have understood because of language differences), Pelagius was acquitted of heresy. This was unacceptable to Augustine and the bishops in North Africa, and after condemning his teaching in two councils, they asked Pope Innocent in Rome to rule on the teachings of Pelagius and Caelestius. After much maneuvering the African bishops were able to bring Rome over to their side, and in January 417 Innocent accepted their verdict. Some months later Augustine preached a famous sermon in which he said: "the case is finished" (*causa finita est*). And then added: "Would that the error were finished also."

In fact there was more to come. Innocent died in March 417 and was succeeded by Zosimus, who reopened the case. But Augustine and the Africans continued to press the matter, and in April 418, Emperor Honorius condemned the Pelagians. A council of bishops was held in Carthage, and Pope Zosimus issued a formal letter confirming the decision in Carthage. It was signed by most, but not all, of the Italian bishops and promulgated across the empire. After this Pelagius disappears from our view, and we do not know what happened to him. But the controversy did not die. A gifted, well-educated, urbane, and married bishop from Eclanum in Italy named Julian refused to sign the letter, and in the years that followed he mounted an aggressive literary campaign against Augustine's teaching. Reluctantly, Augustine took up his pen again to write a series of new works in response to Julian.

It is sometimes said that Pelagianism was a creation of Augustine. That means, that it was Augustine's interpretation and presentation of Pelagius's teachings that shaped the understanding of Pelagianism down the centuries. There is some truth to this, yet there were real issues at stake: the significance of Christ's death and resurrection, the role of the Holy Spirit in the turning of the heart and mind to God, sin and grace.

Augustine wrote out of a deep well of experience and a nuanced understanding of the Scriptures, including some of the more difficult passages. One text that made a deep impression on him, for example, was a passage from Exodus cited by Saint Paul. "I [God] will have mercy on whom I have mercy and I will have compassion on whom I have compassion" (Exodus 33:19). To which Paul responds: "So it depends not upon man's will or exertion, but upon God's mercy" (Romans 9:15–16). God's grace is an unfathomable mystery that cannot be forced into conventional human categories of justice and fairness.

The Pelagian controversy took place largely in the West among Latin-speaking Christians. Pelagius found his strongest support in the East. Julian of Eclanum was befriended by Theodore of Mopsuestia, a Greek-speaking bishop in southeastern Asia Minor, where he wrote his treatises against Augustine. Augustine's theology of grace never gained traction among Eastern Christians, but in the West it set the terms of all later discussion during the Latin Middle Ages and in the Reformation.

In September 426, when Augustine was seventy-two years old, he made the solemn decision to hand over his responsibilities as bishop to a new successor, Eraclius. In a sermon preached on that occasion, he said:

> In this life we are all bound to die; and for everyone his last day is always uncertain. Yet, as babies, we can look forward to being boys, and, as boys, to youth, as youths, to being grown up, and as young men to reaching our prime, and in our prime, to growing old. Whether this will happen is uncertain; but there is always something to look forward to. But an old man has no further stage of life before him. Because God wished it, I came to this town in my prime: I was a young man then, now I have grown old.

Augustine died four years later as the Vandals were overrunning North Africa, and the labor of a lifetime was soon to go up in flames.

Augustine wanted to die alone, and his biographer, Possidius, who had once lived in his monastery in Hippo, and who remained a close friend all his life, in an unforgettable passage, described Augustine's last days in a biography written shortly after his death.

As Augustine lay dying, wrote Possidius, "he ordered those psalms of David which are especially penitential to be copied out [for example, 'Have mercy on me according to thy steadfast love . . . For I know my transgressions, and my sin is ever before me,' Psalm 51], and when he was very weak, he used to lie in bed facing the wall where the sheets of papers were put up, gazing at them and reading, and copiously and continually weeping as he read."

The Great Controversy over Christus

Eloquence without wisdom is hazardous. In 428 a famous preacher from Syria named Nestorius was consecrated patriarch of Constantinople. Though fluent of speech, he lacked prudence and soon found himself at odds with the imperial family and monks in the city. The misstep that sparked his troubles was a sermon preached by his private chaplain denouncing the use of the term *theotokos,* God-bearer, or mother of God, as a title for the Virgin Mary. Mary is but a woman, he said, and God cannot be born of a woman. In defending his presbyter, Nestorius preached a series of sermons that rankled the faithful. A more appropriate description, he said, would be *Christotokos,* mother of Christ. His remarks set off a furor in the city, and news of his sermon was soon spread abroad.

The epithet *theotokos* was an ancient and venerable term of honor for the Virgin Mary, well documented in early Christian prayers and Christian writers at least from the third century. Here, for example, is the text of a prayer from third-century Egypt:

> To your protection we flee, holy *Mother of God.*
> Do not despise our prayers in our needs,
> But deliver us from all dangers,
> Glorious and blessed Virgin.

Even though the expression *theotokos* carried no explicit doctrinal content, and therefore was used by bishops with differing views, Nestorius thought its pious sentiments disguised faulty theological ideas about the relation of Christ to God. Mary gave birth to a man, who was united with God, not to the divine Son of God. God cannot have a mother, he said.

Within weeks a copy of the controversial sermon had made its way to Alexandria. The patriarch at the time was Cyril, a native Egyptian born in 378 in a small town about seventy miles east of Alexandria. His mother was the sister of Theophilus, who had served as secretary to Athanasius, the stalwart defender of the Council of Nicaea in mid fourth century. When Theophilus became bishop of Alexandria in 385 he took Cyril under his wing, preparing him for clerical office. Later Cyril wrote that from his youth he had been immersed in the Scriptures, and many of his mature writings are commentaries on biblical books, the Pentateuch, Isaiah, the Minor Prophets, the Gospel of John, the epistles of Saint Paul. In 403, he accompanied his uncle Theophilus as secretary to a synod in Constantinople at which John Chrysostom, the bishop of the city, was deposed. He served his uncle for nine years, during which time he learned the art of politics and was able to observe the skills of a wily and pugnacious polemicist. Theophilus was known as the Egyptian Pharaoh, and Cyril proved as redoubtable in governing the Church in Egypt as he was formidable in argument and debate. He was, in the words of a British scholar, one of those "strong characters that excite the animosity of less successful controversialists." He became bishop of Alexandria in 412.

The debate between Cyril and Nestorius centered on the interpretation of the Scriptures. In speaking of Christ, Cyril and the Alexandrian tradition favored the language "God became flesh," and highlighted biblical passages such as John 1:14, "the Word became flesh." In the Incarnation the divine Son, the eternal Word of God, begotten of the Father from eternity, had become man. Christ is the Son of God under the conditions of human life. So it is fitting to call Mary the God-bearer.

The tradition Nestorius represented drew on passages in the New Testament that spoke of God indwelling in Christ, such as Colossians 1:19, "in him all the fullness of God was pleased to dwell." Nestorius's thinking had been shaped by Theodore, a bishop in the city of Mopsuestia (d. 428) in southeastern Anatolia, not too far from Antioch. Hence the theological perspective of Theodore and Nestorius (who also came from a city close to Antioch) is called Antiochene. In their view, the Incarnation, God becoming flesh, meant that the divine Son had united with the man Jesus, with Christ who was born of Mary. Hence "mother of Christ" was preferable to "mother of God." In Cyril's view, by rejecting the term *theotokos,* Nestorius was portraying Christ as an inspired man—unique to be sure—rather than God become flesh.

Each way of thinking could make sense of certain passages in the Scriptures, but had difficulty with others. For example, the gospels say that Jesus increased in wisdom and stature (Luke 2:52), that he grew tired (John 4:6), that his soul was sorrowful (Matthew 26:38), that he suffered pain and died. Who is the subject of these experiences? If it is the man Jesus, they pose no problem. But if it is the divine son of God, the question arises: Can God grow in wisdom or die? Conversely, when the gospels say that Christ stilled the sea, raised Lazarus from the dead, healed the sick, are these the work of the man Jesus, or should they be attributed to the Son of God?

To the Alexandrians it seemed that Theodore and his disciples divided Christ into two persons, the divine Son and the man Jesus, attributing some passages in the gospels to the Son and others to the man Jesus. On the other hand, the Antiochenes thought that Cyril so emphasized the divinity of Christ that he could not take Christ's humanity with full seriousness. The challenge each faced was to find theological language to express the Church's belief that in Christ the divine and human were united in a mysterious way. There were no easy solutions; hence the controversy.

When a report of Nestorius's sermons made its way to the monks living in the deserts of upper Egypt, Cyril decided to prepare an encyclical (general) letter to them explaining why the term *theotokos* is not only appropriate for the Virgin Mary, but absolutely necessary. The designation, wrote Cyril, safeguards the union of God and man in Christ and excludes any notion that Christ is simply a man who has been united with the divine Son of God. The person we read about in the gospels, Jesus of Nazareth, is "of one substance with the Father," as the Creed of Nicaea testifies. Therefore Mary is rightly honored as the theotokos.

Copies of Cyril's letter were forwarded to Constantinople, and Nestorius was offended that the patriarch of Alexandria presumed to instruct him, the patriarch of Constantinople, on a doctrinal matter. There was, however, more at stake than doctrine. According to ancient tradition, the church in Alexandria was founded by the apostle Mark. This meant Cyril stood in a succession that went back to Saint Mark, just as the bishop of Rome stood in a succession stretching back to Saint Peter. During the first three centuries Alexandria and Antioch—two of the first cities outside Palestine to have a Christian community—were, along with Rome, the principal Christian centers in the empire. With the founding of a new city by Constantine in the early fourth century, Constantinople, though a latecomer and not an apostolic city, had risen in prominence in the Christian world to become second in honor only to Rome.

In mounting a broadside against the patriarch of Constantinople, Cyril was not only defending the theological tradition of Alexandria, he was also upholding the ancient prerogatives of his see against what he considered an upstart and rival. In the earlier confrontation between the two cities, Cyril's uncle, Theophilus of Alexandria, had brought charges against Chrysostom, patriarch of Constantinople, because he had sheltered a group of Egyptian monks suspected of heresy. In any account of the controversy over the person of Christ, the political rivalry between Alexandria and Constantinople must always be kept in mind. Yet, at the end of the day, the conflict was driven more by theological differences than political aspirations.

From the outset neither Cyril nor Nestorius was willing to give way, and each moved swiftly to build support among neighboring bishops and gain favor at the imperial court. When Nestorius's sermons reached Rome they were read with alarm, and Pope Celestine was drawn into the controversy. A council was hastily called, and Nestorius's views were found to be in error. To Cyril's delight, Celestine asked him to carry out the decisions of the Roman synod.

In the meantime, momentum was building to convene a general council of bishops from around the Christian world to adjudicate the matter. Nestorius welcomed a council because he thought it would be held in Constantinople. But to his dismay Emperor Theodosius II (408–450)—under pressure from his older sister Pulcheria—decided to hold it in Ephesus, a city with a long history of devotion to the Virgin Mary. According to pious tradition, the Virgin Mary spent her last days in Ephesus, and Nestorius's views on the theotokos were unlikely to receive a favorable hearing there.

Cyril, however, overplayed his hand. Shortly before the council was to convene, he dispatched a letter to Nestorius with a list of twelve propositions outlining the Alexandrian position in provocative language acceptable only to his own followers. For example: "If anyone dares to say that Christ is a God-bearing man and not truly God, being by nature one Son, because the *Word was made flesh* [John 1:14] and shared in flesh and blood like us, let him be anathema." These propositions, known as the *Twelve Chapters,* were to bedevil efforts to work out a compromise in the next two decades. When Nestorius received Cyril's letter he immediately sent a copy to his principal ally, John, patriarch of Antioch, who rallied his bishops in Nestorius's defense.

The council was to convene on June 7, 431, and Nestorius was the first to arrive, with a company of bishops. But he was received coldly by the bishop of Ephesus, Memnon. A few days later Cyril and his supporters, including a powerful Coptic monk, Shenoute, arrived in Ephesus. About the same time a group of bishops from Palestine led by Juvenal, the bishop of Jerusalem, reached the city. The delegation from Rome had not arrived, and neither had the large group of bishops from Syria headed by John of Antioch, Nestorius's learned and articulate ally.

After waiting almost two weeks for John's arrival, Cyril decided to convene the council, a right he could claim because he was the ranking bishop. He persuaded the imperial commissioner to read aloud the imperial document authorizing the council. Since Constantine it was the custom for the Roman emperor, not the bishops, or the bishop of Rome, to convene a general council. Once the official document (called the *sacra*) was read, the council was solemnly declared in session and the bishops took up the matter at hand.

Ephesus is the first church council for which we have minutes that allow us to follow the course of events. Nestorius was not present at the opening assembly, and the assembled bishops sent a delegation asking him to appear before them. When he refused, the bishops turned to the theological question that had brought them together, Nestorius's rejection of the theotokos. In the course of the discussion the creed of Nicaea, the standard of orthodoxy acknowledged by all, was read aloud. But the bishops also had read two letters from Cyril to Nestorius, as well as a dossier of excerpts from the works of earlier Christian writers (called a *florilegium*, a collection of flowers) and a number of passages from the writings of Nestorius. In a letter written home to Alexandria, Cyril reported that the entire city of Ephesus had stood outside the church the whole day awaiting the decision of the bishops. The outcome was never in doubt, and by the end of the day Nestorius's teaching was condemned as contrary to the Church's faith.

When the bishops from Syria arrived in Ephesus a few days later, they were outraged that the council had met without them. So Ephesus became the scene of the sad spectacle of a different group of bishops convening a second council to condemn the teaching of Cyril and the bishop of Ephesus. The principal charge was that Cyril was tainted with the error of Apollinaris, a bishop who had been condemned several decades earlier for teaching that Christ was not a fully human person.

Faced with the dilemma of reconciling two competing councils, the emperor responded by seizing both of its horns. In the stifling heat of August, he sent a high-ranking imperial official to Ephesus to place Nestorius, Cyril, and Memnon under arrest. Then he called together a small group of bishops—seven on each side—to discuss the issues. The results were inconclusive. In the meantime Nestorius had lost the will to fight, and he returned to his monastery in Syria. Cyril sailed for Alexandria, where he was greeted like a conquering hero.

Although the unhappy events of the summer ended in a stalemate, one thing had been secured. The Syrian bishops who had supported Nestorius agreed to the use of the epithet *theotokos* for the Virgin Mary, thereby ensuring that it would become a permanent fixture of Christian prayer and devotion, especially in the Eastern churches.

Although the council at which Cyril presided was eventually considered official and recognized as the Third Ecumenical Council, in the months that followed Cyril realized his political position was vulnerable. Many resented his high-handed behavior and insisted that no progress toward union could be made unless he withdrew the *Twelve Chapters*. At this point Cyril displayed another side to his character. Whereas in Ephesus he was truculent and uncompromising, here he became conciliatory and flexible, seeking language that would be acceptable to his opponents. In a masterful letter to one of Nestorius's defenders, Cyril explained his own views in terms that the Syrian bishops found persuasive.

An embassy was sent to Alexandria headed by a respected bishop, Paul of Emesa, accompanied by an imperial legate to work out a joint statement. After lengthy negotiations, during which Cyril was ill, they were able to reach agreement. The language came largely from the Syrian bishops, but the honorific *theotokos* was retained and the condemnation of Nestorius was allowed to stand. On Christmas day, 432, Paul preached in the cathedral in Alexandria and to thunderous applause proclaimed: "Mary the Theotokos gives birth to Emmanuel" (a familiar name for Christ, from the Hebrew for "God with us," Isaiah 7:14). The congregation shouted in response: "This is the true faith!"

In spring the agreement was signed, and Cyril announced from the pulpit that communion had been reestablished. Known as the *Formula of Union,* this brief creed-like statement also served as the basis for the conciliar decree at Chalcedon two decades later.

Several things were noteworthy about the *Formula of Union.* First, it clearly affirmed that Christ and the divine Son are one person, that the one born of Mary is the "unique Son of God." It also affirms that Christ is fully God and fully man, that the divine nature and the human nature are united as one: "We confess one Christ, one [divine] Son, one Lord." Yet to satisfy the Syrians it goes on to say that, although Christ is one, in reading the gospels it is sometimes necessary to distinguish between those things that are proper to his human nature and those that are proper to his divine nature. Hence one can say that Christ is "of [or 'out of'] two natures." The phrase "out of two natures" also proved controversial. Some thought it should read "in two natures."

At this point the controversy moves into a new stage. Although the dispute had centered on the term *theotokos,* in the next phase it focused on the term "nature." For the Alexandrians, "nature" designated a specific entity, as the name Samuel refers to an individual person named Samuel. Hence the Alexandrians could say that Christ was "one nature of God the Word incarnate." "Nature" meant the concrete person. The Syrians, however, used the term "nature" to mean a characteristic that belonged to a person, such as brown hair or blue eyes, traits that an individual shares with other persons. Hence they said Christ had two natures, one divine and one human. This difference in the understanding of the term "nature" would foil efforts to preserve unity.

John of Antioch died in 441, and Cyril three years later. On his death one of his opponents, Theodoret of Cyrrhus, wrote: "His departure delights the survivors, but possibly disheartens the dead; there is some fear that under the provocation of his company they may send him back again to us. . . . Care must be taken to order the guild of undertakers to place a very big and heavy stone on his grave to stop him coming back here." Unfortunately Cyril's successor, Dioscorus, was an ambitious and impetuous figure whose zeal to humiliate Constantinople was matched by his want of sound judgment. When a dull-witted monk in Constantinople named Eutyches was condemned for teaching that after the Incarnation there was "one nature" in Christ, Dioscorus came to his defense. By working his connections at the imperial court Dioscorus was able to persuade the emperor to convene a council to reverse the decision against Eutyches.

In the meantime, Pope Leo weighed in with a long letter (called the *Tome*) arguing from the Scriptures that "two natures" remained after the union. "The nativity of the flesh shows forth the human nature; the Virgin's childbearing indicates divine power. . . . The one Herod impiously plans to slay is like humanity in its beginnings; but he whom the Magi rejoice to adore on their knees is Lord of all." Although Rome had supported Cyril, Leo's letter seemed to tilt toward Antioch. He sent the letter to the emperor, expecting that it would be read at the council and would settle the matter. But Dioscorus, who had been given authority to preside at the council, arranged for it to be pushed to the bottom of the agenda, and it was never read. He was able to strong-arm the bishops into submission to his will. Leo dubbed the council a *latrocinium*, a den of thieves, and ever since it has been known as the "Robber Council."

To undo the damage, Leo appealed to the emperor to call a new council in Italy, but Theodosius was unbending. A few months later, however, while out riding, he was thrown from his horse and died. At once his sister Pulcheria grasped the reigns of power, married a military man named Marcian, and had him proclaimed emperor. While Marcian turned his attention to the Huns who were threatening the northeastern borders of the empire, Pulcheria, working with Leo, made plans for a new council to meet at Chalcedon, in the East, not, as the pope wished, in Italy.

The council met in the beautiful church of the martyr Saint Euphemia, a large, imposing complex with a spacious sanctuary, a columned forecourt open to the sky, and a round building holding the relics of the martyr. It stood on a high promontory, from which one could see the city of Constantinople across the dark blue waters of the Bosporus. There were 520 bishops in attendance, and supporters of Leo sat on one side, allies of Dioscorus on the other. Because of the rowdy behavior of the bishops at the Council of Ephesus in 449, the emperor and empress entrusted the leadership of the council to a group of nineteen laymen.

After a few days of maneuvering, Dioscorus found himself in the position of the accused for supporting Eutyches and also for his imperious actions at Ephesus. Though some pleaded for leniency, most bishops, with the support of the emperor, turned against him, and he was officially deprived of his office. To announce the decision, placards were set up in Chalcedon and Constantinople.

Then the assembly turned its attention to theological matters. Although most thought the creed of Nicaea, confirmed at Constantinople and reaffirmed at Ephesus (431), was sufficient as a confession of faith, the bishops knew that they would have to formulate a new doctrinal statement to address the disputed matters. So a commission was appointed to work on a draft of a new decree, which was presented to the council fathers on October 21. Unfortunately, the actual text is not recorded in the minutes, but it seems, from the discussion that ensued, that it did not include the term *theotokos* and used the phrase "out of two natures." Some, particularly the Roman delegation, found the draft unacceptable because "out of two natures" seemed to be a concession to Dioscorus. So a new committee was formed, and a few days later a revised statement was read aloud to the bishops. It was received with hearty shouts of approval. Little did the bishops realize it would be one of the most divisive doctrinal statements in the Church's history.

After a preface on the desire for peace in the Church, the decree gives the text of the original creed of the Council of Nicaea in 325, followed by the text of the revised form adopted at the Council of Constantinople in 381, what is today known as the Nicene Creed. By including the original version as well as the later version, with the additional section on the Holy Spirit, the bishops let it be known that as Constantinople had gone beyond Nicaea to deal with issues that had arisen after Nicaea. So they were justified in formulating a statement to deal with questions that had emerged since the Council of Constantinople seventy years earlier.

> Following then the holy fathers, we all confess in harmony one and the same Son, our Lord Jesus Christ; the same one perfect in divinity and perfect in humanity, truly God and truly man, of a rational soul and a body; of one being with the Father as regards his divinity and of one being with us as regards his humanity; like us in all respects except sin; begotten before the ages from the Father in divinity, and in the last days the same one for us and for our salvation born from Mary, the virgin theotokos in humanity; one and the same Christ, Son, Lord, only begotten; acknowledged in two natures without confusion, without change, without division, without separation; at no point was the difference between the natures taken away because of the union, but rather the distinctive character of each nature being preserved, and each coming together in one person and a single subsistent being; he is not divided or separated into two persons, but is one and the same Son, only-begotten God, Word, Lord Jesus Christ as the prophets of old and the Lord Jesus Christ himself taught us about him, and the creed of the fathers handed down to us.

By invoking the authority of the "fathers," faithful Christian teachers of earlier generations, the bishops wished to affirm that their confession of faith was in continuity with earlier Christian teachers. The decree then states that Christ is fully God and fully man with a "rational soul and body." This phrase was included to make clear that Christ had a human consciousness. He was not a divine being who inhabited a human body. As God he was "begotten of the Father before the ages," and as man he was born of the Virgin Mary, the theotokos "in the last days," a reference to Hebrews 1:1, "In many and various ways God spoke of old to our fathers by the prophets; but in these last days he has spoken to us by a Son."

Then come the controversial words: "in two natures." Note, however, that the decree does not say that Christ *existed* in two natures, but that he was *acknowledged* or *known* in two natures. This subtlety was, however, lost on the Alexandrians, who wanted the expression to read "out of two natures," not "in two natures."

The definition was a composite document, the work of a committee drawing on the writings of bishops representing the two traditions of thought, of Alexandria and of Antioch. It is less a fully worked out doctrine of the person of Christ than a series of signposts or markers to indicate the boundaries to be respected in teaching about Christ. Because the decree was a series of statements in juxtapositions, it included something for all and lent itself to different interpretations. The phrase "two natures" represented the thinking of the Antiochenes, but the inclusion of theotokos hearkened back to Cyril's defense of the term against Nestorius. Some phrases in the decree are taken directly from Cyril's writings: "the same one . . . born of the Father before all ages according to deity and, the same one, born . . . of Mary the Virgin . . . according to humanity." Nevertheless, to many, most notably the Alexandrians, the phrase "in two natures" seemed to favor the Antiochenes.

At the sixth session of the council the emperor himself, Marcian, and his wife Pulcheria, who had promoted the council, made an appearance. Marcian was hailed as the "new Constantine," and 452 bishops signed the definition of faith. The dissension that followed the council, however, suggests that some, if not many, signed the decree with reservations.

Like other councils, the Council of Chalcedon issued a series of canons dealing with administrative, liturgical, and jurisdictional matters. These canons give a vivid picture of the inner life of the churches, and not so incidentally they are a reminder that the Church was no longer a small community of fervent believers; it was a large and unruly institution very much immersed in the world. Here, for example, are some of the rulings: clergy are forbidden to take secular employment; clergy should not bring suits against other clergy in secular courts; ordinations should not be performed for money; a cleric cannot hold appointment in two churches; no woman under forty is to be ordained as a deaconess; no one should be ordained without having been appointed to a city or village church or the shrine of a martyr; monasteries are not to be turned into hostels.

Many of these canons were routine, but one dealt with a sensitive matter, the ecclesiastical standing of the see of Constantinople, the "new Rome." Although it was acknowledged by all that "old" Rome was first among Christian cities, some thought that as capital of the empire Constantinople should be recognized as equal to Rome. At Constantinople in A.D. 381 the bishops had adopted a canon ruling that the bishop of Constantinople should "enjoy the privileges of honor after the bishop of Rome." Rome, of course, had been opposed to any elevation of the see of Constantinople. But the emperor wished for the ruling of 381 to be restated and confirmed by the council.

So a new canon was adopted, number 28, that gave the bishop of Constantinople the privilege of ordaining bishops in the civil dioceses of Pontus, Asia, and Thrace, roughly eastern and northern Asia Minor along the Black Sea and the lower Balkans. But it also ruled that because Constantinople was the imperial capital and enjoyed privileges "equaling older imperial Rome," the city should be elevated in ecclesiastical affairs and "take second place after [Rome]."

The canon was opposed by the Roman legates, but it also did not go down well among the Alexandrians, who thought that after Rome, Alexandria was the most venerable patriarchate. In the months following the council, Leo made known his displeasure in letters to the patriarch of Constantinople and to the emperor. Constantinople, he wrote, was a great and imperial city, but it was not founded by an apostle: "Secular matters are one thing, divine things another." But the deed was done, and the issue continued to bedevil the efforts of Rome and Constantinople to work in tandem in the centuries that followed.

Like the Council of Nicaea, the Council of Chalcedon was the beginning, not the ending, of debate. But unlike Nicaea, whose creed came to be accepted by most of the Christian world and was confirmed at the Council of Constantinople in 381, the controversy over the decree of Chalcedon lasted for more than two hundred years. As we shall see in chapters to come, every effort to bring about peace and restore unity only led to greater division.

Egypt and the Copts; Nubia

When the bishops from Egypt returned home from the Council of Chalcedon they knew what awaited them. "Every district of Egypt will rise up against us," they said. The actions of the council struck Alexandria like a huge wave from the sea. Dioscorus, the patriarch of Alexandria, had been deposed and the council had adopted a formal theological statement using language alien to the Alexandrian tradition. And by reaffirming the privileges of Constantinople as second to Rome, thereby relegating Alexandria to third place, Chalcedon had offended the dignity of the ancient apostolic see of Saint Mark.

Emperor Marcian ordered that an election be held to replace Dioscorus, but the city still recognized him as its "pope" and resisted the consecration of a new bishop. Nevertheless, the imperial will prevailed and the choice fell on a man named Proterius. Though he had been a presbyter under Dioscorus, he was known to be sympathetic to Chalcedon, and many of the faithful felt betrayed.

Marcian died in 457. Within months a group of monks and bishops persuaded a man named Timothy, nicknamed "the Cat," to be consecrated bishop of the "believing community," the non-Chalcedonians. So intense was the feeling against Proterius that the Alexandrian mob, notorious for its violence, seized him in the baptistery of one of the churches in the city and ran him through with a sword. After dragging his body through the streets of the city it was burnt in the hippodrome.

Although Proterius's gruesome death was more sensational, for the future of Christianity in Egypt the consecration of Timothy the Cat was the more portentous action. By installing a second patriarch in Alexandria, a rival to the historic line of bishops, the non-Chalcedonians were establishing an alternative hierarchy. In effect they were creating a parallel church in the city and the region, a precedent that would have far-reaching consequences for the future of Christianity in the Middle

East. Though some remained loyal to Chalcedon and to the imperial Church, the majority of Christians in Egypt stubbornly resisted the "two-nature" terminology of Chalcedon, and they came to be identified as monophysites (or "miaphysites"), those holding to "one nature."* When the Muslims conquered Egypt in the seventh century, most of the people were miaphysites alienated from Constantinople.

Founded by Alexander the Great in 334 B.C., the city of Alexandria had never seemed fully part of Egypt. It was a Greek-speaking city located on a narrow strip of land facing the Mediterranean Sea, separated from the rest of the country by a small lake. To a traveler coming from the south it appeared as an island off the coast of Egypt. To a visitor coming by sea from Constantinople or Rome, it was the gateway to a country that stretched south on a narrow strip of land on either side of the Nile River. The river's annual flood that began in June and lasted until September brought fresh water and rich silt from the highlands of Ethiopia to create a fertile belt hugging the river. In places one can stand on a low rise on one bank of the Nile and look over to the other side where a sharp line divides the green cultivated area near the river and the shimmering sand beyond.

In the heart of the country the language was Coptic, a term based on the Arabic word for Copts, *Qibt*, a shortening of the Greek *Aigyptos* with the initial "ai" and the suffix "os" dropped off. Coptic is the native Egyptian language, the language of the pharaohs that had been written with hieroglyphics, but by the third century of the Christian era it was written in Greek letters. Coptic would become the language of Egyptian Christianity, and the Christians of Egypt are known as the Copts.

Because the city of Alexandria produced so many distinguished Christian teachers and leaders—most famously the biblical scholar and theologian Origen of Alexandria, along with Athanasius, its forceful bishop in the great dispute after Nicaea, and Cyril who defended the theotokos against its detractors—the Greek-speaking Christianity of Alexandria is better known than that of the Christians who spoke Coptic. Beginning in the third century, however, the Coptic-speaking Christians in upper Egypt began to form their own distinctive Christian culture. The Bible was translated into Coptic, and a language that had been spoken largely by peasants and the lower classes became a literary language. Besides original works in Coptic, such as lives of the saints, homilies, and monastic rules, earlier Christian writings written

---

*In Greek, *physis* means "nature," and *monos* means "only" (only one nature); *mia* means one. So the proper term for the non-Chalcedonians is miaphysites, though in past historical writing monophysites has been more widely used. Whatever the term, the non-Chalcedonians did not believe that Christ had only a divine nature. Like the Chalcedonians, they held that he was fully human as well as fully divine, but they thought the expression "two natures" suggested that the divine Logos and the man Christ were two distinct persons, and for that reason they rejected Chalcedon.

in Greek were translated into Coptic and are known to us today only in their Coptic versions. The most notable among these writings is the gnostic library found in the mid twentieth century at Nag Hammadi (Chenoboskion), a city on the west bank of the Nile eighty miles north of Luxor. The early leaders of the monastic movement, Antony and Pachomius, spoke Coptic, and most of the men and women who left their homes to live the solitary life in the deserts of Egypt were Coptic speakers.

The patriarchs of Alexandria had long cultivated relations with the Coptic-speaking monks of upper Egypt. Athanasius had written the famous *Life of Antony* celebrating the solitary life in the Egyptian desert, and in the controversy over the person of Christ, Cyril kept in close touch with the monks to the south. The events of the fifth century cemented the ties between the great city on the Mediterranean and the rest of the country. A little incident at the Council of Ephesus can illustrate the point.

When Cyril sailed to Ephesus he was accompanied by a group of Coptic-speaking monks, among whom was a man named Shenoute, the archimandrite (abbot, or head) of an enormous monastery in upper Egypt. Known as "the prophet" to other monks, he was a man of iron will and great physical strength, and Cyril may have brought him along less for his brains than for his brawn. According to Shenoute's biographer, a fellow monk named Besa, when "impious Nestorius" came into the chamber at the Council of Ephesus, the book of the gospels was lying on a chair. Nestorius picked up the book, set it on the ground and sat in the seat. When Shenoute saw what Nestorius had done he leaped to his feet "in righteous anger," seized the gospel book, and struck Nestorius in the chest, saying, "Do you want the Son of God to sit on the ground while you sit on a chair?" To which Nestorius replied, "What business do you have in the synod? You are certainly not a bishop, nor an archimandrite, or a superior, only a monk." After the encounter, Cyril came up to Shenoute, kissed him, and put a stole on him as archimandrite of a monastery.

The exchange between Shenoute and Nestorius may be a bit of local lore, yet the story is illuminating. For Shenoute was the most powerful monastic leader in Egypt, and he would become a revered figure among Egyptian Christians. His assault on Nestorius symbolizes the deep hostility in Egypt against Nestorius's teaching and the broad support the patriarch of Alexandria had among the monks of Egypt in challenging the patriarch of Constantinople.

Shenoute was born in the mid fourth century in a village in upper Egypt near Akhmin, a town on the Nile some 250 miles south of present-day Cairo and 90 miles north of Luxor. His uncle, Pjol, was superior of a monastery at Sohag, and at a young age Shenoute was entrusted to his care. In the mid 380s, when Shenoute was in his thirties, he became abbot of the monastery. Under his stern and demanding rule the White Monastery—as it is called because of the color of its stone—became a vibrant monastic city of 2,200 men and 1,800 women.

Although Shenoute is one of the most memorable and colorful leaders in early Christian history, his life and accomplishments are not well known. In part this is due to the neglect of sources written in Coptic. Until recently most of our knowledge of early Christian monasticism was based on Greek and Latin writings. He seems to have known Greek, but all his writings are in Coptic. Few of his works have been made available in modern editions, and his elaborate rhetorical style is extremely difficult to render into English.

Shenoute was a forbidding figure whose military-like discipline, including corporal punishment, is alien to modern sensibilities. He has been called "authoritarian," "harsh," even "violent." At the same time he was also a charismatic leader who inspired fierce loyalty and lasting devotion among the many monks of the White Monastery. He lived to be at least 115 years old and ruled over the monastery for seventy years, from his late thirties until his death. No small feat! He was a man of compassion and an advocate of the poor and helpless. When thousands were driven from their homes by a Nubian invasion, Shenoute had his monks provide food, shelter, and medical treatment. The bakeries of the monastery worked day and night, turning out large baskets of loaves of bread for the refugees. Under his leadership the huge monastic complex, with its carpenters, smiths, potters, weavers, basket makers, became a thriving economic center in the region, producing goods and wares more cheaply than craftsmen in the villages.

An energetic evangelist, Shenoute was a fierce critic of the paganism that lingered in the customs of rural Egyptians. He censured the faithful for wearing amulets and talismen, a snake's head tied to the hand, a crocodile's tooth hanging from someone's arm, a fox claw on the leg. In an effort to efface all remnants of the old religion he set his monks to the task of scraping hieroglyphs off the walls of ancient temples, then consecrated them anew as Christian sanctuaries. "Where there was once blasphemy, now blessings and hymns will sound forth," he said.

Shenoute was the first major writer in Coptic, and his letters and sermons display a Christianity stripped of the sophisticated theology of the great thinkers of the early Church. Though he sailed to Ephesus with Cyril to do battle against Nestorius, his spiritual home was rural Egypt, far from the intellectual struggles taking place in the great cities of the empire. The accent was on a disciplined moral life, the virtues of humility, truthfulness, continence, control of anger, repentance, charity. On entry to the monastery one had to agree to a "covenant" promising not to steal, lie, defile the body in any way, bear false witness, or act deceitfully or secretly. Most of the members of the community were poor peasants from the surrounding area, and the monastery offered a precious commodity, order and stability, to their lives.

Yet Shenoute was critical of extreme asceticism, and some even thought he was too lenient. He knew that deprivation of the body was not an end in itself; its aim

was to achieve inner freedom. Understandably, he laid great stress on obedience—
to God as well as to the abbot—and his writings have more to say about the
freedom of the will than about grace. But his sermons are permeated with the Bible,
and his biographer, Besa, says that he "bore Christ," and his "teachings were sweet
in everyone's mouth, like honey to the heart of those who seek to love eternal life."

The White Monastery was organized on the communal, or coenobitic, model
pioneered by Pachomius several generations earlier. The monks lived in individual
houses under the guidance of a housemaster (or housemistress) and spent their
time gathering reeds, making baskets, baking bread, sewing clothes or sandals.
Much of the day was spent in manual labor and prayer. The complex had a central
church, a refectory, and an infirmary, and the monks gathered early in the morning,
an hour and a half before light, for a service of psalms and reading from Scripture.
They took a meal of vegetables and bread once a day in midafternoon, then came
together for another service of psalms and Scripture. Before retiring they gathered
for a vigil service. The Eucharist was celebrated once a week. All the activities of the
monks, time of prayer and meals, work and dress, and living arrangements were
closely regulated and supervised.

Of the more than four thousand monks of the White Monastery at its height,
approximately forty percent were women. There were also children and members of
the same family, though men and women lived separately. Shenoute was the abbot
for the entire community, and the members were called the "people of Apa Shenoute," although he seems to have had difficulty keeping control over the women's
houses. Among his letters there are at least ten that deal directly with problems he
faced dealing with the women. They range from disputes about food and clothing,
homoeroticism among the younger women ("who run after their companions in a
fleshly desire"), resistance to superiors appointed by Shenoute, relations with family members, such as husbands or sons among the male monks, malicious gossip,
jealousy, and the like. In some cases the women rebuffed his interventions.

No doubt similar problems arose among the men, but the women lived apart,
almost as members of daughter houses of the main monastery, and they had their
own women superiors. The physical separation made it more difficult for Shenoute
to exert his authority, and it seems that the women preferred things that way. The
disputes suggest that they wished to shape their own lives as female ascetics independent of the abbot, just as later in the West the practice of "cloister" kept the
bishop at a distance. In the end, however, the structure of authority proved elastic
enough for the monastery to hold together. The bold experiment to build a single
monastic community made up of men and women under one leader continued
under Shenoute's successor, Besa.

The success of Egyptian monasticism was part of the larger growth of a Coptic
Christian culture in Egypt. Beginning in the fourth century, Coptic Egypt entered

on a great period of building. As in other parts of the Christian world, the architectural focus shifted from temples, baths, stadiums, and gymnasia to churches and monasteries. The walls of white stone churches rising up in the towns and villages were an emphatic marker of the new order.

The imprint of the new Egyptian Christian culture is also evident in paintings and tapestries. A fascinating example is a beautiful sixth-century icon of Christ and Saint Menas, an early Egyptian saint. The icon features two figures, Christ on the right and Menas on the left. They stand side by side facing the viewer, the head of each surrounded by a nimbus with a cross superimposed on the nimbus of Christ. Christ holds a book bound in leather decorated with precious stones. The bodies are slightly shortened and their forms disguised by their garments. This simplification of the figures, the enlargement of the heads, and the prominent oval eyes create a strong sense of presence. What is most striking, however, is that Christ rests his arm on Menas's shoulder, almost as one would put an arm around a dear friend. In contrast to the majestic and august representations of Christ in Byzantine art, as a remote figure enthroned in heaven, here he is depicted as touchingly human, making a warm personal gesture.

There is, however, more to this icon than meets the eye. The gesture of a divine figure putting his arm around someone's shoulder is not original with the artist. It can be found on an Egyptian burial shroud from the Saqqara necropolis in Cairo, now in the Pushkin Museum in Moscow. On the shroud one sees the jackal-headed god Anubis standing to the right with his arm over the shoulder of a deceased young man to his left. A third figure is the Egyptian god Osiris. On the icon Christ looks out at the viewer, whereas on the shroud Anubis is looking at the young man as he leads him into the afterlife. The icon of Christ and Menas is clearly Christian, but at the same time it is distinctly Egyptian, using a gesture that is found in Egyptian funerary art. Another example of the Egyptian influence on Coptic Christian art is a statue of the Virgin Mary and Jesus that borrows from Egyptian representations of the female goddess Isis and her offspring Horus.

Because of Egypt's dry climate, many examples of ancient textiles have been preserved there. Several display the transition from the older Egyptian culture to the new Christian culture. As any reader of the Bible knows, Egypt had a major role in the history of the ancient Israelites. The book of Genesis, for example, devotes fourteen chapters to Joseph, the son of Jacob who rose to become governor of Egypt under one of the pharaohs after being abandoned by his brothers. Joseph was a favorite biblical hero among Coptic Christians. Medallions and bands sewn on tunics include incidents from the life of Joseph: Joseph thrown into the pit, his tunic dipped in goat's blood, being sold to the Ishmaelites, and his dreams.

The rejection of the Council of Chalcedon coupled with the emergence of a distinctive Egyptian, or Coptic, national Christian culture, set Egyptian Christianity on a course independent of the imperial Church. These developments would alienate Egypt from Constantinople, but after the Muslim conquest their deep attachment to the Coptic language and culture gave Christians in Egypt the wherewithal to persevere, albeit in reduced numbers, under Muslim rule.

Although Egypt is part of the African continent, it was oriented more toward the Mediterranean world and the Middle East than to Africa. Nubia, however, the region to the south of Egypt, was a land of dark-skinned people who lived in the large area along the Nile stretching from the first cataract at Aswan to the foothills of Ethiopia. At the cataracts the river is shallow and its surface broken by rocks that make it difficult for boats to navigate, and the first cataract had been a political, cultural, and linguistic divide since the time of the pharaohs, cutting off Nubia from the civilizations to the north. Unlike Alexandria and Egypt, where Christianity arrived at the end of the first century, and Ethiopia, which embraced Christianity in the fourth century, the first evidence of Christian penetration in Nubia does not appear until the fifth century, and it is only in the sixth century that the ruling family of one of the Nubian kingdoms was converted.

The first organized mission to Nubia came from Constantinople during the reign of Emperor Justinian (527–565). According to an ancient account, Theodora, Justinian's shrewd and strong-willed wife, an ardent miaphysite, persuaded her husband to send a mission to Nubia. Justinian, however, was a firm adherent of the Council of Chalcedon, and when he learned that the person she had chosen to lead the mission, a presbyter from Alexandria named Julian, was miaphysite, he was displeased. So he wrote a bishop sympathetic to Chalcedon in the Thebaid in upper Egypt with orders to proceed to Nubia, adding that to assist the mission he was sending ambassadors "with gold and baptismal robes and gifts of honor" for the king of the Nubians. Persuasion was not the only tool of evangelization.

But Theodora was a step ahead of the emperor and schemed to have his ambassadors delayed. The result was that Julian arrived in Nubia before the Chalcedonian embassy and was warmly received by the king. When the emperor's representative finally reached the distant kingdom, the new Christian king rejected the "wicked faith" of the Chalcedonians. Not that he would have been able to distinguish one from the other! But he knew who his benefactress was. The king, whose name was Silko, then proceeded to conquer the people to the south on the eastern side of the Nile, and they too adopted Christianity in its miaphysite dress.

In a very short time the traditional culture was displaced by the beliefs and practices of the new faith. Within a generation an old temple at Qasr Ibrim was transformed into a church and, significantly, burial customs also changed. Before the adoption of Christianity, when someone was buried grave goods were included in tombs with the body, but archaeological evidence shows that after Christianity took hold the Nubians buried their dead without objects in the tombs. Within decades of the mission to the Nubians the new faith was adopted by the people of the region as far south as Ethiopia.

Although these new Christian kingdoms were miaphysite, they maintained close ties with the imperial Church in Constantinople, and Byzantine influence is evident in art and architecture. In their liturgy they used Nubian (with some Greek prayers), and the Church became the guardian of national Nubian culture and language.

A spectacular witness to the vibrancy of Nubian Christian culture was discovered at a place named Faras, south of Aswan, in present-day Egypt. The region is now underwater because of the building of the dam that created Lake Nasser, but in the 1960s a team of Polish archaeologists excavated the site. During the Christian period Faras flourished as the capital of one of the Nubian kingdoms, and in the seventh century a large cathedral was built near the Nile. An earlier church of sun-dried brick had stood there, but it was replaced by a much larger and more opulent building. The original church had two rows of columns with three aisles and an apse, but the new building had four rows of columns (as did the Anastasis in Jerusalem), making four aisles and a nave.

But it is not only the grandeur of the building that is imposing. What is even more remarkable is that the walls of the cathedral were covered with well-executed frescoes. A simple listing of some of the subjects depicted indicates the scope of the artistic project: a scene of the nativity of Christ, Madonna and Child with a Nubian princess, Christ being worshiped by two angels, the archangels Gabriel and Michael, Saint Anna, Saint John Chrysostom, the fourth-century bishop and preacher, a cross with symbols of the four evangelists, a bishop named Petros, paintings of other bishops and saints.

The painting of the Madonna and Child with the Nubian princess is particularly memorable. The virgin is a largish figure with a violet mantel decorated with grayish blue spots. Her large eyes are turned toward the child who sits on her arm with his right arm on her shoulder. His eyes are turned toward Mary and in his hand he holds a scroll. His head is surrounded by a nimbus with a cross imposed on it. With both hands the Madonna is holding up a smaller figure, the Nubian princess, whose feet do not touch the ground. She is wearing a gold chain as necklace and a crown with a cross in the middle. The face of the Madonna and the child are cream colored, but the face of the princess is a dark brown. The artist not only wished to paint Mary and Jesus, who were the focus of veneration and worship, he also wanted to represent his own people who were dark-skinned.

The same brownish tones are used for other figures, kings and bishops, who were Nubian. One of the most striking is a painting of Peter, the bishop of Pachoras. It shows the bishop with a dark brown face standing looking at the viewer. Behind and above him stands the apostle Peter, with a cream-colored face and a nimbus around his head. His two hands are resting on the shoulders of Bishop Peter, who holds a gospel book in his left hand and his right hand is raised in blessing with an *encheirion,* a thin strip of embroidered cloth, wrapped around his index finger. Another fresco pictures the Virgin Mary with a cream-colored face standing full front holding the child Jesus. To the left is a Nubian bishop, Marianos, with a light brown face holding a gospel book and his right hand raised in blessing with an encheirion.

The architects of the cathedral were also interested in leaving a record of the history of the church in Faras. On the wall in a chapel of the cathedral the names of twenty-seven of the bishops of the city are recorded with the years of their episcopates. Though the list is not complete, it suggests that the first Nubian bishop about whom information was available was consecrated in 625, less than a century after the mission from Constantinople. The garment worn by one of the bishops marks him as an adherent of the miaphysite tradition.

The cathedral is only one example of the rapid growth of Christianity in the region. Many other churches were built during the eighth and ninth centuries, and Nubian Christian culture reached its zenith in the tenth century. With their own language and cultural traditions, the Nubians were able to resist Muslim advances and remain independent far longer than most territories in the Middle East. But Islam eventually established a strong presence in the northern part of the country. By the twelfth century Christianity in Nubia was in decline, and by the fifteenth century the Nubian language had largely given way to Arabic. Today the memory of these ancient Christian kingdoms lives only among a small company of scholars.

African Zion:
Ethiopia

To the ancient Greeks, Ethiopia was the land of the "burnt-faced people" who lived far to the south of Egypt, near the headwaters of the Blue Nile, the great river that joins the White Nile at Khartoum in Sudan. The Greek historian Herodotus called its people "the most distant of men," and Aeschylus, the ancient Greek playwright, dubbed it a "land far off, a nation of black men . . . who lived hard by the fountain of the sun where is the river Aethiops."

Viewed from the perspective of the Mediterranean world where Christianity first made its way, Ethiopia was indeed a distant land. From Alexandria on the coast of Egypt it is more than fifteen hundred miles by air. But if one comes from Arabia, it is only twenty miles by sea across the Strait of Bab el-Mandeb, which separates the Horn of Africa from present-day Yemen. In antiquity South Arabia and Ethiopia were part of a single Red Sea culture, and the Ethiopians spoke a semitic tongue, Geez, that belongs to the linguistic family including Arabic. In ancient times Ethiopia was reached from Egypt by sailing south down through the Red Sea, landing at one of its ports, and then making one's way up the plateau where its principal city, Aksum, was located.

Ethiopia (including present-day Eritrea) has had a continuous history for more than two thousand years, and for the first seven centuries A.D. Aksum was the center of a prosperous, well-organized, and technologically advanced civilization. It carried on extensive trade with the Arabian peninsula in ivory, rhinoceros horn, tortoise shell, apes, incense, and slaves. The Ptolemies, rulers in Syria during the Hellenistic period, sent out emissaries to Ethiopia to obtain African elephants to be used in warfare.

Yet Ethiopia remains largely unknown in the West, and few realize that it is the home of one of the oldest Christian civilizations. The name occurs several times in the Old Testament, for example in the psalms, "Let Ethiopia hasten to stretch out her hands to God" (Psalms 68:31), and the book of Acts includes the famous story of the conversion of the Ethiopian eunuch. The Ethiopia mentioned in this passage was actually the kingdom of Kush in ancient Nubia (modern-day Sudan), which sits between Egypt and Ethiopia.

According to the Acts of the Apostles, Philip, a Christian deacon who supervised the distribution of food to widows in Jerusalem and had proclaimed the gospel in Samaria (Acts 8:5), was told by an angel to go down the road from Jerusalem to Gaza. On the way he met an Ethiopian, a eunuch, minister to Candace, "queen of the Ethiopians," who had come to Jerusalem to worship and was returning home. The Ethiopian was reading the book of Isaiah, and Philip asked him: "Do you understand what you are reading?" To which the Ethiopian replied: "How can I, unless someone guides me?" The passage he was reading was this: "As a sheep led to the slaughter or a lamb before its shearers is dumb, so he opens not his mouth . . ." (Isaiah 53:7–9). Who is the prophet speaking about, asked the eunuch? In reply Philip told him the "good news of Jesus." As they talked further, they came to some water, and the Ethiopian asked to be baptized. Commanding the chariot to stop, he stepped down and Philip baptized him. When Philip left him, according to Acts, he "went on his way rejoicing" (Acts 8:26–40).

The account in Acts would suggest that the Christian gospel reached distant Ethiopia already in apostolic times. But this account stands alone and has no follow-up in the ancient sources. As far as we know, the Candace mentioned in the story, queen of Meroe in Nubia, did not convert to Christianity, and the faith reached Nubia only in the sixth century through missionaries encouraged by Theodora, wife of Emperor Justinian. Nevertheless the biblical story is noteworthy, for it shows that dark-skinned African people south of Egypt had links to ancient Israel. This memory lives on in the Ethiopian Church, and the Ethiopians are unique among Christian nations in adopting certain Jewish practices and giving ancient Israel a distinctive role in their national epic.

Even if Christianity did not reach Ethiopia in the apostolic age, it did arrive there early. The account of its beginnings can be found in the *Ecclesiastical History* of Rufinus, written at the end of the fourth century. Here is how he tells the story:

Meropius, a Christian philosopher from Tyre, came to Ethiopia accompanied by two boys he was tutoring named Frumentius and Aedesius. Their goal was India, and as they followed the customary route along the African coast of the Red Sea they ran short of provisions and put in at a port, most likely Adulis. The local inhabitants, however, were hostile to outsiders, and they killed Meropius and everyone aboard the ship, sparing only the two boys, who became slaves of the king of Aksum. Over time they won his confidence, and Aedesius became his cup-bearer and Frumentius was made secretary and treasurer.

On the death of the king, Frumentius and Aedesius were given leave to return to their own country, but the queen mother begged them to remain to help her administer the kingdom until her son grew up. The young men agreed, and as the years passed Frumentius sought out Christians among the merchants settled at Aksum and the port, encouraging them to establish meeting places for prayer. The young king himself became a convert and offered royal support and buildings for Christian worship.

When the king was old enough to rule the country alone, Frumentius and Aedesius asked him for permission to leave. Aedesius returned home to Tyre, but Frumentius went to Alexandria and laid the whole affair before the newly appointed patriarch, Athanasius, begging him to appoint a bishop to minister to the needs of the growing Christian community at Aksum. Athanasius summoned a council of clergy, and it was agreed that no one was more suited to the task than Frumentius, who was then consecrated the first bishop of Ethiopia, probably in the late 340s. On his return he took the name Abba Selama, "Father of Peace."

Rufinus ends his account by assuring the reader that he had gained information about Ethiopia from Aedesius himself, not third hand, and his narrative of the beginning of Christianity, at least in its general outline, is confirmed by other sources. The name of Frumentius, for example, is mentioned in a letter of the emperor Constantius II (337–361) to King Ezana of Ethiopia, and an Ethiopian inscription from this period attributes Ezana's victories in war not to the tutelary god Mahrem, but to "the Lord of the Heavens who has power over all beings in heaven and on earth." It seems, then, that the introduction of Christianity to Ethiopia took place during the reign of King Ezana (320–356), who goes down in history as the first African king to embrace the Christian faith and adopt it as the religion of his people.

Two things are worth observing. First, the bishop of Aksum was consecrated by Athanasius, the patriarch of Alexandria in Egypt. This meant that Ethiopia would be closely linked to the Egyptian Church, and its principal bishop would be appointed by the bishop of Alexandria. In fact, until recent times the bishop was an Egyptian. The close ties to Egypt also explain why the Ethiopian Church, which was not part of the great dispute over the person of Christ in the fifth century, aligned itself with the non-Chalcedonian communions, the miaphysites.

Second, the conversion of Ethiopia follows a pattern that would mark the Church's mission in the centuries to come. During the first three centuries Christianity spread slowly in the Roman world, from the ground up, as men and women, through personal contacts, family, neighbors, and friends, learned of Christ and eventually asked to be enrolled as catechumens and be baptized. But beginning in the fourth century and extending for the next six or seven centuries, Christianity was established from the top down. First the king or queen was attracted to the new faith—not always for spiritual reasons—and after the baptism of the king the people were baptized, often en masse. There were no revivals, no individual conversions; conversion was a communal event that encompassed the people as a whole.

A sign of the cultural shift appears early in coins minted by Ethiopian kings. Ethiopia was the first African country in antiquity to issue gold coins, rare for any kingdom. The only other gold coins were minted in the Roman Empire and in the Persian Empire. Before the adoption of Christianity, the coins bore an image of the king and a disc or a crescent, divine symbols, above the king. But following the conversion of King Ezana, a cross appears above his head. On one coin there are four crosses, and on another a single cross sits at the center of the coin with the legend, "May this please the country," "this" referring to the cross. In the same period inscriptions begin to appear with the legend, "In the faith of God and the power of the Father and the Son and the Holy Spirit." One coin from the late fourth century pictures the king with a cross above his head and a cross on the reverse side, with a small center of gold surrounded by a beaded circle and the legend, "By this cross you shall conquer."

In the early years Christianity in Ethiopia was restricted to the port city of Adulis and a narrow corridor between Adulis and the capital at Aksum. But in the late fifth century a group of monks, known as the Nine Saints, came from the Roman Empire and began to spread the faith in the villages and rural areas. It is likely that they were opponents of the doctrinal decree of the Council of Chalcedon and were seeking to widen the outreach of what was becoming a separate Christian communion. Besides their missionary efforts they also planted the first monasteries in Ethiopia, using the rule of Pachomius, the Egyptian monk who had organized solitary monks into communal houses.

They also began to translate the Bible from Greek into Geez, the language of the Ethiopians. Here too they established a pattern that would be repeated by missionaries in the East, namely to put the Bible, the liturgy, and the lives of the saints into the vernacular, the language of the people. In the West, as we shall see, the monks took a quite different approach: they retained the Latin language for worship and for rituals such as baptism, and they taught the new converts Latin.

Christianity grew steadily in Ethiopia, and by the sixth century a traveler reported that everywhere in the country there were "churches of the Christians . . . where the gospel of Christ was proclaimed." So vital was the Christian kingdom of Ethiopia to Christianity in the region that Justin, the Byzantine emperor (518–527), wrote to Caleb (note the Old Testament name, from Numbers 14), the king of Aksum, to come to the aid of Christians being persecuted in the kingdom of Yemen. Evidence of Christians in the Arabian peninsula goes back at least to the third century. Eusebius mentions a bishop from Bostra, at the head of the Persian Gulf. But Yemen is located in the most southern part of the peninsula, on the

Arabian Sea. Christianity had spread among the Arabic-speaking tribes in the peninsula in the fourth century primarily through the presence of monks who had penetrated deep into the desert. Several ancient sources mention a monk named Moses whose holy life so impressed the head of an Arab tribe that he was allowed to live among them. Some of the Arabs were converted to Christianity.

The most extensive documentation of Arabic-speaking Christians in the Arabian peninsula before the rise of Islam comes from Yemen. By the sixth century there was a well-established Arabic-speaking Christian community in Najran with a full ecclesiastical organization, bishop, presbyters, deacons, and deaconesses. In the fourth century the region had come under the control of the Aksumite kingdom of Ethiopia. Sometime about 520, however, a South Arabian prince named Dhu Nawas carried out a successful revolt against the Ethiopians. He had converted to Judaism and knew Christians in the region were sympathetic to the Ethiopians. He also hoped to convert the people in his kingdom, including the Christians, to Judaism. When the people of Najran refused, he laid siege to the city and offered the residents a choice, either conversion or death. The Christians were asked to declare that "Christ is a man and not God." He treacherously promised to grant the Christians amnesty if they surrendered, but then gathered them into a church, barred the doors, and set fire to the building. Many were martyred, including Arethas, the leader of the Christians, and a prominent woman named Ruhayma. By good fortune we have a full account of the persecution and a list with the names of three hundred martyrs. Significantly, most of the names are Arab.

The Arabian peninsula was a significant buffer between the Persian Empire and the Byzantines, and the Arabic-speaking Christians had been shielded by the Byzantines. When the emperor Justin in Constantinople learned of the massacre he wrote to Caleb, the Ethiopian king, and asked him to intervene on behalf of the Christians in Yemen. Caleb overthrew and killed Dhu Nawas, but he was not able to restore Aksumite rule. With the rise of Islam, Christianity in the Arabian peninsula went into decline.

By the time of the rise of Islam, Ethiopia was a strong and vibrant Christian kingdom in the Horn of Africa, with hegemony over southern Arabia. When Islam spread through the region in the seventh century, Ethiopia, unlike Syria and Egypt, was not conquered. It may have been spared because an Ethiopian king had come to the aid of the prophet Muhammad at a difficult period in his life. When the first disciples of Muhammad were being persecuted by their fellow Arabs, Muhammad sent some of the members of his family and disciples to safety in Ethiopia. In A.D. 615 they arrived across the Strait of Bab el-Mandeb and were warmly received by the Christian king of Ethiopia. Among the group were Muhammad's son-in-law, Uthman ibn Affan, his daughter Ruqayya, and two of his future wives. The total company numbered about a hundred. The Prophet was much gratified by the support and kindness of the Ethiopians, also known as Abyssinians, and said that they should be left in peace.

Ethiopian Christianity has certain Judaic features that are not present in other Christian communions of the East. The Ethiopians observe Saturday as a holy day, not only Sunday. They follow Old Testament rules regarding ritual cleanliness, especially in sexual relations, observe certain dietary laws, and circumcise male children on the eighth day. Another distinctive feature of Ethiopian Christianity is its Bible. The "canon" of scriptural books is larger than the canon accepted in the Greek and Latin churches. The traditional canon of the Old Testament follows the Septuagint, which includes such books as Wisdom, Sirach, Judith, Susanah, 1 and 2 Esdras, and the four books of Maccabees. But the Ethiopian canon includes several other books, notably Enoch, Jubilees, and the Ascension of Isaiah. In fact, a number of these ancient Jewish books have come down to us only in the Ethiopian language. The canon of New Testament books is also broader and includes such early Christian writings as the Shepherd of Hermas and 1 and 2 Clement.

Scholars have debated the historical origins of these Judaic features of Ethiopian Christianity. Was it a matter of imitating Old Testament practices, or were there direct Jewish influences? The question cannot be answered. It is possible that Ethiopian Christians learned of these customs from Jews living in Ethiopia or the Arabian peninsula, but the "Judaizing" features of Ethiopian Christianity may have been embraced from a literal reading of the Old Testament. They appear only later in the history of the Ethiopian Church.

Still it is clear that something unique had arisen among Ethiopian Christians. For the Ethiopians claimed the mantle of ancient Israel. This identification is most evident in the national epic, *Kebra Nagast* (Glory of the Kings), which builds on the scriptural account of the queen of Sheba and King Solomon (1 Kings 10:1–13) and apocryphal literature, such as the book of Enoch. According to the Bible, when the queen of Sheba heard of the fame of Solomon she came to Jerusalem with a great retinue, camels bearing spices, much gold, and many precious stones. She had heard of his wisdom and wanted to "test him with hard questions." King Solomon was able to answer her questions, and when the queen of Sheba had "seen all his wisdom" and the house he had built, the food of his table, his many attendants, the temple and the sacrifices in the house of the Lord, "there was no more spirit in her." Solomon lavishly bestowed gifts on the queen and "gave her all that she desired." So she returned to her own land.

In *Kebra Nagast,* the queen of Sheba is identified with Makeda, the queen of Aksum, who learns from a merchant about the wisdom of Solomon. Crossing the Red Sea, she travels to Jerusalem where she meets King Solomon. So impressed is she with Solomon's wisdom that she embraces the religion of the Israelites. "From this moment I will not worship the sun, but will worship the Creator of the sun, the

God of Israel." Solomon shared more than his wisdom with the queen. When she departed she was pregnant, and Solomon gave her a ring so that the child could identify himself to Solomon. On her return to Ethiopia the queen gave birth to a son named Menelik.

Years later, when the boy was in his twenties, he returned to Jerusalem and met his father. He was anointed king, and Solomon tried to persuade him to remain in Jerusalem. But Menelik wished to return home. Before departing he was given instruction in Jewish law, and when he returned to Ethiopia he brought with him a company of Israelite families. On the journey home Menelik discovered that the Israelites had brought the Ark of the Covenant, a small wooden chest containing the two tablets of the law.

Christians in other parts of the world had long appropriated the history of Israel as their own and saw its fulfillment in Christ and the growth of the Church. Eusebius, for example, begins his chronicle of world history with Abraham, and in Augustine's *City of God* the historical career of the city of God begins with biblical history. But Ethiopia created a past in which there is a direct line of descent from King Solomon to Ethiopian kings. Ethiopia was the "new Israel" not only in a spiritual sense, but physically, because its rulers were descended from Solomon. The presence of the Ark of the Covenant gave the Ethiopian kings a preeminent position among Christian kings. Ethiopian tradition believes that one of its first churches, Our Lady of Zion, contained the Ark of the Covenant.

Replicas of the ark became a distinctive feature of Ethiopian churches. When a new church is consecrated, the bishop gives the people a "tabot," a replica of the Ark and the tablets of the law. It is kept in a special place and on certain festivals it is carried about accompanied by song and dance, as David and the legendary king Menelik son of Solomon danced before the ark.

Ethiopia is a particularly vivid example of the way Christianity took distinctive shape as it was embraced by different peoples. Though Ethiopia was influenced by Egyptian Christianity, and was neighbor to Nubia, it created its own distinct Christian culture. The historian Peter Brown coined the phrase "micro-Christendoms" to describe this phenomenon. Each national church possessed all the marks of Christian faith, bishops, creed, liturgy, Scripture, sacraments, monasticism, and in this sense created an entire Christian world, yet the form that Christian life and institutions took varied profoundly.

Ethiopia remained independent in another sense. Even though it was in the cultural orbit of Arabia, it was never conquered by the Muslims. The two countries to the north, Nubia and Egypt, succumbed early, as did greater Syria. But Ethiopia is the only nation in the Middle East that withstood the advance of Islam and did not become subject to Muslim rule. When Ethiopian Christianity was first "discovered" by travelers from the West, they were astounded by what they saw. A visitor from Counter-Reformation Portugal in the seventeenth century had this to say: "No country in the world is so full of churches, monasteries, and ecclesiastics as Abyssinia; it is not possible to sing in one church without being heard in another, and perhaps by several. . . . [T]his people has a natural disposition to goodness; they are very liberal of their alms, they much frequent their churches, and are very studious to adorn them; they practice fasting and other mortifications. . . . [They] retain in a great measure the devout fervor of the primitive Christians."

Syriac-Speaking Christians:
The Church of the East

Unlike the Egyptian bishops who left Chalcedon in defeat, many from Syria, particularly in the orbit of Antioch, returned home with the satisfaction that the "two natures" formula was now enshrined in a solemn declaration of an imperial council. One bishop in particular had reason to rejoice. His name was Ibas, the Syriac-speaking bishop of the city of Edessa, east of Antioch. An energetic spokesman for the Antiochene tradition and a sharp critic of Cyril, Ibas had been deposed by Dioscorus at the "Robber Council" in Ephesus in 449. But two years later at Chalcedon he was restored to his office.

Ibas was a minor player in the great controversy over the person of Christ, although a letter he wrote at the time was the subject of heated debate at the council and was eventually condemned at another council a hundred years after Chalcedon. The significance of the letter, however, is more cultural than doctrinal; it was written in Syriac and addressed to Mari, who was the principal bishop of the Christian community in the Persian Empire. Ibas had been appointed by the bishop of Antioch, but Antioch was located to the west, near the Mediterranean. There the language was Greek, though on market days the streets were crowded with Syriac-speaking peasants from the countryside. As one traveled eastward into ancient Mesopotamia, the region between the Euphrates and Tigris Rivers, the landscape was dotted with Syriac-speaking towns and villages.

Edessa, where Ibas lived, was located a little over 150 miles northeast of Antioch, in the most eastern region of present-day Turkey. Sitting at the top of the Fertile Crescent in the plain between the Tigris and the Euphrates, it was on the route from Mesopotamia to the Mediterranean coast. Abraham is believed to have traveled through the region on his way from Ur of the Chaldees near the Persian Gulf to the Promised Land. One road came down from Armenia, heading south to Harran, and another ran eastward along the Silk Road to Persia (Iraq and Iran), India, and China. By the sixth century the region east of Edessa, Tur Abdin, the mountain of the servants of God, was the home of dozens of monasteries.

In the first century B.C., Edessa had become the capital of an independent kingdom, but as the Roman Empire expanded eastward the city came under Roman hegemony. In the third century a new ruling family, the Sasanids, came to power in Persia and established a vast empire stretching from Sogdiana in Central Asia south to Arabia, and east all the way to China. From the middle of the third century until the Muslim conquest in the seventh, Persia was Rome's most formidable foe. As the two great powers vied for domination in the region, Edessa was drawn one way and then another. By the time Ibas became bishop in the 430s, Edessa was part of the Roman Empire, though its Christians had strong ties to the Syriac-speaking community in the Sasanid Empire.

In Edessa a semitic form of Christianity arose that differed from that of the Greek- and Latin-speaking Christianity in the lands encircling the Mediterranean. The Syriac poet Ephrem (d. 373), whose divine hymns we have already encountered, spent his last years in Edessa. Ephrem stands at the beginning of the Syriac literary tradition. Its flowering came later, with such writers as Narsai (d. 503), a poet and biblical commentator, and Jacob of Serug (d. 521), also a poet and bishop. But all looked back to Ephrem and drew on his writings. His hymns became part of the Syriac liturgy and set the standard for later Syriac hymnography, and his influence spread far beyond the Syriac Christian world. Ephrem lived before Syriac Christians had extensive contact with Greek thought and represents an original form of Christian thinking whose language, manner of expression, and patterns of thought are semitic.

Twenty years after Ephrem died, Jerome reported that he was so revered in the West that his writings were "read in some churches after the scriptural readings." Some were translated into Greek, and Jerome had read a work of his on the Holy Spirit. Even in translation Jerome could recognize Ephrem's "lofty intellect." Another Western writer, Palladius, called Ephrem the "greatest ornament of the Catholic Church." In a translation of Palladius's book into Syriac several centuries later, the translator adds a paragraph of his own in which he tells of a dream of "one of the holy fathers." A band of angels had brought a scroll down from heaven at God's behest, asking to whom it should be entrusted. Some said one person, others another, but finally they all said: "No one can be entrusted with this apart from Ephrem," for "Ephrem teaches as if a fountain was flowing from his mouth."

In the controversy over Christ in the fifth century, Rabbula, the bishop of Edessa, had supported the condemnation of Nestorius, the patriarch of Constantinople, at the Council of Ephesus in 431. But when Ibas became bishop in 435 he favored the teaching of Theodore of Mopsuestia. Theodore had died in 428 on the eve of the controversy between Cyril and Nestorius, but his writings influenced the thinking of Cyril's opponents, including Nestorius, John the bishop of Antioch, and Theodoret the bishop of Cyrrhus, a Greek-speaking city among Syriac-speaking Christians northeast of Antioch. So revered was the bishop of Mopsuestia as a biblical commentator that he was called simply "the Interpreter," and in his letter to Mari, Ibas calls him "the blessed Theodore, a preacher of the truth and teacher of the faith." Many of his writings have come down to us only in Syriac translations.

At his death Theodore was a respected bishop and scholar held in high regard by other bishops in the imperial Church. But because he had written polemical works against Cyril, his reputation suffered a reversal after his death. Some of his writings were eventually condemned. Yet to many it seemed that the decree at Chalcedon vindicated his teaching, or at least supported his interpretation of the language of two natures. As Cyril became the authoritative teacher for the Copts in Egypt, Theodore became the teacher par excellence of Syriac Christians in the Sasanid Empire and Central Asia. There is some irony here; Cyril and Theodore both wrote in Greek.

Because Chalcedon became the standard of orthodoxy in the Byzantine world (and also in Rome), the Copts became alienated from the Greek and Latin churches. In Syria, however, the situation was more complex. By the beginning of the sixth century the bishops in western Syria, the region closer to the Mediterranean, had become critics of Chalcedon and looked to Cyril as their teacher. Even Antioch, Alexandria's theological rival in the fifth century, came over to the miaphysite side in the early sixth century during the patriarchate of Severus (512–518), a disciple and defender of Cyril's teaching.

The controversies of the fifth century shattered the tenuous unity of Christianity in the East, and the one Church confessed in the Nicene Creed ("I believe in one holy catholic and apostolic Church") was on its way to division into several distinct communions, each with its own hierarchy:

> 1. Those who held to the Council of Chalcedon. In the Middle East these Christians, many of whom spoke Syriac, came to be called Melkites, from the Syriac word for king or emperor, because they were in communion with the emperor in Constantinople. There was also another Chalcedonian communion, the Maronites, named after a monk called Maro who died in the early fifth century. After his death a monastery was founded in northern Syria, and during the controversy over Christ these monks and their followers accepted the Council of Chalcedon.
>
> 2. The Copts in Egypt, who now had their own patriarch, distinct from the Chalcedonian patriarch. The Copts were joined by the west Syrians, those living in the vicinity of Antioch, in the early sixth century. They came to

be called Jacobites, because Jacob Baradeus, bishop of Edessa (543–578) traveled throughout the region consecrating bishops and establishing an independent hierarchy in Syria. With the Copts they formed the second major grouping, the non-Chalcedonians, or miaphysites.

3. The Syriac-speaking Christians in the Sasanid Persian Empire and Central Asia. They are often called Nestorians, because they rejected the Council of Ephesus in 431, where Nestorius was deposed, but the proper term for this large body of Christians is the Church of the East. Their patriarch, or *catholicos,* resided at Seleucia-Ctesiphon, a city occupying both sides of the Tigris, and later at Baghdad.

Because the city of Edessa had become part of the Roman Empire, it was under constant pressure from Constantinople to conform to the doctrinal standards of the imperial Church even as the emperors tilted one way, then another. In 489 the emperor Zeno, in an effort to end the divisions caused by the controversy, drove from the city those teachers and students who held to the teachings of Theodore of Mopsuestia. They fled to Nisibis, a Syriac-speaking city northeast of Edessa where Ephrem was born, today known as Nusaybin in eastern Turkey, where they established a new school.

The school at Nisibis played a key role in the life of the Church of the East. Its reputation reached to the Latin West, and in the sixth century in southern Italy, Cassiodorus (d. 580) modeled his educational program on it. With its own building, faculty, and formal rules for instruction, the school of Nisibis provided elementary instruction in grammar as well as advanced training in reading and interpretation. Students began with the psalms, and as they progressed they studied the commentaries of Theodore on the Scriptures.

Though the school of Nisibis offered a disciplined intellectual program of study, its goal was not simply to understand the Scriptures; the aim was to form the lives and morals of the students. Like a monastic community, the company of students and faculty had a regular regime of prayer, meditation, and worship. Reading was a kind of ritual act in which the Scripture was relived through recitation. The importance of chantlike recitation among Syriac Christians is illustrated by an account of the dedication of a church in the monastery of Beth Abhe, some twenty-five miles east of Mosul in present-day Iraq. At the celebration of the "Holy Mysteries" during the dedication, a monk named Jacob was asked to go to the lectern and read the psalms; at the same time, there was "a learned priest who had gone out to the porch of the church to meditate upon the outline of the sermon" he was preparing to deliver. "But when the deacon, Mar Jacob, had begun to recite the psalm, the sweetness of his voice so greatly attracted the attention and mind of everyone, that the eyes of all were fixed upon him and were looking at him." When he had finished his psalm, and had come down from the lectern, the learned priest cried out with a loud voice: "Fie on you, young man, for the sweetness of your voice and the beautiful manner of your singing have driven out of my mind the thoughts which I had wished to gather together."

Over the generations Syriac-speaking Christians in the Sasanid Empire forged a distinct sense of their identity. This was the work of geography, politics, and religion. When the Sasanids overthrew the former rulers, the Parthians, they established Zoroastrianism as the official religion of the kingdom. Zoroastrianism was an Iranian religion that traced its roots back to Zoroaster (Zarathustra), who lived in the second millennium B.C. Its distinctive feature was the worship of the one god Ahura Mazda, creator of the universe, and the twin spirits Spenta Mainyu and Angra Mainyu, the first one good and beneficent, the latter evil and destructive. Human history is a tale of the cosmic struggle between these two spirits. The Zoroastrians had a singular devotion to fire as one of the seven good creations of Ahura Mazda. Fire was the symbol of God, who is "pure undefiled light," and they built temples in which a fire burned continuously. To stand before the fire was to be in the presence of God. For Christians living in the Persian Empire, the advent of Zoroastrianism as the official religion would eventually lead to persecution.

When Constantine became emperor of the Roman Empire it appeared to the Sasanid rulers that Christianity was the official religion of the Roman world. As a result, Christians came under suspicion for being devoted to a religion practiced by a foreign and rival kingdom, that of the Romans. As emperor, Constantine assumed he had responsibility for all Christians wherever they lived, and in an imprudent letter to Shapur II, the Sasanid king, he asked him to look after the Christians in his realm. Constantine wrote that the "fairest districts of Persia" are filled with Christians, and prayed that they might enjoy prosperity and that Shapur "will experience the mercy and favor of that God who is the Lord and Father of all." With this kind of intercession by the Roman emperor it is understandable that Christianity was called the "religion of Caesar" by the Sasanids, and shortly after Constantine came to power the Persian rulers doubled the tax on the "Nazarenes." When the head of the Christian community refused to agree to the increase, he was arrested and executed.

Two factors led to the persecution, the suspicion that Christians were loyal to Persia's historic enemy, Rome, and the clash between Zoroastrianism and Christianity. In a revealing official document the Sasanid king had this to say about Christianity: "These Christians destroy our Holy Teaching, and teach men to serve one God, and not to honor the Sun or Fire. They defile water by their ablutions, they refrain from marriage and the propagation of children, and refuse to go to war with the King of Kings [the Sasanid ruler]. They have no rules about the slaughter and eating of animals; they bury the corpses of men in the earth. They attribute the origin of snakes and creeping things to a good God. They despise many servants of the King and teach witchcraft."

The persecution lasted for more than two decades, beginning in 341, and some reckon the number of martyrs in the thousands. But with the death of King Shapur in 379, the Christians enjoyed a period of toleration, and under later rulers they were granted the right to follow their way of life as a legitimate religious community within the empire. The *catholicos,* the head of the Church in the Sasanid Empire, was officially recognized by the emperor and made responsible for the conduct of Christians in the realm. A mixed blessing indeed! The churches were also asked to pray for the welfare of the "king of kings," the honorific title of the Sasanid ruler. The Church of the East, like the Church in the Roman Empire, had passed through the fires of persecution stronger and more confident of its place—restricted to be sure—within the Persian Empire.

With the return of peace, the Church in Persia worked to solidify its identity as a distinct Christian communion, one in faith with the Church in the Roman Empire, but ecclesiastically independent. In 410 at a conference in Seleucia-Ctesiphon the bishops in Persia met in their first official council. Under the leadership of its principal bishop, Izhaq, the council adopted the creed and canons of the Councils of Nicaea (in 325) and Constantinople (in 381). In another council, in 424, the bishops in Persia ruled that they were able to govern themselves without interference from the West. Initially the Christians in Persia were under the jurisdiction of Antioch, but now they declared that they would manage their own affairs. No longer, they said, shall any matters be referred to the "western patriarchs," those in the Roman Empire. The "catholicos of the East" would not be judged by those under him or by another patriarch. At the end of the sixth century the catholicos took the title "patriarch" of the Church of the East, and the bishops invoked Christ's words to Peter, "on this rock [*petra*] I will build my church" (Matthew 16:18), acclaiming him as "our own Peter."

In the telling of the early history of Christianity it is customary to highlight the role of the major cities, Alexandria, Antioch, Rome, and Constantinople, all of which eventually were accorded the title of patriarchate. And as the centuries passed, Rome and Constantinople, the one in the West with its face turned toward northern Europe, and the other in the Greek-speaking East facing the Slavs in the Balkans and Russia, symbolize the two great cultural and ecclesiastical worlds of Christianity. But this way of remembering the Christian past is myopic, for it ignores the other major center of Christianity in the East, the Church centered in the Sasanid Empire.

The Church of the East kept its own counsel in its internal affairs. A good example is the marriage of bishops. Celibacy was of course a necessary condition for the monastic life, but neither in the West nor in the East was it required of the clergy. By the fifth century, however, celibacy was widespread among the clergy across the Christian world, especially bishops, and a controversy erupted in the Church of the East over the marriage of bishops. At a council in the year 486 under the presidency of Acacius, who was the catholicos at the time, the Persian bishops adopted a canon approving the marriage of bishops. It affirmed the right of all Christians to marry, whether laymen, priests, or bishops, though following ancient custom it ruled that a priest or bishop could not be married after ordination.

In defense of their action the bishops offered support from the Scriptures, citing the words of Saint Paul to Timothy: "If anyone aspires to the office of bishop, he desires a noble task. Now a bishop must be above reproach, married only once . . ." (1 Timothy 3:1–2). They also said that enforcing celibacy on those who are not called to the solitary life had led to abuse and immoral behavior, citing the authority of Saint Paul: "It is better to marry than to burn" (1 Corinthians 7:9). No doubt the attitudes and sensibilities of Persian society were a factor in the council's decision. The practice of virginity irked the Persians. The people looked down on celibate clergy, and some took the practice as a repudiation of Persian culture. In any case the council's decision was another instance of the independence of the Church of the East from the imperial Church.

The Church of the East moved in a different cultural environment from Christians in the Roman Empire, and its geographical location gave it a unique place in Christian history. The center of the Church of the East was in the lowlands and hill country on the eastern side of the Tigris River, in present-day Iraq, but it reached much farther east. If one looks at a map of the Middle East today, the Church of the East was spread across southeastern Turkey, Azerbaijan, Iraq, Kuwait, eastern Saudi Arabia, Bahrain, the United Arab Emirates, Oman, Iran, Turkmenistan, Uzbekistan, and Afghanistan. It had a large vision of the Christian mission, and its monks and bishops carried the gospel to lands far more distant than those reached by missionaries from the Latin-speaking West or the Greek-speaking East. As we shall see in a later chapter, Syriac-speaking Christians from the Church of the East brought the new faith as far away as India, China, and islands in the Indian Ocean, including Ceylon (Sri Lanka).

Armenia and Georgia

Armenia is a large mountainous region west of the Caspian Sea and north of Mesopotamia (Iraq), bordering eastern Anatolia (Turkey). It is a land of lofty mountain ranges and river valleys with few lowlands. The average altitude is 5,900 feet above sea level, and its most famous geological feature is Mount Ararat, a towering peak of 16,000 feet, where according to the book of Genesis (8:4) the Ark of Noah came to rest when the floodwaters receded. The region around the great saline sea, Lake Van, was inhabited as early as the thirteenth century B.C., but it was not until the first century B.C. that a strong independent kingdom was established. Under Tigranes the Great (95–55 B.C.), the Armenian empire stretched from the Caspian Sea to the Mediterranean.

In the early centuries of the Christian era Armenia was divided into three distinct geographical areas. The western region, known as Armenia Minor, had been incorporated into the Roman Empire in the first century A.D. The second, to the east, was linked culturally and politically to Persia, and when the Roman emperor Jovian ceded the territory to Persia in the fourth century it became part of the kingdom ruled by the Sasanids. The third area, to the south, was linked culturally to the Aramaic-speaking world of Mesopotamia. These cultural and political factors had a profound influence on the development of Christianity among the Armenian people.

In his *Ecclesiastical History,* Eusebius says that there were Christians in Armenia at the beginning of the fourth century, but how Christianity first reached Armenia is uncertain. The traditional account dates the conversion of the Armenian people to the efforts of a man named Gregory ("the Illuminator"), the son of an Armenian nobleman. According to an early Armenian historian, Gregory's father was put to death for assassinating the king, but the boy's life was spared and he was taken to the city of Caesarea in Asia Minor to be raised among Christians. When he reached maturity he returned to Armenia, joined the army, and eventually worked his way up to become secretary to the king. But when Gregory refused to sacrifice to Anahit, the goddess of fertility venerated by the Armenians, the king, Tiridates III (d. 330), was enraged and confined Gregory to an underground dungeon.

Gregory was kept in prison for more than a decade, but on his release he was brought before the ailing king, whom he miraculously healed. In gratitude the king and his court embraced Christianity, and Gregory returned to Caesarea where he was consecrated bishop. He came back to Armenia in A.D. 314 to baptize the king and the people in the Euphrates River. At once Tiridates set about destroying the pagan shrines and building churches across the land. Gregory consecrated other bishops, who adopted the creed and canons of the Council of Nicaea.

This account is a bit too tidy. It sheds light on certain aspects of the early history, notably the close ties between the western Armenians and the Greek-speaking Christians of Anatolia. And it highlights the importance of Gregory's family. For over a hundred years the head of the Armenian Church, the catholicos, would be one of Gregory's descendants. Bishops in Armenia were married. But Christianity also entered Armenia from the Syriac-speaking area around Edessa to the south before the consecration of Gregory as the first bishop of the Armenians. In the early years the semitic influence was more profound than the Greek due to the proximity of Armenia to the Syriac-speaking Christians to the south and to the east in the Persian Empire.

In contrast to the urban culture of the Roman Empire, with its rich literary traditions, Armenia was largely rural and its literature was made up of heroic oral epics. Christian faith required books, and the spread and establishment of Christianity among a new people needed a written language. In Armenia in the early decades the language of the liturgy and the Scripture was Greek or Syriac, and an interpreter translated the readings into Armenian for the "oafish peasants," as one ancient historian put it. The practice was similar to the custom in synagogues of Aramaic-speaking Jews. There readings from the Torah in Hebrew were translated orally into Aramaic. Eventually some were written down (called *targums*), and these can be read today.

The translations into Armenian, however, were not written because there was no Armenian script. If Christianity was to put down deep roots among the Armenians and create a Christian culture, a written language was essential. The problem was felt most keenly by an extraordinary Armenian named Mashtots, who was born in 361 in Hatsekats. He was learned in Greek, Syriac, and Persian and had been employed in the chancery of the king drafting official documents, royal decrees, and letters. But he was also an intensely spiritual person, and eventually he left the chancery to become a monk.

According to his biographer, Mashtots spent much of his time living alone in the mountains, sleeping on the ground, fasting, and practicing techniques of mystical prayer. But he kept his ties with the court, and when he learned that a Syrian bishop named Daniel had proposed a set of letters for writing Armenian to the king based on a semitic script, he became interested in the project. For two years Mashtots worked with a group of students to write down the Armenian language using the letters. But when they read and reread what they had written for legibility and ease of understanding, they concluded that the proposed alphabet was not suitable for Armenian.

Mashtots then visited other places as an itinerant monk, and in Edessa, while caught up in ecstatic prayer, he had a vision of a different set of letters. He was, however, a practical man and realized that before he could actually put the letters to work transcribing Armenian he needed the help of a calligrapher to give them proper form. In the city of Samosata in Syria he met a Greek scholar by the name of Rufinus, who showed him how to write the strokes clearly and simply.

He engaged two students to help him, and they began to translate the Scriptures into Armenian. The first book of the Bible to be translated was Proverbs, which begins with the words, "To know wisdom and instruction, to perceive the words of understanding." Proverbs seems an unusual choice as the first book to be translated, and modern scholars are puzzled as to why it was selected. Yet Christianity is a form of wisdom, and wisdom sayings, whether from Proverbs, the Psalms, Wisdom of Solomon, or Sirach, had a central place in Christian life, especially among the monks. So it is perhaps an inspired choice to begin with the wisdom of Proverbs.

When Mashtots returned to Armenia, it was said that he was received like Moses coming down from Mount Sinai with the Ten Commandments. He set about the task of teaching the letters to the people so they could become familiar with the "laws and commandments" that set Christians off from those who lived around them. The creation of an Armenian alphabet made it possible for the Armenian Christians to have their own religious books, the Scriptures, commentaries on the Bible, and the lives of the saints, to celebrate the liturgy in Armenian, and to translate other Christian writings from Greek and Syriac. In time they produced original writings in Armenian. As an ancient Armenian writer put it, a fountain of divine knowledge was opened up for the Armenian people and the "world sustaining gospel became Armenian speaking."

The new alphabet was a huge success. By the end of the fifth century, less than a hundred years after its creation, there were Armenian monks living in the Judean desert east of Jerusalem reciting the psalms in Armenian. Although Armenia was a long way from Jerusalem, Armenian solitaries had been drawn to the Judean desert near the holy city of Jerusalem. The first and most famous Armenian monk was Euthymius (known as "the great" among Eastern Christians), who made the long journey from his native land to settle permanently in the desert of Jesus and John the Baptist at the beginning of the fifth century. Through his humble and rustic life, Euthymius drew dozens, then hundreds, finally thousands to the desert east of Jerusalem. His presence transformed the Judean wilderness into a thriving Christian community, and established a permanent Armenian presence in the Holy Land. The liturgical language of the Judean monks was Greek, but the Armenians who had come to live the ascetic life in Palestine did not know Greek. At the monastery of Sabas (Mar Saba today, in the Judean desert), they recited the psalms in Armenian in a little chapel. As the number of Armenians multiplied, they moved into a larger church. There they celebrated the early part of the liturgy, the service of readings, in Armenian and joined the other monks for the "holy sacrifice" in Greek.

The Greek and Armenian monks, however, came into conflict over the wording of a popular hymn, the Trisagion (thrice holy). In the traditional version it read: "Holy God, Holy and Strong, Holy and Immortal, have mercy on us." But at the end of the fifth century, the non-Chalcedonian patriarch of Antioch, a man known as Peter the Fuller, added the words, "who was crucified for us." The Armenians adopted the hymn with the addition, and the other monks were "indignant," demanding that they chant it "according to the ancient tradition of the Catholic Church."

The Trisagion was addressed to the Holy Trinity. The addition implied that the Holy Trinity had been crucified—a theological idea without foundation in the Scriptures and contrary to Christian tradition. In its defense, the miaphysites argued that the hymn was addressed to the Son, one of the Holy Trinity, who *was* crucified. In this interpretation the addition could be understood in an orthodox way. The dispute was, however, not simply about the wording of a liturgical hymn. It touched on a much broader matter, how the Christians of Armenia related to the great dispute over the person of Christ.

In the early fifth century, when the controversy between Cyril and Nestorius broke out, the Armenian Church, part of which was located in the Persian Empire, was closely aligned with the Antiochenes and west Syrians. They looked to Theodore of Mopsuestia as the interpreter par excellence of the Scriptures and followed his thinking on matters related to Christ. When Mashtots was searching for a script to write down the Armenian language, he spent time in Edessa and other cities in Mesopotamia where the "two nature" Christology of Theodore was regnant. He returned to Armenia with a profound respect for the Antiochene theology.

At the time Sahak, great grandson of Gregory the Illuminator, was the catholicos, the premier bishop of the Armenians. Sahak served in this office for fifty years (387–438) and was instrumental in establishing an Armenian liturgy; with Mashtots and Eznik, an Armenian scholar, he worked on the translation of the Bible into Armenian. His episcopal see, however, was located in the city of Dvin, in the part of

Armenia ruled by the Persians. So he was a subject of the Sasanid king, called the "king of kings," and lived under the eye of the Persian governor whose residence was in Dvin. Which is to say that he dwelled among Syriac-speaking Christians who were solidly in the Antiochene camp, and therefore held to a two-nature Christology.

Until the Council of Ephesus in 431, Sahak the Armenian sided with the Antiochenes. A few years after the council, however, Sahak sent an embassy to Constantinople with writings of Theodore, asking for an opinion on Theodore's teaching. In response, the patriarch Proclus wrote a substantive letter, known as the *Tome of Proclus,* sharply criticizing the language of the two natures and setting forth an interpretation of the person of Christ along Cyrillian lines. Although Proclus did not condemn Theodore by name, he spoke of the "newly invented impieties of those who divide Christ into two," phraseology that could only refer to Theodore. From this point on, Sahak began to turn away from the "two nature" teaching of Theodore to embrace the theology of Cyril of Alexandria, Theodore's trenchant critic.

By aligning himself with the patriarch of Constantinople, Sahak brought down the wrath of the Persian authorities on the Armenian Church. Political loyalty and religious conformity were inseparable, and to the Persians it appeared that the Armenians were making common cause with a foreign power, the Romans who were ruled from Constantinople. And by agreeing to the condemnation of Nestorius, the Armenians were implicitly making a judgment against the orthodoxy of Theodore of Mospuestia, the most revered teacher of the Syriac-speaking Christians in the Church of the East. It is unlikely that Sahak was able to impose Constantinople's will on the Armenian Church as a whole, but by siding with the critics of Nestorius he let it be known that the Armenians were independent of the Church of the East.

As the most dominant political and religious power in the Tigris and Euphrates valleys, Persia sought to limit contacts between the Armenians and Greek-speaking Christians in the Roman Empire and to thwart the growth of a strong national Church in Armenia. In 450 the Persian king tried to impose Zoroastrianism on the people, deporting and executing Armenian leaders, including Sahak. A Syriac-speaking bishop was appointed catholicos, with authority to oversee the collection of taxes, administer the law courts, and regulate other secular institutions. Understandably the Armenians deeply resented Persian intrusion in the life of their churches. As an Armenian catholicos put it a few decades later: "The accursed barbarian Nestorians [the Syriac-speaking Persian Christians], who came and dwelt in our countries . . . and gained influence . . . up to the point of appointing a pseudo-bishop as leader of their filthy opinion . . ."

Armenia, especially what was called Persarmenia, was a long way from the great cities in the Roman Empire where the battle over how to formulate the Church's teaching on the person of Christ was waged. In the years leading up to the Council of Chalcedon, the Armenians were too much involved with their own internal affairs to take an active part in the debates. In fact, the Council of Chalcedon came and went without their participation. In the decades after the council, the Armenian Church, in contrast to the Egyptians, did not take an official position either for or against the decree of Chalcedon. In time, however, the Armenians gradually abandoned their allegiance to the "two nature" thinking of Theodore and embraced the thinking of Cyril of Alexandria, which had gained favor in Constantinople.

In 482, in an effort to reconcile the two theological traditions, Emperor Zeno issued a new document called the Henotikon (statement of union). The strategy behind the Henotikon was to raise up the Nicene Creed (the version adopted at the Council of Constantinople in 381) as the standard of orthodoxy, to affirm the theotokos, and to accept the condemnation of Nestorius (and by implication Theodore) at the Council of Ephesus in 431. However, it said nothing about the contentious formula of "two natures in one person." Although the Henotikon seemed a masterful diplomatic stroke, by ignoring Chalcedon it was doomed to failure.

The Armenians were sympathetic with the emperor's decision to tilt in the direction of the "one nature" language of Cyril of Alexandria. The decree of Chalcedon, with its "two nature" language, reflected the teaching of Theodore of Mopsuestia and was tainted with the errors of Nestorius. In other words, the council appeared to support the teaching of the Church of the East that was imposing its will on the Armenian people in Persia. So it happened that at a council in Dvin in 506, the Armenians accepted the Henotikon of Zeno, which condemned Nestorius (and hence Theodore), and some Armenian bishops openly repudiated the Council of Chalcedon. A century later, the Armenian bishops formally anathematized the Council of Chalcedon and the Tome of Pope Leo that was received at Chalcedon. These decisions would reverberate down the centuries, signaling that the Armenian Church, like the Church of Egypt, would take its place among the non-Chalcedonian Christian communions.

The Armenians, however, are unique and do not fit snugly within the conventional portraits of the Eastern Christian communions, whether Chalcedonian or non-Chalcedonian. In contrast to the practice in other Eastern churches, the Armenians use unleavened bread in the Eucharist. As one Armenian put it: "We will not eat the oven baked bread of the Greeks." They do not mix wine with water in the Eucharist, the common (and ancient) practice in East and West. Although the Armenian liturgy is similar to that of the other Eastern churches, their churches do not have an iconostasis, the screen that divides the altar from the rest of the church. They do not observe Christmas as a separate feast, but celebrate it on Epiphany in early January. And they make the sign of the cross in the Western manner, from the left shoulder to the right.

Armenian church architecture is also distinctive. In the early years the churches were modeled on the basilica style found in Anatolia and Syria. But in the sixth and seventh centuries many new buildings were constructed with a centralized plan. One church, Saint Hripsime at Vagharshapat, has a dome mounted on an octagonal structure. On four sides of the octagon arms extend out that terminate in four apses, forming a kind of cross. In each corner there is a sacristy, an area for sacramental vessels, vesting of clergy, and so on.

This octagonal plan was duplicated again and again in churches over the next several centuries. Domed churches were built in Anatolia, but it is likely that the Armenian buildings reflect a distinctly Near Eastern style of architecture used by the Sasanids in Persia and earlier by others in Central Asia. The buildings in Armenia use squinches, a small arch placed across the corners of a square to form an octagon suitable for carrying a dome. This technique was not known to the Romans and was rare among the Byzantines. As the distinguished architectural historian Richard Krauthammer observed: "Of all the border countries of the Empire Armenia is the only one to deal with Byzantine architecture on an equal footing. But the differences between Byzantine and Armenian buildings—in design, construction, scale, and decoration—cannot be too strongly stressed." That puts things well. In Armenia, a unique Christian culture arose in a small country that stood on equal footing to the larger Christian communions in the East.

To the north of Armenia lived the Georgians, an ancient people whose country reached from the eastern shore of the Black Sea to the Caucasus Mountains in the north and almost to the Caspian Sea in the east. With the exception of a large and fertile coastal plain, most of the country is mountainous. The Georgian people settled in the region in the second millennium, and between the seventh and fourth centuries B.C. two kingdoms, one in the west in the coastal area along the Black Sea and another in the east known as Iberia, were established.

Because Georgia could be reached easily by sea, it attracted Greek sailors and merchants and came under the cultural influence of the Greeks living in Asia Minor. In the first century, Nero annexed the region on the east coast of the Black Sea called Colchis, and it became part of the province of Cappadocia in Asia Minor. By the end of the third century, Christianity had made its way to the region, and two bishops from the area were present at the Council of Nicaea in 325.

The conversion of the kingdom of Iberia (Georgia) in the east was the work of a saintly woman named Nino. The historian Rufinus, writing in about the year 400, gives us an account of her impact on the royal house based on what he had learned orally from a Georgian prince he came to know in Palestine. Here is the story as told by Rufinus.

Nino had been taken captive by the Georgians and made a slave. She lived a chaste and virtuous life and offered her prayers to Christ as God. The Georgians were amazed at her austerity and her persistence in following her religious ways, which especially aroused the curiosity of the womenfolk. It was the custom among the Georgians that if a child fell ill it was carried by its mother from house to house to see if someone knew a trustworthy remedy. After a certain woman had made the rounds of her neighbors without finding a cure, she went to the captive woman. Nino said she knew no "human remedy" but would pray to "her God Christ." Placing the infant on a bedcover of horse's hair, she offered prayers and returned the child to her mother healed.

When news of the healing reached the queen, Nana, who was ill, she asked for the captive woman to be brought to her. But Nino refused, because it was not right for her to break her regime of prayer and fasting. So the queen was carried to the captive, and like the infant she was laid on the bedcovering. Nino called on the name of Christ; the queen was healed, and Nino told her that "Christ, Son of God Almighty" had healed her, and she should acknowledge him as "the source of her life and health." When the queen returned home, the king, Mirian, was overjoyed and ordered that presents be sent to the woman, but the queen said that Nino would have nothing to do with gold and silver; she was sustained by fasting, and the only reward she would accept was for the king and queen to worship the God Christ.

The king ignored her request, but a few days later on a hunting trip he got lost in a forest. Finding himself wandering in thick darkness, he remembered the name of Christ and prayed to him for deliverance. At once he was able to find his way back to the city. When he returned home, he summoned the captive woman and asked her to instruct him in Christian rituals and forms of prayer. Then he called together the Georgian people and instructed them in the faith, and though he was not yet baptized, he "became the apostle of his own nation." Then he set his architects and workmen to building a church at Mtskheta, near modern Tbilisi, according to a plan suggested by Nino. On her advice he sent an embassy to Emperor Constantine asking that priests be sent to them "to complete the work God had begun."

Rufinus's account of Nino and the conversion of the Georgians is overlaid with legendary details, but the basic outline is sound. Through the efforts of Nino, Mirian the king was baptized in 337, and the princes and some of the people followed his example. The king asked Constantine for clergy, and a bishopric was established in the capital city of Mtskheta.

The conversion of the Georgians (and Armenians) followed a pattern that was repeated elsewhere in the ancient world as Christianity spread beyond the borders of the Roman Empire. In the early centuries Christianity grew slowly as individuals were drawn to the Church, instructed in the faith, taught Christian prayers, and baptized. But when Christianity spread among the peoples living on the borders of the empire or beyond, conversion took place beginning with the king and queen.

Adoption of Christianity and consolidation of political power went hand in hand. In the early centuries in the Roman Empire the Church formed a body independent of the social and political order. But in Georgia and Armenia, in Nubia and Ethiopia, political rule and ecclesiastical institutions complemented one another. Still the Church retained a kind of independence; the king had to request bishops from more established churches to oversee the Church in his realm and to ordain priests. A charismatic person such as Saint Nino could convert the king and queen, but the king could not found a Church that claimed apostolic authority. Continuity with the past and communion with the Church throughout the world could come only through the succession of bishops.

The adoption of Christianity by a new people had less to do with the reorientation of the soul than it did with rituals and behavior and the customs and laws of the society. In his account Rufinus says that the "Iberian nation" (Georgians) accepted the "laws of God's word." In Georgia, as in Armenia, Christianity led to the creation of an alphabet for writing down the language that eventually made possible the growth of a national literature. The conversion of the royal house was a cultural as well as a religious event.

In 506, at the council in Dvin, twenty-four of the thirty bishops in attendance joined with the Armenians in condemning Chalcedon. The Georgian king Vakhtang I (d. 522) made an alliance with Emperor Zeno and accepted the Henotikon. In return the emperor recognized the Iberian (Georgian) Church as independent, though it remained under the jurisdiction of the patriarch of Antioch. At the beginning of the seventh century, however, during the reign of the catholicos Cyrion I (d. ca. 609), the Georgians officially accepted the Council of Chalcedon and broke free of Armenian authority. In the eighth century the Georgian Church became fully free of any other ecclesiastical jurisdiction.

These two national churches east of the Byzantine Empire would have different relations with the rest of Christendom. Even though they were geographical neighbors, the Armenians would be aligned with those Christian communions that did not accept the theological statement of the Council of Chalcedon, and the Georgians would be in fellowship with Constantinople and the Western churches that held to Chalcedon.

Central Asia, China, and India

In the mid sixth century, a merchant set out from Egypt to sail to the southern coast of India. Like earlier visitors from the Roman Empire, he had undertaken the long journey to bring home peppercorns from the Malabar coastal region, and he called India the land where "pepper grows." Pepper is indigenous to India, and it was one of the most prized spices in the ancient world. The Romans loved it as do we. In his *Natural History,* Pliny the Elder said that pepper had nothing pleasing about it except its pungency, yet "we go all the way to India to get it."

The name of the sixth-century traveler was Cosmas, and because of his journey to India he is known to historians as Cosmas Indicopleustes, Cosmas the Indian Navigator. Cosmas was a Christian, and in his *Christian Topography* he reports on Christian communities discovered in his travels. He spent some time in Malabar, the southwestern coast of India, in present-day Kerala, where he found a church with a bishop appointed from Persia. He also visited Socotra, an island in the Arabian Sea, approximately two hundred miles south of Yemen and east of Somalia, where there were Christians with clergy who received their ordination from Persia. But even more striking, he got as far as Ceylon (present-day Sri Lanka) and there he discovered a church composed of "Persian Christians" with, in his words, the "full ecclesiastical rite," presumably including baptism, the Eucharist, and bishops in apostolic succession.

It is revealing that Cosmas says that on islands in the Indian Ocean, on the subcontinent of India, and in Ceylon the clergy had been commissioned by the Church in Persia. We are familiar with the adventurous missionaries who went to northern Europe at the bidding of the pope, such as Saint Augustine of Canterbury, who traveled to the British Isles to spread the gospel to the English people, or Cyril and Methodius, who were sent to the Slavic peoples by the Byzantine emperor. But our histories tell us little about the mission to the Far East. As the spread of Christianity to northern Europe was the work of Latin-speaking monks, and the spread of Christianity among the Slavs was the work of Greek-speaking monks, so the spread of Christianity to the East was the work of Syriac-speaking monks from the Church of the East.

The principal route from the Mediterranean world to the Far East was the Silk Road, an extensive commercial network that began at Antioch near the Mediterranean, traversed the Middle East to Persia, from there passed through the cities of Sogdiana (present-day Uzbekistan), continued east through Kyrgyzstan to the Turpan oasis in western China, and finally reached all the way to the Great Wall of China and Xi'an. Besides carrying goods to be sold or traded, including silk, spices, jewels, perfumes, and glassware, the Silk Road was the bearer of ideas, culture, and religion. In caravans along the entire length of the route, Christian merchants were active. Their role in the historic spread of Christianity, and that of the monks and clergy who followed them, is singular; they carried the gospel to lands far more distant than those reached by missionaries from the Latin-speaking West or the Greek-speaking East. Already in the fifth century there was a bishop at Merv, an oasis on the Silk Road near the city of Mary in present-day Uzbekistan. Located twelve hundred miles east of Syria, Merv became the base for the mission to the Turkish tribes east of the Oxus River and eventually to China.

In the long history of Christian missions, no one was more visionary than Timothy I (d. 823), catholicos of the Church of the East at the end of the eighth and the beginning of the ninth century. Timothy was the driving force behind the mission to the East. As a young man he was groomed for high office in the Church. He received a thorough education in biblical interpretation, and at the famous monastery of Bet Abhe near Mosul in present-day Iraq he learned Greek and was tutored in Greek philosophy. He also learned Arabic and Persian. His native language was Syriac and he was a prolific author in that language, but at the behest of the Muslim caliph he translated Aristotle's *Topics,* a work on dialectical reasoning, into Arabic. His most famous writing is an account of a debate that took place in the presence of the Muslim caliph on the similarities and differences between Christianity and Islam.

But it was his promotion of the Christian mission to the East that made his tenure as catholicos memorable. At the time the Church of the East was under Muslim rule, and Timothy cultivated cordial relations with the caliph. Remarkably, he was allowed to organize a mission to Central Asia and to repair churches that had been destroyed or fallen into ruin. He took a lively interest in the mission to the Turks east of the Caspian Sea, and after the king of the Uighurs was converted he appointed a metropolitan to oversee the churches in the region. He was in contact with monks who had traveled to China and India, and when a bishop wanted to retire in comfort in Baghdad Timothy reminded him that monks were walking to China and India with only a staff in hand and a satchel. In a letter he mentions that he had plans to ordain a bishop for Tibet: "In these days the Holy Spirit has anointed a metropolitan for the Turks and we are preparing to consecrate another one for the Tibetans." Whether the project met success we do not know, but that Timothy planned to send a bishop to such a distant land is a testimony to the largeness of his vision and his untiring devotion to the Church's mission.

In a book written by a contemporary, Thomas of Marga, we learn that Timothy also ordained bishops for the Dailamites and Gilanians, Iranian people living southeast of the Caspian Sea. "These bishops," writes Thomas, "were ordained by the holy Catholicos Timothy the Patriarch to the countries of the savage peoples, who were devoid of every understanding and civilization. No missionaries and sowers of the truth had till then gone to their regions, and the teaching of the gospel of our Savior had not yet been preached to them; but why should I say the teaching of the Christ, our Lord, while they had not even received, like the Jews and the rest of the gentiles, the knowledge of God, creator and ruler of the worlds, but were worshipping trees, graven wood, beasts, fish, reptiles, birds and such like, along with the worship of fire and stars." The rationale, to preach the gospel throughout the world, is ancient, but for Timothy the call was fresh and urgent.

A striking example of the spread of Syriac-speaking Christianity to the East can be found on an ostracon, a piece of pottery broken off a vase or some other object, uncovered a few decades ago in Panjikent, a town in Central Asia in the present state of Tajikistan. Located on the Silk Road, Panjikent was a thriving commercial center of the Sogdians, an Iranian people who had been brought into contact with Greek culture through the conquest of Alexander the Great.

The text on the ostracon contains three verses from Psalm 1 written in Syriac: "Blessed is the man who walks not on the path of the impious, and does not stand in the convictions of sinners, and does not sit in the gatherings of ridiculers, but his delight is in the law of the Lord." Certain features of the orthography have led scholars to think that the text was written from dictation; for instance, letters that are silent when spoken in Syriac (such as aleph) are omitted. Certain grammatical peculiarities in the text suggest that it was written not by a native Syriac speaker, but by someone whose language was Sogdian. The psalm may have been written down as part of a student's exercise in learning to write Syriac script.

In the Syriac-speaking Christian world the basic education, often in a school associated with a monastery, was memorizing and reciting the psalter. Narsai, the Christian poet in Nisibis, the great center of Syriac learning in Mesopotamia, said that he went to a school for boys at seven and began to learn the psalter. After a few years he had learned the psalms by heart and could "recite all David."

The ostracon has another curious feature that confirms its possible use. The last two lines are written in a different hand and seem to be a "test of the pen"—a kind of trial run. They include part of a doxology taken from the Syriac liturgy: "Your glory, God of Hosts, which fills heaven and earth."

Panjikent, the city where the ostracon was found, was part of Sogdiana, a civilization built by Iranian peoples with their own language, Sogdian. Their principal city was Samarkand, in present-day Uzbekistan. Alexander the Great's conquest of the region in the fourth century B.C. formed ties to the West, and in the second century B.C. an embassy of the Chinese envoy Chang Ch'ien brought the Sogdians into contact with China. By that time the Sogdians had come to the attention of Christians in the Middle East, but Christianity did not arrive in the region until the sixth century. By the eighth century, the date of the ostracon, Christianity was well established there, and Samarkand was the seat of a metropolitan, an archbishop in communion with the catholicos in Baghdad. Besides archeological evidence, there are literary texts, fragments of books of the New Testament written in Sogdian. Other manuscripts include writings in Sogdian and Syriac.

Archaeologists have also uncovered examples of Sogdian Christian art. A noteworthy piece is a silver dish that depicts a besieged castle with people garbed in local Turkic dress. The dish includes scenes from the Old Testament in narrative sequence: the siege of Jericho with Rahab (Joshua 2:1–16), the carrying of the ark (Joshua 6:4–20), the sun standing still (Joshua 10:13–14). Apparently the Sogdian castle represents the city of Jericho. Art historians have noted that the scene on the dish is reminiscent of a Buddhist depiction of Kushinagar, the city that kept the relics of the Buddha after his death. If so, this would indicate a very early encounter of Christianity with Buddhism. Another silver dish, now in the Hermitage Museum of Saint Petersburg, includes three medallions depicting scenes from the gospels of the suffering, death, and resurrection of Christ, Peter's denial, soldiers guarding the grave, the robber Jesus forgave, Mary and Mary Magdalene, and angels.

As the Silk Road brought Christians to Sogdiana in Central Asia, so the same route brought Syriac-speaking monks from Persia to China. The T'ang dynasty that ruled China from the seventh to the tenth centuries had diplomatic and mercantile relations with Central Asia as well as political hegemony over Manchuria, northern Korea, Mongolia, Tibet, and other neighboring countries. China was home to a cosmopolitan culture open to outside influences, and it welcomed Christians. According to Chinese sources, Christians first appeared in the capital city, present-day Xi'an, during the reign of Emperor T'ai-tsung (626–649). An official decree of the emperor mentioned Christianity explicitly: "The Persian monk A-lo-pen has come from afar bringing scriptures and teaching. . . . The meaning of the teaching has been carefully examined; it is mysterious, wonderful, calm; it fixes the essentials of life and perfection; it is the salvation of living beings; it is the wealth of man. It is right that it should spread through the empire. Therefore let the local officials build a monastery in the I-ning quarter with twenty-one regular monks."

In another royal decree a century later, the religion of the Christians is called "the Persian religion" or the "Iranian religion." This decree also mentioned monks, and it is reasonable to assume that in the Far East, as well as in the West, it was monks, some of whom were no doubt ordained, who established a Christian presence among new peoples. They may have been preceded by merchants, but the founding of Christian communities required clergy. And we know that the Church of the East had a well-ordered institutional structure that allowed bishops in distant lands to keep in touch with the catholicos in Baghdad. These imperial decrees also show that Christianity was sanctioned, even supported, by Chinese rulers. At least in the initial stages! One scholar even surmised that there were economic motives behind the patronage of Christians. Giving support to Christians from Persia would encourage more Christian merchants to come to China. Persuasion was not the only tool of these enterprising monks.

The most impressive evidence of the presence of Christianity in ancient China is a large stone monument discovered in the seventeenth century on the precincts of a temple in Sian-fu, not too far from Xi'an. This monument of black limestone is ten feet high and three and a half feet wide, with seventeen hundred Chinese characters, interspersed with Syriac words and Syriac names with Chinese characters indicating how they are to be pronounced. It was erected in 781 on the site of a monastery of the Church of the East. When the news of its discovery reached the West, some doubted its authenticity. Voltaire thought it a pious fraud of the Jesuits who, inspired by the example of Francis Xavier, had been sending missionaries to the Far East. But today the monument is considered genuine.

The author of the text was a Persian priest named Adam, whose Chinese name was Ching-Ching. He is identified in the Syrian text as "Adam, priest and bishop of the countryside and spiritual master of Zinistan [China]." He was also a monk at the monastery where the monument was found. It was erected to honor a monk named I-ssu, who is said to be learned and skilled in teaching, but also adept in military matters, including spying on the enemy. He restored churches that had fallen into disrepair, cared for the sick and needy, and was overseer of the monks living in the region.

The monument also includes a brief account of the history of the "luminous religion" in China, including the appearance of the first Christian monk A-lo-pen from Persia. He was apparently given a grand reception, suggesting that something was known of Christianity before his arrival, and the books he carried with him were translated into Chinese so the emperor could read them. Without giving names, the text says there are twenty-seven books of Scripture, and mentions baptism, worship, keeping the Sabbath, and rules for the monks, notably that they do not hold slaves, do not accumulate wealth, and are generous to others. On the monasticism of the Syriac-speaking monks it says: "Purification is made perfect by solitude and meditation; self restraint grows strong by silence and watching."

Besides this inscription and official Chinese records, a cache of Christian documents was found in a walled-up chapel in Tunhuang early in the nineteenth century. These include writings in Chinese by Christian monks, some translated from the Syriac, others original contributions. There is a hymn in adoration of the "Transfiguration of our Lord," a work entitled *Jesus Messiah Sutra* that outlines the fundamental teachings of Christianity, a *Discourse on the Oneness of the Ruler of the Universe,* and another on almsgiving. According to those who have studied them, these writings are difficult to understand because they were written by someone who did not know Chinese well. Nevertheless, they show that Christian monks were consciously attempting to present Christianity in a way that would be intelligible to Chinese. For example, they emphasize virtues such as ancestor worship, filial piety, even veneration of the emperor. Other documents written 150 years later display a surer knowledge of the Chinese language, a more accomplished literary style, and skillful presentation of Christian beliefs.

Though the introduction of Christian ideas and the translation of Christian writings were welcomed by the T'ang rulers, and monasteries were dependent on imperial favor, as the years passed Chinese authorities began to withdraw their support. Chinese sources display mounting criticism of Christianity. Buddhism was likened to the clear water of the Ching River, and Christian teaching to the muddy water of the Wei River. By the middle of the ninth century Christians as well as adherents of other foreign religions were subject to repression and persecution. A Chinese text from A.D. 845 says that aliens making known the religions of foreign countries, including the Ta-ch'in (Christians) and the Mu-hu-fu (Zoroastrians), must "return to lay life and cease to confound the customs of China."

By the end of the tenth century Christians in China were almost extinct. In 987 an Arab writer in Baghdad said that he had met a monk who had been sent to China by the catholicos to attend to the affairs of the Church in China. The monk reported that most Christians had perished and their churches were destroyed. He found no people to whom he could minister and returned to Baghdad.

There is no continuous history of Christianity in China to the present day; in India things took a different course. As the voyage of Cosmas the Indian Navigator shows, India was accessible by sea from Egypt. In the memory of Christians in India, Thomas the Apostle brought the gospel to the subcontinent already in the first century. For centuries the story of his journey and adventures has been told in song and verse by Indian Christians, and to this day it enjoys a kind of canonical status.

The tale of Thomas's journey to India is found in an ancient Syriac document, the Acts of Thomas, written in the third or fourth century. According to this work, after the ascension of Jesus the apostles drew lots to see who would go to which part of the world to preach the gospel. India fell to Thomas, but Thomas said he did not know the language of the people living there and refused to go. But Jesus appeared to him in a dream and told him to make the journey. Soon afterward Thomas met a wealthy merchant from India with orders from Gundaphar, a king in Punjab in northwestern India and Afghanistan, to bring back skilled architects and builders to construct a royal palace. Thomas agreed, and when he arrived the king provided money to build the palace.

But when Thomas learned of the poverty of the people in India, he used the king's money to serve their needs. Not a prudent decision! On the king's return, Thomas explained that he had spent the money to heal the sick, drive out demons, and teach the people about the true God. Understandably, the king was outraged, but Thomas was rescued from the king's wrath when his deceased brother appeared to him in a dream to say that he saw a copy of the palace in heaven. Soon afterward the king decided to become a Christian. The people followed and were anointed with oil and baptized, and Thomas celebrated the Eucharist. He then went on a journey to other places in India and was killed by the spears of soldiers on the orders of another king. The traditional place of his martyrdom is a hill outside of Mylapore (Mailapur), a suburb of Madras, present-day Chennai, on the eastern coast of India. The location is noteworthy because there was a Roman trading colony on the eastern coast of India at Arikamedu not far from Mylapore.

It is difficult to uncover the historical kernel behind the story of Thomas. There was a king named Gundaphar who ruled over a large kingdom in northwest India in the first century. Coins attest to his reign, and they lend plausibility to the account. Some early Christian traditions identify Thomas as the apostle to Parthia (Persia), and he was venerated in Edessa. The shortest route to India from Mesopotamia was down the Euphrates to Basra on the Persian Gulf and from there by sea to the mouth of the Indus River in northwest India, where Gundaphar was king.

Some early traditions trace the establishment of Christianity in India to the apostle Bartholomew. In his history of the early centuries Eusebius says that Pantaenus, a Christian philosopher and teacher of Clement of Alexandria, traveled to India in the late second century to proclaim the gospel to the "peoples of the East." When he arrived he found Christians were already living there, and they possessed a copy of the Gospel of Matthew in Aramaic characters.

Eusebius's account would suggest that Christianity arrived in India from Roman Egypt. Travel to India had become relatively easy, because Roman sailors and merchants discovered that monsoon winds off the east coast of Africa favor sailing from Egypt to India in summer and returning in winter. According to Pliny, the monsoon winds would bring ships to the Muziris, or Malabar, a city on the southwestern coast, the "first trading station in India." This Indian city even appears on an ancient Roman map with a Roman temple.

The direction and timing of winds in the Indian Ocean made it possible for ships to sail regularly to India and return laden with pepper and other goods for sale. Berenike, a port city on the Red Sea, became a major center for trade with India. By the first century there were Greco-Roman settlements on the southwestern coast of India, and thousands of Roman coins document the presence of settlers from the Roman Empire.

Because of these mercantile relations with southwestern India, it is possible, even likely, that Christians were among those who made their way to India in the first or second century. By the third century the Red Sea trade between Egypt and India declined, and the ties between Christians in India and those living in the Roman Empire were cut off. Christian communities had been established in the north of the country by Christians from Persia, and Christians in the south began to orient themselves to the Syriac-speaking Christian world. In the late third century David, a bishop of the Church of the East and metropolitan of Basra, made a journey to India, and it is likely that he visited communities not only in the north of the country but also in the south. The Church of the East had a network of churches around the Indian Ocean. Though the Church in India was founded by Greek-speaking Christians sailing from Roman Egypt, in the third and fourth centuries, as trade between Egypt and India declined, it came under the influence, and eventually the jurisdiction, of the Syriac-speaking Church in Persia.

More than any other ancient Christian communion the Church of the East made Christianity into a global religion. The vitality of its monastic centers, the zeal and fortitude of its monks, its well-oiled institutional structure, and its regular synods of bishops gave it the resources to reach out beyond familiar geographical and cultural boundaries. The route from Persia to India was dotted with monasteries that provided lines of communication between the catholicos in Mesopotamia and bishops in distant lands. Though bishops in India and China were not required to attend the general synod of the Church, they were expected to prepare a report every six years informing the catholicos of the situation in their dioceses.

The Church of the East planted Christian communities among peoples and cultures beyond the horizon of the West. In the Latin West the great mission to the north took place among the Germanic peoples, who had been known to the Romans for centuries. In the Greek-speaking East, missionaries went north among the Slavic peoples in the Balkans and in Russia and south to Nubia bordering Egypt and Ethiopia. But Syriac-speaking monks in the East had a more ambitious agenda, to carry the gospel not only to peoples who worshiped trees and stones, but to lands with ancient cultures and religions, notably China and India. By any calculus the missions of the Syriac-speaking Church of the East deserve an esteemed place in the history of Christian missions.

A Christian Empire:
Justinian

As Christianity was spreading eastward among new peoples, Christians in the Roman Empire were fashioning a Christian society. This work had been under way since the fourth century, but it was not until the sixth that it was realized, if only imperfectly. As recently as a hundred years earlier, a significant minority of people clung to the old ways and worshiped the Roman gods.

In the early fifth century, several major Christian writers had written apologies in defense of Christian belief to the cultured despisers of the new religion. Most famous, of course, was Augustine's great work, *City of God* (ca. 413–427), which carried the telling subtitle, *contra paganos,* "against the pagans." And Cyril of Alexandria, though preoccupied with the protracted struggle over the teaching about Christ, found it necessary to compose a large work in defense of Christianity (ca. 433) in response to Emperor Julian's biting and derisive treatise, *Against the Galilaeans* (ca. 360), written several generations earlier. Cyril took up Julian's challenge because his book was still being read in the fifth century and its arguments thrown in the face of Christians.

By the sixth century, when Justinian became emperor, the transition from the Rome of "Caesar Augustus" (Luke 2:1), under whose rule Jesus was born, to a Christian empire was complete. It was, however, not a new empire, but a later stage in the history of the same Roman Empire that had been inaugurated by Augustus. Though it was now ruled from the great city of Constantinople in the East, not from Rome, its emperors understood themselves to stand, and indeed did stand, in direct continuity with the Rome of Augustus and Trajan and Marcus Aurelius, even of wicked emperor Domitian, the persecutor of Christians in the early fourth century, and of course the Christian emperors Constantine and Theodosius. When, for example, Justinian set out to revise the legal code of the empire, he instructed his commissioners to collect statutes beginning with legislation from the time of the emperor Hadrian (A.D. 117–138) up to the present.

Nevertheless, what had come into being by the sixth century was new, and to mark the transition from the earlier Roman Empire to the Christian Roman empire, historians call the latter the Byzantine Empire. The Byzantines, however, called themselves *Romaioi,* Romans. Byzantium was the name of the city occupying the site emperor Constantine had chosen to found a new capital. Graced by geography and history to be the center of a great empire, Byzantium stood on a triangular peninsula surrounded by water on two sides. The inlet to the north, a kilometer wide and six kilometers long, was called the Golden Horn because of the way it turns gold in the rays of the setting sun. Two major roads headed toward Europe, the Via Egnatia going directly west toward Thessalonica in northern Greece, the other leading northward to Adrianople and the Danube provinces. To the east was the Bosporus, a narrow waterway separating Europe and Asia and connecting the Black Sea to the Sea of Marmara, the Dardanelles, and the Aegean Sea. Sitting astride one of the most important waterways in antiquity as well as in modern times, Constantinople linked the Mediterranean world to the Black Sea, to Georgia on its eastern shore and the steppes of Asia farther east. Across the Sea of Marmara stood the city of Nicomedia, present-day Izmit, from which a network of roads led to points east in Asia Minor, Armenia, Syria, and Mesopotamia.

Constantinople's strategic location between Europe and Asia gave the city a singular role in Christian history. In the early centuries Carthage in North Africa (Tunisia), Alexandria in Egypt, Caesarea, near present-day Tel Aviv on the Mediterranean coast, Antioch in Syria, and Rome were the stages on which the drama of Christian history was played. But with the rise of Islam these cities, save Rome, came under Arab rule. Had Constantine chosen a site farther east than Byzantium, or made Alexandria or Antioch or Caesarea the location of his capital, it would have been conquered by the Muslims in the seventh or eighth century. But because it was located far from the Middle East by land and by sea, Constantinople was able to resist Arab efforts to conquer it, and its political, cultural, and religious life continued—interrupted by the devastation of the Fourth Crusade (1202–1204) and the Latin kingdom that followed—until the city was conquered by the Ottoman Turks in 1453. When Crusaders from western Europe saw the city in the twelfth century they were filled with wonder at the "rich palaces" and "lofty churches."

Though Latin was still used in Justinian's day and Justinian was himself a Latin speaker, the principal language of the city was Greek. In fact, in 535, shortly after rising to the purple, Justinian decreed that the language of the state should be Greek. As Rome came to symbolize Western Latin-speaking Christianity, Constantinople, the "new Rome," was the premier city of Greek-speaking Christianity.

In the sixth century Constantinople was a large cosmopolitan city of some

500,000 residents covering an area of five square kilometers. Though the metropolis celebrated by visitors and depicted by historians was a city of monuments, churches, and the imperial palace, most of the land inside its walls was given over to vineyards, orchards, and the growing of vegetables. In it lived a medley of diverse communities set apart by language, culture, and in some cases religion. There was, for example, a Jewish neighborhood with its own synagogue. On the streets of Constantinople one could hear many languages besides Greek—Latin, Syriac, Armenian, Coptic, Ethiopian, Gothic, and more. The rhythm of the city's life was governed by the pomp and majesty of the imperial court and the annual calendar of celebrations, for victories in war, religious festivals commemorating martyrs and saints, and the major Christian feasts, Christmas, Easter, and Pentecost.

Justinian was born in 483 in Tauresium, present-day Caricin Grad in Serbia. As a youngster he was brought to Constantinople and adopted by his uncle, Justin, who became emperor in 518. Justin saw that the youth received a good education in Greek and Latin and was schooled in military matters. As Justinian observed the wiles of palace intrigue he gained a sure grasp of how imperial administration and politics worked. He also married Theodora, a showgirl and dancer of great beauty, intelligence, and pluck. Her exploits were narrated with relish by a contemporary historian, Procopius, who deliberately intended to discredit Justinian and Theodora.

After her marriage, however, Theodora became a model of piety and respectability, and a trusted, though sometimes duplicitous confidant of her husband. As we saw in the section on Nubia, Theodora, a miaphysite, got the jump on Justinian and dispatched missionaries to Nubia ahead of Justinian's Chalcedonian emissaries. In 527 Justinian was made co-emperor by his uncle, and when Justin died four months later, Justinian assumed the throne. He would rule for thirty-eight years, until his death in 565, almost as long as Augustus, the first Roman emperor.

Justinian had a zeal for conquest, and during his reign the Mediterranean became a Roman sea again. Since the fifth century, Roman North Africa had been overrun and ruled by the Vandals, Arians who had crossed to Africa at the Strait of Gibraltar. Italy was ruled by Ostrogoths. Within less than a decade Justinian's armies conquered Carthage, the chief city in North Africa, Sicily, Rome, and even Ravenna in northern Italy.

Justinian was an enterprising builder, and the historian Procopius wrote a book on his reign titled simply *Buildings*. Procopius imagined that in future ages people would refuse "by reason of their number and magnitude to believe [the buildings] are the work of one man," and he wished to provide irrefutable proof of the scale of Justinian's accomplishment. What remains even to this day in Constantinople and around the Mediterranean and the Middle East is indeed astonishing: aqueducts, bridges, fortifications, monasteries, and most notably churches. Judging by the attention Procopius gave to the churches and his detailed description of their design and decoration, it seems that Justinian considered the building of churches his greatest and most illustrious accomplishment.

Up until the age of Justinian most church buildings had been constructed on the basilical plan, a rectangular structure with a timber roof, often with two rows of columns, a narthex and atrium on the western end, and an apse on the eastern end. In the medieval West, builders added a dimension of verticality, but they left the basic basilical floor plan unchanged. Justinian's architects, however, broke with this tradition and turned to vaulted centrally planned structures with a dome carried on massive piers buttressed by semi-domes. The placing of a dome over the nave of the church created a different kind of interior space, lofty and spacious, airy and filled with light, more circular than rectangular. So different was the design of these churches that to this day church architecture remains a visible sign of the cultural divide between Eastern and Western Christianity.

Among churches in Constantinople constructed with domes during Justinian's reign, three stood out: the Church of Saints Sergios and Bacchos, the Church of Hagia Eirene (Holy Peace), and the Church of Hagia Sophia (Holy Wisdom), and all are still standing. In its magnitude, however, in the sophistication of its architecture, and in the refinement of its decoration, Holy Wisdom overshadows all of Justinian's buildings, and it has symbolized the creative energy and technical skill of Byzantine architects.

The structural plan of the Church of Holy Wisdom was as simple and straight-forward as it was innovative. Instead of a rectangle, the core of the building is almost a square with four large piers, one in each corner, on which the dome of the nave is set. Between the piers are arcades with five bays on either side surmounted by another set of arcades of seven bays on the gallery level. Above these are seven windows on the clerestory. Behind the pillars the aisles are broken up into galleries created as places to view what happens in the nave; everything in the design was intended to draw the eye to the large area beneath the dome. It is, wrote Procopius, "more extravagant than the buildings to which we are accustomed and more noble than those that are merely large." It is filled with "light and sunshine," so that one would say "the place is not lighted by the sun from without, but the radiance is produced from within, so abundant is the light pouring into the sanctuary." Above the arches is raised a "huge spherical dome . . . that seems suspended from heaven."

The construction of churches on a central plan was in part a response to developments in Christian worship. In the first part of the Liturgy, the book of the gospels, adorned with precious metal and stones, was carried in procession to the ambo, a raised platform in the center of the nave. Churches had no pews, and the open space allowed the faithful gathered in the nave and in the side galleries to behold the spectacle. According to ancient accounts, as the book of the gospel passed by, "the surging crowd strove to touch the sacred book with their lips and hands while moving waves of people crowded around."

Later in the Liturgy a second procession took place, bringing the bread and wine to the altar. At Holy Wisdom the procession began outside the church proper, in a small building nearby called a *skeuophylakion,* "place where the sacramental vessels are kept," moved into the church through a door to the left of the apse, and from there into the center of the nave as clergy held the bread and wine aloft in gold and silver vessels accompanied by incense and candles. When the procession reached the center of the church it turned toward the apse and proceeded on a raised walkway, called *solea,* to the bishop, who was standing at the altar behind the chancel screen, a low wall of marble panels topped by columns, with a marble beam stretching across the columns.

When the emperor was present at the Liturgy, he and the empress met the procession at the ambo in the center of the church. In a tenth-century document the scene is described this way: when the imperial party reached the ambo "the sacred vessels are waiting for them," and "lighted torches are placed in the hands of the sovereigns who march in front of the gifts with the senators and chamberlains." Then the emperor and empress proceed "via the solea to the holy doors [of the chancel screen], the first to the right, the second to the left and affix their torches to the balusters of the holy doors." They pause with the "holy things" as the archdeacon censes the sovereigns and the patriarch, and the holy table, or altar. After the holy things are brought forth and all have entered, the sovereigns greet the patriarch and exit on the right side.

Besides Holy Wisdom, Justinian commissioned the building of the monastery of Saint Catherine in the Sinai desert. The Sinai had long been a place of pilgrimage for Christians. In the fourth century the pilgrim Egeria had made the long and arduous journey from the West to see and climb what she called the Holy Mount of God, the traditional place where Moses had received the tablets of the law from God (Exodus 19–20) and the plain where the Israelites made the golden calf (Exodus 32). Nearby was also the "place of the Bush" (Exodus 3:1–6), where God had appeared to Moses in a bush that burned without being consumed. When Egeria reached the mountain, she discovered that there were "cells" of monks living there.

Justinian took an interest in this community of monks in the desert for reasons of security as much as piety, and the monastery was constructed as a fortress. He also provided a company of mercenaries to protect it. Procopius gives us a contemporary account: "A precipitous and terribly wild mountain, Sinai by name, rears its height close to the Red Sea. . . . On this Mount Sinai live monks, whose life is a kind of careful rehearsal of death [see Plato's *Phaedo*], and they enjoy without fear the solitude which is very precious to them. . . . [T]he emperor Justinian built them a church which he dedicated to the Mother of God, so that they might pass their lives in it praying and celebrating the liturgy. He built this church, not on the mountain's summit, but much lower down. . . . And at the base of the mountain this emperor built a very strong fortress and established there a considerable garrison of troops, in order that the barbarian Saracens [Arabic-speaking Bedouins] might not be able from that region, which, as I have said, is uninhabited, to make inroads with complete secrecy into the lands of Palestine proper."

The monastery included a church that is still in use today, with its original walls (now plastered) and roof beams in place, though the interior decoration has changed. In this case the architect followed the traditional basilica plan and constructed a longitudinal structure with two aisles and a nave. Its huge portal with double doors, almost four meters high, is one of the few ancient church doors to have survived. It has twenty-eight panels set into grooves and is decorated with vines, peacocks, plants, and animals. The apse has a large mosaic of the Transfiguration of Christ on Mount Tabor (Matthew 17:1–8), a spectacular display of Christ's glory that was seen as a fulfillment of God's appearance to Moses in the burning bush. Christ stands in the center in the midst of an aureola with radiating silver beams, with Moses and Elijah on either side, and the disciples Peter, James, and John are huddled on the ground. They are surrounded by busts of twelve apostles and sixteen prophets. Above the apse mosaic, Moses is depicted taking off his sandals before the burning bush and receiving the law in the form of a scroll—not tablets!

Although churches were only one part of Justinian's ambitious building program, more than anything else they show that Christianity had changed the spatial architecture as well as temporal rhythms of the ancient city. Churches took the place of temples, and statues to the gods and goddesses of Rome gave way to icons of Christ, the Virgin Mary, and the saints. But religion is not all of life, and Justinian put his mind to many other things, most notably law. In some ways his most enduring project was the publication of a new code of law for the Roman Empire based on a revision of previous statutes. It was a prodigious undertaking: the commissioners had to read three million lines of legal documents and gather them into a coherent whole. To deal with the flow of excerpts from earlier laws, carpenters were instructed to build a system of 432 pigeonholes in the room where the commissioners worked. The result was a cultural monument that combined the wisdom of the past with an eye toward the future. Edward Gibbon, the eighteenth-century historian of Rome, wrote that "the vain titles of the victories of Justinian are crumbled into dust, but the name of the legislator is inscribed on a fair and everlasting monument," for the "public reason of the Romans has been silently or studiously transfused into the domestic institutions of Europe."

The *Corpus Iuris Civilis,* as the collection of legal writings is known, was a revision, expansion, and rearrangement of an earlier revision that had been made during the reign of Emperor Theodosius in the fifth century. Though it bears the title "civil law," it is really a collection of Roman legal sources dealing with civil and criminal law. It is made up of four different works: the Codex, a library of imperial pronouncements going back to the time of Hadrian; the Digest (or Pandects), a gathering of selections from the writings of classical jurists; the Institutes, an introduction to the Corpus and a summary of the laws and the basic principles guiding the revision; the Novels (novellae), more recent laws, particularly decrees of Justinian himself. Taken as a whole, the Corpus of Justinian is a written testimony to the continuity of Roman institutions reaching back to their roots in the Latin-speaking West and into the Greek-speaking future.

Law has its own integrity, and in most of the material collected in the Corpus the influence of Christian beliefs and ideas is slight. There is little evidence of a systematic effort to Christianize the substantive principles of classical Roman law. Still under Justinian's hands, all the laws that were included in the Corpus were issued "in the name of our Lord Jesus Christ" and by the authority of a Christian emperor obedient to Christ. Though the specifics of the laws were unchanged, they were set within an explicitly Christian framework. In one instance, a law dealing with the corruption of provincial magistrates, Justinian instructed the bishops to read out the law to their congregations on festival days. In another case, also dealing with corruption, Justinian instructed the bishops to deposit a copy of the law in the churches so the people could see that it was "consecrated to God" and "enacted for the benefit of the men created by him." He further instructed that the law be inscribed on stone and posted at the entrance to the church so it would be known to the people.

One of Justinian's most significant and long-lasting innovations had to do with judicial procedures. Before any trial or judicial hearing the participants, the litigants, and the legal officials were required to swear an oath of Christian faith while laying a hand on the book of the gospels. To ensure that in legal proceedings God would be present as witness, Justinian ordered that the book of the gospels be placed in every Roman courtroom.

Early in his reign Justinian set in motion punitive legal machinery to constrict the profession of pagan beliefs within the empire. The most famous instance was a decree in 529 forbidding anyone to teach philosophy in Athens. The law was directed at the ancient school of philosophy that had been in existence there for centuries. Unlike the school in Alexandria, which was made up chiefly of Christian philosophers, the school in Athens was largely pagan and the inheritor of a Platonic philosophical tradition critical of Christianity.

In modern times, some historians have seen the date as symbolic. In the same year that Justinian moved against the school in Athens, Benedict of Nursia founded the monastery at Monte Cassino in Italy. The emergence of the distinctive form of monasticism in the West, coupled with the closing of the school in Athens, seemed to mark the boundary between the brilliant culture of ancient Greece and Rome and the lesser civilization being created by Christians. The truth is much less dramatic.

The law about the academy in Athens was part of an initiative to impose Christian beliefs on the society as a whole. In the ancient world religion was inextricably interwoven with social and political life, and it was assumed that each city, each people or state, had its own distinctive religious practice. In the fourth century, the emperor Julian had prohibited Christians from teaching in the schools, arguing that if they did not believe in the gods of ancient Greece and Rome, they had no business teaching grammar and literature—in which the gods figured large—to the young.

Christian leaders stridently protested Julian's reforms, as earlier bishops and apologists had opposed efforts of Roman authorities to impose the traditional religion on Christians. But after Christianity was decreed the official faith of the Roman world in the late fourth century, and the majority of citizens in the empire became Christian, the power of the state was put at the service of Christian doctrine, and law was used to constrict the practice of paganism, by forbidding sacrifice, for instance.

Nevertheless, Justinian's measures against pagans, and also heretics, were unusually harsh. Even Byzantine writers were critical of shutting down the school of philosophy. "By making the teachers redundant," said one writer, Justinian was responsible for a new level of "boorishness." The punishment for noncompliance was severe: confiscation of property and banishment from the empire. And that leads to a tale.

At the time of Justinian's decision to close the academy in Athens, the king in Sasanid Persia, Chosroes I, was an enlightened prince. His reputation had reached Athens, and seven teachers from the city decided to settle in the Persian capital and cultivate their philosophical heritage under Sasanid royal patronage. Though Chosroes was generous and genuinely interested in philosophy, the scholars from Athens soon became disillusioned with life among the Persians. Within a year they were ready to return home, and the king gave them leave. Surprisingly, according to the historian Agathias, Justinian granted them safe passage home and allowed them to live within the empire.

How much of this story is to be taken at face value is a matter of debate among scholars. But we do know that the philosophers did return and several continued to write philosophical works. Apparently imperial authorities in Athens did not carry out the law to the letter. Decades later the school still retained possession of some of its property and had access to its endowment. Understandably the pagan philosophers chafed under the atmosphere created by Justinian. In their writings they drop hints that they are living at a "time of tyranny and crisis" and that the "prevailing circumstances" make it difficult to carry on their work. But carry on they did, if not in the style they had been accustomed to. One of the philosophers who had gone to Persia, Simplicius, wrote a number of learned commentaries on Aristotle in the years after his return to Athens. From the citation of ancient sources in his commentaries it is evident he had access to a well-stocked library.

No less significant are the works composed by other philosophers during Justinian's reign. Most notable was the Christian philosopher Philoponus (490–570), who wrote commentaries on Aristotle as well as original works. His most significant contribution was a critique of Aristotle's physics and cosmology, and he proposed fresh ideas about motion. He argued that a projectile is moved not simply by the push of air behind it, but by an "immaterial kinetic power" imparted by the initial impetus. His ideas were developed later by Islamic philosophers and scholastic thinkers in the Middle Ages. Although Justinian shut down the academy in Athens, the demand for a philosophical education did not diminish, and a considerable body of philosophical works was composed during his long reign.

Justinian also had to deal with the continuing debate spawned by the Council of Chalcedon. In his *Divine Comedy,* Dante depicts Justinian's efforts to resolve the controversy over the person of Christ, and he has Justinian say that he had set his mind to "that hard task." It is an apt phrase to describe what Justinian faced.

By the sixth century the Church had been developing its own system of law, what came to be called "canon law." But the line between civil and church law was not drawn cleanly. Already during the reign of Theodosius I at the end of the fourth century the confession of God as triune had become the law of the empire. Justinian built on this tradition. In one of his Novellae, he rules that the "canons of the holy Church which were enacted or confirmed by the four holy councils [Nicaea, Constantinople, Ephesus, and Chalcedon] shall have the force of law." What had been decided by the bishops in council now become civil law.

Although Justinian decreed that the decisions of the four ecumenical councils were the law of the land, not everyone saw things that way. The Council of Chalcedon was still an affront to many bishops, especially in Syria and Egypt, and the rift spawned by its dogmatic decree had widened in the intervening years. Justinian's predecessors had sought to bridge the differences and establish unity, the Henotikon of Emperor Zeno in 482 being the most notable effort, but with each passing decade the divisions became more intractable.

The strategy of Emperors Zeno (474–491) and Anastasius (491–518) was to raise up the authority of the Councils of Nicaea and Constantinople (381), on which everyone agreed. But by ignoring Chalcedon and Pope Leo's Tome, with its "two nature" language, they only drove the parties further apart. The supporters of Chalcedon felt betrayed, the anti-Chalcedonians wanted outright condemnation of

Chalcedon, and Rome took any slight of Leo's teaching as an affront. The result was a schism between Rome and Constantinople, known as the Acacian schism after the patriarch of Constantinople, Acacius (471–489), lasting more than three decades.

The contretemps between Rome and Constantinople was not simply an affair of theology. Pope Gelasius (492–496) made resistance to imperial meddling in church teaching a matter of high principle. "For you know, most gracious son," Gelasius wrote to Emperor Anastasius, "that although you hold the chief place of dignity over the human race, yet you must submit yourself in faith to those who have charge of divine things." In other words, the emperor has no business telling the pope what the Church should teach. The rule laid down by Gelasius, making a clean distinction between secular and sacred authority, would be invoked often in the West; in the Byzantine world, however, the line between sacred and secular was much finer. As Justinian put it in one of his Novellae, "the difference between priesthood and empire is small." Responsibility for protecting orthodox teaching lay with the emperor. Justinian hoped that a unified Church would help him achieve other goals, chief of which was to restore the empire to its former glory by reestablishing Roman rule over the Vandals in Africa, the Lombards in Italy, and the Franks in Gaul.

In a meeting between Chalcedonian and anti-Chalcedonian bishops, Justinian gave both parties an opportunity to state their case. He thought that if the participants could focus on the writings of certain individual bishops, instead of the decree of Chalcedon itself, he would be able to distance himself from Chalcedon without repudiating the council itself. He reminded the company that Chalcedon had condemned those who held an extreme "one nature" position, such as Eutyches. Everyone, he reasoned, could agree on that. Further, if writings of certain "two nature" bishops (long dead) were condemned, specifically those of Theodoret of Cyrus, Ibas of Edessa, and Theodore of Mopsuestia (all celebrated in the Church of the East), perhaps the quarreling parties could come together. Predictably, the proposal was rejected on familiar grounds: it ignored the Council of Chalcedon's "two nature" formula. The controversy did not die, and it resurfaced again a few years later.

The writings of Theodoret, Ibas, and Theodore came to be known as the "Three Chapters," and in 545 Justinian announced plans to convene a council to condemn these works. Rome was opposed to the proposal because it viewed the three thinkers as theological allies, but Justinian's campaign to retake Italy was in full swing and he needed Rome's support. So he had the pope, Vigilius, arrested and brought to Constantinople. At first Vigilius resisted the pressure to join in the condemnation of the Three Chapters, but eventually he gave in, to the dismay of leaders in the West, where he was denounced as a traitor. The bishops of North Africa excommunicated him.

In 551 Justinian issued an edict titled the True Faith, setting forth his theological views on the matter at issue and thirteen anathemas. It was a curious document, affirming the two-nature formula of Chalcedon, yet at the same time approving of the controversial phrase "one nature of God the Word Incarnate" used by Cyril of Alexandria. The text was posted at the Church of Holy Wisdom in Constantinople and elsewhere.

The council called by Justinian finally met in Constantinople in May 553 under the presidency of Eutyches, the patriarch of Constantinople. Only 165 bishops were in attendance, largely from the Eastern dioceses. Realizing that the West would view the condemnation as a betrayal of Leo, the mercurial Vigilius refused to attend. The council issued fourteen anathemas, twelve of which were directed against Theodore of Mopsuestia, the theologian par excellence of the Church of the East. But the bishops were not thinking about Christians in the Persian Empire; they were myopically focused on the internal affairs of their own empire. In the end the pope agreed to accept the council, but it was not recognized in certain jurisdictions of Italy, including Milan and Aquileia. Nevertheless it went down in history as the Fifth Ecumenical Council.

In truth it was far too late to bring about a reconciliation of the contending parties. Too much had happened in the century since the adjournment of Chalcedon; the bishops in Egypt and Syria had begun to take things into their own hands independent of the imperial Church in Constantinople. Alexandria had a miaphysite patriarch, and Severus, bishop of Antioch (512–518), had begun to ordain anti-Chalcedonian bishops.

Justinian's grandest dream, to unite the quarreling ecclesiastical parties into one confession of faith, failed. By the end of the sixth century, on the eve of the rise of Islam, the fissure between Syriac- and Coptic-speaking Christians and the imperial Church had hardened into separate communions. The unity of the imperial Church was destroyed as language, regional loyalties, and theological formulas gave large regions of the Christian world a new sense of identity independent of Constantinople.

New Beginnings in the West

What the Syriac language was to Christians east of Jerusalem, Latin was to Christians in the West. Its geographical reach was not as wide as that of Syriac, but it would bind the peoples living in Germany, France, the Low Countries, Poland, Scandinavia, the British Isles, Spain, and Italy into a distinctive Christian civilization that we know as Europe. Latin became the language of learning and of law, of civil administration and royal decrees, and of the Church's principal rituals, baptism and the Eucharist. The language in which the poet Virgil sang the glories of Rome was the tongue in which monks chanted the psalms of David, and the speech of Cicero the Roman statesman and moralist became the argot of Christian philosophy and theology. In the thirteenth century Thomas Aquinas, the great medieval theologian, wrote in Latin; the poet Dante, who wrote his *Divine Comedy* in Italian, also composed works in Latin; and later the Protestant reformers Martin Luther and John Calvin wrote treatises in Latin. To this day all official texts issued by the bishop of Rome, the pope, are in Latin.

Latin Christianity was dynamic, not monolithic. When the peoples of northern Europe embraced the new faith, they did not simply transplant the culture of the Latin-speaking cities of the Mediterranean world to the lands north of the Alps. As the religion moved north it not only changed the mores of the people; the people brought new vitality and diversity to the religion. The Latin Christianity of the British Isles is a different thing from the Latin Christianity of Augustine's North Africa.

The early history of Christianity in the West takes place largely within the boundaries of the Roman Empire, the world of Cyprian of Carthage, Ambrose of Milan, Augustine of Hippo, and Leo of Rome. Though the empire extended beyond the Alps, the two great rivers, the Rhine flowing northwestward on the edge of Gaul and the Danube in the Balkans flowing east into the Black Sea, provided a natural boundary between the Roman world and that of the "barbarians" who had settled on their banks. So profound was the division in northern Europe between the regions in which the Germanic languages were spoken and the empire, where Latin was the lingua franca, that to this day a linguistic fault line separates French-speaking Belgium from areas that speak Flemish.

During the early centuries Christian leaders in the West displayed a studied disinterest in the world beyond the frontiers of the empire. One noteworthy exception was a <u>Goth named</u> Ulfila (little wolf), the "apostle to the Goths", who embraced Christianity in the fourth century at the height of the Arian controversy. He was ordained by an Arian bishop in Constantinople and served as "bishop of the Christians in the Gothic land" beyond the Danube River. During his years among the Goths he founded churches and ordained bishops, and most remarkably translated parts of the Bible into the Gothic language. With the exception of the books of Kings! These he omitted because, as an ancient historian put it, the "Gothic people are lovers of war and needed something to restrain their passion for fighting rather than incite them to it." Because of his efforts many of the Germanic peoples living on the borders of the empire adopted an Arian, or non-Nicene, form of Christianity. And it is these peoples, the Ostrogoths, the Visigoths, the Burgundians, the Lombards, who occupied and ruled the territories in northern Italy, Spain, and Gaul that had once been part of the Roman Empire.

Ulfila is singular. There is no other evidence of bishops being sent to preach the gospel to people living in the lands beyond the frontiers of the empire. When Christianity gained a foothold, as in Armenia, the king *sent* for bishops, but the initiative came from the king, not from leaders of the empire. In fact, with the accession of Constantine to the imperial throne many Christians assumed that the destiny of the Church was merging with that of the Roman Empire. That certainly was the opinion of Eusebius, the church historian, who saw in Constantine the fulfillment of the history that had begun in Christ. Rome and the Church were conflated into a single Christian kingdom. In this understanding of Christianity there was no place for a mission to the peoples beyond its frontiers. The Spanish poet Prudentius wrote that "Roman and barbarian are as distinct one from the other as are four-footed beasts from humans."

Prudentius's world was not, however, to last. He died in 410 and in the same decade Roman rule in Spain came to an end, and for the next century Spain would be ruled by the Visigoths, a "barbarian" people. Spain was not alone. Direct imperial rule over Italy, North Africa, and Gaul had ended earlier in the century, and the last emperor in the West, Romulus Augustus, was deposed in 476, by the German Odoacer. Though this date is sometimes called "the fall of Rome," it was a minor change of rule, more a political coup that allowed Odoacer to be proclaimed "king" by his troops than a major event in world history. By the end of the fifth century local kings ruled over territories in the West once ruled by Rome, the Franks in Gaul, the Ostrogoths in Italy, the Visigoths in Spain, and the Vandals in North Africa. The settled urban society of the Western empire was a thing of the past.

Within the empire the principal actors had been emperors and bishops. But with the decline of Roman rule in the West, kings (and queens) came to occupy center stage. So in turning to the peoples living beyond the Alps, the story must begin, as it did among peoples in the East, with a king. His name was Clovis, and he was the first among the Frankish kings to embrace Catholic (that is, Nicene) Christianity, rather than continue to practice the Arianism favored by the Germanic peoples.

Clovis was born into one of the Frankish groups that had settled along the banks of the Rhine River north of Tournai in Belgium in the third century. The name Clovis is derived from the German Chlodovech, which became Ludovicus in Latin, and Louis in French, the honored name of many kings of France up to the eighteenth century. When the Franks settled on the Rhine frontier they first fought with the Romans, but as the years passed, they adopted Roman ways. Among the finds in the tomb of Clovis's father, Childeric, discovered in the seventeenth century, was a signet ring with the face of a long-haired warrior in Roman military uniform and an inscription in Latin: *Childerici regis,* "by order of the king Childeric." Childeric's father was named Merovech, from which the term Merovingian is derived, the name for the Frankish kingdom that would rule Gaul until mid eighth century.

The center of Childeric's domain was in Belgium, but under the leadership of Clovis, a bold and cunning warrior, the Frankish kingdom overcame neighboring rivals and expanded into southern France. His success earned him the respect if not the affection of the rulers in Constantinople, and he was given the title of honorary consul. Like other Germanic kings, Clovis had first converted to a form of Arian Christianity, but under the influence of his wife he adopted Nicene Christianity. The story of his conversion is told in the *Ten Books of History* (often called the *History of the Franks*) written by Gregory, bishop of Tours, in the sixth century. The details of his account cannot be confirmed by other sources, but it shows how Gregory thought the story of the conversion of a king should be told and, most important, how Clovis's adoption of Catholic Christianity would be remembered in the medieval world. Here is Gregory's version of Clovis's baptism.

Against the objections of the king, his wife, Queen Clotild, had her son baptized by a Catholic bishop. But the child died shortly afterward, and Clovis reproached his wife for her rash and imprudent act. If the boy had been dedicated to my gods, said Clovis, he would not have died. When a second son was born, Clovis again opposed his baptism, predicting that his brother would suffer a similar fate. Sometime afterward, in the midst of a military battle, when his situation became desperate, Clovis called on Christ and soon his army was victorious. When he told the queen that he had triumphed by appealing to Christ she ordered Bishop Remigius of Rheims to meet with the king. Clovis agreed to be instructed, but reminded the bishop: "The people under my command will not agree to forsake their gods." Nonetheless he decided to go ahead.

In preparation for Clovis's baptism the public squares were draped with colored cloths, the church adorned with hangings, candles were lit and the air was filled with the fragrant odor of incense. On Christmas day, 508, Clovis confessed his faith in "God Almighty, three in one" and went down into the baptismal pool like a "new Constantine," writes Gregory. Significantly more than three thousand of his army were baptized with him as well as his sister Albofled.

The baptism of a king was a public and communal event, and Clovis's resolve to be baptized in the Nicene faith followed a prolonged process of deliberation among the members of his court and his military leaders, weighing what was to be gained as well as the risks. The decision was as much political as it was religious, a break with the past, a determination to change public practice and modify the mores of his people. Hence Clovis's hesitation. He knew his people would resist giving up their gods and familiar way of life. "Conversion" not only meant adopting new beliefs; it would bring changes in customs, such as marriage practices, impose new laws, alter the rhythms of communal life—Sunday as a holy day, festivals such as Easter and Christmas—reconfigure public space, construct a new past informed by Christian history and the Bible, introduce new words into the local language, and require the learning of some Latin to participate in the Church's rituals. The conversion of Clovis was the first step in the building of a new Christian society with the king as the head of the Christian people. The modern distinction between church and state has as little relevance to early medieval Europe as it had to life in the Roman Empire.

Clovis, king of the Franks, stands at the beginning of a new epoch in the history of Christianity in the West. His conversion set in motion forces that would advance the establishment of Catholic Christianity among the Germanic peoples living north of the Alps. Other Germanic peoples would soon follow: the Burgundians in southern Germany abandoned Arianism in 516, the Visigoths in Spain in 589. A new direction was being set. On his death Clovis left behind a Christian kingdom whose bishops were in fellowship with Rome, and in the next century the alliance between Christian kings and the papacy would set the course of medieval history for centuries. Clovis died in Paris in 511 and was buried in the Church of the Apostles (later known as Saint Genevieve).

In the same decade that Clovis was baptized, a young Italian nobleman set out for Rome to study the liberal arts. His name was Benedict, and he came from Nursia, a small town in Umbria, to the east of Rome. When he reached nineteen or twenty years (ca. 500), growing weary of literary studies and the dissolute life of his fellow students in Rome, he gave up his books and inheritance and resolved to find a place where he might serve God alone. At first he remained in the city but then settled, with a company of "devout men," at Enfide (modern-day Affile), some forty miles east of Rome.

Still Benedict was not satisfied and soon moved to a "lonely wilderness" near modern-day Subiaco in the Simbrucini mountains east of Rome. There he met an elderly monk named Romanus who supplied him with a monastic habit. Under a cliff on the side of a mountain Benedict found a narrow cave some ten feet deep and lived there as a hermit, unknown to anyone save Romanus, who set aside bread from his own portion and visited Benedict regularly. Because there was no path to the cave, Romanus would tie bread to a rope to let it down, and a small bell attached to the rope let Benedict know the bread had arrived.

After three years living alone, Benedict had gained the respect of other monks in the vicinity, and on the death of the abbot of a local monastery he was asked to become abbot. But things did not go well, and he set out on his own again. Now, however, he began to think more about communal life and put his mind to establishing monastic communities in the region. As his thinking matured he came to realize that the renewal of the individual was best reached not by the path of solitude but by living and working together in community under a common discipline. For two decades he devoted himself to this work and established twelve monastic houses.

About 530 he decided to leave the region and settle on the summit of Monte Cassino, a small mountain some eighty miles to the south. There he organized a monastery that would live in one "house" under a single abbot, not be spread around the countryside as at Subiaco. And it was at Monte Cassino that he wrote his famous *Rule,* one of the most influential books in the history of Christianity. It has proven to be singularly durable and to this day guides the life of religious communities all over the world.

The *Rule* is a short document written in vernacular Latin for the ordering of the life of a community of men (or women) who desire to follow the way of life presented in the gospels. Its language is simple and direct, "remarkable for its discretion and clarity of language," said Gregory the Great. Early Christian monasticism was a lay movement and its directives are addressed to laymen, not to clergy. The *Rule* deals with all aspects of the life of the community: times of prayer, which psalms are to be recited at different times of the day, the role of the abbot, governance of the community, formation of novices, correction of faults, sleeping arrangements, food and drink, clothing, work, reception of guests, caring for the sick, the practice of the virtues, most notably humility and obedience. "The first step of humility is unhesitating obedience." In the Prologue, Benedict says that he intends to set down "nothing harsh, nothing burdensome," and his *Rule* is a wise and discerning book that displays a spirit of moderation and a keen understanding of human nature.

Benedict called the monastery a "school for the Lord's service" where the monks could learn to serve the Lord in obedience to the abbot, who held the place of Christ. He wished to bring men back to God by the practice of obedience, because it was through the "idleness of disobedience" that they had turned away. Yet when he begins to list the "tools" for a virtuous life, he first mentions "love," citing the words of Jesus, "Love the Lord God with your whole heart, your whole soul and all your strength, and love your neighbor as yourself" (Matthew 22:37–39). Only after he has set the love of God before the monks does he enumerate the commandments and quote sayings of Jesus and the apostles on how one is to live; "Renounce yourself in order to follow Christ," for example, and "do not repay evil for evil."

For Benedict the religious life was social, and the genius of the rule was to provide guidelines for the formation of a distinct kind of community. Though he calls the monastery a "school," unlike a school it was not a place one entered for a fixed period of time; he envisioned a community in which one would live permanently with others. "Stability" (*stabilitas loci*), remaining in one place, was a key element in the growth in holiness. Besides stability, the monks took a vow of conversion of one's life (*conversio morum*) and obedience to the abbot. A better term than school to describe the monastery would be family or household, a company of men or women bound together for life under the direction of an abbot.

The daily life of the community was centered on regular hours of prayer. The day began with the "night office," a service of psalms and readings from Scripture and the writings of the church fathers on Scripture, at "a little past the middle of the night," says Benedict, when the evening meal is "fully digested." Then, appealing to the words of the psalmist, "Seven times a day have I praised you" (Psalms 119:164), Benedict prescribed seven times of prayer, which included Lauds at daybreak and Vespers at the end of the day. During the course of the day there were four short offices, Prime, Terce, Sext (midday), and None. These terms refer to the first, third, sixth, and ninth hours of the day. Finally, before retiring the monks would come together for "compline," in Latin, *completorium,* close of day. Each office included psalms and a reading from the Scripture, and Benedict is very explicit about what psalms are to be read at the different offices. The entire psalter was recited in the course of a week.

The primary "work" of the community was to pray. The monastery was not established to engage in any other activity, as for example teaching the young or caring for the sick or needy. In Benedict's words, "Nothing is to take precedence over the work of God," by which he meant the regular hours of prayer. "On hearing the signal for an hour of the divine office," writes Benedict, "the monk will immediately set aside what he has in hand and go with utmost speed." At the same time the monks had to support themselves, so work became an integral part of their life, tending the garden, cooking and baking, practicing useful crafts such as shoemaking, caring for the buildings, and the like. Manual labor was held in high regard. Though later some monastic communities became centers of learning, Benedict was more interested in the increase of virtue than growth in learning.

When Benedict wrote his *Rule,* monasticism was already well established in the West. To mention only a few notable leaders: Saint Martin of Tours (d. 397), who founded a monastery at Ligugé in southern France, the first to be established north of the Alps; Honoratus (d. 430), who founded a monastery on the island of Lerins off Cannes in the Mediterranean; John Cassian (d. ca. 430), who founded two monasteries in Marseilles and wrote a book setting forth rules for the monastic life; Caesarius (d. 541), who began his monastic life at Lerins and as bishop of Arles promoted monastic life and wrote two rules drawing on the traditions of Lerins. Benedict's *Rule* had many rivals, and its reception was slow. Over time, however, its practical insight, clarity, moderation, and adaptability gained favor, and like leaven, it worked its way into the growing monastic culture of northern Europe. But it was not until the eighth and ninth centuries that it began to receive royal support. The key figure was another Benedict (d. 821), a monk who founded a monastery at Aniane in southern France, where he adopted the *Rule* of Benedict after practicing a more severe form of monasticism.

Both Charlemagne (d. 814) and Louis the Pious, his son, were interested in reforming monastic life and set out to impose the *Rule* on the monasteries in the Carolingian realm. They enlisted Benedict who, with the authority of the crown behind him and timely legislation, was able to persuade other monastic houses to adopt the *Rule* and adapt it to local conditions. The aim was to bring the monasteries under a uniform observance and to institute regular visitations to ensure that the new order was observed. Monks and nuns began to think of themselves as part of a single fellowship rather than members of independent houses, what later came to be called a religious order. Benedict of Aniane and the Carolingian rulers are the true founders of Benedictine monasticism. Because of their efforts the *Rule* of Benedict would become the primary instrument fashioning monasticism in the West until the emergence of new forms of religious life in the High Middle Ages. Even so, the *Rule* proved remarkably fecund and adaptable throughout the Middle Ages and into modern times. It is understandable that Benedict is sometimes called the patron of Europe.

Two events then, the conversion of Clovis the Frankish king to Catholic Christianity and the writing of the *Rule* of Benedict, can be taken as signs of the new beginnings of Christianity in the West. Clovis was baptized in 508, and the *Rule* was written some three decades later. In the decades leading up to the year 500 and in the years that followed several other noteworthy figures in the making of a Latin

Christian culture flourished in the West. One of the more remarkable was a man named Anicius Boethius (480–524), who was born in Rome the same year as Benedict. Boethius was a man of the world, a statesman, philosopher, and educator, widely recognized as one of the fashioners of Western Christianity.

Boethius came from a noble family and as a young man studied in Athens and Alexandria, where he learned Greek, a rare achievement by someone living in the West at that time. His father had been consul under the Arian king of the Ostrogoths, Theodoric, who ruled over Italy from the city of Ravenna on the Adriatic Sea. In 510 Boethius became consul at the court of Theodoric, and by 520 he was the head of the civil administration. Boethius, however, was a Catholic Christian, and his theological views led to tension with the king when the emperor Justin in Constantinople began to champion the Nicene cause and persecute Arians. What brought about his downfall, however, was an ill-considered attempt to defend a senatorial colleague who had been charged with disloyalty to the king. Boethius was implicated in a widespread conspiracy and summarily tried, condemned to death, and imprisoned at Pavia, a town in northern Italy not too far from Milan. While awaiting death he wrote a treatise entitled the *Consolation of Philosophy,* one of the most beloved, influential, and widely read books of medieval times. Already in the ninth century it was translated into Anglo-Saxon for King Alfred the Great.

The *Consolation of Philosophy* is a meditation on the transitory fortunes of this life and the quest for true happiness. It is a profound and eloquent book, a work of philosophy not theology, interspersed with original Latin poems. Even Gibbon, the Enlightenment historian, called it a "golden volume, not unworthy of the leisure of Plato or of Tully [Cicero]." The book takes the form of a dialogue in which philosophy, Lady Wisdom, leads Boethius out of his despair and despondency to lift his mind to what alone can bring true happiness. Step by step she lays before him the catalogue of goods for which human beings strive, riches, honor, power, fame, pleasure, to show that they all can be lost in a sudden change of fortune.

Boethius had "pledged himself to fortune," says Wisdom, and thought he could find stability and happiness in human affairs. But it is folly, says Lady Wisdom, to put one's trust in man's "tumbling fortunes." Once one has submitted to the fetters of fortune one "must take calmly whatever she can do to you." Every change of fortune "brings with it a disquiet in the soul," and in a revealing line Boethius acknowledges that even when things were going well his mind was never at rest. He thought he could rely "on things that come and go," but nothing that comes into being lasts. When engulfed by the "stormy sea of fortune," says Lady Wisdom, the one good that endures, the supreme good, is God. In the central poem in the book Boethius prays: "Grant, Oh Father, that my mind may rise to Thy sacred throne. Let it see the fountain of good; let it find light, so that the clear light of my soul may fix itself in Thee." True freedom, he writes, is found only in hope and prayer, the bonds that form the basis of our relation to God.

Had he only written the *Consolation of Philosophy* Boethius's reputation would have been secured. But he also wrote more specialized works in philosophy and theology and translated and commented on ancient Greek philosophical writings. Boethius's philosophical essays and translations exemplify a feature of the emerging Western tradition, a sustained and systematic attempt to preserve the learned inheritance of Greek and Latin antiquity.

In any roll call of the fashioners of a Western Christian culture, an honored place belongs to Cassiodorus, a contemporary of Boethius. Cassiodorus was born in 485 in Calabria in southern Italy to a senatorial family. Like Boethius he served at the court of Theodoric, putting his literary skills to work compiling edicts and official letters and recording notable events. More politic than Boethius, he lived to a ripe old age and at seventy returned to his native village of Squillace on the southernmost coast of Italy to found a monastery. He had traveled in the East and was impressed by the Syrian Christian theological school in Nisibis and hoped to create something similar in the West. In contrast to Benedict he made scholarship and study integral to the monastic life.

In Augustine's day educated Christians were the beneficiaries of an educational system that had been in place for hundreds of years. When he wrote his treatise *On Christian Doctrine* (an essay on interpreting and expounding the Scriptures) Augustine could assume that his readers knew Latin grammar and were familiar with standard rhetorical techniques. But a hundred years later such knowledge could no longer be taken for granted. In the generation of Boethius and Cassiodorus the challenge was no longer how to transform what had been received; it was rather to preserve and transmit what was forgotten.

Cassiodorus's most important work, *Institutes of Divine and Human Letters*, a compendium of sacred and secular learning, was written to aid the monks in reading and understanding the Scriptures and in copying manuscripts. He begins by listing the books of the Bible, the order and division of the books, how they are to be interpreted, and brief comments on Christian teachers, including Hilary, Ambrose, Jerome, and Augustine. Note that all are Latin church fathers; the Greek writers are largely ignored.

In the second part of the *Institutes,* dealing with "secular letters," he includes sections on the "arts" necessary to interpret the Scriptures, grammar, dialectic, rhetoric. Secular letters, he writes, are indispensable for the study of the Bible, and grammar is "the foundation of liberal studies." When he was ninety years old he wrote a book titled *On Orthography,* a spelling handbook for monks to aid them in their work of copying older books. Christian thinkers had begun to assume responsibility for managing the mechanisms of the Latin language.

Latin was also the language of Christianity in Spain, and in the generation after Cassiodorus, the most learned person in Spain was Isidore, the bishop of Seville. Born into the landed gentry of Cartagena in 560, he was educated in an episcopal school in Seville under the supervision of his brother Leander, bishop of the city. In the year 600 he succeeded Leander, and as bishop Isidore had a profound influence on the liturgy and laws of the Church in Spain. He also commands our attention because of his interest in language and in organizing the knowledge that had been inherited from the past.

The work that best represents his genius is known as *Etymologies,* a vast encyclopedia that attempted a summary of all branches of knowledge by drawing on the deep reservoir of classical writers: Aesop, Apuleius, Aristotle, Caesar, Catullus, Cicero, Demosthenes, Herodotus, Hesiod, Homer, Horace, Juvenal, Livy, Lucretius, Ovid, Pindar, Plato, Plautus, Quintillian, Virgil. In this work Isidore deals with grammar, rhetoric, mathematics, medicine, law, ecclesiastical books and offices, languages, kingdoms, human beings, animals, weights and metals, agriculture, ships, architecture, clothes. Isidore was engaged in an enterprise not unlike the movement of "cultural literacy" in our time. To engage in such an apparently simple task as reading a book or newspaper, one must know certain things.

Like Quintilian, the famous Roman grammarian and rhetorician, Isidore recognized that grammar is "the science of correct speech and the interpretation of the poets." It is not simply a matter of knowing which case goes with which preposition or when to use the subjunctive; it is a study of the features of language and the rules that govern the relation of words and concepts. Grammar teaches students to make distinctions and to use words accurately, introduces concepts such as analogy, and explains the different figures of speech. By taking responsibility for elementary education, he encouraged clear and cogent thinking, and this in turn lent solidity, authority, and elegance to writing. For Isidore grammar and lexicography were instruments of culture. Indeed, to produce writings that drew on examples from ancient literature, especially in the conditions of his time, required uncommon perseverance, discipline, and a well-organized scriptorium for copying earlier books. His library was inscribed with the words *Sunt hic plura sacra, sunt mundialia plura* (There are many things here dealing with sacred matters, and many more dealing with secular matters).

As necessary as retrieval and preservation were in the sixth century, they are only a part of the story of the transition from ancient to medieval culture. While Isidore and Cassiodorus were copying manuscripts and passing on the wisdom of the ancients, an original Latin poet came on the scene. His name was Venantius Fortunatus (ca. 530–609), and in measured lines and resonant verses he voiced religious sentiments that were fresh and original and distinctly Western. So popular did several of his hymns become that to this day two are still sung across the

Christian world during Holy Week: *Vexilla regis prodeunt* (The Royal Banners Forward Go) and *Pange lingua* (Sing, My Tongue, the Glorious Battle).

Venantius was born in Italy and as a young man he crossed the Alps, spending most of his life in Gaul, where he died as bishop of Poitiers. At first he gained attention by writing flattering verses for kings, queens, and bishops; then he became spiritual adviser to a Frankish queen, Radegunda, who had found refuge from her coarse and bloodthirsty husband in the peace of a monastery in Poitiers. In 569 the emperor Justin II had sent as a gift to Radegunda the most precious relic in Christianity, a remnant of the True Cross. For the solemn procession when the relic would be carried from Tours to the monastery at Poitiers, Venantius wrote *Vexilla regis prodeunt*. This was no ordinary hymn about the crucifixion; it breathes a kind of "cross" piety, a devotion to the "wood" of the cross on which Christ was crucified. Here is the first stanza in Latin, then in a verse translation:

> Vexilla regis prodeunt
> Fulget crucis mysterium
> Quo carne carnis conditor
> Suspensus est patibulo
>
> The royal banners forward go.
> The cross shines forth in mystic glow;
> Where he in flesh, our flesh who made
> Our sentence bore, our ransom paid.

It is, however, the fourth stanza where the fertile imagination of Fortunatus is most apparent.

> Arbor decora et fulgida,
> Ornata regis purpura
> Electa digno stipite
> Tam sancta membra tangere

In translation:

> O lovely and shining tree,
> adorned with the purple of a king,
> chosen from a worthy trunk,
> to touch those sacred members.

For Fortunatus the tree itself (on which Christ was crucified) has become an object of devotion. As by the fruit of a tree sin came into the world, so by the fruit of a tree came salvation. This "noble wood" bears the "new fruit," the body of Christ. Fortunatus's warm and tender feelings toward the cross are developed more fully in the second hymn, *Pange lingua*. Here are several stanzas in John Mason Neale's translation and Fortunatus's Latin:

"Faithful Cross! Above all other,
One and only noble Tree!
None in foliage, none in blossom,
None in fruit thy peer may be;
Sweetest wood and sweetest iron!
Sweetest weight is hung on thee.

Bend, O lofty Tree, thy branches,
Thy too rigid sinews bend;
And awhile the stubborn hardness,
Which thy birth bestow'd suspend;
And the limbs of heav'n's high Monarch
Gently on thine arms extend!

Crux fidelis, inter omnes
Arbor una nobilis
Nulla talem silva profert,
Flore, fronde, germine
Dulce lignum, dulci clavo,
Dulce pondus sustinens!

Flecte ramos, arbor alta,
Tensa laxa viscera
Et rigor lentescat ille
Quem dedit nativitas,
Ut superni membra regis
Miti tendas stipite

Something new is at work here that will shape Western piety for centuries. Reading Fortunatus's hymns, one understands why the crucifix became the most prominent object of devotion in Western Christianity and the ritual of kissing a wooden cross part of the Church's liturgy on Good Friday.

Latin Christianity Spreads North

The daunting task of carrying Christianity to the peoples living north of the Alps and in the British Isles was carried out, in the main, by brave and hardy Latin-speaking monks and bishops. It is a story—in truth many stories—stretching over hundreds of years, roughly from the fifth to the eleventh centuries. A case can even be made that the great period of Christian expansion in Europe did not come to an end until the fourteenth century, when Jogaila, the grand duke of Lithuania, adopted the faith.

In the century after the demise of the empire in the West, there was no organized effort to Christianize the north. The first mission to England was initiated by Pope Gregory the Great at the end of the sixth century. His project was an unusual undertaking for a pope; only after Gregory did the popes take an active interest in the mission to peoples of the north. In most regions the initiative came from enterprising monks and bishops in alliance with local kings. Most kingdoms were small and many kings were itinerant; where the king was, there was the seat of political power. It was a diffuse and divided world with no central authority, whether political or religious. The adoption of Christianity proceeded piecemeal without any systematic plan, and it was not until the time of Charlemagne at the end of the eighth century that a unified political and spiritual order came into being. This chapter highlights some of the more memorable figures.

Ireland had never been part of the Roman Empire, though its harbors were known to the Romans through trading, and it was probably merchants who brought Christianity to the island in the fourth century. In 431, Pope Celestine sent a man named Palladius from Gaul to the Christians in Ireland "as their first bishop." Unfortunately, almost nothing is known of Palladius, and his role in the spread of Christianity in Ireland is overshadowed by the indomitable Patrick.

The story of Patrick's life is overgrown with legend, and some of the tales that are told about his work among the Irish appear only in very late sources. The vignette that he used the leaves of the shamrock to illustrate the doctrine of the Holy Trinity is not found until the seventeenth century. However, we do have two brief writings from Patrick himself, and they give a vivid account of his adventures and of his convictions. The first, the *Confessio,* is a kind of personal statement filled with autobiographical details written in simple and often obscure Latin by someone who had little formal education. He calls himself "unlearned" and admits he has difficulty with the "idiom" of this "foreign tongue."

Patrick was born in Britain sometime in the late fourth century. At the age of sixteen he was captured by Irish raiders and brought to Ireland, where he became a herdsman. After six years he had a vision urging him to flee, and he made his way to a port where he boarded a ship sailing to his home country. While in Ireland, Patrick underwent a moral and spiritual conversion, and after returning to Britain he began to have thoughts of returning to evangelize the Irish people. He tells of a dream in which a man named Victoricus had appeared to him with a bundle of letters from Ireland. As he read the letters one by one they began to speak with a single voice, "the voice of the Irish," as he put it, calling him back: "We beg you, holy youth, that you come and walk again among us."

Patrick resolved to return to Ireland and may have gone to Gaul on the continent to prepare for ordination. But there was opposition, perhaps because of his meager education. In his *Confessio* he also mentions an incident thirty years earlier when he was only fifteen that was thrown in his face by his detractors. But Patrick was able to stand down his critics and was soon ready to begin the "devout and wonderful work" of preaching the gospel to the Irish people.

The task was arduous. Patrick was "insulted" by people, most likely Druids who worshiped other gods, persecuted by local kings, subjected to cold and deprivation. Yet he persisted and made his way to "remote districts" where no one had heard the gospel, and according to his testimony he baptized "thousands" of people. He also began to lay the foundations for the institutional structures that would allow the new faith to put down roots and flourish. He established monasteries and made provisions for the teaching of the Latin language. In Gaul and Italy and Spain, the spoken language, the forerunners of French, Italian, and Spanish, had developed out of Latin. For the Irish, however, Latin was a foreign tongue. Without Latin, the clergy could not celebrate the Church's rituals or read the Scriptures or communicate with Christians on the continent. One story told of Patrick relates than when he baptized a convert to Christianity he handed him the ABC, a Latin grammar.

A fascinating artifact of how Latin was transmitted in the early Middle Ages was found in County Antrim in 1914. An Irishman cutting turf for fuel uncovered a Latin schoolbook four feet deep in a bog located not far from the remains of an ancient monastery. Inside were six wooden leaves lined with wax and bound to-gether with leather straps. On the leaves were written psalms 30 and 31 in the Latin Vulgate (31 and 32 in English Bibles). As in the Syriac-speaking world, the Psalms were the first textbook studied by youngsters. The tutor would read the Latin verses to the student, whose language was Irish, and he would write them on the waxed leaves that allowed his mistakes to be corrected. By slow methodical ex-ercises Latin was taught to the young and gradually became the language of the monks, clergy, and educated classes. With the arrival of bishops and monks came the makings of a Latin Christian culture.

There were no towns in Ireland, and the population was dispersed widely. In the Roman Empire the bishop resided in a city and had close relations with the local civil administration. In Ireland the basic social unit was a tribe or clan under a king without any fixed territory. In a revealing line in his *Confessio,* Patrick mentions "the sons of kings who travel with me." There were many kings—as many as 150—and the territory each ruled over was tiny. By making alliances with the local dynasties Patrick was able to advance the Christian mission. And the one institution that proved most adaptable to the social world of fifth- and sixth-century Ireland was the monastery. With land endowed by local kings, buildings, farms, animals, bak-ery, church, and sturdy walls, the monasteries became centers not only of religious but also of social life. And it was there that the art of writing, copying, and decorat-ing books, as well as woodworking and stone carving, were cultivated.

From Ireland monks crossed the North Channel to Scotland. One of the first was a man named Columba (520–597), son of a royal family, who had founded a monastery at Derry in Ireland in the mid sixth century. In 563 he sailed, as a "pilgrim for Christ," in the words of his biographer, to Iona, a small island off the west coast of Scotland in the Hebrides to establish a monastery. In truth he was driven out after his clan lost a key battle. Eventually he became an evangelist to the Picts of northern Scotland. Steep and rugged mountains divided the northern part of Scot-land from the south, and, according to the English historian Bede, the Picts living in the south were evangelized by Ninian, "a Briton who had received orthodox instruction at Rome in the faith and the mysteries of the truth."

The most enterprising of the Irish monks was Columbanus—a different person than Columba—who joined the monastery at Bangor in County Down in the middle of the sixth century. Like Columba, he desired to be a pilgrim for Christ and in the 580s left Ireland for Gaul, where he founded several monastic houses. Even-tually he traveled over the Alps to Italy to establish yet another monastery at Bobbio, where he died in 615. His aim was to renew Christian life in areas where the old Roman Christian culture had been destroyed by the Germanic invasions of the fifth century. Ironically, monks from a far-off mission field returned to the continent to "re-christianize" regions where Christianity had once flourished.

Columbanus was fiercely independent and ignored the local bishops, bringing along his own bishop to carry out episcopal functions. He even gave Pope Gregory the Great a piece of his mind over the date of the celebration of Easter. The Irish, like the Romans, celebrated Easter on a Sunday, but if the vernal equinox fell on a Sunday, Easter was celebrated on that same Sunday, whereas Rome kept the festival on the next Sunday. "How can you keep a dark Easter," Columbanus asks the pope, by celebrating it when there is no moon? Though the letter is deferential to the pope's authority, calling him "the fair ornament of the Church," by the time he reaches its end Columbanus senses he may have spoken too bluntly and apologizes for his "forwardness." Significantly in his address to the pope he uses the phrase "the whole of Europe," implicitly recognizing the pope as the head of the Western Latin Church.

Besides transporting the Irish tradition of celebrating the date of Easter to the continent, Columbanus also introduced a new form of penance. In the early Church the only form of penance was a public ritual for grievous sins, such as murder or adultery. Offenders were set apart from the community, made to stand in a separate section in the church during services, listen to the prayers of the faithful on their behalf, fast, and remain chaste. A person could be admitted as a penitent only once in a lifetime, and the practice was so harsh that penance was postponed until the end of life.

Columbanus was one of the architects of what eventually would be known as "private" penance. Unlike the practice in the early Church, it could be administered by a priest, not only a bishop, and repeated a number of times. The confessor determined the gravity of the sin and imposed an appropriate penance. The practice was not really "private," because the acts of penance were known by family, neighbors, and friends, but it did fill a spiritual void by providing for a personal act of contrition before a priest. Over time books called "penitentials" were written to serve as manuals for the clergy to determine what penances fit what sins, and also to provide spiritual guidance to the penitent. Because it allowed for a personal and compassionate way to deal with sin, the practice caught on and became characteristic of Western Christianity. The penitentials are a fascinating window on the mores of societies in which they were written.

In the same decade, the last of the sixth century, when Columbanus had traveled from Ireland to Gaul, a monk from Rome had journeyed in the opposite direction to the British Isles to evangelize the Anglo-Saxons living in southeastern England. His name was Augustine, and he has gone down in history as Saint Augustine of Canterbury because he founded an episcopal see there, in the capital of Kent.

Christianity had arrived in the British Isles in the third century, most likely carried by merchants or soldiers. Tertullian, the North African who wrote early in the century, mentions that "Christ's name" is confessed in Britain, but gives no details. And much later in his *Ecclesiastical History of the English People,* Bede (d. 735), a monk at the monastery in Jarrow in northern England, tells the story of the martyrdom of a certain Alban at the beginning of the third century.

Bede was one of the most learned men in the early medieval world and a skilled Latin stylist. Like Cassiodorus and Isidore of Seville, he wrote works on grammar and spelling, and on Latin metrics, but also on chronology (to calculate the date of Easter). He was a diligent, if not original, commentator on the Bible who drew widely on the writings of the Latin church fathers, Augustine, Jerome, Ambrose, and Gregory the Great. His history is our principal source for the planting and growth of Christianity in England from its beginnings until the early eighth century.

According to Bede's account, Alban hid a priest who had converted him in his home to escape persecutors. When the ruse was discovered Alban was taken prisoner and beheaded. The date of his martyrdom is uncertain, but it seems to have taken place in the latter part of the third century. By the fourth century the Church in Britain had an ecclesiastical structure and was able to send three bishops, Restitutus of London, Eborius of York, and Adelphius of Lincoln, to a council at Arles in Gaul (Francia).

Toward the end of the fourth century, however, the Roman settlements were besieged by Picts, who came across the northern frontier and breached Hadrian's Wall, and by Scots and Saxons who arrived by sea. Early in the fifth century, during the reign of Emperor Theodosius, the Romans began to withdraw and Roman rule came to an end, leaving the Britons to provide for their own defense. In the years that followed, Saxons, with the encouragement of local kings, began to settle in the eastern estuaries and to mingle with the local peoples.

With the arrival of the pagan Saxons, Christians were driven into Wales, and Christianity went into steep decline. It is against this background that Pope Gregory mounted his project to evangelize the English. The fullest account of Augustine's mission England is told in Bede's history. For Bede the arrival of Augustine in England is a pivotal event in English history.

Here is how he introduces his account: "In the fourteenth year of [Roman emperor] Maurice and about fifteen years after the coming of the Angles to Britain, Gregory [the Great], prompted by divine inspiration, sent a servant of God named Augustine and several more God fearing monks with him to preach the word of God to the English race."

To explain why Gregory had taken an interest in "that place cut off at the very world's end," in Virgil's words, Bede tells this story: one day in the marketplace in Rome before he had become pope, Gregory saw some boys "with fair complexions, handsome faces, and lovely hair" on sale. He asked where they had come from and was told their home was the island of Britain. When he inquired whether the people of the island were Christian, he was told they were heathen and called "Angli." To which he responded, "Good, they have the face of angels and such men should be fellow-heirs of the angels in heaven."

Bede seems to have had some doubts about the veracity of this story, because he emphasizes before he tells it and again afterward that it was handed down as a "tradition of our forefathers." But from one of Gregory's letters we know that for a long time he had in mind a mission to the British Isles, whose people, as he put it, live in a "remote corner of the world [and] are still worshipping trees and rocks."

Gregory commissioned Augustine, a monk from his own monastery on the Celian Hill in Rome, and a company of monks to make the long journey over the Alps and through Gaul to the English Channel for the crossing. But when they reached Francia, says Bede, they were "paralyzed with terror" at what they were facing, a barbarous people in a strange country whose language they did not know. So they turned back and begged Gregory to allow them to abandon "so dangerous, wearisome, and uncertain a journey." But Gregory was not one to give in so readily, and he wrote bishops and kings in Francia urging them to give Augustine whatever aid he needed. With their help Augustine was able to enlist interpreters who spoke the language of the Anglo-Saxons, and he continued on his way.

Augustine and his company of monks arrived in England in spring 597, on the island of Thanet off the east coast of Kent. Augustine sent a messenger to Ethelbert, the king of Kent, to inform him of their arrival, and the king ordered them to remain on the island "until he decided what to do about them." Ethelbert was familiar with Christianity because his wife, Bertha, the daughter of a Frankish king, was a Christian. A few days later the king came to the island to meet with Augustine. Augustine told him that he had come to proclaim good news, and the king, after listening politely, said he could not accept what he heard because it was "new to him and doubtful." He did not believe his people would give up the ways they had followed for so long. He did, however, give them a dwelling in Canterbury, the chief city in his realm.

According to Bede's account, Augustine and his monks approached carrying "the holy cross" and "an image of our great King and Lord, Jesus Christ," and singing a litany in Latin. I have always been charmed by this passage, but it is likely that the story of Augustine's arrival as told by Bede is largely the work of his imagination. Nevertheless there is a precious bit of information embedded in it. Bede says they were singing the following responsorial verse (or antiphon): "We beseech Thee, O Lord, in Thy great mercy, that Thy wrath and anger may be turned away from this city and from Thy holy house, for we have sinned. Alleluia." This is an ancient liturgical text, and by good fortune we know two of the melodies it was sung to, one from England and the other from Francia and Italy.

When Augustine arrived there were some Christians living in Kent, and a church building near the city from Roman times was still standing. The king put it at the disposal of Augustine's monks. The presence of Christians in Kent suggests that Gregory's aim in sending Augustine was not only to evangelize the native population but also to bring ecclesiastical order to the region and establish "Roman" Christianity in the British Isles.

Augustine arrived with forty monks—a very large number—and a few years later Gregory sent four other monks to join them. Clearly the mission to England was a major undertaking. It was also well equipped. According to Bede, when the reinforcements arrived they brought with them sacred vessels for celebrating the Eucharist, altar cloths and church ornaments, vestments for the clergy, relics of the apostles and martyrs, and many manuscripts. They also carried a letter from Gregory instructing Augustine to organize the bishops in Britain.

As soon as they began their work, the monks had questions about how to deal with native customs and religious rites. Dutifully Augustine wrote Gregory for advice. He asked what should be done with temples housing statues of pagan gods. At first Gregory said the temples and the "idols" in them should be destroyed, but he soon discovered that, even after King Ethelbert had become a Christian, he could not simply compel the people to abandon their old ways. As reports on the progress of the mission were brought back to Rome, Gregory began to reconsider the matter.

In a sagacious letter to a bishop in Francia who was traveling with the monks returning to England from Rome, Gregory asked him to carry a message to Augustine: "I have long been thinking about the case of the English and have decided that the temples should not be destroyed, but only the idols within them. Let holy water be sprinkled on them, altars constructed, relics deposited in them, so that if well built the temples may be converted from the cult of demons to the worship of the true God." If the buildings are not destroyed but allowed to stand, explained Gregory, the people will be more likely to go to them to worship God than they would to frequent a new structure.

Gregory adopted a similar approach in the matter of animal sacrifices. Although it was the custom of the people to roast animals as sacrifices to the gods, the practice should not be discontinued. Rather, Augustine should let the people enjoy such celebrations "but in a changed form." Instead of calling these feasts "sacrifices," they should be occasions for thanksgiving to God who gives all things, and, one can imagine, the occasion for a good party. The joy in material things, said Gregory, would incline their hearts to spiritual joy, for it is only by gradual steps that we can ascend to God.

Gregory's wisdom, prudence, and sound judgment have endeared him to later generations of Christians. Yet his approach to the English was not idiosyncratic. As Christianity expanded among new peoples in different parts of the world, it adapted to local customs and made them part of the Church's life. At the same time, Christianity changed the mores of the people in such matters as marriage, consanguinity, how they prayed and buried their dead, the ordering of space (by constructing churches), and the marking of time (Christian festivals and saints days). As in other parts of the Christian world, Christianization brought about a gradual transformation of communal life. New institutions were established, such as bishoprics and monasteries, and distant peoples became part of a larger ordered society, what Gibbon called the "union and discipline of the Christian republic."

The success of Augustine and the monks from Rome had far-reaching consequences for the future of the Church in the British Isles. This is most evident in a council held in 664 at the monastery of Whitby under King Oswiu of Northumbria. His aim was to unite those who followed the Celtic observance of Easter and those who followed Roman practice. The king kept the Celtic practice, but Eanflaed, the queen, came from Kent, where the Roman date was kept. Which meant that Easter was observed at different times by the members of the royal family; the king would break the Lenten fast to celebrate Easter while the queen and her company were still in Lent observing Palm Sunday.

According to Bede's account of the council, after opening remarks by the king on the unity of the Church, Colman, a bishop from Ireland, laid out the case for the Celtic practice, and Agilbert, a bishop from Gaul, was asked to set forth the Roman view. But he yielded the floor to a local priest named Wilfrid who had studied in Rome and, said Agilbert, "can explain our views in the English tongue better and more clearly than I can through an interpreter." The debate was held in the vernacular, Old English, not Latin. Wilfrid's chief argument was that the Roman practice, resting on the authority of Peter, was observed across the Christian world, whereas the Celtic tradition was kept only on "the two remotest islands of the Ocean." At this insult Bishop Colman rose to defend the Celtic way, and the debate was joined.

In the end the king decided the council should follow Peter because, says Bede, he held the keys to the kingdom of heaven. The council did not, however, put an end to the Celtic practice. Bishop Colman and his clergy returned to Ireland and held fast to their traditions. But Whitby did lay the foundations for a unified ecclesiastical structure in England under the bishop of Rome in communion with the churches on the continent.

In the decade before the Council of Whitby a pious father in Wessex, England, handed over his young son to a monastery at Exeter. His name was Wynfrith, and he would be celebrated in Christian memory as Boniface, the "apostle to the Germans." As a boy he joined a monastery at Nursling, where he excelled as a student—he later wrote a Latin grammar—and found in himself a fervent desire to become a "pilgrim for Christ." When he was forty years old his abbot gave him permission to undertake a mission to Frisia, the area west of the Rhine along the North Sea in present-day Netherlands. His first effort was unsuccessful, but he made his way to

Rome, and in 719 Wynfrith received a formal commission from Pope Gregory II to evangelize the heathen and was named Boniface after an early Christian martyr. His new name was an ominous portent as to how he would end his life. Boniface worked for a few years in Frisia with Willibrord, another monk from England, but he was strong-willed and wanted to do things his own way. After another visit to Rome he was consecrated bishop by the pope, with a mandate to evangelize the German-speaking people east of the Rhine.

On returning to the north he paid a visit to Charles Martel, mayor of the palace at the Frankish court, seeking his support. Without the protection of kings and princes the missions of the monks would never have gotten off the ground. Boniface carried letters from the pope to princes in Thuringia, and for the next fifteen years he worked in the dense forests of central Germany. There were some Christians living in the region, but Boniface's biographer, Willibald, says they did not accept the teachings of the Church "in their entirety," meaning they continued in their pagan ways while confessing Christ.

According to Willibald the Germans worshiped trees and springs, and he tells the fabled story about Boniface and the sacred oak tree in Geismar. The tree was "of extraordinary size and in the tongue of the pagans it was called the Oak of Jupiter." When Boniface saw that the people reverenced the mighty oak, he boldly stepped forward with an axe in hand, a large crowd looking on, and began to cut it down. In Willibald's telling, after Boniface had made a few cuts, a "mighty blast of wind" split the tree and it fell to the ground. At this "extraordinary spectacle" the people stopped reviling Boniface and began to bless the Lord. Prudently Boniface used the timber from the huge oak to build a chapel to serve as the heart of a new monastery.

In truth Boniface's principal activity—and that of other monks and bishops— was more prosaic, cultivating good relations with local royalty and aristocracy, establishing new monasteries, most famously Fulda in Hesse, copying the books of the Scripture, baptizing, preaching, and teaching. It was the slow follow-up that really mattered among new peoples. In many ways monks had their greatest impact by providing pastoral care (*cura animarum*) before there were parishes with a resident priest.

Boniface was not working on his own. He kept in close touch with the pope in Rome, who commissioned him to organize the bishops in the new region and establish bishoprics. With the support of the Frankish king he revived the custom of having councils to enforce disciplinary standards. Eventually he would be appointed archbishop of Mainz.

But Boniface was a restless soul with a keen sense of the urgency of the Church's mission. In a letter he quotes the words of Saint Paul in 1 Timothy, "God desires all men to be saved and to come to the knowledge of the truth" (2:4). When he was in his seventies Boniface set out again to Frisia on the North Sea, accompanied by

Eoban the bishop of Utrecht and a group of monks. After a year of work they had camped on a riverbank near Dokkum for the "laying on of hands" (confirmations), but they were surprised by a group of hostile Frisians brandishing weapons and seeking loot. Several monks grabbed for their swords to defend themselves, but Boniface told them to lay down their arms. Without mercy the plunderers massacred Boniface and more than fifty companions. When the thieves opened the chests hoping to find treasures, to their great chagrin they found only books.

Boniface's body was taken to Utrecht, then to Mainz, and was finally laid to rest at Fulda, where it remains to this day. The monastery soon became a place of pilgrimage, and there one can see a gospel book with two deep gashes. It is piously believed that Boniface used the book to defend himself when he was attacked.

By the eighth century the Christian mission had reached the North Sea, and in the ninth century another enterprising monk, Anskar (801–865), known as "the apostle to the north," pressed into Denmark. But he met with little success. A few years later he reached Birka, near present-day Stockholm in Sweden, but again his labors did not bear fruit. A century and a half later, though, about the year 1000, thanks to the efforts of Sigfrid, an English monk, the Swedish king Olov Skoetkonung was baptized.

Christianity also reached Norway from England. The Norwegian king Olaf II (d. 1030) provided strong, though seldom gentle, support for the establishment of Christianity in his realm. In the twelfth century an Englishman, Nicholas Breakspear, was sent by the pope to Norway to organize the churches and establish new bishoprics, most notably at Trondheim (Nidaros), where a great cathedral was built. Nidaros, the most northern episcopal see in the Western Church, would become a famous pilgrimage site in the Middle Ages.

From Scandinavia monks sailed to Iceland, and the ruling council of elders adopted the faith in the year 1000. About the same time, as we shall see in a later chapter, Poland adopted Christianity from the West—not from Byzantium as did other Slavic peoples—and episcopal sees were founded first at Gniezno and then at Cracow, under the jurisdiction of the pope in Rome.

In the course of seven or eight centuries, most of western Europe embraced Christianity, and the foundations were laid for a distinctive Western Christianity in which Latin was the language of learning and of worship, bishops were in fellowship with Rome, and monks followed the *Rule* of Benedict.

The Sacking of Jerusalem;
More Controversy over Christ

Although Constantinople was the political, administrative, and economic center of the Roman Empire, the hearts of Christians were fixed on Jerusalem, the city of King David where Solomon built the first Jewish temple, the stage for the Hebrew prophets, and the place of Jesus's death and resurrection. To mark the site of Christ's burial, Constantine's architects had constructed a shrine with twelve enormous columns encircling the tomb. Across from the tomb they placed a courtyard to enclose the rock of Golgotha where Christ was crucified, and next to it they raised a huge basilica with four aisles and a nave. The buildings were so splendid they could not be looked on "without exciting wonder." Each year thousands of pilgrims came to Jerusalem to walk the streets where Jesus walked and kiss the tomb where his body had been laid.

In the early centuries Jerusalem had been overshadowed by the greater cities of Alexandria in Egypt, Antioch in Syria, and Rome and Carthage in the West, but by the fifth century it had been elevated to a patriarchate with jurisdiction over churches in the region. Its spiritual potency, however, transcended its ecclesiastical stature. Jerusalem was the Christian city par excellence, the "holy city," as it came to be called. Several decades ago archaeologists uncovered the floor of a church built in the eighth century in Jordan with a mosaic panel depicting buildings of Jerusalem. Above the panel is written a Greek legend: THE HOLY CITY.

Jerusalem was also the repository of the holiest relic in Christianity, a fragment of the wood of the cross on which Christ was crucified. In the fourth century, Cyril, bishop of Jerusalem, reminded the faithful that the "holy wood of the Cross . . . is seen among us to this day." Each year on Good Friday the bishop sat in a chair with the rock of Golgotha behind him and a table before him. Deacons brought out a gold and silver box, and the precious fragment of the cross was taken out and placed on the table. As the deacons held firmly to each end of the wood, the people came forward one by one, bent over to touch the "holy Wood" with their forehead and their eyes, then kissed it.

Viewed from the perspective of the West, Jerusalem seems perched on the edge of the Mediterranean world, far closer to Mesopotamia than to Rome. Though the Romans had extended their empire into the Middle East, for centuries they had fought with the Persians over control of the vast area extending from the Mediterranean Sea to the Euphrates River. On several occasions the Romans had reached the Persian capital of Ctesiphon, and the Persians, under Sasanid rule, had pillaged Antioch and other cities in greater Syria.

In the early seventh century the Byzantine Empire, divided politically by rival claimants to the throne, weakened economically, and threatened by the Avars and Slavs settling in the Balkans, was vulnerable to invasion from the East. So precarious did things seem when Heraclius became emperor in 610 that he contemplated moving his headquarters to Carthage, far to the west. The patriarch of Constantinople and the people steadfastly resisted the move.

Already in 603 the Persians had begun to move against Roman frontier fortresses in northern Mesopotamia, capturing Mardin, a thriving center of Syriac-speaking monasticism, whose populace was loyal to Constantinople. In hopes of stemming the Persian advance, one of Heraclius's first actions was to withdraw troops from the Balkans and send them east. But the reinforcements made little impact, and at the end of 611 the Persians had captured Antioch. Heraclius was forced to retreat into Anatolia, cutting Constantinople off from cities to the south, Damascus, Caesarea, Jerusalem, and Alexandria.

The Sasanid armies quickly took Damascus and headed toward Caesarea, the capital of the Byzantine province of Palestina Prima. Caesarea capitulated without a struggle, and in April 614 the Persian general Shahrbaraz marched his army up to Jerusalem to begin the siege of the holy city. He dug large trenches under the walls and built wood scaffolding to support the walls. After the wood was set afire, the walls came crashing down, and the Persian army stormed the city "with unbounded fury." They massacred men, women, children, and the elderly, destroyed churches, and profaned the holy places, killing priests, monks, and holy women.

The most detailed account of the conquest, *The Capture of Jerusalem,* was written by an eyewitness, a monk named Strategos from the monastery of Mar Saba in the Judean desert. His treatise is important not only for what it tells us about the siege and its aftermath, but also for how Christians viewed the occupation of their holiest city, "that great city, the city of the Christians, Jerusalem, the city of Jesus Christ," as Strategos put it. In a Georgian version of the work, Jerusalem is described as "that city which was a refuge for all Christians and a bulwark of their empire."

For Strategos the conquest of Jerusalem was not the sacking of an ordinary city;

it was an event in the framework of biblical history. He likens what happened in the seventh century A.D. to the destruction of Jerusalem in the sixth century B.C. by the Babylonians. No longer, however, was the Jewish temple the religious center of the city; now it was the Church of the Resurrection and the true cross. His subject is the "capture of the true cross and plundering of the church's sacred vessels and the captivity of the flock and the capture of Zachariah the patriarch."

In the early centuries Christians drew a contrast between the "heavenly city" of Jerusalem and the city on the edge of the desert. Echoing Saint Paul (Galatians 4:26), Melito of Sardis, a bishop in Asia Minor in the second century, had written: "The Jerusalem below was precious but it is worthless now because of the Jerusalem above." Over the centuries, as the Christian population of the city had grown and churches were built at the holy places, Christian attitudes toward Jerusalem underwent a profound transformation. The earthly city had become a thriving Christian metropolis; like a mother welcoming her children, Jerusalem drew Christians from all over the world to pray at its shrines, live in its sacred precincts, or practice the solitary life in the Judean desert. For Christians of the seventh century its capture was a fearful calamity, and Strategos, reversing the sentiments of earlier generations, wrote: "The Jerusalem above wept over the Jerusalem below." So great was the sorrow in heaven that "on that day a great darkness came over the city," reminding people of the darkness at the time of Christ's crucifixion.

The central character in Strategos's story is Zachariah, the patriarch of Jerusalem at the time of the Persian conquest. It was his unhappy lot to be taken into exile by the Persians for fourteen years. As Zachariah was led out of the city he was followed by the faithful down into the Kidron Valley and up the Mount of Olives. As they took one last look at Jerusalem before descending down the other side of the Mount of Olives, they began to weep. "Some struck their faces, and others threw ashes over their heads, and some threw dirt in their faces, and some pulled hair from their scalps. They were not grieving over their own sins but over the destruction of Jerusalem, and some struck their breasts and others lifted their hands to heaven crying out and saying, 'Have mercy on us, O Lord; have mercy on your city, O Lord, have mercy on your altars.'"

Before being led down the mountain, Zachariah turned to Jerusalem, extended his arms and cried out, "O Zion, with a sorrowful word that makes one weep I speak peace to you; peace be with you O Jerusalem, peace be with you O Holy Land, peace on the whole land." And then, making the words of the psalmist his own, he said: "O Zion, do not forget me, your servant, and may your creator not forget you. For if I forget you, O Jerusalem, let my right hand wither. Let my tongue cleave to the roof of my mouth if I do not remember you [Psalms 137]. Peace on you, O Zion, you who were my city, and now I am made a stranger to you. I adore you, O Zion, and I adore him who dwelled in you." After he had given his final blessing over the city, Zachariah was led through the Judean desert, across the Jordan River, and on to Damascus.

There is no more doleful scene in the Church's early history, no event that evoked such an outpouring of grief among the Christian people. The only thing comparable was the sack of Rome by the Visigoths in 410, a catastrophe that stunned the Christian world. Rome's fall was an intellectual challenge, for pagan critics charged that Christians were to blame for abandoning the worship of the gods of their ancestors. The sack of Jerusalem, however, was an event of another magnitude. For the Jerusalem occupied by the Persians was the city celebrated in the Psalms, denounced by the prophets, Zion, the city of David celebrated in the Church's prayers and sung in its hymns, the city of Christ's death and resurrection.

The most eloquent laments over the city are two poems written by Sophronius, who became patriarch of Jerusalem after the city was recaptured by Heraclius. Written in acrostic with a fixed meter, they belonged to a showy and affected genre of poetry favored by orators in his time. Here is how one poem begins:

> Holy City of God
> Home of the most valiant saints
> Great Jerusalem
> What kind of lament should I offer you?
> Children of the blessed Christians
> Come to mourn high crested Jerusalem
>
> In the face of such tragedy
> The flow of my tears is too brief
> The dirge of my heart
> Too measured before such suffering
>
> Nevertheless, I shall sound forth a lament
> Weaving my garment of groans for you
> Because you have suffered such brigandage
> Concealing the rushing forth of my tears.

Sophronius's poems are without parallel in early Christian poetry. Pilgrims left many depictions of Jerusalem and the holy places, but no one wrote about the city with such tenderness and feeling as Sophronius. In another poem he sang:

> Let me walk your pavements
> And go inside the Anastasis [Church of the Resurrection]
> Where the King of all rose again
> Trampling down the power of death

And as I venerate that worthy tomb,
Surrounded by its conches
And columns surmounted by golden lilies,
I shall be overcome with joy.

Prostrate I will kiss the navel point of the earth,
That divine Rock
In which was fixed the wood
That undid the curse of the tree

How great your glory, noble Rock,
In which was fixed
The Cross, the redemption of mankind.

The Sasanid occupation of Jerusalem was, however, a temporary interruption of Christian rule. Heraclius was not prepared to concede Jerusalem by abandoning the city and the territory surrounding it. Realizing he could not meet the Persians face to face in Palestine, he shrewdly launched a counteroffensive through Armenia and northern Syria into the heart of Persia itself. The Persians met the Romans near Mosul in northern Iraq and were decisively beaten. The way was now open to the Persian capital, Ctesiphon, and when Heraclius arrived he learned that his foe, Chosroes, the king, had died. In disarray, the Sasanids sued for peace. By the spring of 630, Heraclius had returned to Palestine, bringing with him the holy cross, and in March of that year he entered Jerusalem in triumph. The empire had survived, and its authority seemed uncontested in the Middle East. The victory, however, was short-lived.

Before turning to the Muslim conquest of Jerusalem, a brief word needs to be said about the final stages in the great controversy over Christ that erupted after the Council of Chalcedon. After Heraclius's victory, with the borders of the empire apparently secure, theological matters that seemed secondary when survival was at stake again came back into public view. It may seem late in the day for Christian thinkers to be debating a central point of Christian doctrine, but the issues that had divided at the Council of Chalcedon in the fifth century were still very much alive. In the seventh century, however, a thinker of uncommon brilliance, spiritual depth, courage, and sheer doggedness took in hand the great question of the divine and human in Christ. In a series of essays he argued that Chalcedon's language of "two natures" was, in fact, a powerful affirmation of the unity of Christ. But in the charged religious world of early Byzantine society Christology had become a deadly game of imperial politics, and he wound up on the losing side. Nevertheless, though he knew defending two wills in Christ would lead to exile and perhaps death, he fearlessly faced down the emperor and his imperious officials. He would be vindicated only after his death.

His name was Maximus, known in Christian history as Maximus the Confessor, and he was born in Palestine in 580. His gifts were recognized early, and as a young man he served as a secretary of Emperor Heraclius. But he soon found life at court shallow and unsatisfying. In 614 he joined a monastery at Chrysopolis, a city across the Bosporus from Constantinople, and later moved to another monastery in Cyzicus on the southern shore of the Sea of Marmara. It was an unwise decision, for after their victories in the Middle East the Persians set their sights on Constantinople, the capital of the empire. As their armies drew closer, Persian ships patrolled the shipping lanes that led from the Aegean through the Sea of Marmara to Constantinople. Fearing for their lives, Maximus and a group of monks fled from the monastery. After lengthy sojourns in Crete and Cyprus, they eventually found a home in the great city of Carthage in North Africa. Though Maximus was a native Greek speaker, and his writings are in Greek, he lived in a Latin-speaking world for almost two decades.

Maximus was drawn into the controversy over the person of Christ when Sergius, the patriarch of Constantinople, floated some new theological ideas on the unity of Christ. In an effort to overcome the duality implied by the formula "in two natures" at Chalcedon, some had suggested that in Christ there was a single "activity" or a single "will." At first these proposals met little opposition, and Maximus was sympathetic to the new approach. But as he studied the Scriptures more carefully he began to have doubts. In particular one event in the gospels caught his attention, the scene in the Garden of Gethsemane after the Last Supper, what is sometimes called the "agony" of Christ, when he prayed: "Father, if thou be willing, remove this cup from me; nevertheless not my will, but thine, be done" (Luke 22:42).

For centuries Jesus's prayer was taken as hypothetical. No one believed that he would refuse to drink the cup and not go willingly to his death. Maximus, however, asked whether the second part of Christ's prayer, "Nevertheless not my will, but thine, be done," makes sense if the words "let this cup pass from me" were not spoken in earnest. He is of course quick to observe that the key element in the passage, and in the narrative of Christ's passion in the gospels, is that he *did* drink the cup and submitted to the will of the Father.

What Maximus was getting at—and here he went beyond earlier thinkers—is that the Agony of Christ shows indubitably that he had a human will. There was no question that as the Son of God he had a divine will that was one with the will of the Father. Maximus's point is that he also had a human will. Therefore it is proper to speak of two wills in Christ, a divine will and a human will. Those who adopted this position were called dyothelites, from the Greek *duo,* two, and *thelesis,* will; those who held to one will were called monothelites. According to Maximus, Christ, acting in freedom, submitted to the will of God by conforming his human will wholly to God's will. Though there is no opposition between the two wills, the distinction between them must be maintained. For Maximus the doctrine of one will placed in jeopardy the full reality of the Incarnation.

As one of the Church's greatest thinkers was pondering the mystery of Christ, the world that he had grown up in was being swept away. As we shall see in the next chapter, by 640 Arab armies had overpowered the Byzantine provinces in the Middle East, capturing Damascus, Antioch, Caesarea, and Jerusalem, threatening Constantinople itself. Unlike the Persians, the Arabs would not be driven back, and Byzantine rule would not be restored in the Middle East.

As Christian cities were submitting to the Arabs, the emperor, the leading bishops, and theologians valiantly pressed for a resolution of what had become an intractable theological problem: how to hold to the "two natures" of Chalcedon and still affirm that Christ is one. Because the teaching of one will had support in some quarters, and even brought a temporary truce between the miaphysites in Alexandria and the Chalcedonians in Constantinople, the emperor issued a statement of faith (known as the *Ekthesis*) affirming that the two natures were united in a single will. On Heraclius's death in 641, the new emperor, Constans II, tried to impose this teaching on the empire as a whole.

The *Ekthesis* did not go down well in Rome, though a few years earlier Pope Honorius (d. 638) had accepted the imperial formulation of one will in Christ. But his successors realized that the teaching of one will compromised the doctrine of "two natures" that had been vigorously defended by Pope Leo the Great in the fifth century. Rome found a new ally in Maximus, who arrived in the city in 645. In the meantime the emperor had issued a new decree called the *Typos,* which prohibited any discussion of "one will and one energy or two wills and two energies." When Martin I became pope in 649, he convened a council in the Lateran basilica to render a judgment on the matter. Most of the bishops were from the West, but Maximus, neither a bishop nor a priest, served as adviser to the pope and helped frame an official statement that confirmed Chalcedon and affirmed that Christ had two wills.

With this, the issue between Rome and Constantinople was joined, and as soon as the emperor learned of the decisions of the Lateran council he dispatched the exarch of Ravenna, the ranking imperial official in Italy, to Rome to arrest Martin. But Martin was able to bid for time. A few years later, however, a new exarch was more decisive. He arrested Martin, even though the pope was ill, and arranged for his transfer under guard to Constantinople. After a long trip by sea, interrupted by stops at islands on the way, Martin arrived in Constantinople in September 654. There he was brought before a tribunal and condemned for treason.

To humiliate him further, the emperor forced the pope to stand before the jeering people of the city as he was stripped of his episcopal robes and the pallium, a strip of lamb's wool marked with six black crosses worn over the shoulders, a symbol of his office. Then he was led through the city in chains to prison, where he was held until banished to the Crimea, on the northern shore of the Black Sea. In the end even the faithful in Rome abandoned him and elected a successor while he was still alive. A year later in September 655 he died in exile from cold and starvation. For his faithfulness in the face of deposition, humiliation, exile, and death, later generations bestowed on Pope Martin the venerable title of martyr, the last pope in history to have been given that honor.

Maximus suffered an equally cruel fate. Like Martin, he was arrested and brought to Constantinople to stand trial. By good fortune we have a detailed account of the proceedings that sheds unexpected light on the relation between political and religious authority in the Byzantine Empire. In the West, due to such resolute bishops as Ambrose of Milan and Pope Gelasius, the authority of the bishop had been vigorously defended against that of the emperor. But in the East the emperor's prerogatives allowed him to intrude deeply into ecclesiastical matters, as was evident during the reign of Justinian.

So it happened that during the trial Maximus was asked whether the emperor should be considered a "priest." What was at issue was not whether the emperor could celebrate the sacraments, but whether he had the authority to make judgments on doctrinal matters. For it was the emperor who had imposed the teaching that Christ had one will on citizens of the empire. But, Maximus responded, only a priest can "define the saving teachings of the Catholic Church." The imperial official answered that Melchizedek, the mysterious king who meets Abraham in the book of Genesis (14:21), was a "king and priest." Maximus demurs: Melchizedek was unique, not a model for other kings or emperors. The emperor is a layman; he does not stand at the altar with the priests. In the great prayer over the bread and wine in the Eucharist, the emperor is mentioned with the laity, and even Constantine, the first Christian emperor, was included among the faithful departed laymen.

This exchange provides us with a luminous moment in the midst of controversy, showing how theological truth had become captive to shifting political coalitions. Not only did Maximus address the great theological issues with uncommon clarity and depth; in his trial he took on a second role, a courageous voice against the pretensions of political power in religious matters. Christian doctrine, he asserted, is not determined by "orders of the emperor." Maximus's fate, however, was never in doubt. He was brought to Constantinople to be convicted, and after the trial ran its course he was condemned to exile in Bizye in Thrace in the lower Balkans.

But the story does not end there. Even though he was condemned for refusing to obey the imperial edict forbidding discussion of the wills of Christ, Maximus continued to write and speak against the teaching of one will. So he was brought out of exile to face yet another trial. This time his tormenters made sure he would neither write nor speak any more. The tongue that had taught two wills in Christ was ripped out of his mouth, and the hand that held the pen that defended the two wills was cut off. He was exiled to Lazica on the eastern shore of the Black Sea, where he died. Because of his witness to Christ under great suffering, he is remembered in Christian tradition as Maximus the Confessor.

In 680, two decades after the death of Maximus, a new emperor, Constantine IV, called a churchwide council to meet at Constantinople to render final judgment on the matter. By this time, opinion had turned in favor of the teaching of two wills, and the bishops, in union with Rome, solemnly declared the doctrine of two wills and two energies in Christ as the Church's official teaching. In the end Chalcedon triumphed (at the Council of Constantinople in 681), in part because of the labors of Maximus. Still, it had been more than two hundred years since Chalcedon adjourned, and the Christian East was deeply and irretrievably divided. It was a bitter legacy that Christians would have to live with as the world they knew crumbled away, and a new civilization was built in its place.

No God but God:
The Rise of Islam

No event during the first thousand years of Christian history was more unexpected, calamitous, and consequential than the rise of Islam. Few irruptions in history have transformed societies as rapidly and irrevocably as did the conquest and expansion of the Arabs of Islam in the seventh century. And none came with greater swiftness. Within a decade three major cities in the Byzantine Empire, Damascus (634), Alexandria (639), and Jerusalem (636), fell to the Arabs. There had been reports that something large was happening in the Arabian peninsula early in the seventh century, but the Byzantines were preoccupied with the Sasanids in Persia, who had sacked Jerusalem in 614 and made off with the relic of the cross, and the Avars, a people who had settled in the Balkans in the sixth century and were now threatening Constantinople.

Even on the eve of the conquest of Jerusalem, when Arab armies had encircled the holy city and blocked the road to Bethlehem, Sophronius the patriarch of Jerusalem assured the faithful: "We will laugh at the demise of our enemies the Saracens [as Christians called the Arabs] and in a short time see their destruction and complete ruin." A century and a half later, a Byzantine chronicler grasped more fully what Islam meant for Christians. He began his account with a lapidary notice about its founder, Muhammad: "I think it necessary to discuss his ancestry in full."

Muhammad was born in 570 in Mecca, an important trading center in the Arabian peninsula. His father died before he was born, and his mother a few years later. He was raised by his uncle. As a young man he came into the employ of an older woman, Khadijah; later, he married her and she had five children by him. Three daughters survived to maturity. Like others from his tribe, the Quraysh, Muhammad engaged in trade, traveling on occasion to neighboring Syria. As a young man he began to withdraw from society to be alone in a cave on a mountain outside Mecca. During one of these retirements, when he was about forty, he began to have visions and to hear a voice that summoned him to give devotion to God alone. Encouraged by his wife, he responded to the summons that came from the one God (in Arabic *Allah*), the God who had created the world and spoken to the prophets of old, to Moses and to Jesus.

The voice instructed him to "recite" (Qu'ran means recitation) what he heard, and the words came out in solemn and majestic Arabic prose, in "a clear Arabic tongue," as the Qur'an puts it (16.103). Even in English the power of its words is palpable.

> When the sun shall be darkened,
> When the mountains shall be set moving,
> When the stars shall be thrown down,
> When the pregnant camels shall be neglected,
> When the seas shall be set boiling,
> When the souls shall be coupled,
> When the buried infant girl shall be asked for what sin she was slain
> When the scrolls shall be unrolled,
> When heaven shall be stripped off,
> When Hell shall be set blazing,
> When Paradise shall be brought nigh,
> Then shall a soul know what it has wrought. [Qur'an 81]

At first Muhammad shared his message only with his wife and a few friends, but after a few years he began to urge his fellow tribesmen to join him in worshiping the one God. The Arabs worshiped many deities, some protectors of particular tribes, others associated with a tree or a grove or a stone or the stars. Special honor was shown to three female goddesses, Allat, al-Uzza, and Manat, whose shrines were in neighboring districts. Behind all these gods was a vague and shadowy figure named Allah, who was associated with a sacred stone structure in Mecca called the Kaaba. It was the custom among the Arabs to circle the Kaaba a number of times on foot and touch a black stone in one corner. Muhammad exhorted his fellow Arabs to give up the worship of many gods and serve the one God alone, the God of Abraham. In the words of the opening surah (chapter) of the Qur'an:

> Praise belongs to God, the Lord of all Being,
> The All-merciful, the All-compassionate,
> the Master of the Day of Doom.
>
> Thee only do we serve. To Thee alone do we pray for succor.
> Guide us in the straight path, the path of those whom Thou hast blessed,
> Not of those against whom Thou art wrathful,
> Nor of those who are astray.

Understandably, Muhammad met with opposition. Some said he was "possessed"; others charged him with proclaiming the "word of an accursed Satan." Yet some were moved by his words. One Meccan said: "I thought it would be a good thing if I could listen to Muhammad. . . . When I heard the Qur'an [what was being recited] my heart was softened and Islam entered into me. By God [said another], his speech is sweet."

In proclaiming that there is one God, Muhammad was saying to his fellow Arabs that the deities they venerated are no gods at all. But his affirmation of the one God carried another claim: God's word had been sent to them through a new prophet, and that prophet was Muhammad. Hence Islam came to be defined by the simple testimony (*Shahadah* in Arabic): "There is no God but God and Muhammad is his messenger." The message called for a personal response: it was the duty of all human beings to surrender to God and to order their lives according to God's will.

In Arabic the term *Islam* means submission to God, and *Muslim* means the one who submits. Muhammad taught that each human being faced an inescapable choice. Either worship the one God and obey his will, or choose to follow one's own desires and designs. The responsibility for choosing rightly lay in one's own hand, but in mercy God will direct and guide the lives of those who turn to him.

At the time Muhammad began to preach there were Christians and Jews living in Mecca and in the Arabian peninsula. From the Qur'an it is clear that Muhammad was familiar with certain aspects of Christianity (possibly through Syriac-speaking Christians) and had some acquaintance with the biblical tradition. The most striking instance is the story of Joseph in the book of Genesis; an entire surah of the Qur'an (12) is devoted to the biblical figure of Joseph (Genesis 37–50). In the Qur'anic version some of the details are different, but the outline of the biblical story is intact. The tale, however, has a quite different feel. In the Scriptures Joseph is a pivotal figure in the covenantal history of ancient Israel; in the Qur'an Joseph stands alone as a moral exemplar who urges others to give full devotion to the one God.

The Prophet's message, as enshrined in the Qur'an, was often expressed in vivid images reminiscent of the Hebrew prophets. Muhammad had no direct knowledge of their writings, though on occasion he appealed to the literary tradition behind Judaism and Christianity. In the Qur'an the voice of God says to Muslims: "If you are in doubt about what We have sent down to you, ask those who were reading Scripture before you."

Muhammad was convinced that neither Jews nor Christians practiced a form of religion befitting the worship of the one God. Christian teaching is held up for critique in the Qur'an. At one point phrases from the Nicene Creed are alluded to in order to distinguish the Islamic understanding of God from the Christian teaching that God is triune. "Say, 'He is God, One, God the Everlasting. . . . He did not beget and is not begotten. And none is his equal'" (Qur'an 112). Elsewhere Christians are called "associators," because they believe God has an associate, Christ, the eternal Son and God.

The Prophet's message was directed chiefly at his fellow tribesmen, not to Christians and Jews. When, however, he pressed the inhabitants of Mecca to give up the worship of many gods, most rebuffed or ridiculed him. Although he won some converts, he was forced to emigrate to a neighboring town, Medina, where, with a small group of followers, he found sanctuary. This emigration (*Hijrah* in Arabic) took place in 622, and the date came to be considered the first year of the Islamic era. From this event Muslims reckon time as Western civilization dates events from the birth of Christ.

Muhammad's mission in Medina was as much political as religious. He sought to form a new kind of community whose life would be governed by the revelations he received. From the beginning Muhammad taught that Muslims—those who had submitted to God—should live devout lives not only as individuals but as a society. In the words of the Qur'an: "You have become the best community ever raised up for mankind, enjoining the right and forbidding the wrong, and having faith in God" (3.110). This community was not limited to the tribe, and became, at least in principle, a universal fellowship that transcended tribal divisions among the Arabs as well as bonds of race or ethnicity. The word Muhammad used for the company of believers was *Ummah* (Arabic for community or people). In the decades after his death it would take on the features of an independent state with a distinctive form of worship, including prayer five times a day and an annual monthlong fast, *Ramadan*.

At first the Ummah took the form of a tribe. To establish its independence the Muslims carried out raids against Muhammad's own tribe, the Quraysh. After several military battles stretching over eight years, Muhammad was able to gain authority over the Quraysh, and to claim the Kaaba in Mecca (which was said to have been built by Abraham and his son Ishmael [Genesis 16:15]) as the most sacred shrine of the new religion. In 632 he made a peaceful pilgrimage to Mecca, thereby establishing the form of pilgrimage that would be adopted by Muslims. Kissing the black stone at the Kaaba was seen as an act of submission and devotion to the one God, the God of Abraham. A few months later, as he was preparing for a military expedition to Syria, he died.

The society Muhammad formed was held together by the person of the Prophet, and his death plunged the fledgling state into a time of uncertainty. But the leaders quickly chose a man named Abu Bakr, a rich merchant from Mecca, one of the first to believe in the mission of the Prophet, and the father of Aisha, the favorite wife of the Prophet. The choice was disputed by some who thought that Ali, Muhammad's son-in-law, should be named his successor. The new leader was called caliph: successor of the Prophet. This decision was far-reaching, for it meant that Islam would constitute itself as a single body, and no distinction would be made between religious and political authority. Abu Bakr died in 634, only two years after he had become caliph, but he named Umar ibn al-Khattab, one of his most loyal supporters, to succeed him. Umar was the first to assume the title "Commander of the Faithful." The rapid succession of caliphs secured the principle that the new community required a single head to whom all would be loyal.

The goal now was to extend Muslim rule over the entire population of Arabia. This was done through military and diplomatic means. But the Muslims also began to move out beyond the Arab lands into the settled and populated regions to the north. They first set their sights on greater Syria, the fertile and arable lands close to the Mediterranean ruled by the Byzantines, present-day Jordan, Israel and Palestine, Syria and Lebanon. Syria is a geographical extension of Arabia, and the Arabs viewed it as a kind of paradise on earth, a land of prosperity and plenty blessed with regular rainfall. The majority of the inhabitants of the region were Syriac-speaking Christians, and in the decade after Muhammad's death they had their first contact with Islam.

Because Abraham had lived in Syria after leaving Mesopotamia and eventually settled in the region of Hebron (where he is buried), thirty miles south of Jerusalem in Palestine, Muslims believed they had a claim on the land of the Bible. Jerusalem was also revered by the Muslims as the city of the prophets, including Jesus, and it became the *qibla,* the direction in which Muslims turned when they prayed. Later the qibla would be changed to Mecca. Jerusalem was important for another reason. According to Muslim tradition, Muhammad was brought to Jerusalem by the angel Gabriel, to the site of the ancient temple of Solomon, from where he ascended into the heavens.

So it is not surprising that Muslims had designs on Syria and Jerusalem. An Armenian chronicler reports that they "sent an embassy to the emperor of the Greeks [Heraclius, the Byzantine emperor] saying; 'God has given this land as an inheritance to our father Abraham and his posterity after him. We are the children of Abraham. You have held our country long enough. Give it up peacefully, and we will not invade your country. If not, we will retake with interest what you have withheld from us.'"

During the caliphate of Abu Bakr the Arabs carried out minor military expeditions in southern Syria, but with the arrival of a force from Iraq under the command of an able general, Khalid ibn al-Walid, the campaign began in earnest. The first city in Syria to fall was Bostra south of Damascus. After a brief siege the inhabitants submitted and agreed to pay their new rulers an annual tax. The bulk of the Byzantine army was a long way off in northern Syria, and when Damascus and other cities were taken the emperor Heraclius gathered a huge force that hurried south to meet the invaders. The decisive battle took place at the Yarmuk River, a tributary of the Jordan, some four miles southeast of the Sea of Galilee on the eastern slopes of the Golan Heights. Though vastly outnumbered, the Arabs prevailed, in part because a large segment of the Byzantine army was made up of Arab auxiliaries who went over to the Muslim, or Arab, side. The date was August 636. With the defeat of the Byzantine army, the Muslim armies were able to force the capitulation of the other cities in Syria. Most cities did not resist, and public buildings and churches remained standing with little or no damage.

Although Jerusalem, the great prize, had not yet been captured, the conquest of Syria was effectively over. Only the coastal cities of Gaza and Caesarea, which could be supplied from the sea, resisted. The other cities and towns had little choice but to submit. Jerusalem, however, refused to negotiate and fell subject to a long siege. In the end the residents, realizing resistance was futile, demanded that the caliph himself, Umar, enter the city to make a treaty with the inhabitants. The unhappy task of negotiating a surrender with the conquerors was given to Sophronius, the patriarch of Jerusalem. The meeting between the representative of the Roman Christian civilization and the leader of the new regime was so filled with drama and historical significance that several detailed accounts have come down to us. One, composed by a Christian chronicler who wrote in Arabic in Egypt in the tenth century, tells us how Christians of the East under Muslim rule remembered the meeting several centuries later.

According to the Christian account, when the gates of the city were opened, Caliph Umar and his companions went directly to the courtyard of the Anastasis, the great Church of the Resurrection, known today in its shrunken form as the Church of the Holy Sepulcher. When it came time to pray, Umar said to Sophronius the patriarch, "I would like to pray." Sophronius said: "Pray wherever you wish." But Umar would not pray in the church. So the patriarch directed him to another church. But Umar said he could not pray there. He explained that if he prayed in the church it would be taken from the Christians and made into a shrine because "Umar prayed there." So Umar wrote out a document granting Christians the right to hold on to their churches and forbidding the Muslims to pray in their churches or even in front of the churches.

Then Umar asked the patriarch to show him a place where he might build a mosque, and according to the story, Sophronius took him to a high elevation on the eastern edge of the city facing the Mount of Olives. Once the Jewish temple had stood there, but now it was a desolate and deserted dung heap. When they arrived Umar gathered up the edge of his garment, filled it with dirt, and threw it over the high retaining wall into the valley of Gehenna to the east. When the other Muslims saw what he had done they also gathered up their garments or used their cloaks or shields or baskets to clear the site.

The Muslim account of the conquest puts things differently. Umar does not engage in an aimless quest for a proper site to build the mosque. He knew exactly where he wanted the building to stand, and he found each suggestion of the patriarch unacceptable. It was only when they reached the site of the temple of Solomon that he said, "By him in whose hands is my soul, this is the place described to us by the Apostle [Muhammad] of God." The Muslim version makes clear that Muslims had a religious interest in Jerusalem and wished to claim the city as their own and to consecrate its most ancient and holy site to the God of Islam. Two generations later, the beautiful domed mosque that dominates the skyline of the Old City of Jerusalem to this day, the Dome of the Rock, was built on this location.

The Arab conquerors of Jerusalem were not simply belligerents. They were the vanguards of a new religion that made a spiritual as well as a political claim on Jerusalem. The commanders of their armies were heralds of the Prophet as well as soldiers, harbingers of a new civilization that would displace the language, transform the institutions, and remake the architecture of a region that had been dominated for centuries by the cultures of Israel, Greece, Rome, and Christianity. Once the Mediterranean had been a western lake joining the deserts of Egypt with the cities of Italy and North Africa, but with the coming of Islam it became an immense moat dividing the Muslim East from the Christian West. In two hundred years many of the Christians of the region would be speaking Arabic, and territories that were once provinces of the Roman Empire would be ruled from Baghdad, not Constantinople.

One of the first tasks of the conquerors was to work out suitable social and legal arrangements to make a place for the huge population they now ruled—millions of people who were neither Arab nor Muslim. Most were Christians divided among the three rival Christian branches: the Melkites, who were in communion with the Byzantine emperor, the non-Chalcedonians who were strongest in western Syria and Egypt, and the Syriac-speaking Christians who were concentrated in the former Persian Empire, modern-day Iraq and Iran. The Muslim advance took place against a background of divided loyalties among the Christians that would have consequences for Christian life under Islam. At this point in Muslim history there was no attempt to convert Christians.

To deal with the non-Muslim population the Arabs adopted a system similar to what had been in effect in the Persian Empire: the imposition of a tax on a segment of society. The Arab Muslims were considered privileged, and non-Muslims were required to pay a tribute, called *jizyah,* levied on males of military age, including Christians, Jews, Zoroastrians, and Samaritans, collectively known as the "people of protection" (*ahl al-dhimma* in Arabic, or *dhimmis*). The basis for the legislation was found in a passage in the Qur'an: "Fight those who believe not in God and the last Day and do not forbid what God and his messenger have forbidden—such men as practice not the religion of truth, being of those who have been given the book—until they pay the tribute readily and have been humbled" (Qur'an 9:29). Christians were allowed to live in the lands that were formerly theirs and to follow their own laws on matters that concerned their religious life—on the condition that they submit to Muslim law in civil and criminal matters and pay the jizyah. The several Christian groups became societies within society, and in the early years they were able to carry on their affairs largely independent of the Muslim rulers.

Initially the conquerors had to rely on the conquered, especially those who were educated and skilled in governmental affairs, to carry on public business. The caliphs needed Greek and Syriac speakers to administer the new state and to deal with the Christian population. A conspicuous example is the father of John of Damascus, the distinguished theologian. John's father was appointed to high office by the caliph and put in charge of financial affairs in Syria.

By the end of the century, however, the Muslim leaders were less willing to allow Christians to have positions of authority. Under the caliph Abd al-Malik (684–705) a process of "organization and adjustment," according to Arabic historians, was undertaken. The administrative patterns that had been maintained since the conquest were replaced by new structures, and Arabic displaced Greek as the language of administration. For the first time the Arabs struck gold coins—previously only the Byzantines had gold coins—and printed legends on them written in Arabic and derived from the Qur'an. One coin included the words from the Qur'an that challenged Christian teaching: HE IS GOD, ONE, ETERNAL; HE DOES NOT BEGET NOR IS HE BEGOTTEN (112).

At the same time the Arabs began to give Jerusalem a Muslim face by constructing the Dome of the Rock on the site of the Jewish temple. This building, along with the mosque on the southern edge of the temple platform, Al-Aqsa mosque, are the first major buildings constructed by Muslims in the formerly Christian city. As Constantine built the monumental Church of the Resurrection in Jerusalem in the fourth century, so the new rulers of Jerusalem built a dazzling and imposing mosque at the highest point in the city, on the site of the ancient Jewish temple. The building was to be a symbol of the Muslim triumph, and it towered over every other building in the city, most notably the Church of the Resurrection. Jerusalem would become, along with Mecca and Medina, one of the three holiest places in Islam.

The Dome of the Rock, an octagon covered by a dome, is modeled on Christian buildings constructed over a sacred place, like a shrine or a burial site. It was a center of pilgrimage, not a congregational mosque. The architects and workmen were Byzantine Christians, and the decorative themes, such as vegetal figures and vases, are commonplace in church architecture. But what is most significant are the inscriptions found in the interior. All come from the Qur'an. The verse from surah 112 appears here again, and also a verse from surah 33.56. "Verily God and His angels bless the Prophet; O ye who believe, bless him and salute him with a worthy salutation." And even more explicit: "O ye people of the book, overstep not bounds in your religion; and of God speak only truth. The Messiah Jesus, son of Mary, is only an apostle of God, and his Word which he conveyed into Mary, and a Spirit proceeding from him. Believe therefore in God and his apostles, and say not 'Three.' It will be better for you. God is only one God." The inscription is followed by the prayer: "Pray for your Prophet and your servant, Jesus, son of Mary" (4:170).

Two decades later a large mosque was constructed in Damascus on the site of a Christian church dedicated to John the Baptist, where once a pagan temple had stood. At first the Muslims shared the church with the Christians, the Muslims praying in the eastern section and the Christians in the western side. But when the building became too small to accommodate the growing Muslim population the caliph took over the church, promising to spare the other churches in the city. All signs of Christianity were removed to accommodate Muslim worship, and a large courtyard was added.

Several generations later the Arab geographer Al-Maqdisi, who had visited the mosque in Damascus, reported on a conversation that explains why this mosque and the Dome of the Rock were built. One day, he said to his uncle that the caliph was "wrong to squander the wealth of the Muslims on the mosque of Damascus. Had he spent his money to maintain the roads and the water cisterns and to restore the fortresses, that would have been more apposite and more meritorious. 'Don't you believe it, my son. Al-Walid was right and he did something important. He saw that Syria, the land of the Christians, was full of beautiful churches of seductive appearance and vast renown, like those of the Anastasis [in Jerusalem], of Lydda [in Palestine] and Edessa. He therefore gave the Muslims a mosque to divert their attention from these churches, and made it one of the wonders of the world. In the same way Abd al-Malik, when he saw the immense and dominating dome of the Church of the Resurrection, feared that it would dominate the hearts of the Muslims, and he therefore erected the Dome which we see on the Rock.'"

The arrival of the Muslims did not, however, mean the displacement of the Christians or the end of Christian life. At first things went on with little disruption, but soon it became clear that Islam had shifted the center of gravity of the world, and Christians faced an uncertain future.

Images and the Making of Byzantium

Constantine's decision in the fourth century to build a new capital of the Roman Empire at the site of the ancient city of Byzantium was serendipitous. Had he chosen to locate it in one of the major cities in the eastern Mediterranean, at Antioch in Syria, at the great port city of Caesarea on the Palestinian coast, or at Alexandria in Egypt, the empire would surely have collapsed in the face of the Arab conquest of the Middle East. Constantinople's advantage was that it was located far to the west, and to an attacking army from the east it was on the other side of the Bosporus.

Nevertheless, the capital of the empire was the grand prize, and after taking several islands in the eastern Mediterranean, including Cyprus and Rhodes, the Arabs set their sights on Constantinople. First they captured Cyzicus, a Greek city in Asia Minor across the Sea of Marmara from Constantinople, then in 674 a Muslim force under the command of Yazid, son of the Arab caliph, besieged Constantinople. The blockade lasted almost four years and ended in failure after the Arabs suffered heavy losses from "Greek fire," a kind of crude petroleum similar to napalm.

Constantinople by this time was the capital of a much diminished empire embracing central Asia Minor, the lower Balkans and Greece, southern Italy, and Sicily. It had lost its wealthiest provinces and now faced a larger and determined empire to the east. The ancient lands on the southern coast of the Mediterranean, Egypt, Libya, North Africa, were now under Muslim rule. Though the Arabs called the empire "Rum" (Rome) it was well on the way to becoming a regional state. But the city had survived, and because of it, the empire survived. For Christianity, this historical fact reverberated down the centuries.

The changed circumstances in the wake of the Muslim conquest led to a profound soul searching in the Greek-speaking Christian world. The old certainties had been shattered. Once Constantinople ruled over an empire that stretched from North Africa in the west to Syria in the Middle East. The rise of Islam not only cut off the great cities in the Middle East, Antioch and Alexandria, from Constantinople; Carthage fell in 698, bringing an end to Byzantine rule in Africa. In the East, the non-Chalcedonian communities had long been alienated from Constantinople; now they fell out of the consciousness of Christians in the Greek East. The Church in Egypt was governed by a Coptic patriarch, and any notion that Constantinople was the center of a worldwide Church was a fading memory. Even the ties with the Melkites, Chalcedonian Christians in the Middle East loyal to Constantinople, were weakened as many began to speak Arabic. And in the West a new society was being built; the pope looked more to the Franks north of the Alps than to Constantinople in the East.

In the eighth and ninth centuries the empire of the "Greeks," as the Franks called the Byzantines, went through a sustained period of consolidation and renewal as its leaders came to terms with their new situation. The Roman Empire of old was a thing of the past, but what was the character of the new entity coming into being? How did it relate to its Roman and Christian past? Once Constantinople thought of itself as the greatest power in the world; now it looked more like a satellite of the Muslim empire. Initially Christians thought they would drive back the invaders and reestablish Christian rule in Syria, but with each passing decade that dream seemed more illusory. Even Jerusalem, the "holy city" of the Christians, was under Muslim rule, and by the eighth century a symbol of the triumph of Islam, the Dome of the Rock, had arisen on the Temple Mount at the highest point of the city, looking down on the shrine and great basilica at the place of Christ's resurrection. What was to be made of the Muslim empire in light of the Christian past and hopes for the future?

Constantinople also assessed its relation to Christianity in the West. This became evident at a council in the city in 692 called by the emperor, Justinian II, to deal with pastoral and administrative matters. Neither the second Council of Constantinople in 553 nor the third Council of Constantinople in 680–681 had issued any "sacred canons"; they dealt only with doctrinal issues. Confident that the threats to Constantinople had passed, the emperor decided to convene a council to clarify, interpret, and expand on older legislation. They bishops met in the domed room (*trullus*) of the imperial palace, and for that reason this council is known as the Synod *in Trullo*, or the Quinisext (Fifth–Sixth), because it took up matters that had been left hanging by the two previous general councils.

In the mind of the emperor and the bishops in attendance the council in Trullo was considered an ecumenical council of the whole Church; in truth it was a gathering of Eastern bishops, and its canons display the marks of Greek Christian tradition. The first order of business was to affirm what had been taught at earlier ecumenical councils: Nicaea, Constantinople, Ephesus, Chalcedon, Constantinople II and III. In citing regional councils whose canons they considered authoritative, however, the bishops listed only Eastern councils in Asia Minor or Syria. Likewise, in naming church fathers whose writings were sources for ecclesiastical legislation, they mentioned only bishops from the Greek-speaking East: Basil of Caesarea, Gregory the Theologian (Nazianzen), Gregory of Nyssa, Cyril of Alexandria, and so on. Writers from the West are ignored—Augustine is not mentioned —though they did invoke Cyprian, "archbishop of the country of the Africans and Martyr."

When the council turned to the primary order of business, the conduct of the clergy, liturgical practices, and the like, the first topic addressed was the marriage of the clergy. The council fathers stressed that their practice differed from that of the "most holy Church of Rome," Christians in the West. Rome, they said, follows the "rule of perfection," celibacy of the clergy, but Constantinople follows the way of "kindness and consideration" by allowing clergy to be married. With certain conditions. Those who are twice married cannot be ordained, and those who are already ordained may not marry. Bishops, however, may not marry, and if they are already married they cannot live with their wives. The presumption—no doubt not shared by the wives—is that on separation the bishop's wife would betake herself to a monastery. The decisions of *in Trullo* reflect long-standing tradition; in the early centuries the clergy were often married. In the West, however, celibacy of the clergy had become widespread, though it was not formally mandated until the twelfth century. The divergence between East and West on this matter continues to this day.

In other canons the bishops made clear that their ways differed not only from those of the West, but also from other Christian communions in the East, most notably the Armenians. In canon 55 they chided the West for failing to keep the traditional practice that forbad fasting on Saturdays (except for the great Sabbath on Easter eve); but in canon 56 they censured the Armenians for eating eggs and cheese on Saturdays and Sundays during Lent. The "whole Church of God throughout the world," intoned the bishops, should follow "one rule" and abstain from anything that has been killed. Eggs and cheese fall into this category because they are the "fruit and produce" of animals, from which they abstained during Lent.

The Council in Trullo claimed to speak for the Church at large, but as one reads through its canons it is apparent that it is describing a distinctly Byzantine Christian world that was emerging in the years after the hammering it had taken from the Arabs. And it is this feature that gives the council its historical significance: it offers us a glimpse of the form of Christian life that would define the Greek East and later the Slavic Christian world, what came to be called Eastern Orthodoxy.

The Council in Trullo addressed the topic of religious art in two canons. One dealt with the cross, by which, in the words of the bishops, humans were "saved from the ancient fall." The issue was whether images of the cross were due veneration. The bishops said yes, but roundly condemned the practice of setting crosses into the floor, lest they be desecrated when people trampled on them.

In another canon they dealt with the image of a lamb. In the Scriptures, Christ is called the "lamb of God," and the lamb served as an image of Christ (John 1:29; Isaiah 53:7; 1 Peter 1:19)). In some churches, such as Saint Vitale in Ravenna, Christ was depicted in the form of a lamb. A lamb is, however, a symbol drawn from the Old Testament that points to Christ; it is not the thing itself. In the view of the bishops, since the ancient types such as the lamb had given way to the full revelation, the proper way to represent Christ is to portray him as a human person. Here is how they put it: "We decree that from now on the figure of the Lamb of God who takes away the sins of the World, Christ our God, should be set forth in images in human form, instead of the ancient lamb; for in this way we apprehend the depth of the humility of the Word of God, and are led to the remembrance of his life in the flesh, his passion and his saving death, and the redemption which thereby came to the world."

The two canons on religious images occur in the midst of 102 canons dealing with everything from whether water should be mixed with wine in the Eucharist, adultery, abortion, long-haired monks, and kneeling on Sundays. Religious images come up in the course of routine business; they were not central to the work of the council. But by the seventh century images had become objects of veneration in the Greek East and engendered an intensity of devotion that would lead to a rift within the society.

Of course Christian art had long favored visual representations. The walls of the catacombs had been adorned with images picturing events in the Bible (Jonah and the great fish, Moses striking the rock in the desert, the baptism of Christ), as well as non-biblical images (the lamb bearer and the orant, a person with hands uplifted in prayer). In the fourth century, when church buildings sprang up across the Christian world, the apse and walls were often decorated with religious images. In the grand church of Saint Mary Major in Rome, panels in the architrave above the columns depict scenes from the history of Israel. In Santa Pudenziana, also in Rome, the apse has a mosaic with a figure of Christ garbed in a golden toga with purple trim flanked on either side by several of his disciples.

The eyes are more learned than the ears, and Christian leaders welcomed images on the walls of the new churches. In the fourth century, Basil of Caesarea commended artists for the way they depicted Saint Balaam, a martyr during the persecution of Diocletian early in the century. "Fill out with your art the faint image of this leader. Illuminate with the flowers of your wisdom the crowned martyr whom I have only portrayed indistinctly. Let my words be surpassed by your drawing of the heroic deeds of the martyr." And his younger brother Gregory of Nyssa said that he could not look on a painting of the sacrifice of Isaac without "shedding tears."

The pictures in churches were, however, affixed to the walls and by their size and location were removed from the faithful. Smaller portraits of holy persons that could be viewed at closer range were another matter. A fascinating story in the apocryphal Acts of the Apostle John, written in the third century, offers insight into the practice. According to this account, certainly legendary, Lycomedes, a prominent figure in Ephesus during the lifetime of John, wanted to have a picture of the apostle. So he arranged for a painter to have John sit for the artist, and after the painting was finished Lycomedes put the image in his bedroom and decorated it with garlands and lit lamps before it. When John saw the picture, he was puzzled, for it seemed that Lycomedes had a painting of "one of his gods." To John it appeared that Lycomedes was "still living as a pagan."

As the story in the Acts of John suggests, portable paintings with Christian images seemed to mimic pagan practice. To some these more intimate pictures crossed an invisible line, inviting a kind of idolatrous veneration that Christians associated with the pagan society around them. The use made of the picture was objectionable, not the picture itself.

The pull of images was, however, irresistible. Unlike the pictures on the walls or in the apse of churches, these smaller images could be kept in the home or workplace and viewed at close range. By making the saints visible and palpable, these images enabled a more intimate relation between the believer and the holy person. There is nothing more astonishing than a human face, and when painted on wood with piercing eyes it called for a response, a bow or a simple touch of the finger. In time images acquired an almost numinous quality.

Some, however, questioned whether such devotion was pleasing to God. In the fourth century one bishop had compared the veneration of images by Christians to the practices of the pagans. "When images are put up the customs of the pagans do the rest." But until the eighth century there was no sustained opposition to images. Islam was opposed to making images of holy persons, and Islamic art revels in geometric or floral patterns and the stately unfolding of elegant Arabic letters. Christians living under Muslim rule were sensitive to Muslim criticism of images, and archaeology attests that some of the mosaics in churches were altered after the rise of Islam. A good example is the famous mosaic map of the holy land discovered on the floor of a church at Madaba in Jordan early in the twentieth century. Two boats with oarsmen sail across the briny waters of the Dead Sea, but the oarsmen have no faces; the tiles have been rearranged so that their human features have vanished. Nevertheless there is scant evidence that the presence of Islam and Islamic ideas had a direct influence on Christian critics of images.

The first official steps to ban the veneration of icons were taken during the reign of Emperor Leo III (d. 741), in 726 and 727. A terrible volcano had erupted on the island of Thera (Santorini) in the Aegean Sea, spewing ashes into the sky and sending boiling lava into the fields and villages, even darkening the heavens above Constantinople. The emperor thought the empire had been abandoned by God because the people had fallen into idolatry through venerating images. But there was no official prohibition and no systematic destruction of icons. Still the campaign against images had come from the highest authority in the empire.

The term for image in Greek is *eikon,* "icon" in English. The word could designate any sort of image, but as used by art historians today it refers to a religious image, usually on a wood panel, intended for veneration. Those who opposed the veneration of images were called iconoclasts, from the Greek term for breaking images; those who defended the practice were called iconodules, ones who serve images, or iconophiles, lovers of images.

In 741 Leo was succeeded by his son Constantine V, who took a firmer line against the veneration of images. He had been victorious against Arab forces in Syria without parading icons before his troops. In the wake of his victories he decided to convene a council at Hieria, across from Constantinople on the Asian shore, in 754. More than three hundred bishops were in attendance—a very large number. The mood at the council was hostile to icons, and the bishops ruled that the veneration of icons was contrary to the Church's ancient tradition. Those who venerated images had broken the commandment of God and would be subject to the laws of the empire. The council, however, fearful of the violence that might follow its actions, forbade the destruction of sacramental vessels, vestments, other sacred objects, and churches that displayed images.

The bishops also anathematized John of Damascus (d. 750), a stalwart defender of the veneration of icons. Although his monastery was located in the center of the Muslim empire, and Christians were coping with the alien society being formed around them, John was deeply troubled by the attack on icons, not least because, like Maximus the Confessor two generations earlier, he thought the emperor had no business dictating what the Church teaches. John had written a series of essays, *Against Those Who Denounce the Sacred Images,* to show that the veneration of icons was not a recent "invention" but the "ancient tradition of the Church."

In his treatises on images John distilled the Church's teaching about Christ and focused it brilliantly on the matter at hand. His signal contribution was to show that the prohibition of icons challenged the Christian belief in the Incarnation, that God who is before time and beyond space became man in the person of Jesus Christ and lived at a particular time and place in history. Because the divine Word, the eternal Son of God, had taken on human flesh, writes John, it is possible, indeed necessary, to "draw his image and show it to anyone willing to gaze at it." For John images were not a useful appendage to Christian teaching; without images the truth about Christ could not be grasped fully. At the same time he recognized that the veneration of images was different from the worship due only God. Drawing on the language of the Bible, "God only shall you worship" (Luke 4:8; Deuteronomy 6:13), he made a clean distinction between the adoration due to God and the honor and veneration appropriate for images.

For John the controversy over icons was a dispute about how God is made known to human beings, not a debate about religious art. His views provided a theological rationale for the veneration of images. Throughout history God had been revealed in historical events, and in the last days he had "spoken to us through his Son" (Hebrews 1:2). John readily granted that the Scriptures forbid the making of images of God, but the command against making graven images was given in ancient times to the Jewish people before the coming of Christ. Because God clothed himself in human form and became visible, says John, "you may draw his likeness." In Christ all things are new; after his coming we are able to *see* what is uncircumscribed and invisible.

Again and again he highlights the role of "seeing" in Christian faith and calls sight "the noblest sense." Only by seeing are human beings brought into intimate relation to God: "I have seen God in human form, and my soul has been saved. I look at the image of God, as Jacob did, but in a different way." Jacob saw only with "spiritual sight" what was to come in the future; his vision was limited (Genesis 32:30). Now we are able to see God "visible in human flesh," and the image of God has been "burned into my soul." Icons are the Church's most palpable way of confirming that God appeared in human flesh in the person of Jesus Christ.

John's arguments are not only theological; he has a keen appreciation of the sensuous nature of experience. He wrote that he was a human being with a body, and as a human being "I desire to communicate physically with the things that are holy and to see them." A piece of cloth is a lifeless thing, no more valuable than the stuff of which it is made, but if it is a shirt or a blouse of someone I love it is something more than a piece of cloth. "I have often seen lovers gazing at the garments of their beloved," he wrote, "embracing the garments with their eyes and their lips as if the garment were the beloved one." In the same way the faithful kissed the wood of the cross that held the precious body of Christ, knelt in adoration at the rock where he was crucified, and kissed an image of the infant Christ in the arms of the Virgin Mary. Only by turning to what can be seen and touched do we learn to see the God who cannot be seen. Christianity is an affair of things.

John died in 750, and it is unclear how much influence his writings had on the course of the controversy. Their significance was not recognized until later. Yet he was a herald of what was to come. In 775 the iconoclastic emperor Constantine V died, and he was succeeded by his son Leo IV. When Leo died a few years later, in 780, his wife Irene became regent for her nine-year-old son Constantine.

Although iconoclastic sentiment had dominated the imperial family for half a century, Irene did not share her family's views and moved swiftly to reverse imperial policy. The elderly patriarch of Constantinople, Paul IV, had sided with the iconoclasts, and he was forced to resign and retire to a monastery. In his place Tarasius, a layman and first secretary of the government, was elected and consecrated bishop in December 784. At once he let it be known that he favored the calling of a general council to revoke the iconoclastic decrees of the Council of Hieria two decades earlier.

He also knew that it was essential to gain the support of the pope. Irene and Tarasius wrote to Pope Hadrian I (772–795), informing him of the forthcoming council and asking him to send a delegation. In his response, Hadrian criticized Tarasius's uncanonical elevation from layman up the ecclesiastical hierarchy in a matter of days, and demanded the recognition of the primacy of Rome. But he applauded the decision to convene a council, and dispatched two legates to represent him.

The council convened in August 786 in the church of the Holy Apostles in Constantinople, in the presence of Irene and the sixteen-year-old emperor, Constantine. Things did not go well; the iconoclastic bishops realized that if the council proceeded they would come out the losers. So they gathered in a separate conclave to reaffirm the decisions at Hieria, but their proceedings were broken up by imperial troops and forced to disband.

In May of the following year, a second summons went out for a council to convene at Nicaea, across the Bosporus from Constantinople in Asia Minor. Nicaea had been the setting for the first worldwide council in the Church's history, and by a happy coincidence the emperor at the time of second Nicaea was also named Constantine.

Tarasius, the patriarch of Constantinople, presided, and the first order of business was to call the iconoclastic bishops to account. Some wanted them to be treated harshly, but the majority agreed to restore the iconoclasts to fellowship out of a desire to achieve "unity and concord." One session was devoted to a point-by-point refutation of the iconoclastic decree of the Council of Hieria. The bishops also adopted a formal theological definition supporting the veneration of icons:

> We decree . . . that like the figure of the honored and life-giving cross, the venerable images, whether painted or made of mosaic or of other suitable material, are to be exposed in the holy churches of God, on sacred instruments and vestments, on walls and panels, in houses and by public ways; these are the images of our Lord, God and savior, Jesus Christ, and of our Lady without blemish, the holy theotokos, and of the revered angels and of any of the saintly holy men. The more frequently they are seen through pictorial representation, the more those who see these images are drawn to

remember and to have an earnest desire for those who serve as models, and to honor them and give them respectful veneration. This is not the full adoration that according to our faith is properly paid only to the divine nature, but it is similar to the veneration given to the relic of the precious and life-giving cross, and also to the holy books of the gospels and to other sacred objects. Let these images be honored with the offering of incense and lights, as was piously established by ancient custom. The honor paid to an image is conveyed to the model, and the one who venerates the image, venerates the person represented in that image.

More than 350 bishops were in attendance at the council, and it would seem that their solemn declaration in support of the veneration of icons settled the matter once and for all. For a time it did. But opposition to icons ran deeper than the confident dismissal of iconoclastic arguments suggests. Unfortunately, most of the writings of the iconoclasts were destroyed, and their views can be reconstructed only on the basis of their critics. For that reason it is difficult to judge how widespread the sentiment against images was in the final decades of the eighth century. But iconoclasm certainly had not died out, for early in the next century another emperor, Leo V (813–820), began a new campaign against images. As in the first phase of the controversy, the spiritual issues often seem secondary to political and military matters. The Bulgars, a Slavic people, had crossed the Danube, overrun towns and villages in Thrace in the lower Balkans, and threatened Constantinople itself. Nevertheless, the iconoclasts were not without arguments, and they revived the ethical theory of icons, the view that the most authentic image of a holy person was a virtuous life modeled on that of the saint.

The commanding theological voice on the side of the iconodules was a clearheaded monk, Theodore of Studium (d. 826), from a monastery in Constantinople. Like John of Damascus he drew on theological ideas developed in the course of the Christological debates, but his thinking ran deeper. He was convinced that the iconoclasts thought much too abstractly about Christ, as though the divine Word had assumed humanity in general. A symbol can depict an idea or concept or abstract quality, or an aspect of a person, but only an image can display the person of Christ in his fullness. In his paradoxical language, unless there is an image of Christ there is no Christ. As a shadow is inseparably bound to the body that cast it, so an image is indivisible from the original. Hence the icon of Christ "is the most visible testimony of God's saving plan."

As in the earlier stage of the controversy it was the mother of a young emperor, a woman named Theodora, who moved to turn back the policy of the new generation of iconoclastic emperors. When her husband, the emperor Theophilos (829–842), died she assumed imperial power for her son, Michael III. A new patriarch was installed, and on the first Sunday of Lent in 843 the decisions of the Council of

Nicaea II were reaffirmed and the veneration of icons officially sanctioned. The day was long remembered, and the churches of the East celebrated it as the Triumph of Orthodoxy.

Although the iconophiles viewed their victory as a vindication of ancient tradition, in truth they had accomplished something new: they had secured an enduring place for the veneration of images at the heart of Eastern Christian piety. The image brought the person it depicted into the presence of the believer; hence it became customary to prostrate oneself before an icon, light a candle, or burn incense as though honoring the person himself or herself.

The victory over the iconoclasts also led to a rethinking of how churches would be decorated. In the early centuries images were placed principally on the walls above the columns, in the apse, and on the triumphal arch. But in the centuries after the iconoclastic controversy the walls of the churches hummed with saints and angels, some pictured full-length, others displaying the face gazing at the worshipers. On entering the church one was surrounded by holy men and women welcoming the faithful into their company.

Architects also took a more systematic approach to the presentation of the events of the life of Christ. In earlier churches key events were highlighted, such as the annunciation to Mary or the baptism of Christ, but now the walls of churches displayed a succession of images that set forth the gospel narrative in its fullness: the presentation in the temple, the transfiguration, Christ's entry into Jerusalem, the washing of the feet of the disciples, the betrayal of Judas, the burial of Christ, the resurrection, and more. It is fitting that the most enduring legacy of the great debate would be in pictures, not words. Each time one entered a church, the truth of Christ's humanity was set before the eyes of the faithful in images of vivid color.

Even though the iconoclastic controversy took place in the Greek-speaking East, it had repercussions in the West. The acts of the Council of Nicaea were sent to Rome and forwarded to the court of Charlemagne in a garbled Latin translation. The pope's legates had supported the decree of the council, but Charlemagne's advisers were critical of the council's decisions. They agreed that images should not be smashed, but they did not think they should be objects of adoration. Theodulph, a learned biblical scholar and theologian, prepared a lengthy refutation of the acts of the Council of Nicaea. And in 794 the Carolingian bishops convened their own council in Frankfurt, where they ruled that the veneration of images was to be rejected. The reaction was less a judgment about images than a different sensibility about the place of images in Christian devotion. The crowning of Charlemagne as emperor by the pope in the year 800, thereby establishing a rival to the emperor in Constantinople, only deepened the political, cultural, and religious divide between East and West.

Arabic-Speaking Christians

By the middle of the eighth century more than fifty percent of the Christian world had fallen under Muslim rule. In the span of less than a hundred years, the Arabs had conquered greater Syria (including the Holy Land and Jordan) and Egypt, and made their way from the western edge of Egypt along the North African littoral until they reached the Atlantic Ocean. From the Arabian peninsula they advanced northeast through Persia and across the Asian steppes to India. In 711 they reached Sind, today a province in Pakistan. Within the same decade, they crossed the Strait of Gibraltar into Spain and in midcentury established an independent Muslim kingdom in the peninsula.

In these disparate and distant regions Muslims created a new society formed by common beliefs, practices, and language, held together in a loose unity by the caliphate established in the ancient city of Damascus and moved to Baghdad after 750. As new territories were conquered, garrison towns arose. The Arabs brought their wives and children, built mosques, and founded new cities such as Basra and Kufah in Iraq, Fustat (old Cairo) in Egypt, and Kairouan in Tunisia. By keeping themselves apart initially from the local societies, they were able to maintain their identity in a sea of strange people and gradually displace the culture that had dominated the region for centuries.

At first Arabic was spoken only by the Arabs, but by the end of the seventh century, during the caliphates of Abd al-Malik and his son Hisham, Arabic was becoming the language of administration, commerce, and learning, as well as of religion. Coins were minted with legends carrying a reproach to Christians: THERE IS NO GOD BUT GOD ALONE. HE HAS NO COMPANION. A public cult supported by political authority was established, calling for prayer five times a day, recitation of the Qur'an on Fridays, an address before prayers, the *khutba,* and an annual month of fasting (Ramadan).

The successors of Muhammad planted a permanent political and religious rival to Christianity and made Christians a minority in lands that had been Christian for centuries. Four hundred years later, when the Crusaders arrived in the East, an Arab historian observed that they had entered "the lands of Islam."

In adapting to Muslim rule, language was a key factor. In Egypt, as Arabic became the everyday language, Christians held on to the ancient Egyptian language, Coptic, giving them distance from Muslim society and helping them to preserve their distinctive way of life. In time they adopted Arabic, but there is no significant body of Christian literature from Egypt written in it until the end of the tenth century. In Spain some Christians embraced Arabic, even enthusiastically, but others made a strenuous effort to hold on to the traditional Latin Christian culture. In other countries, such as Armenia and Ethiopia, Arabic was never adopted by the Christian communities.

In Palestine, Syria, and Mesopotamia the lingua franca was Aramaic (or Syriac), and at first there was little reason for most Christians to learn Arabic. By the beginning of the eighth century, however, Arabic had become the public language of the society. Even road signs displayed the Muslim creed, the Shahadah, in Arabic: "There is no God but God and Muhammad is his prophet." By the middle of the century, when a new dynasty, the Abbasids, came to power, Christian leaders began to realize that Islam was here to stay, and they took up the challenge of translating Christian writings into Arabic, defending and explaining Christian practices, such as the veneration of icons, to Muslims.

The transition from Greek and Syriac into Arabic over several generations can be seen by comparing the lives of three Christian thinkers who lived in the early centuries of Muslim rule. One is John of Damascus (655–750), the theologian who defended the veneration of icons against the iconoclasts; another is Timothy I (728–823), patriarch of the Church of the East; and finally, Theodore Abu Qurrah (755–825), bishop of Harran, a city in the vicinity of Edessa in northern Syria.

John was the son of a prominent family, the Mansurs, in Damascus. His father had served at the court of the caliph, and as a boy John received a traditional education in Greek and learned Arabic. As a thinker John was the heir of the long tradition of Greek-speaking theologians, including Athanasius of Alexandria, Gregory the Theologian, and Cyril of Alexandria; his major work, the *Fount of Knowledge,* a compendium of Christian theology, became a handbook of Christian teaching in the East. He was the first Christian to write an appraisal of Muhammad.

The earliest recorded comment of a Christian reaction to Muhammad dates from only a couple of years after the Prophet's death. When tales of a prophet among the Arabs reached Christian Syria, someone asked an old man, "What can you tell me about the prophet who has appeared with the Saracens?" The old man groaned deeply and said, "He is false, for the prophets do not come armed with a sword."

John's account is more substantial and based on his own study of the Qur'an. It can be found in a section of *Fount of Knowledge* devoted to Christian heresies. John presents Muhammad and Muslim teaching in the light of Christian doctrine. In trying to explain why Muslims reject Christian belief in Christ as God and say God has no "associate," he depicts Muhammad as a descendant of the arch-heretic Arius, a teacher who truncated Christian truth. With his knowledge of Arabic, John was able to cite specific passages from the Qur'an to support his argument, but his intellectual horizon is shaped wholly by ideas that had been formed before the rise of Islam. He is dimly aware that something new had entered his universe, but he is unequipped to deal with Islam except in terms of Christian beliefs. Even though John had first-hand experience with Islam and lived in a society that was being transformed by the beliefs and practices of the new religion, he viewed the Prophet Muhammad and his teaching as a deviation from Christian teaching.

Timothy was born of well-to-do parents in Hazza (in northern Iran) in the middle of the eighth century. His uncle, a bishop, took charge of his early education, and after his elementary formation he studied with a monk named Abraham bar Dashandad at a monastic school, learning the Scriptures, liturgy, philosophy (particularly Aristotle), Greek, and Arabic. For a short time he was a monk near present-day Mosul in Iraq, but in his early thirties he succeeded his uncle as bishop of Beth Bagash on the Zab River in Iraq. A few years later, after a much contested election, he was consecrated catholicos (patriarch) of the Church of the East, whose see was in the Abbasid capital, the newly founded city of Baghdad. As we have seen in an earlier chapter, Timothy was an energetic promoter of the Christian mission to Central Asia, India, China, and even Tibet.

Besides his administrative and diplomatic skills Timothy was a gifted writer. Although he was fluent in Arabic, all of his writings are in Syriac written to the clergy and monks under his jurisdiction. Among other things, he wrote a book on astronomy, works on canon law, a collection of homilies, a commentary on writings of Gregory Nazianzen, and a large body of letters. Timothy was also active in the intellectual life of the Abbasid capital. Shortly after he became patriarch, Caliph al-Mahdi asked him to make a translation of the section in Aristotle's work on logic that deals with dialectics. Apparently there was a Syriac version, and Timothy, with the help of another Christian, translated the Greek text into Arabic for the caliph. Timothy's translation of Aristotle is an early example of influential collaboration between Muslim intellectuals and Christian scholars who knew Greek as well as Syriac.

In 781 Timothy was invited to take part in a debate at the court of al-Mahdi, the third Abbasid caliph in Baghdad, on differences between Christianity and Islam. As was to be expected in the circumstances, Timothy was at a distinct disadvantage; he even used the word "futility" to describe the debate. Yet the discussion focused on substantive issues, and it is clear that the caliph was well informed about Christianity and took Timothy's arguments seriously. The caliph asked, for example, how someone so learned could say that God married a woman and begot a son. Timothy replied that no Christian would say that. But, said the caliph, did you not say that Christ is the son of God? True, Timothy answered, but how this could be is beyond our grasp; we can only speak in analogies. As light is born of the sun and the word of the soul, so Christ who is Word is born of God before all worlds.

After debating Christian theological concepts, the discussion turned to Muhammad. The caliph said that passages in the gospels, such as John 14:16, 26, that mention the coming of the Paraclete (Counselor) refer to Muhammad. But Timothy responded that Muhammad cannot be the Paraclete (the Holy Spirit), because the Spirit has no body and Muhammad had a body. The caliph also charged Christians with corrupting the Scriptures so that the references to Muhammad are eliminated. Timothy would not grant that Muhammad is mentioned in the Scriptures, but he praised the Muslims for abandoning idolatry for the worship of the one God.

The debate was very cordial, and each side knew a great deal about the other. The caliph could cite the Scriptures and argue about how texts were to be interpreted, and the patriarch knew the Qur'an and used passages from the Muslim sacred book to buttress his arguments. Of course we do not have a stenographic account of the debate; what we have is Timothy's summary written for Christians living in the Muslim world. The text was written and circulated in a Syriac version, and was soon translated into Arabic and expanded. It was very popular among Arabic-speaking Christians, because it provided arguments in defense of Christianity against Islam.

Timothy lived in a bilingual world of Syriac and Arabic. Though he spoke Arabic, he wrote in Syriac. He is a reminder that even as Arabic was being adopted by many Christians in the Middle East, Syriac continued to be used as the language of scholarship and worship among others. In the ninth century one of the most distinguished biblical scholars in the early Christian world, Ishodad of Merv, wrote commentaries on the Bible in Syriac. So prized were his writings by Syriac-speaking Christians that he was esteemed not only by scholars in his own communion, the Church of the East, but also by the miaphysites (the Jacobites). Among later Christian writers in Syriac, Michael the Syrian, Jacobite patriarch of Antioch at the end of the twelfth century, and Bar Hebraeus, bishop of Aleppo in Syria in the mid thirteenth century, stand out. Michael wrote a chronicle of world history that began with the creation of the world and came up to his own day. It is still read today for its many citations of sources that no longer exist. Bar Hebraeus, a scholar of uncommon breadth, wrote an encyclopedia of human knowledge based on Greek, Syriac, and Arabic authors, commentaries on the Old and New Testaments, and works on ethics, canon law, history, and poetry. Each writer bears witness to the vitality of Syriac as a Christian language long after the Muslim conquest.

Theodore Abu Qurrah's native language was Syriac, but his major writings are in Arabic. He was born in Edessa (present-day Urfa in Turkey), a center of Syriac-speaking Christianity. Though he learned Greek, he did not write in that language. Little is known of his life, but he became the Melkite (or Chalcedonian) bishop of Harran, some twenty-five miles from Edessa in northern Syria. In other words, Theodore and Timothy were representatives of two of the three divisions among Christians of the East that had arisen after the Council of Chalcedon.

Theodore was a skilled debater and polemicist, and he traveled throughout the Middle East explaining and defending Christian faith against Muslims and Jews. A number of his works deal with points of Christian doctrine: the Holy Trinity, the person of Christ, the Incarnation, and so on. But he also wrote an essay on the veneration of images, and this work gives us a good picture of the social world Christians inhabited and the challenges they faced in a Muslim society.

The treatise was written in response to the request of Abu Yannah, a member of the family in charge of the church in Edessa that held the famous image of Christ "not made with hands." "You have informed us," Theodore wrote, "that many Christians are abandoning prostration before the image of Christ . . . and the images of his saints . . . because non-Christians, and especially those who claim to be in possession of a scripture sent down from God, rebuke them for their prostration to these images. For this reason they charge them with worshipping idols, and breaking the Law given by God in the Torah and the prophets. They even sneer at them."

From the way Theodore approached the topic, it is evident that Jews as well as Muslims were critics of the Christian veneration of images. With the end of Byzantine rule Christians no longer enjoyed the protection of the political authorities, and Jews saw an opportunity to attack Christians on a point where they were vulnerable. So a section of the treatise is given over to the defense of the Christian practice against Jewish critics. But the heart of the argument has to do with the believers of Islam—in Theodore's words, those "who claim possession of a scripture sent down from God."

Although the Qur'an includes no explicit prohibition of the making of images of human persons, in the early centuries its expositors interpreted its condemnation of idolatry as a strict prohibition of religious images. Muslims were offended at the proliferation of images that adorned the walls of Christian churches. As Muslim rulers eliminated symbols of Christianity from public places and issued orders that pictures in churches be removed, the Christian people became fearful and began to abandon the veneration of images. In this setting, Theodore took up his pen.

To convince Christians who were persuaded by the arguments of Muslims against the veneration of images, Theodore shows that in some cases Muslims recognize that it is proper to bow down before a human being. In an allusion to a passage in the Qur'an (2:34) in which angels bow down before Adam, he says that according to the

Qur'an "God commanded all the angels to prostrate themselves to Adam, and they prostrated themselves." Further, Muslims should not mock Christians when they bow before a bishop because, and here he quotes the Qur'an's surah "Joseph" directly: Jacob and his sons "bowed down to Joseph as one making prostration" (Qur'an 12:100).

Theodore's aim in the treatise was to convince wavering and conflicted Christians that the traditional practice of venerating images is supported by the Christian Scriptures and can be defended against Muslim critics on the basis of their holy book. He understood that matters of practice were as vital to the survival of Christianity in a hostile world as was Christian teaching. The veneration of images was not a pious custom that could be abandoned without grave consequences for the spiritual health of the Christian body. Hence his defense was twofold: to preserve a traditional form of devotion that nurtured Christian faith and to assert the distinctive features of Christian teaching in a Muslim society. This task he carried out with polish in the Arabic language. His writings were read by Muslims, and we know of one Muslim thinker, Abu Musa Isa ibn Subayh al-Murdar (d. 840), who wrote a treatise "against Abu Qurrah, the Christian."

While Theodore and other Christians were defending Christian practice and teaching, some were engaged in an equally vital undertaking, the translation of Christian writings, the Scriptures, liturgical texts, lives of the saints, and writings of the church fathers, into Arabic. The principal places of translation, and hence the intellectual centers of the emerging Arabic-speaking Christianity, were monasteries, in particular Mar Saba and Mar Chariton in the Judean desert to the east and southeast of Bethlehem, and Saint Catherine in the Sinai. Originally Greek-speaking, the monasteries welcomed Syriac-speaking monks, and as Arabic became the new lingua franca of the Middle East they mastered Arabic.

By good fortune we know the names of several of these pioneering translators, though details of their lives are sparse. Anthony David of Baghdad arrived at Mar Saba in the late ninth century, and his name appears in the colophon (a brief notice at the end of a manuscript identifying the copyist or translator, place, or date of translation) of two manuscripts written there in 885–886. One manuscript includes translations of the lives of the most famous Palestinian monks, Saint Euthymius and Saint Sabas, as well as of writings of Greek fathers, Basil of Caesarea, Gregory of Nyssa, and of the Syriac writer Isaac of Nineveh.

Here is how Anthony identifies himself in the colophon:

> The poor sinner, Anthony David the son of Sulayman of Baghdad, copied this volume in the laura [term for the kind of monastery common to Palestine] of the holy Mar Saba. The monk Abba Isaac asked him to copy it for the monastery of the hallowed Mount Sinai. I, the feeble sinner who has copied it, ask and beseech everyone who reads the holy fathers and others in it

to beseech and ask Jesus Christ, our God and savior, to forgive my many sins and offenses. By the intercession of the honorable Lady Mary, and of our father Saba and all his pious holy ones, may God have mercy on the ones who have produced, copied, asked for a copy, read, heard or said "Amen" to this work. It was copied in the month Rabi' al-Awwal, of the year 272 [885–886].

That Anthony David came from Baghdad is worthy of note. The city is a long way from Palestine, and his presence at Mar Saba near Jerusalem suggests that with the transfer of the Muslim capital from Damascus to Baghdad, the monasteries of the Holy Land had begun to look more to the East than to Byzantium as they had done earlier. As Christians became part of the cultural world of Islam, they laid a foundation to support intellectual life in a new environment. The colophon to the manuscript copied by Anthony David shows that the monks in the several monastic houses depended on one another to build their collection of Arabic manuscripts. Anthony copied the manuscript at the request of Isaac, a monk at the monastery of Saint Catherine in the Sinai desert. By good fortune, the librarians at Saint Catherine preserved these precious Arabic Christian manuscripts over the centuries until modern times.

Another translator and copyist, Stephen of Ramla, was a monk at the monastery of Mar Chariton, not too far from Mar Saba. Stephen's name appears in the colophon of two Arabic manuscripts, one in the British Museum dated 877, and the other from the monastery of Saint Catherine in the Sinai dated 897. In the colophon to the manuscript in the British Museum, Stephen wrote: "The book is finished. . . . Stephen . . . son of Hakam, known as ar-Ramli, wrote it in the laura of Mar Chariton for his teacher Anba Basil." The other manuscript gives the same information. Stephen's name al-Ramli marks him as a native of the city of Ramla in Palestine. When the Muslims conquered the Holy Land they built a new city named Ramla near the ancient city of Lydda on the fertile plain of Sharon in central Palestine and made it the center of the military district. Growing up in Ramla, Stephen learned Arabic, but he also spoke Syriac and learned Greek from Christian tutors.

One of the two manuscripts copied by Stephen of Ramla is a complete translation of the four gospels, the earliest that we know of. There was a pressing need to provide translations of the Scriptures and liturgical books for the growing Arabic-speaking Christian population. The translation is based on a Greek text of the gospels that is closely related to the Syriac translations that were used in the churches in Palestine. It is not a lectionary, a selection of readings for liturgical purposes; however, passages to be read in the liturgy in Jerusalem during the course of the year are clearly marked off so the manuscript could be used liturgically. By offering the full text of the gospels, the manuscript could be used for scholarly purposes as well.

The other manuscript is quite different. It contains a short treatise outlining

Christian teaching in terms that would be intelligible to an Arabic speaker. It is titled "A Summary of the Ways of Faith in Confessing the Trinity of the "One-ness" of God, and the Incarnation of God, the Word, from the Pure Virgin Mary." The content is similar to what is found in Timothy's debate with Caliph al-Mahdi. The manuscript also includes Theodore Abu Qurrah's treatise defending the veneration of images.

It is clear from this small selection of Arabic Christian manuscripts that there was a concerted effort on the part of these learned monks to build a library of Christian writings in Arabic. Though they loved the languages in which Christian tradition had been handed on to them, principally Greek and Syriac, they were looking to the future. By translating Christian writings into a new language and creating an Arabic Christian idiom, they took part in a scholarly ritual that has been repeated again and again in the Church's history.

Arabic, however, posed a unique challenge because its religious vocabulary came from the Qur'an; still, Christian translators boldly appropriated its language for Christian use. To illustrate: Each surah in the Qur'an begins, "In the name of God, the Merciful, the Compassionate." In Arabic the phrase "in the name of God" is *bi-ism Allah*. When Christians translated the invocation of the Holy Trinity into Arabic, the phrase began in the same way, "Bi-ism Allah," "in the name of God," and continued, "Father, Son, and Holy Spirit." Christians used the same word for God as did the Muslims, "Allah," which has the same root in Hebrew and in Syriac. The term "come down" used for Muhammad's visions is used by Christians to refer to the revelation in Christ. They also use the Muslim word *Iblis* for Satan, and even the word "islam" to signify obedience. In some writings phrases from the Qur'an, such as "Praise be to God" (*al-hamdu-li-llah*) or "Lord of mercy," are taken over and put to Christian use.

Translators like Anthony David of Baghdad and Stephen of Ramla were concerned primarily with providing Arabic translations for use in the churches and monasteries. But there were other Christian thinkers, philosophers, physicians, mathematicians, who were engaged in translating other kinds of writings. The impetus came from the Muslim court and Muslim intellectuals who did not know Greek and were interested in ancient Greek writings. Christian scholars who spoke Arabic and read Greek were engaged as translators.

But there was more at work in these translations than a service to Muslim readers. The Christian translators themselves had an interest in the content of the texts they translated and began to write original philosophical works. Syriac-speaking Christian thinkers had long been interested in philosophy, particularly the writings of Aristotle. In the sixth century a scholar from Edessa, Sergius of Resh'ayna (d. 536), had studied Aristotle with Christian philosophers in Alexandria and carried their ideas to Syriac-speaking scholars in northern Syria. Timothy I also had a lively interest in Aristotle and borrowed some of his works on logic, including the Organon, from a monastery near Mosul in Iraq.

This interest in philosophy followed a familiar path that Christians had traversed for centuries. Christian thinkers were interested in philosophy as a way to provide rational support for what was believed and to serve in interpreting and explaining the Scriptures and Christian teaching. Without the study of logic, it was said, one could not understand the sacred books. Muslim thinkers worked with similar convictions, and this led to fruitful collaboration between Christian and Muslim scholars.

The list of Christian philosophers working in Baghdad under the Abbasids is long, but one person can stand as exemplary. He is Hunayn ibn Ishaq, who was born in 808 and died in 873. His native language was Syriac, but he mastered Greek and spoke Arabic; his interests were philosophical, scientific, and medical. Hunayn came to the attention of the caliph through his translations, but he also had medical training and became the court physician for Caliph al-Mutawakkil (847–861). While at the court he oversaw a workshop of translators, but he wrote original philosophical works in defense of Christianity, a treatise on proofs for the existence of God, and another on criteria for determining whether a religion is true. One treatise bears the title "gnomic sayings" or "instructive anecdotes" and is a collection of quotations from wise men of antiquity on the moral life.

The Christian scholars and thinkers who wrote in Arabic were engaged in a major intellectual project that stretched over three hundred years, from the middle of the eighth century up to the Crusades at the end of the eleventh century. They were faced with the challenge of making Christian faith intelligible in the emerging Arabic Muslim culture. What made their situation unique is that the language they translated Christian writings into and the idiom they explained Christian beliefs and practices in was the language of another religion with universal ambitions. Islam was not one religion among others, it was the religion of the society in which Christians lived.

Their accomplishment is all the more remarkable when one realizes that Arabic-speaking scholars were isolated from Western Christians, those who spoke either Greek or Latin. They wrote in a language unknown in the West, and contacts with Christians outside the Muslim world were infrequent. Even when visitors did make their way to Jerusalem, they came as pilgrims to pray at the holy places and had little interest in the local churches. Few ventured into the desert to visit the monasteries where the translators were working, and most were unaware of the intellectual vitality of Christian life in Muslim society. The Christian world east of Jerusalem had begun to fade in the memory of Christians in Byzantium and the West.

Christians Under Islam:
Egypt and North Africa

After the triumphant march through greater Syria and Iraq, the Muslim commanders turned west, to Egypt, the most obvious next goal of their conquest. The Nile Valley was the granary of Constantinople, and Egypt the portal to the North African coast and points westward. The task fell to Amr Ibn al-As, one of the "companions" of Muhammad. As a merchant in Egypt he came to know the country well and had led the Muslim advance on Gaza bordering Egypt. In making the case to Caliph Umar that his forces should turn to Egypt, he is reported to have said: "The conquest of Egypt will give great power to the Muslims and will be a great aid to them, for it is the wealthiest land and the weakest in fighting and war power."

The invasion began in 639. This is astonishing when one considers that Muhammad died in 632; Seleucia-Ctesiphon, the capital of the Sasanid Empire, fell in 637; and Jerusalem was taken in 638. After seizing the coastal cities, Amr began a siege of Babylon (old Cairo), a fortress commanding the junction of the Nile Valley and the Delta. The army arrived in late spring in 640, and by December of the same year it was victorious. A portion of the army then headed south to subdue the cities up the Nile, but another force made its way to the great city of Alexandria on the Mediterranean coast.

When the Arabs arrived in Alexandria, the magnificent cathedral of Saint Mark stood at the center of the city, and in the harbor they could see the great lighthouse of Pharos, one of the seven wonders of the ancient world. It was like arriving in New York and seeing the Statue of Liberty for the first time. In March 641 the Muslims laid siege to Alexandria, and though their numbers were fewer than the Byzantines, by early fall this ancient Christian capital was in Muslim hands. After the conquest Amr wrote to Umar the caliph: "I have captured a city . . . with four thousand villas and with four thousand baths." The Muslims, however, chose the fortress of Babylon, near present-day Cairo on the Nile River, as their capital, not Alexandria, and gave it the name al-Fustat.

At the time of the conquest Cyrus, a bishop from the Caucasus, was the Melkite (Chalcedonian) patriarch of Alexandria and prefect of the Byzantine military forces in the country. He proved to be duplicitous in dealing with the Muslims, and the emperor removed him from the position and recalled him to Constantinople. The head of the Coptic Christian community, the largest Christian communion in Egypt, was Benjamin. At the time of the Muslim invasion he was in hiding—not for fear of the Muslims, but to escape harassment by Cyrus, who had been sent to Egypt to subdue the Coptic Christians and bring them over to the imperial Church. During his exile Benjamin moved from one monastery to another with a small company of followers, but he spent most of his time at the famous White Monastery of Shenoute at Sohag in upper Egypt. After Cyrus left Egypt, Amr learned that Benjamin was the principal leader among Christians, and ordered him to Alexandria to head up the Egyptian Christian community.

Benjamin was a native Egyptian who had been born in a village west of Alexandria in the Nile Delta. As a young man he had become a monk, but when Andronicus (616–622), the patriarch of Alexandria, recognized his gifts he ordained him priest and made him his personal assistant. When Andronicus died Benjamin succeeded him and governed the Egyptian Church until his death in 661. Though he is a major figure in Coptic history, revered with the likes of Athanasius and Cyril of Alexandria, he is hardly known in the West. His name does not merit an entry in the major encyclopedias of Christian history. Yet he guided Egyptian Christians through three major upheavals, the Persian occupation of Egypt in 618–629, the repressive years under Cyrus, the Byzantine governor, and the early years of transition to Muslim rule.

By good fortune we possess the Coptic text of a sermon on the wedding at Cana (John 2:1–11) preached by Benjamin shortly after he returned from exile. The occasion was the liturgical celebration of the wedding at Cana in the Coptic calendar. It is at once a winsome meditation on the biblical story (Benjamin has the disciples say to the host, "If you can't provide wine for the wedding why did you invite us?"), a robust defense of the Egyptian theological tradition, and a valuable account of his trials while in exile. Yet what is striking about the sermon is that Benjamin makes no mention of the Muslim conquest or the challenges facing Egyptian Christians. Like Sophronius, the patriarch of Jerusalem, Benjamin imagined the Muslim occupation was a temporary interlude and would soon come to an end. The sermon gives no hint that the mountains had been shaken and the waters roared.

Benjamin soon realized that the ground on which he stood had shifted. Egypt was no longer under Byzantine rule and the Chalcedonian minority had lost its privileges. He was made the sole representative of Egyptian Christians. This put him and his successors in a compromising position, for the new rulers quickly put in place a fiscal system that imposed a poll tax and a land tax on the conquered, and Benjamin was charged with collecting the taxes. The new position of the patriarch, intermediary between the Muslim rulers and the Christian people, was an early sign of the social order that would shape the future of Christianity in Egypt in ways large and small. The Muslims had little interest in having Christians convert to Islam; they were needed to run the government, to provide financial support, and to till the fields.

As in Syria, the Christians in Egypt were able to go about their lives and manage their affairs with minimal interference. One of the first items of business was to repair and restore the churches and monasteries that had been damaged during the invasion. Benjamin gave himself energetically to the task. The cathedral of Saint Mark had been destroyed by fire, and Benjamin realized that this church among all others in Egypt carried the memories of Egyptian Christians. So he moved quickly to rebuild it and claim Saint Mark as the founder of the Coptic Church, and to assert that as patriarch, or bishop of Alexandria, he was in a direct line of succession from the apostle. Benjamin's last action as patriarch was to celebrate the liturgy in the restored cathedral.

In the early years relations between the Christian communities and the Muslim rulers remained cordial. But gradually as Muslim rule reached into more areas of society, the Christians found their freedom restricted and their activities more closely regulated. For example, the Muslim governor took an interest in the election of bishops and in particular the election of the Coptic patriarch. In one case when the patriarch Isaac (689–692) was asked to consecrate a bishop for Ethiopia he replied: "I cannot ordain a bishop for you without the command of Amir, the governor of the land of Egypt." In another case when the bishops elected a patriarch who was not Egyptian they were summoned to appear before the governor and account for their decision. When asked they said: "The matter belongs to God, and in the second place to you." Though the bishops stood their ground, it was clear that a principle had been established: the Muslim governor had a role in the selection of the patriarch of Alexandria.

In Egypt the people spoke Coptic, the native language of their land, unrelated to Arabic. In the early eighth century, however, a series of laws were passed requiring the use of Arabic in public documents. The aim was to further the "Arabization" of the society. The increasing use of Arabic for administrative, legal, and mercantile purposes began to displace Coptic as the language of daily life among Christians. One Christian writer had this to say about the use of Arabic by Christians: "They are abandoning their beautiful Coptic language, in which the Holy Spirit has spoken many times through the mouths of the holy spiritual fathers, and they are teaching their children from infancy to speak the language of the Arabs, and to take pride in it! Even the priests and monks—they as well!—dare to speak in Arabic and take pride in it, and that within the sanctuary! Woe upon woe!"

Nevertheless, the Coptic language and culture gave Christians of Egypt a precious inheritance that helped to sustain their communal identity under Muslim rule. Yet in the tenth century, Severus, a Coptic bishop and historian, wrote his *History of the Patriarchs of the Coptic Church of Alexandria* in Arabic. In the monasteries, however, the monks continued to chant the psalms in Coptic, a practice that continues to this day. The monasteries also preserved the Coptic literary heritage by copying and producing books in Coptic, even writing grammars to teach the Coptic language. At the same time the monasteries served as centers of economic life, sacred places of pilgrimage, havens in times of trouble, and cultivators of Egyptian Christian culture. In the centuries that followed, Christianity in Egypt proved to be remarkably resilient, and today the Coptic Church of Egypt is the largest Christian communion in the Middle East.

The story is quite different in North Africa. After the Punic Wars between Rome and Carthage in the third and second centuries B.C., Rome formed a new province, Africa (present-day Tunisia and Algeria), across the Mediterranean Sea from Italy. Over time a Latin-speaking culture was established in the cities, and at the end of the second century A.D. the first evidence of Christianity appears. The Acts of the Scillitan Martyrs is a concise, even austere account of the martyrdom of seven men and five women executed in the city of Scillium, not too far from Carthage (Tunis), for refusing to renounce Christianity. This precious document, written in 180, is the first Christian writing in Latin and the first to give evidence of a Latin Bible, or at least of a Latin translation of the letters of Saint Paul. The Acts of the Scillitan Martyrs stands at the beginning of a long and illustrious tradition of Latin-speaking Christianity in the large territory north of the Sahara desert.

The first theological treatises in Latin were written by Tertullian of Carthage, a native of Africa, who lived in the early third century. Tertullian forged for the first time a vocabulary to express Christian teachings in Latin that is used to this day. Christianity flourished in Roman Africa, and by the time Cyprian became bishop of Carthage in the mid third century the city was a major Christian metropolis. Christianity reached its zenith in the early fifth century when Augustine was bishop of Hippo (Annaba in present-day Algeria). But the rise of the Donatists, a tenacious rigorist movement spawned by the persecution of Emperor Diocletian in the early fourth century, led to schism. So vigorous were the Donatists that they were able to create an alternate church with its own bishops and ecclesiastical buildings, often in the same city as the Catholic churches. After a major showdown in which Augustine wrote several of his most influential works, Donatism was condemned by a series of church councils. The schism, however, did not end, and the Donatists remained a source of division until the Arab invasion in the seventh century.

Unlike Egypt, where Christianity developed a distinctive culture among the native Coptic-speaking populace, the strength of Christianity in Africa was found, with some exceptions, largely in the urban Latin-speaking areas. Even the monasteries were located in or near the cities and towns. In several sermons Augustine mentions that the people in the countryside spoke a different tongue, but there is no evidence of translations of the Bible into local languages. Some of the Berbers who lived up against the Atlas Mountains to the south converted to Christianity, but they remained largely independent of the Latin Christian culture and of the Roman administration. Evidence for an indigenous Christian culture in North Africa is slim; the contrast with Egypt is vivid.

In 430, as Augustine was dying, the Vandals, a Germanic people, who had adopted an Arian, non-Nicene form of Christianity, crossed the Strait of Gibraltar from Spain to invade North Africa. Once on the African continent they moved eastward toward the great prize, the ancient city of Carthage. In 430 they reached Hippo and after a long siege, during which Augustine died, they entered the city, burned churches, monasteries, and public buildings, and terrorized the population. A decade later Carthage was in Vandal hands, and the entire region remained under Vandal rule for a century.

The aim of the Vandal invasion was to establish an Arian Christian kingdom independent of Constantinople and of Catholic ecclesiastical authority, and the first Vandal king, a man named Gaiseric, inaugurated harsh and punitive measures against the Catholic (and Donatist) population. Some of the Catholic churches, most notably the cathedral in Carthage, were taken over and put under the control of Arian clergy, and Catholic clergy were prohibited from serving their people or sent into exile. The new rulers prevented the election of bishops, and in some cities the episcopal throne was left vacant. In Carthage the city was without a bishop for four decades.

Yet the Church, though weakened, was able to survive and to raise up intelligent and courageous leaders. The most notable was Fulgentius of Ruspe, who was born (ca. 462) into the landed aristocracy of Roman Africa. Remarkably, given the times in which he lived, he received a traditional grounding in the Latin classics and in the Scriptures. For a time he served in the Vandal administration, but after several years he resigned and took up the monastic life. Quickly he learned he was unsuited for seclusion and solitude.

After a visit to Rome, he was consecrated bishop of Ruspe, some hundred miles south of Carthage on the Mediterranean coast. No sooner had he taken up residence in Ruspe than Thrasamund, the Arian ruler, sent him into exile in Sardinia with sixty other Catholic bishops. During an exile of thirteen years he wrote a series of theological treatises influenced by Augustine. Finally he was allowed to return to Africa and took part in a public debate with Arian clergy, but was again banished, returning two years later in 523. Fulgentius is not a major figure in Christian history, and his writings lack originality, but he is a pointed reminder that the venerable Latin Christian tradition of the North African Church was alive in the dark and perilous years of Vandal rule.

Shortly after Fulgentius returned to Africa, Justinian became emperor, and he set out at once to reconquer lands in the West that had historically been part of the Roman Empire, most notably in Italy and North Africa. Under the leadership of his able general Belisarius, Byzantine rule was restored to North Africa in 534. With the return of Byzantine authority and the largesse of the emperor, the Church in Africa entered a period of growth and consolidation. Churches were repaired, new ones built, monasteries founded. But the Vandal occupation had left its mark, and Christianity in Africa would never regain the stature and prominence it enjoyed in the early centuries.

Nevertheless Christians in Africa were able to rejoin the larger Christian world and again become part of the Eastern Roman Empire. They were even drawn into the ecclesiastical controversies that were dividing the East, in particular the acrimonious and extended debate over the "will" of Christ. In 628, as the Persians were approaching Constantinople, Maximus the Confessor, the bold Greek theologian who defended the doctrine of "two wills," fled to Carthage, residing there for the next two decades. In 645 he took part in a prominent debate with Pyrrhus, the deposed patriarch of Constantinople, on the will of Christ. That Maximus would flee the capital to live in Carthage for twenty years, and participate in a debate with historic repercussions across the Christian world, shows that Christianity remained vibrant in North Africa in the seventh century.

We know that traditional Christian practices continued to be observed. One example will suffice: in 636, at Cirta (Constantine), a city in Numidia (northeastern Algeria), four bishops from the region went in solemn procession to deposit the relics of five holy persons, Stephan, Focas, Theodore, Victor, and Corona. A lead tablet, now displayed in the museum in Cirta in Algeria, documents the deposition. A few years later another deposition took place in a neighboring city where a chapel was dedicated. In the mid seventh century, even after the Muslim conquest of Jerusalem, life went on in North Africa, and Christians had no reason to think that their way of life was threatened or to fear that another catastrophe was imminent.

But the Arabs were on the march westward. The decisive battle for control of Byzantine North Africa took place in 647 at Sbeitla (ancient Sufetula), a small city in central Tunisia approximately 125 miles southwest of Carthage. The Byzantines were routed, but it would take another fifty years, and seven campaigns, before the

Arabs were able to take Carthage. In 698 the Muslim commander Hassan ibn al-Nu'man breached the walls and laid waste the city. Some inhabitants escaped by ship to Sicily and Spain, but most were killed and the city was destroyed. Though Africa did not fall as quickly to the Arab invaders as did Syria and Egypt, by the beginning of the eighth century another major Christian capital was in their hands.

As in Syria and Egypt, the Christians were classified as a "protected people" (dhimmi), persons who were "sheltered" as long as they submitted to Muslim rule and paid a tax. They were allowed to practice their religion without interference, but were kept apart from the new society that was being formed around them. Soon after the conquest the new rulers began to issue coins with Latin legends directed at the Christian population. Some of the legends were deliberately provocative: "Non est Deus nisi unus cui non socius alius similis" (There is no God but the one God and he has no associate like him), referring to the famous passage in surah 112 of the Qur'an ("He did not beget and is not begotten"). Eventually coins would be stamped with Arabic legends, but in the early years the new rulers wished to assert in a public way the superiority of Islam over Christianity, using the Christian language, Latin.

After the fall of Carthage many Christians from North Africa fled by sea to Italy, Spain, and islands of the Mediterranean. Their exodus deprived the local communities of the cream of Christian society, its educated and elite members. This may explain the lack of written sources after the conquest. A great silence descends on Christianity in Africa. Whatever the reason for the silence, the lack of Christian writings and the paucity of other evidence on the internal life of the churches has fueled speculation that Christianity in North Africa went into steep decline from the beginning of Muslim rule.

But in recent years, thanks to the work of Arab historians drawing on Arabic sources, a different picture has emerged. Kairouan, a city in central Tunisia, was founded by Muslims in 670. Though it was not an ancient Roman city with a long-standing Christian population, by the end of the eighth century Christians had settled there. The community was well organized and its leader, a man named Qustas (Constans), had good relations with the Muslim authorities and was granted permission to build a church. As late as the eleventh century there are Christian epitaphs from North Africa with the Latin expression *anno domini,* a system of reckoning time learned from Latin-speaking Christians in Europe. The spelling of Latin words on inscriptions shows that Latin had remained a spoken language among Christians.

Though cut off from Constantinople, the churches in Africa remained in communication with the Latin West, in particular the pope in Rome. At the end of the eighth century Pope Hadrian I (772–775) mentioned the Church of Africa along with the churches of Spain and Gaul and appointed bishops for the region. In the next century Pope Leo IV (847–855) observed that African Christians followed the same calendar in observing Lent as in Rome, and another pope mentions envoys from Africa who had asked for Rome's help in a schism "between the bishops of the African provinces." But there was a precipitous decline in the number of bishops, confirmed by the dearth of written documents, letters, sermons, and the like. By the eleventh century the bishop of Carthage could not muster two other bishops to make up the required number of three to ordain a bishop.

As the correspondence of several popes demonstrates, the Christians of Africa were not forgotten. And something of its former glory still inspired Christians in other parts of the world. At the end of the ninth century a group of pilgrims from Brittany had gone to Rome, Jerusalem, and Egypt as an act of penance. From Egypt, according to an ancient account of the pilgrimage, the company "turned their steps to Africa to visit the tomb of Saint Cyprian, archbishop and martyr of Christ, who lies at rest near the sea at the second milestone from the city of Carthage where many great works and many miracles are very often revealed by the Lord." From Carthage the pilgrims returned to their homes in Brittany.

In the centuries immediately after the Muslim conquest, Christianity remained alive in North Africa. But through a combination of social constraints, the displacement of Latin by Arabic as the language of government and commerce, the atrophy of ecclesiastical structures, and lack of leadership, the number of Christians dwindled, and by the twelfth century this most ancient Christian region had become wholly Muslim. Unlike the Middle East and Egypt, today there is no indigenous Christian community in North Africa that can trace its history back to the time of Tertullian, Cyprian, Augustine, and Fulgentius of Ruspe.

Christians Under Islam:
Spain

At the end of his letter to the Romans, Paul wrote that after visiting the Christians in Rome his plan was to go on to Spain (Romans 15:28). But he died before he could make the journey, and there is no evidence that Christianity reached Spain in the first century. But it did arrive early and most likely from North Africa. The first mention of Christians in Spain appears in a writing of Tertullian of Carthage at the end of the second century. By the middle of the third century an ecclesiastical structure was in place embracing bishops from its several regions, and the churches in Spain looked to Carthage for guidance, not to Rome. Among Cyprian's letters one is addressed to two Spanish bishops who had sought his counsel on a local matter. One was the bishop in Asturias, in the northwest of the country, and the other in the southeast, and Cyprian mentions another bishop in Saragossa in the northeast. Forty-three bishops were present at a council in Spain in the early fourth century.

In most histories of the early Church, Spain plays a minor role. Yet it has a singular and illustrious history. In the fourth century, a Spanish bishop by the name of Hosius of Cordoba (d. 358) was invited to become a member of Emperor Constantine's inner circle and had a hand in the emperor's conversion. After Constantine embraced Christianity, Hosius served as a kind of ecclesiastical adviser to the emperor. When the Arian controversy erupted he counseled Constantine to call together bishops from all over the world, and at this convocation, the Council of Nicaea in 325, Hosius, a Spanish bishop, presided. Later he presided over several other councils and became a staunch defender of Athanasius, the articulate exponent of the creed of Nicaea, against Emperor Constantius. In a famous letter Hosius rebuked the emperor for meddling in ecclesiastical affairs. It is the business of bishops, not the emperor, he wrote, to decide theological matters: "You have no authority to burn incense."

Roman Spain was the birthplace of the poet Lucan and the essayist and philosopher Seneca, and Christian Spain was to make its own distinctive contribution to the republic of letters. The most celebrated figure, a gifted poet still read today, was Aurelius Prudentius Clemens, a Latin writer, who flourished at the end of the fourth century. Prudentius began a tradition of Christian poetry that stretches from antiquity through the Middle Ages to the *Faerie Queene* of Edmund Spenser in the sixteenth century and beyond. His most famous work was a long allegorical poem called *Psychomachia,* or "spiritual warfare." For the history of the Church in Spain, his collection of poems titled *Peristephanon* (Crown of Martyrdom) is his most memorable work. Of the fourteen poems, six are devoted to martyrs from cities in Spain, one celebrating eighteen martyrs from Saragossa in the third century. Though the *Crown of Martyrdom* also depicts more famous Christian martyrs, including Lawrence, Cyprian, Peter, and Paul, by inscribing in measured verse the names of Spanish cities and Spanish saints Prudentius gave his native land an honored place in Christian memory.

In the early centuries Spain was part of the Roman Empire, but in the fifth century, as the Western empire was invaded by Germanic peoples, Spain was left to fend for itself. Eventually the Visigoths, a people that had adopted Arianism, were able to defeat their rivals, establish a capital at Toledo, and bring a measure of order and stability to the region. For several decades, by persuasion as well as coercion, they sought to impose Arianism throughout the realm, but when Reccared became king in 586 he converted to Catholicism, and Arianism soon ceased to be a force in the land.

After the embrace of Catholicism, with its rich cultural traditions, the Spanish Church entered an age of intellectual vigor. Its most acclaimed thinker was the scholarly bishop of Seville, Isidore (d. 636), whom we have already met as the author of the encyclopedia *Etymologies.* Isidore understood that the rebuilding of a Christian culture required a solid foundation in Latin learning, and his many writings are an unprecedented effort to preserve the remains of ancient wisdom. His books deal with elementary matters of language such as grammar and spelling, but also with rhetoric, geography, architecture, ecclesiastical matters, Christian doctrine, canon law, and more. He put himself to the task of establishing monastic and cathedral schools to educate the young and train the clergy. The intellectual and educational achievements of the seventh century helped the Church in Spain meet the challenges of Arab rule in the centuries to come.

The growing self-confidence of the Church and the efforts of the Visigothic kings to bring unity to their kingdom had negative consequences for the Jews who had begun to settle in Spain before the Christian era. Their presence is well documented in the early centuries of the Roman Empire, when they were able to go about their way of life and practice their religion without interference. At a Spanish council in the city of Elvira in the early fourth century, however, several canons were directed specifically at the Jews, including one forbidding marriages between Jews and Christians. Later, under the Visigothic king Reccared, the rights and liberties of the Jews were severely restricted. They were prohibited from holding public office and forbidden to build synagogues, for example.

Under Reccared's successor the legislation became harsher. One royal decree ordered Jews to submit to baptism, though it is doubtful such legislation was actually carried out or could be carried out. Nevertheless the prevalence of such laws in the seventh century indicates that church leaders and kings made a concerted effort to hinder the practice of Judaism. One king actually issued decrees outlawing the celebration of Passover and prohibiting circumcision. Though there was little overt hostility to the Jews, the language of ecclesiastical councils and royal decrees shaped the perceptions and sentiments of Christians. With the onset of Muslim rule the political and legal status of the Jews changed, and over the next several centuries Jewish intellectual and literary life flourished. Maimonides (1135–1204), the great Jewish philosopher and legal scholar, was born in Cordoba and received his initial formation in Spain. Later he moved to Morocco and eventually settled in Egypt.

A little over a decade after the fall of Carthage in 698, Muslim armies had reached the Atlantic Ocean and the Strait of Gibraltar. We assume a great divide between the northern shore of the Mediterranean Sea and the lands on its southern coast, but the ancients did not see things that way. The distance between Carthage in North Africa and Sicily was not great, and the Strait of Gibraltar is less than eight miles wide. For centuries commercial and cultural traffic had kept the two regions in regular communication.

Mauretania, the Roman name for what is today Morocco, was a long way from the Middle East, and as Arab forces had moved across North Africa they picked up recruits from among the Berber tribes. By 710 the Arab province of Ifriqiya (Africa) was sufficiently pacified to undertake the conquest of Spain, and the man who led the expedition was Tariq ibn Ziyad, a Berber freeman, not an Arab. Many of his men were Berbers. When they reached Ceuta (Roman Septa) on the African coast the troops were ferried across the strait, and in 711 they launched raids in the southern part of the country. The Visigothic king, Roderic, mounted a defense, but in 712 he was killed in battle and his forces collapsed and fled. Spain was defenseless before the Muslim advance. Within a short time the invaders were able to occupy a large part of the peninsula and subdue the populace. In the end, however, though seemingly invincible, after crossing the Pyrenees into southern France, they were met by the well-organized and determined opposition of the Franks under the leadership of Charles Martel.

In 733 the Muslim army was routed and its general killed at the famous battle of Poitiers (Tours). The defeat at Poitiers halted the Muslim advance into Christian lands and ensured that the new Christian culture being built in northern Europe would not be stifled under Muslim rule.

In his *Decline and Fall of the Roman Empire,* Gibbon imagined what would have happened had the battle of Poitiers gone differently: "Perhaps the interpretation of the Koran would now be taught in the schools of Oxford, and her pulpits might demonstrate to a circumcised people the sanctity and truth of the revelation of Mahomet." For Christians the battle of Poitiers is celebrated as a victory that changed the course of Western history; for Muslims, Poitiers is remembered as "the Plain of the Martyrs."

Spain's history under Islam took a different course than it had in the other lands conquered by the Muslims. During the first century of Muslim expansion the newly conquered territories came under the rule of the Umayyad caliph in Damascus. But in 750 a new dynasty, the Abbasids, overthrew the Umayyads and systematically killed members of the family. A grandson of Caliph Hisham named Abd al-Rahman was able to escape and make his way to North Africa. From there he continued westward and crossed into Spain in 756. After gathering an army he defeated the Muslim governor and established an independent kingdom at Cordoba in southern Spain. In 703 a woman from England planned to travel to Spain, but Boniface wrote advising her to wait "until the attacks and threats of the Saracens which have lately manifested themselves in the lands of the Romans, should have quieted down." His was a vain hope.

Over the course of several centuries the descendants of the Umayyads forged a distinctive and brilliant Islamic culture in a land far to the west of the heartland of Islam. By all accounts the Spanish Umayyads were remarkable rulers gifted with intelligence, imagination, and longevity. And they were great builders. Muslim Cordoba was a sparkling jewel of a city in contrast to the drab landscape of western Europe. It was graced by grand palaces, public baths, fountains, and gardens, and by night the city was lit by lanterns. Water was piped to homes, public squares, and steam baths. The ornament of the city was the great mosque begun during the reign of Abd al-Rahman. When the Muslims began to settle in Cordoba they appropriated half of the central Christian church of Saint Vincent for use as a mosque. But within two generations the Muslim population outgrew the space, and Abd al-Rahman negotiated with Christian leaders to buy the land. An agreement was reached and he paid them a large sum to rebuild a church outside the city walls for their use. Saint Vincent was demolished and construction of the mosque begun.

The most distinctive feature of the mosque of Cordoba is the forest of horseshoe arches that seem to extend out in every direction like a field of autumn flowers. The alternation of red and cream stones in the arches is reminiscent of Syrian buildings, but the dense march of arches creates a mysterious interior space unlike anything else in the world. The mosque has a central dome of blue tiles decorated with stars, and the *mihrab,* the niche on one wall indicating the direction of Mecca, is adorned with geometric designs and plants. Though the columns and capitals are all taken from earlier Roman or Christian buildings, the architects created a sacred building of singular beauty and religious feeling.

The great mosque is the most majestic and enduring artifact of the grandeur of the Umayyad kingdom in Spain, but an equally conspicuous token of its splendor was its patronage of Arabic literature and poetry. Its cultural life flowed on the great river of the Arabic language. To advance in society, Christians had to learn Arabic. According to one observer, a man named Paul Alvarus, Christian youth had fallen under the spell of Arabic. Though raised as Christians they were more interested in the latest fashions in society than the Latin books that had nurtured Christian culture. They "enthusiastically read and study the Arab books," said Alvarus, "are ignorant of their own language, and have no interest in Christian literature. For everyone who can write a letter in Latin to a friend, there are a thousand who can express themselves in elegant Arabic." Arabic poetry held their fancy, and they became skilled in writing according to the canons of rhythm, meter, and stress of Arabic poetry. Language is a symbol of cultural and religious loyalty, and the attraction of Arabic signaled a loss of Christian identity. Though it appears that for these young men a passion for Arabic poetry was less a matter of religious faith than a desire to be accepted in Cordoban society.

Nevertheless the lure of the Arabic language did reflect a malaise within the Christian community. Even though Christians had few restrictions on their way of life, they were forbidden to build new churches and were prohibited from making a public display of their religion, through the ringing of bells or processions on feast days. As Arabic became the common speech of Christians as well as Muslims (and Jews), and Muslim practices and institutions permeated society, learning Arabic well was a necessity, especially for young men who wished to advance in the civil service or participate in cultural life. Muslim law also worked against Christians. If a Muslim man married a Christian woman she became Muslim, and their children were raised as Muslims. Inevitably Christians began to assimilate to Muslim society, and some converted to Islam.

A good example is a talented and ambitious Christian named Gomez ibn Antonian ibn Julian. When he entered government service he was a Christian and rose swiftly to a high position. He spoke Arabic fluently but he also knew Latin well and was able to act as an interpreter and correspondent for the caliph in dealings with Christian kings in Europe. As Ibn Antonian rose in the bureaucracy the pressure to convert to Islam intensified. The caliph wished to appoint him chief administrator of the government, but was reluctant to entrust a Christian with such a high office. Faced with the choice of giving up his position or embracing Islam, Ibn Antonian chose Islam. Things did not, however, go well. Some at the court were suspicious that his conversion was not sincere, and thought he continued to practice Christianity in secret. Eventually he was dismissed from his post.

The attraction of Arabic language, culture, and religion was a matter of deep concern for some Christians. At the same time Ibn Antonian was moving up the bureaucratic ladder in Cordoba, a small group of Christians resolutely set their faces against any accommodation with Islam. Known as the Martyrs of Cordoba, they initiated a movement that is the most heralded instance of a "spiritual" revolt by Christians against the transformation of society under Muslim rule.

The story begins in June 851, when a monk named Isaac came down from his monastery (Tabanos) in the mountains north of Cordoba to visit the city. Isaac was well-born, fluent in Arabic, and had held office in the Muslim government, but he gave up his post to become a monk. On his visit to Cordoba he came to the palace where he had once been employed and asked the judge (*qadi*) whether he could instruct him on some points of Muslim teaching. But as soon as the judge began to speak, Isaac interrupted him and launched a vitriolic attack on the Prophet Muhammad. The judge thought he had lost his senses, but Isaac made it clear he knew full well what he was doing. In obedience to the truth, he said, he was compelled to speak out against Islam.

Isaac was arrested, and after consulting with the emir the judge sentenced him to death. He was decapitated on June 3, 851, and his body hung upside down on the opposite side of the river in a public place. Previously a few Christians had been condemned to death for blasphemy, but Isaac's action was of a different order. He had deliberately provoked the Muslim governor with the intention of seeking martyrdom. For Christians this posed something of a problem (Isaac had not been coerced to deny his faith; he voluntarily sought death) and opinion was divided as to whether he should be honored as a martyr. The bishop of Seville condemned the movement. But a debate over the fine points of Christian thinking about martyrdom did not deter other zealous Christians from following Isaac's example. Two days after his death a young Christian soldier was executed for the same crime. And within four days of Isaac's death seven others had come forth to blaspheme the Prophet and were summarily decapitated.

A month later, three more Christians presented themselves for martyrdom. One was a deacon named Sisenandus who was studying in Cordoba. He was executed on July 16. Four days later another deacon, Paulus, was executed and a few days later a monk named Theodemirus followed him. We are able to follow the course of the martyrdoms because a priest named Eulogius from an aristocratic Cordoban family kept an account with the names of the martyrs, their background, the circumstances of their "blasphemy," and the date of their deaths. Eventually Eulogius was arrested for his support of the martyrs and was imprisoned, but soon released. A few years later, however, he was arrested again and, because he was a prominent member of the Christian community, brought before a group of royal officials who urged him to back down. "Say something in this hour of need, so that afterward you may be able to practice your faith," they advised him. But Eulogius was adamant and proceeded to instruct his judges on the truth of Christianity. A few days later he was decapitated.

By late summer of 851 the stream of martyrs had slowed, but in the fall nine women came forth seeking martyrdom. The first two, Flora and Maria, denounced Islam together before a judge. But their cases were different. Maria was the daughter of a Muslim woman who had married a Christian and adopted his faith. Maria's brother studied for the priesthood, but in June he had offered himself for martyrdom. Deeply affected by her brother's death, Maria decided to follow his example. While praying in a church in Cordoba she met Flora.

Flora's mother had married a Muslim who died when she was a little girl. Consequently she was raised as a Christian. But children of a mixed marriage (Muslim male and Christian female) were legally Muslims. So Flora practiced her faith in secret. Eventually she was exposed and arrested. In her defense she pleaded that she had been a Christian from birth, that is, from her baptism, and was therefore not technically an apostate. As punishment she was whipped and placed on probation. Later, however, she came forth to profess her faith and was executed. Maria was decapitated for blasphemy.

After these executions there was a six-month lull, but the next summer five more Christians stepped forward and a few weeks later six more joined their ranks. In September, as the emir Abd al-Rahman was dying, two Christians denounced Islam in Arabic in one of the churches in Cordoba, and a few days later a monk from a village near Granada went into a mosque and denounced Muhammad. To magnify their ordeal their hands and feet were amputated before the two men were decapitated.

Over the next several years the martyrdoms continued intermittently, but Eulogius's account ends in early 857 shortly before his death. Other sources, however, indicate that martyrs continued to come forth, though their numbers were fewer. The last martyrdom took place in 931.

However one assesses the martyrs of Cordoba in light of the history of martyrdom—whether they should be ranked with the noble martyrs of Christian antiquity, Ignatius of Antioch, Polycarp of Smyrna, Perpetua and Felicity, Cyprian of Carthage—there can be no doubt that they represented a self-conscious and vigorous public protest against the profound changes that Islam had brought to a traditional Christian society. From the number of monks whose names appear among the martyrs, it appears that the monasteries were fertile ground for cultivating resistance to the accommodation of Christians to Islamic culture.

The protest was also fed, a least indirectly, by learned Christians who were distraught at the decline of Latin learning under Muslim rule. The two most prominent thinkers were Eulogius, who wrote the book on the martyrs of Cordoba, and the layman Paul Alvarus, who wrote a fascinating work drawing on the book of Revelation. Both were keenly aware that the Latin Christian culture was being eroded by the hegemony of Islam and strenuously strove to preserve and nurture Christian identity. Eulogius, for example, made a journey across the Pyrenees to visit monasteries in the Carolingian empire. On his trip he came across manuscripts of Augustine's *City of God,* Virgil's *Aeneid,* the *Satires* of Horace, and other Latin writings, which he brought back to Cordoba. On return he began to instruct his friends in Latin grammar and meter and laid the foundations for a revival of Christian culture.

Although there was no overt persecution of Christians, they were burdened by onerous taxes, hemmed in by Muslim laws (on marriage, for instance), and stifled by government decrees, such as the ban on building new church buildings. As in other lands the Muslim rulers insisted on having a say in the appointment of bishops and had to approve requests to hold a council.

As the decades passed the necessary accommodations to Arab culture led to greater assimilation of Christians into Muslim society, and in turn this led to a spike in the number of conversions. At first there was only a trickle, but as the society changed, Arabic became the lingua franca, and Muslim institutions matured, Christians found it more tempting to convert. As the generations passed the cumulative effect of conversions, especially in the cities, became more evident, and in the tenth century the number mounted. By the twelfth century Muslims had become the majority. This pattern was not unique; it is documented in several other Christian lands that came under Muslim rule.

Language was a factor in the self-understanding of the Christian community. In the Middle East, Christians eventually adopted the language of their conquerors for Christian worship and scholarship. In part this was made possible because of the similarity between Syriac and Arabic, both semitic languages. Latin, however, had nothing in common with Arabic. Though some Christians learned Arabic well, there is little evidence of the development of indigenous Arabic Christian literature in Spain. Nor did Christians adopt Arabic as the language of Christian worship. Spanish Christianity remained Latin in culture and religion.

Yet some Christians learned Arabic very well, and there was a lively interest in Arabic among some learned Christians. Arabic had begun to be studied in the West, and Spain had the largest collection of Arabic manuscripts. Adventurous scholars who desired a deeper knowledge of Arabic science made the journey to Spain. One was an Englishman named Robert of Ketton (fl. 1136–1157), whose interests were not religious. Before coming to Spain he had translated some scientific works from Arabic to Latin, but only in Spain could he have access to larger libraries of texts. By the middle of the twelfth century he was living in northern Spain, studying Arabic manuscripts and working, in collaboration with a friend, on the arduous task of translating Arabic texts. One of his works is a translation of a classical manual on algebra.

In 1141 he met Peter the Venerable, abbot of the famous monastery of Cluny in France. Peter had taken an interest in Islam, and on the invitation of the Christian king of Castille and Leon (in the northern part of the country) he decided to visit Spain to learn about the new religion. His aim was to write a refutation of the teachings of the Prophet. Peter was shrewd enough to realize that there was no point in writing a critique based on ignorance. So he persuaded Robert of Ketton to set aside his "principal study of astronomy and geometry" to work with a team of translators to produce a translation of the Qur'an into Latin. The result was the first complete translation of the Qur'an into a Western language. It was a monumental achievement only possible in Spain. The book, entitled *Lex Mahumet pseudopro-phetae* (The Law of Muhammad the False Prophet), became the standard version read in the West until the sixteenth century.

But there is more to the story. Ketton's translation was very free, in places more a paraphrase than an actual translation. About the same time another Christian scholar, Mark of Toledo, who had learned Arabic as a child, made another, more literal translation. Much later, when knowledge of Arabic was more widespread in the West, Ketton's translation was subject to harsh criticism. So great are its faults, wrote one Orientalist in the eighteenth century, that it does not "deserve the name of a translation" since it scarcely has "any resemblance to the original."

What these critics did not realize is that Ketton knew precisely what he was doing. He was not simply translating the Arabic of the Qur'an, he was interpreting what he found in the text with the help of Muslim commentators on the Qur'an. When his translation is compared with what Muslims saw in the text he is remark-ably on target, often reproducing in Latin what Muslim scholars were writing in Arabic. At an early stage in the confrontation between Christianity and Islam in the West, a Christian scholar, Robert of Ketton, was willing and able to consult Muslim sources to give Christian readers a sense of the Qur'an as it was understood by Muslims. His was an extraordinary feat made possible by the unique situation of Christians in Muslim Spain and in the neighboring Christian kingdoms.

An Emperor in the West:
Charlemagne

Emperors stride again and again across the pages of Christian history, and in the early centuries four of them gave particular shape to the story: Caesar Augustus, during whose reign Jesus was born; Constantine, who signifies the turning of the people of the Roman Empire to Christianity; Theodosius in the late fourth century, who ruled that Catholic Christianity would be the religion of the empire; and Justinian, the great builder and lawgiver of the Eastern Roman Empire. By any measure these four emperors mark major epochs in the Church's history. But there was a fifth, no less significant, no less a shaper of events, and his name was Charlemagne, king of the Franks, who in the year 800 was crowned emperor of the new Christian society that had come into being in northern Europe in the early Middle Ages.

By the eighth century the center of gravity of Christianity in the Latin-speaking West had shifted from the Mediterranean world to the lands north of the Alps. In the large geographical area we know as Europe, between the Seine and the Rhine, roughly modern France and western Germany, was the heartland. In the preceding centuries political and cultural developments had favored the Franks who had settled there. Gaul had come under Roman cultural influence early, and the Frankish kings were able to establish relatively efficient and enduring political and administrative institutions. After Clovis adopted Catholic Christianity, his successors cultivated good relations with the pope in Rome.

Although Rome was historically under the protection of the emperor in Constantinople, its future lay with the West, and in particular with the Frankish kingdom. For centuries the Franks had been ruled by the Merovingian dynasty, but by the eighth century their kings were no longer monarchs in their own right. "Nothing was left to the king," wrote Charlemagne's biographer Einhard (with some exaggeration), "except to be happy with the royal title and to sit on his throne with his flowing hair and long beard and to behave as if he had authority." The "mayor of the palace" ran the administration of the kingdom, appointed men to high office, and exercised patronage over royal lands. Charles Martel (d. 741), after whom the Carolingian dynasty was named (from the Latin for Charles, *Carolus*), even bore the title "prince of the Franks." Known as "the Hammer," Charles is celebrated in Western history for his victory over the Muslims at the famous battle of Poitiers in 733, halting the relentless Muslim advance into Christian lands. When Charles was succeeded by his son Pippin III (known as Pippin the Short), the time was ripe for a change in the government of the kingdom.

In 750 Pippin sent a bishop and a trusted abbot from Saint Denis, a prominent monastery in Paris, on an embassy to Rome to ask Pope Zacharias (d. 752) about "kings in Francia." Pippin had supported the reforms of Boniface among the Frankish clergy, and Zacharias welcomed the embassy. At the time northern Italy was ruled by the Lombards, a Germanic people, whose kings had gradually expanded their rule southward. In 749 Aistulf became king of the Lombards and set his sights not only on Ravenna, the seat of the exarch, the viceroy of the emperor in Italy, but on Rome itself.

Already under Charles Martel the papacy had made overtures to the Frankish ruler, but the Hammer had shown little interest. Now the initiative came from Francia, and Pippin's emissaries were instructed to ask the pope whether it was right for the king of the Franks to continue to bear the title when the kingdom was effectively governed by the mayor of the palace. Zacharias responded that "it is better that he who had the power should bear the royal name than he who remained without power." Armed with the spiritual authority conferred by the pope, Pippin had an assembly of nobles proclaim him king and he was anointed by the bishops of Francia. The legitimate king was sent packing to live out his days in a monastery. So began the royal rule of the Carolingians.

In the same year, 751, the Lombards conquered Ravenna, ending Byzantine rule in northern Italy, and soon they were threatening Rome. In desperation the new pope, Stephen II, took the bold step of making the long and arduous journey over the Alps to Francia—the first by a pope—at the beginning of winter 753 to meet Pippin. He was received as a suppliant at Pippin's court in Ponthion, near Chalons-sur-Marne some hundred miles east of Paris, on the feast of the Epiphany, January 6, 754. Over the next few months Stephen and Pippin had a series of meetings that would shape the future of the Church in the West, the papacy, and the history of Europe.

At Easter, Pippin made a promise to the pope that he would defend the city of Rome and its territories. He agreed to establish a lasting relationship between the king of the Franks and the papacy. This agreement, known as the Donation of Pippin, also guaranteed to the pope temporal authority over the duchy of Rome along with other areas in central Italy, including Ravenna. In return the pope affirmed the legitimacy of Pippin's rule by solemnly anointing him with oil as king and conferring on him the title "patrician of the Romans."

The anointing of the king was consciously modeled on an ancient ritual practiced by the kings of Israel. When the Lord had chosen Saul to rule over the Israelites, the prophet Samuel "took a vial of oil and poured it on his head and kissed him," saying, "you shall reign over the people of Israel" (1 Samuel 10:1). Later, when David ascended the throne, he was anointed as king, as was Solomon and the kings that followed him. Anointing signified divine approval of the king's rule and conferred a spiritual authority not unlike that of a priest. Stephen's successor, Paul I, called Pippin the "new David" chosen by God to protect the Christian people, citing the words of the psalmist: "I have found David my servant; with my holy oil I have anointed him" (Psalms 89:20). The king, not the bishop or the pope, was seen as the head of the Christian people.

Pippin kept his word to the pope. In 755 he gathered his army and marched south to Italy where he made swift work of the Lombard forces. A year later he was able to regain Ravenna and free Rome from Lombard control. Pippin then handed over the territories he had conquered, including the exarchate of Ravenna, to the pope. For centuries the papacy had possessed lands in southern Italy and Sicily, and the wealth they produced was used to maintain the churches in Rome and provide for the needs of its people. But by placing large territories in Italy under the jurisdiction of the papacy, Pippin created something new, a papal state, known as the "patrimony of Peter," territory over which the pope exercised temporal rule. This kingdom would endure until the nineteenth century and the establishment of the modern state of Italy.

About the same time or a few decades later, a spurious document known as the *Donation of Constantine* emerged. It claimed to be a formal legal enactment in which Constantine gave temporal dominion over "all the provinces, places, and cities of Italy and the Western regions" to Pope Sylvester (d. 335). In addition the pope was granted primacy over the churches in the East, notably Alexandria, Antioch, Constantinople, and Jerusalem. In other words the *Donation of Constantine* provided an early legal basis for the pope's universal jurisdiction over the churches throughout the world. The origin of the document is unknown, but it may have arisen at the time of Pippin's "donation" of lands to the pope. It was widely circulated in the Middle Ages and was not exposed as a forgery until the Renaissance in the fifteenth century. Its origin in the eighth century reflects the emerging self-understanding of the papacy.

Pippin died in 768, and the kingdom was divided between his two sons, Charles and Carloman. But Carloman was sickly and died a few years later, at age twenty. On the death of his brother, Charles acted quickly and decisively, proclaimed himself king of the Franks, and seized the territories under his brother's rule. Charles ruled as king of the Franks until 814, and was crowned emperor by the pope in Rome in the year 800, the first Christian king to preside over what later came to be called the Holy Roman Empire. He is a towering figure in Christian history, the most notable Christian ruler after Justinian, and according to his biographer, Einhard, on the inscription over the tomb he was called "Carolus Magnus," Charles the Great, Charlemagne.

In the early decades of his rule, as Charles aimed to extend his kingdom over the neighboring regions, he gave himself wholeheartedly and enthusiastically to military affairs. First he turned to the Lombards, and in 773, with "enormous exertion," according to his biographer, he led his army over the Alps. He captured the Lombard capital at Pavia in Italy and added "king of the Lombards" to his list of titles. By Easter 774 he was in Rome, where he was welcomed by the pope, who conferred on him the title *patricius,* protector of the Romans. In return he acknowledged the pope's political authority over a large part of Italy.

Already in 772 Charles had begun to wage war against the Saxons in northern Germany west of the Elbe River. Though Boniface and his disciples had established monasteries on the edge of the region, such as at Fulda, the border between the Frankish kingdom and the Saxons was exposed and each side harassed the other with raids and pillaging. The insecurity of the frontier led Charlemagne to mount a full-scale assault against the Saxons. With far greater resources at his command than earlier Frankish kings had, he deployed his army in an aggressive and brutal campaign to subjugate the Saxons and force them to be baptized. By 784 Charlemagne's armies had reached the Elbe, and the Saxon leader, Widekund, submitted to baptism.

The military conquest and forced Christianization of the Saxons over the next two decades had little precedent in Christian history, and the incongruity of spreading the faith by the sword was not lost on Charlemagne's contemporaries. An abbot of the monastery at Fulda wrote that Charlemagne converted the Saxons "partly by wars, partly by persuasion, partly even by gifts." And another writer put things this way: "The fierce necks of the Saxons bowed to the light yoke of Christ, though by coercion."

Once victory was assured, the Franks set about the task of introducing Christian ways among the Saxons. Here too coercion was the instrument, and a remarkable document, the *First Saxon Capitulary,* a collection of administrative edicts, outlines in detail measures taken by the Franks to remake the social fabric of Saxon life. Here are some of its regulations: On Sundays and major feast days no meetings or public assemblies shall be held, and the people are expected to go to church to "hear the word of God" and to be free for prayers and good works. Infants should be baptized within a year, and parents who do not comply will be fined. The people were expected to give a tithe of their property and their labor to the Church. The dead were to be buried in the cemetery of the church, not in the "mounds of the pagans." The list of capital offenses was long: refusal to be baptized, eating meat during Lent (though allowance was made for exceptional cases), theft of church property, killing a member of the clergy, burning a corpse (cremation).

Though the *Saxon Capitulary* reflects official policy, some bishops and advisers close to Charlemagne were troubled that Christianity was being imposed by force. The most notable critic was Alcuin, a prominent scholar and teacher at the court. A native of Northumbria in England, he was educated at the cathedral school of York and met Charlemagne in 781. He swiftly became Charlemagne's most trusted adviser. More than any other person he was responsible for the educational reforms that took place during Charles's reign.

But Alcuin believed that coercion was inimical to the gospel. As he put it, "faith arises from the will, not from compulsion. You can persuade a man to believe, but you cannot force him. You may even be able to force him to be baptized, but this will not instill the faith in him." A few years after the Saxon conquest, Charles was faced with yet another foe on the borders of his kingdom, the Avars in the Balkans. After they had been subdued by Frankish armies, it appeared that they too would be subjugated by the same harsh methods used with the Saxons. But Alcuin stepped in to protest. He wrote a letter to Arn, the bishop of Salzburg, imploring him to be a "preacher of piety, not an exactor of tithes; for the new soul must be suckled with the milk of apostolic goodness until it grows in health and strength to take solid food."

Alcuin also wrote directly to Charles. After praising him for his victory, he let the king know that he had serious doubts whether his methods of introducing Christianity among conquered peoples were pleasing to Christ. Though Christ had granted him victory over the Avars, wrote Alcuin, he must now "provide devout preachers for the new people, men who are honorable in their ways, well trained in the knowledge of the holy faith, imbued with the word of God, close followers of the example of the apostles." He was particularly critical of the rapid imposition of "tithes" before the people had any understanding of Christianity, acknowledging that he had difficulty keeping his tithe. Apparently his entreaties were heard. At a meeting in Bavaria, Bishop Arn, Bishop Paulinus of Aquileia, and Charlemagne's son decided not to force the Avars to submit to baptism. Only after they had been persuaded and instructed were they to be baptized. Soon afterward Charles issued a milder capitulary for the Saxons.

By the time Charles was in his late forties he ruled over a Christian kingdom that extended over the whole of what is today France, Belgium, Holland, Germany as far as the Elbe River, Austria, Switzerland, northern Italy, parts of Bohemia, Hungary, and Spain. His domain was not only much larger than the realm he inherited from his father Pippin, it was more diverse ethnically and linguistically. No longer was Charles just the king of the Franks; he was the ruler of all Christians in the Latin

West save Britain and Ireland and some principalities in Spain. The term "Europe" begins to appear in writings from this period, and at the end of the eighth century a poet hailed Charles as the *rex pater Europae,* the "king and father of Europe." A new political entity had arisen, distinct geographically and culturally from Byzantium and Islam, that brought under a common rule the ancient Latin culture of the Mediterranean world and the Germanic peoples of the north.

During the controversy over images in Byzantium, the Carolingian court found itself at odds not only with the Greeks but also with the pope in Rome. Pope Hadrian had sent legates to the Council of Nicaea in 787 carrying a treatise in defense of the veneration of images in which he appealed to the practice of the "Apostolic Roman Church." His legates were well received in Constantinople, and Hadrian approved of the decision to restore the veneration of images. He did, however, demand that the papal patrimonies (ecclesiastical lands and revenues in Sicily and Calabria) be returned—a request that was ignored by the council fathers. Afterward, a hasty Latin translation of the acts of the council had reached the Carolingian court via Rome and was reviewed by scholars there. Though the pope supported the council's actions, the opinion of scholars at Charlemagne's court in Aachen was divided. They agreed that icons should not be destroyed, but the Eastern way of venerating icons was alien to their forms of devotion. Charles asked his most gifted theologian, the Spaniard Theodulf of Orleans, to write a full response—in truth a refutation—of the decisions of the council, the *Opus Carolis Regis contra synodum* (The Work of King Charles in Response to the Council). The Greeks thought the Franks were ignorant barbarians, but Theodulf's treatise was a sophisticated critique of the arguments of the iconodules.

In 794 Charles convoked a "great synod" of "the bishops from his whole kingdom" at Frankfurt to deal with other theological matters and to discuss the decisions taken at Nicaea. Though the Franks were minded to condemn the rulings of the Greek bishops, they knew that Pope Hadrian had given full support to the restoration of icons. Furthermore, his legates were in attendance at the Frankish council. In the end the Latin version of the decrees of the Council of Nicaea offered a way out of the dilemma. The translation they were working with said that the council had ruled that icons could be adored in the same way the Holy Trinity was adored. That was, however, the opposite of what the bishops had said. In rejecting this view, the council of Frankfurt affirmed what Nicaea had taught, resolving the conflict between Charles and Pope Hadrian. The decision, however, had little effect on Western devotion and practice; the veneration of icons, so dear to the Greeks, never became part of Latin piety.

Another sign of the growing divide between East and West had to do with the phrase "and [from] the son" (*filioque*) in the Nicene Creed. At some point in the sixth or seventh century, probably in Spain, the Latin expression *filioque* was inserted into the Nicene Creed. Instead of reading "proceeding from the Father," some Latin versions of the creed contained a fuller clause, "proceeding from the Father *and* the Son [filioque]." To the Greeks the Western formulation suggested a way of conceiving of the mystery of the triune God that was not grounded in the Church's ancient traditions. They believed that God the Father alone was the source and fountainhead of divinity, hence they thought that the expression "from the son" compromised a deep theological principle.

In Rome, however, the ancient version was still used. Hadrian had given his approval to a letter written by the patriarch of Constantinople, Tarasius, to the clergy of Alexandria, Antioch, and Constantinople in which the traditional language of the creed was cited. Charles considered the Greek version heretical and defended the Western insertion, again putting him at odds with the pope. Hadrian, however, stood on firm ground; he knew that the original version was supported by the teachings of the early fathers. But Charles was unmoved and remained resolute in his defense of the filioque. Only later was it inserted into the creed in Rome. Because "filioque" appeared in the creed sung in the Eucharistic liturgy, it became a fixed part of Western Christian tradition, and was a harbinger of deepening differences between Eastern and Western Christianity.

In ways small and large the distinctive features of Western Christianity were becoming evident by the time of the Carolingians. Besides images and the filioque, one might mention Benedictine monasticism, Latin rather than the vernacular as the language of baptism and the Eucharist, unleavened bread in the Eucharist, private penance, celibacy of the clergy, a piety centered on the cross (as in the hymns of Fortunatus), the pope and the emperor as two seats of authority.

With each passing decade of Charles's reign it was clear he was engaged in a much more imposing and far-reaching project than that of earlier kings in the West. He ruled over what was beginning to look like a universal empire, not simply a regional kingdom. Already in 778, Pope Hadrian had hailed him as the new Constantine and the most Christian "emperor," and in letters to Charles, in poems, and in other writings, imperial language began to appear.

As Charles began to envision a grander kingdom, he realized that it needed a fixed center, a "capital," where a stately palace fit for an emperor could be built. He chose Aachen (Aix-la-Chapelle), a former Roman spa on the edge of the Ardennes Mountains, on the border between present-day Germany and Holland. Unlike the capital of Byzantium, Charles's palace was in the countryside, not in a city, yet in building the new complex he had the imperial palace of Constantinople as well as the rising complex at Baghdad in mind. His father had built a royal residence at Aachen decades earlier, and Charles sometimes spent his winters there, but the new palace established for the first time a permanent residence for the king and a political heart for the kingdom.

In designing the buildings, the architect, Odo of Metz, drew on classical Roman treatises as well as Byzantine models. Only the chapel has survived, but the complex included an audience hall or throne room with porticoes that led to an octagonal domed chapel modeled on San Vitale in Ravenna. According to Einhard, the basilica was "adorned with gold and silver, lighting fixtures, and balustrades and doors of solid bronze." Because Charles could not obtain columns and marbles locally, he had them brought from Ravenna. A large mosaic of Christ looked down from the dome, and directly beneath it, on a raised gallery, sat the king's throne, suggesting that he was the mediator between God and the Christian people.

The occasion for Charles's coronation as emperor came, however, not from Charles but from events unfolding in Rome. When Pope Hadrian died in 795, his successor, Leo III, announced his election to Charles and sent him the key to Saint Peter's tomb and the banner of Rome. In his reply Charles told the pope that his role was to defend the Church and promote the faith and that of the pope to raise his arms up in prayer like Moses (Exodus 17:8–16). In Rome, however, Leo was facing stiff opposition to his papacy. Two high officials in the Roman court were against him, and in 799 while he was riding to Mass in a procession he fell into the hands of his enemies. They beat him severely, but he managed to escape and made his way to Charles in Francia. Soon afterward his opponents arrived at the court and set before the king their charges against him.

A year later Charles made the journey to the holy city to investigate the matter. When he arrived, in late November in the year 800, Leo greeted him twelve miles outside the city in a ceremony appropriate for the "advent" (arrival) of an emperor. Early in December, Charles convened a council of Frankish nobles to examine the charges against Leo. From the outset it was clear he would be found innocent; no one thought Charles had the authority to stand in judgment over the pope. So Leo was allowed to affirm his innocence by a solemn oath on the New Testament. A few days later, at Mass on Christmas morning before the tomb of Saint Peter in the great basilica in Rome, Pope Leo "placed a crown upon the king's head as he rose from prayer, and all the people cried out: 'To Charles Augustus, mighty and peaceable emperor of the Romans,'" according to the account in a contemporary chronicle.

Charlemagne's biographer Einhard says that if Charles had known he was to be crowned emperor he would not have gone to the church that morning. That is unlikely. An event of such magnitude does not just happen. Had Charles not agreed beforehand the pope would hardly have inaugurated on his own a ritual without papal precedent. Never had it been the business of the bishop of Rome to crown the Roman (Byzantine) emperor. Pope and king each had had something to gain by the coronation, and they surely knew in advance what was to happen that Christmas morning.

The creation of the office of emperor in the West did not sit well in Constantinople. To the Byzantines the very notion of a second emperor in the barbarian West was risible. A Christian emperor still sat on the throne, though it did complicate things that she was a woman, Irene (797–802). Still, the Byzantine emperor was a direct descendant of the ancient Roman emperors stretching back to Augustus. How could there be two Christian emperors? There is one God, one Christ, one Christian faith, and there could only be one supreme ruler to lead and govern the Christian people. The division between the Eastern and Western empires that came into being in the fourth century was a distant precedent, but for centuries there had been one Christian emperor. Reluctantly, the Byzantines eventually bowed to the new political fact that there was a Christian "empire" in the West. A decade after his coronation, a Byzantine embassy traveled to Aachen and acclaimed Charles using the traditional Greek term, *basileus* (emperor), without, however, adding the qualifier "Roman," the prerogative of the emperor in Constantinople. The Muslims simply called the Byzantine Empire "Rum." Charles responded graciously by saying that peace existed between "the empires of the East and of the West."

Roman was, however, a venerable term, and in the minds of the Carolingians their "empire" was a continuation of the ancient Roman Empire. They had in mind not the pagan empire of Augustus and his immediate successors, but the Christian Roman Empire that came into being in the fourth century, the empire of Constantine and Theodosius and of the great teachers of the Church, Augustine and Ambrose and Jerome. It was, however, not only Rome that inspired the Carolingians. Already in 789 in a general directive (*Admonitio generalis*), addressed to the "ranks of ecclesiastical piety and dignitaries of secular power"—that is, to bishops as well as noblemen—Charles confidently invoked as a model the ancient Israelite king Josiah, who had reformed and centralized religious authority in Israel. As Josiah read out to the people the ancient "book of the law" (2 Kings 23:1–4), so Charles the Christian king was, by correction and admonition, to "recall the kingdom which God had given him to the worship of the true God." The Old Testament, in particular the books of the kings, 1 and 2 Samuel, 1 and 2 Kings, provided a kind of political constitution for the people of God.

A decade later, in 802, Charles, now emperor, called together a "universal synod" at Aachen to "read out" to the bishops, priests, and deacons the laws of the Church and to have them explained and interpreted. He also gathered the abbots and monks and had the *Rule of Benedict* read out to them. Finally he assembled the dukes and counts and representatives of the people so that they might hear the law being read aloud. Though Charles respected the local laws of the people he ruled over, at this convocation he spoke not as king of the Franks but as sovereign of all the Christian people, setting forth laws that applied to everyone in his domain. By drawing on the Bible, the traditions of the Church, the writings of the church fathers, and canon law, Charles wished to establish norms that would govern the Christian society as a whole.

Though Charles was not well educated, he put education at the center of his renewal of Christian society. He respected learning and was comfortable in the presence of well-read bishops and monks, and he recruited talent from abroad to carry out his reform: Alcuin from England, Theodulf from Spain, Peter, a grammarian from Pisa. Charlemagne had a particular interest in Latin, which he learned to speak, though he never mastered the art of writing. He complained that bishops and abbots did not know Latin well and made grammatical mistakes. In the lands where the popular language was close to Latin, such as early French or Italian, even educated people were careless about grammatical blunders. So Charles set his scholars to work preparing textbooks to teach the clergy to speak and write Latin correctly.

Scriptoria were established to produce texts for study, worship, and governmental use, and schools were founded at monasteries and at cathedral churches. At Tours, Alcuin founded a school of calligraphy. By taking responsibility for elementary education, Charles's reforms encouraged clear thinking and lent grace to writing. Latin grammar became an instrument of culture, and his learned advisers persevered in their task with a lively sense of mission and discipline. During his reign there was a great outpouring of works of poetry, histories, and biblical commentaries, religious as well as secular writings.

His most enduring achievement was the introduction of a new and more uniform script, what is known as the Carolingian or Caroline minuscule. In the ancient world, Latin manuscripts had been written solely in capital letters, without punctuation or divisions between words and sentences. To read aloud publicly required great skill and preparation. The new script used small letters, called minuscules, as well as capital letters, majuscules, to mark the beginning of a sentence or a new train of thought. Clearer and more legible, simpler to write, friendly to the reader, it quickly became the standard for the copying of books. Punctuation was added, including commas and periods, and the question mark appears for the first time. Manuscripts from this time begin to resemble the printed page of a modern book.

As more and more books were produced, some with elaborate scripts and luxurious decoration and illustrations, the written word became a sacred thing. When the gospel book was carried in procession it was an object of reverence and devotion, not unlike icons in the East. God had communicated to the ancient Israelites through words, wrote Theodulf, not by images. He chided the Greeks for standing before images and offering incense to them. "We," he wrote, "will search out the commands of our Lord by eager scrutiny in bound books of God's own law."

Words were not only spoken but sung in Christian worship, and Charles's father Pippin had begun a reform of liturgical music. In an effort to bring greater order to the music of the liturgy, he set Frankish singers to work learning Roman chant. Several decades later Theodulf wrote that "there should be no disparity in the way of singing the psalms between churches with an equal ardor of faith." The churches should be "united in one worshipful tradition of chant so that different ways of celebrating the liturgy should not sunder churches joined by devotion to one faith." As Roman chant was appropriated by Frankish musicians, a common repertory of Latin plainchant was adopted, and it shaped the liturgical music of the Western Church up through the Reformation and beyond.

Charlemagne's biographer Einhard wrote that the king "took delight in the books of Saint Augustine and, among them, particularly those entitled the *City of God*." In that book Augustine had written that the "city of God . . . would not have advanced along its goal had the life of the saints not been social." From its beginning Christianity was not just an aggregation of individuals, but a community, a corporate entity, a kind of city. Charlemagne had a vision of a society that was Christian from the ground up, and he consciously sought to give form to the Christian body not only in religious matters, but also in law, institutions, and its political constitution. During his reign, for the first time in the West it is possible to discern the lineaments of what later came to be called Christendom, a society bound together by a common faith, culture, and government spread over a large geographical area. Charlemagne's empire looked back to the early Christian Roman empire, but it was a new creation, uniquely Western, Latin, and medieval, and in various forms what was established by the early ninth century existed until early modern times.

Christianity Among the Slavs

The city of Thessalonica, sitting at the head of the Thermaic Gulf that opens into the Aegean Sea, enters Christian history early. Paul visited it in the late 40s and preached in the synagogue for three weeks. His labors led to the formation of a Christian community, the first on European soil. After leaving the city he wrote two letters to the Christians in Thessalonica, and the First Epistle of Paul to the Thessalonians, written in A.D. 50 or 51, is the earliest Christian writing we possess.

Under the Roman Empire, Thessalonica became the capital of the province of Macedonia and a major port. It was located on the Via Egnatia, the chief east–west road running from the Adriatic Sea to Constantinople, and served as the southern terminus of the principal route from the Danube River to Greece and the Aegean Sea. The Morava–Axios corridor, as this was called, served as a channel for the spread of Byzantine civilization north into the Balkans, the triangular-shaped peninsula between the Adriatic Sea and the Black Sea, and was a passage for peoples pushing southward.

As the Germanic peoples moved westward in the fifth century, the Slavs, an Indo-European people, began to settle in southern Russia, Hungary, Moravia, and the Balkans. By the sixth century they were crossing the Danube to raid and pillage in Macedonia and Thrace, the regions north and west of Constantinople. Some of the Slavs moved into Greece itself and eventually made their way as far as the Peloponnese in the very south of the country. A Western visitor in the eighth century passing through the Peloponnese called it "the land of the Slavs." By that time the Slavs were settled throughout the Balkans and Greece, and the Slavic tongue could be heard on the streets of Thessalonica.

In 862 the Byzantine emperor Michael III received a request from Rastislav, the king of a Slavic state in Moravia, to send a missionary who knew the Slavic language.

The emperor turned to two brothers from Thessalonica, Constantine (Cyril) and Methodius. According to an ancient life of Cyril, when the brothers arrived in Constantinople for an audience with the emperor he said: "You two are from Thessalonica and all Thessalonians speak the Slav tongue well." So began a religious and cultural mission that would advance the establishment of Christianity in the Balkans and among the Rus people, creating a Slavic Christian civilization under the hegemony of the emperor in Constantinople. To this day Christianity in eastern Europe, with some exceptions like Poland, is part of the large family of Orthodox Christians in communion with the Greek patriarch in Istanbul (Constantinople).

In the roll call of great missionaries in Christian history, Cyril and Methodius, the apostles to the Slavs in eastern Europe, hold an honored place alongside missionaries to western Europe, Patrick, Augustine of Canterbury, Columbanus, and Boniface. Their mission, however, had a different strategy; instead of teaching Greek to the new converts as the Western missionaries had taught Latin, their plan was to translate prayers, the liturgy, and Scripture into the Slavic tongue, so the new converts could pray and hear the Bible in their own language. But the Slavic language had no written form; before translation could begin an alphabet had to be devised.

Cyril and Methodius were born into a Greek family early in the ninth century, and both boys received a thorough education. According to his biographer, Cyril studied Homer and rhetoric, geometry with the mathematician Leo, and dialectics and philosophy with Photius, the greatest literary scholar of the day and the future patriarch of Constantinople. Their father held an administrative position in the provincial government, and Methodius, the older of the two, served for a time in the administration of one of the Slav provinces in the Balkans. The emperor, Michael III (842–867), held them in high regard and entrusted them with a mission to the Khazars, a Turkic people living north and east of the Black Sea. On returning, Methodius became the abbot of a monastery on Mount Olympus, and Cyril taught philosophy at the school of the patriarch in Constantinople.

Earlier missionaries to the Slavs had begun to work on an alphabet to write down the Slavic language, but had little success. Too many Slavic sounds could not be rendered using Greek letters. Cyril too had put his mind to creating a Slavic alphabet before he and his brother were summoned by the emperor. So when the call came he was well prepared. His initial effort led to the creation of what is known as the Glagolitic script, an original and distinctive alphabet that was able to express Slavic sounds accurately. Cyril's invention was a major intellectual accomplishment, and scholars of the Slavic language praise him as a philologist of the first order.

About the same time, however, others had begun to take a different approach to the problem. Their idea was to use the letters of the Greek alphabet as a base and to create a number of new letters that were suited to the peculiarities of the Slavic tongue. Because of its simplicity and familiarity this alphabet quickly caught on and was adopted by the Slavic peoples living in Bulgaria, Serbia, and among the Rus. Though the Greek-based Slavic alphabet was the work of disciples of Methodius, it came to be known as the Cyrillic script and is used to this day in many Slavic-speaking countries.

King Rastislav ruled over a kingdom located along the Morava River separating present-day Slovakia from the Czech Republic and Austria, a far distance from Constantinople. In a bid to remain independent of the larger and more powerful German kingdom to the west, Rastislav turned to Constantinople. Christianity was already being practiced in his country, and he asked the emperor to send teachers who would explain the Christian faith in "our language," the Slavic tongue. The Frankish priests, said Rastislav, "do not know our language." His relations with the East Frankish bishops were rocky, and he hoped that an alliance with Constantinople would preserve the cultural as well as political independence of his kingdom.

Cyril and Methodius arrived in Moravia in the fall of 863 and remained in the country for almost four years. The principal aim of their mission was to train a native Slavic-speaking clergy and lay the foundations for a Slavic-speaking Church by translating Christian texts, notably the liturgy and the Bible, into the Slavic language. According to Cyril's biographer, he translated from Greek "the whole ecclesiastical office, matins, the hours [daytime prayers], vespers, compline [prayer before retiring], and the Mass." Cyril's philological and literary work had large consequences. Though his goal was primarily religious and the texts he translated were spiritual writings, he created a literary language that would make possible a Slavic-speaking Christian culture. This language, known as Old Church Slavonic, became the third international language of Europe.

Prior to the arrival of Cyril and Methodius in Moravia, Boris, the khan of the neighboring Bulgars, had made an alliance with Louis the German, king of the eastern part of what had been the Carolingian empire, promising to accept Christianity at the hands of German clergy. This alarmed the Byzantines, who feared the spread of Western (Latin-speaking) Christianity in the Bulgar kingdom. So the emperor dispatched an army to the Bulgarian frontier and moved a fleet of ships into the Black Sea and up the Danube to threaten Boris. His position was precarious, and he decided to renounce the alliance with the Franks and ask for baptism from Constantinople. The date was 865. Boris's sister had already converted, and Boris saw in Christianity a religion that transcended ethnic boundaries and could unite the Bulgars with the Slavs living in his realm and consolidate his authority. Bulgaria became the first major kingdom in eastern Europe to accept Byzantine Christianity. In the East, the emperor rather than the pope united the Christian people, and adoption of Christianity meant becoming part of the Byzantine commonwealth.

Boris, however, was reluctant to become subject to the emperor. He hoped to establish a Bulgarian Church with its own hierarchy and even dreamed of establishing a separate patriarch for his kingdom. But Constantinople was cool to the idea. In a long letter to Boris, Photius, the patriarch of Constantinople, explained the Church's teachings and sketched a portrait of the ideal Christian ruler, discreetly ignoring Boris's request for a patriarch. Nor did he address Boris's concerns about practical matters, such as how Christianity would affect the mores of his people. In frustration Boris decided to renew his ties to the West and sent an embassy to Pope Nicholas I (858–867) in Rome with a series of questions along with a request for priests and a patriarch.

The pope responded with a long letter answering in great detail the many questions put to him by Boris. It is a remarkable document that displays vividly and concretely what a king cared about when adopting Christianity. Augustine of Canterbury had sent a list of nine questions to Pope Gregory I, and Boniface also put nine questions to Gregory III, but Nicholas dealt with over a hundred matters. Before examining Nicholas's letter, however, a few words about Nicholas and Photius, for they represent the growing divide between Eastern and Western Christianity, the one a stalwart defender of the universal authority of the papacy, the other a forceful advocate of the international rule of Constantinople.

Photius (810–895), a venerable figure in the history of the Eastern Church (what later is known as the Orthodox Church), was a major player in the ecclesiastical controversies of the time and a learned and indefatigable scholar. His book *Bibliotheke* (Library) includes excerpts from many lost works, pagan and Christian, with comments on style and content. Though written over a thousand years ago, it remains an invaluable resource on the history of Greek literature. A gifted teacher of philosophy and an accomplished theologian, he became a preeminent expositor of Christian teaching. His writings against the filioque are a definitive statement of the Eastern understanding of the Holy Trinity. As an educator he reorganized the patriarchal academy for the education of the clergy, and as a diplomat he was sent by the emperor as ambassador to the Muslim court in Baghdad.

Photius had considered becoming a monk, but chose a secular vocation instead. He was held in such high regard in Constantinople that in 858 the office of patriarch was thrust on him after the emperor deposed the patriarch, Ignatius. Like Ambrose centuries earlier, Photius was ordained—irregularly—to the lower offices of reader, subdeacon, deacon, and priest within a week and consecrated patriarch in time for him to preside at the celebration of the Nativity that year. His consecration put him at odds with the strong-willed Pope Nicholas I.

Nicholas belongs in the company of the two most accomplished popes in the first millennium, Leo the Great (d. 461) and Gregory the Great (d. 604). Like Photius he was born into a prominent family and as a young man rose quickly to a position of responsibility in Rome under several popes. He was a commanding personality and a student of the writings of earlier popes, including Leo and Gelasius, and by the time he was elected pope he had a well-formed sense of the papacy's role in the Church at large. In a famous confrontation he stood down King Lothair of Lorraine, who had divorced his wife, Theutberga, because she had not given him a male heir. When the archbishops of Cologne and Trier came to Rome with the proceedings of a council that recognized the divorce, Nicholas excommunicated the two bishops. In response the emperor, Louis II, marched troops into Rome, charging Nicholas with "making himself emperor of the world." Nicholas, however, was adamant, and in the end Lothair acknowledged Theutberga as his lawful wife.

Nicholas was no less vigorous in asserting papal authority in the East. In dealing with Photius, however, he found himself face to face with a tenacious opponent. Photius had written to Nicholas to explain and defend the unusual circumstances surrounding his consecration as patriarch. Nicholas then sent envoys to Constantinople to investigate the matter, and on returning they reported that they accepted the consecration. Nicholas repudiated his legates and in 863 he excommunicated Photius. The emperor wrote a forcefully worded letter to Nicholas, and the pope agreed to reconsider the matter.

While this drama was being played out in Rome and Constantinople, Nicholas was actively promoting Western Christian interests in Bulgaria. In an effort to address Boris's concerns, Nicholas responded in the letter mentioned above, *Replies of Pope Nicholas to the Questions of the Bulgars*. Not surprisingly, Boris's questions have to do with matters of practice, not of doctrine. He asks about engagement and marriage, consanguinity, and whether one can have two wives. Nicholas informs him that Christian law forbids polygamy. Nicholas describes in detail the Christian marriage ceremony, the giving of a ring, wearing of crowns, but says that it is the consent of the two people that makes a marriage. He lays down rules for fasting during Lent (eight sections deal with the observance of Lent) and on Friday, but makes clear that he does not lay a "heavy yoke" on the people. The Greeks had told the Bulgarians that one could bathe only on Wednesday or Friday, but Nicholas says they can bathe any day of the week, including Sunday. The people are to refrain from work on Sundays, on major festivals, and on saints' days. Several sections deal with warfare, such as whether an army can go to battle on a festival day, or carry a horse's tail as a military banner. Nicholas says that the soldiers should carry a sign of the cross.

Boris asked about the Bulgarian custom of the king eating alone, sitting on his throne while everyone else, including his wife, sat on stools at a distance. Nicholas had no objection, because it is not a matter of "the faith"; but he reminded the king that Christian leaders should be models of humility, and that Jesus reclined with his friends and ate with publicans and sinners. On matters of food, the Church has no provisions against eating certain animals or birds, though one should not hunt during Lent because meat is not consumed during the fast. Women's heads should be covered in church. One should not make an oath by a sword, only by God. Boris had asked about the burial of someone who has taken his own life. Nicholas says that he should be buried properly but without the customary rites and the "sacrifice" (Eucharist).

Besides accepting a new set of beliefs, putting the Creed and the Our Father to memory, the adoption of Christianity brought changes that reached into every corner of people's public and private lives: the marking of time, relations between the sexes, eating and drinking, the making of war, initiation into the community (baptism), communal rituals (Eucharist), laws on religious and civic matters, the ordering of space as churches were built. In Bulgaria things moved swiftly, and in a little more than a generation a magnificent church, known as the "golden church," was built in the ancient capital of Preslav.

Though Nicholas had supported the Western mission in the Balkans, he was nevertheless very interested in the work of Cyril and Methodius. In 867 he invited the two brothers to Rome, and on their way they stopped in Venice, where they met stiff opposition to the use of Slavonic in the liturgy. The local bishops and clergy informed the two brothers that there were only three sacred languages: Hebrew, Greek, and Latin. Cyril would have nothing of their linguistic imperiousness. "We know of numerous peoples who possess writing," he said, "and render glory to God, each in his own tongue. For example: Armenians, Persians, Abkhasians, Iberians, Sogdians, Goths, Avars, Turks, Khazars, Arabs, Egyptians, and many others. . . . Does not God's rain fall on all equally? Does the sun not also shine on all?" He dubbed their views "the three languages heresy" and "burned them with the fire of Scripture," according to his biographer, most notably the famous passage in 1 Corinthians 14.

By the time the brothers reached Rome, Nicholas had died, but the new pope, Hadrian II, welcomed them warmly. No doubt he saw an opportunity to bring the growing Slavic Christian world under the influence of the papacy. He called those who opposed using Slavonic in the liturgy "Pilatists," because of the inscription on the Cross on Calvary (Luke 23:38), or "trilinguists." From Cyril and Methodius the pope received the Slavic Scriptures and placed them on the altar of the Church of Santa Maria Maggiore in Rome, where "the holy liturgy was sung over them." Then the pope consecrated Methodius bishop and ordained several Slavic-speaking priests. Over the next few days they sang the Slavic liturgy at several other churches in Rome.

Cyril did not live to enjoy the fruits of his success. He died in Rome in 869, and at Methodius's request he was buried in the Church of San Clemente a short distance from the Colosseum. Before he died he implored Methodius not to return to his monastery, but to continue the work among the Slavs in Moravia. Methodius heeded the words of his brother, though his principal supporter in Moravia, King Rastislav, had died and his successor had turned to the West. For a time Methodius was imprisoned, but he persisted and in the last years of his life gave himself to the task of translation. With a group of disciples he translated the books of the Old Testament, writings of the church fathers, and a body of canon law.

In a magnanimous testimony to the achievement of the two brothers—especially since it came from the head of Latin Christendom—Hadrian's successor, Pope John VIII (872–882), had this to say in a letter to a Slavic prince: "It is certainly not against faith or doctrine to sing the Mass in the Slavonic language, or to read the Holy Gospel or the divine lessons of the New and Old Testaments well translated and interpreted, or to chant the other offices of the hours, for he who made the three principal languages, Hebrew, Greek and Latin, also created all the others for his own praise and glory."

Although Cyril and Methodius had labored in Moravia, Slavic-speaking Christianity had its earliest success among the Bulgarians. In large measure this was due to the vigor and intelligence of two disciples of Methodius, Clement of Ohrid (in Macedonia) and Naum of Pliska in Bulgaria. With Boris's support they established theological schools and trained clergy and continued the work of translation. Building on the foundation laid by Cyril and Methodius, they were able to transmit the nascent Slavic cultural heritage to other parts of eastern Europe and to the Rus people living north of the Black Sea.

Christianity reached Slavic-speaking peoples in east-central Europe from the West. Charlemagne died in 814 and was succeeded by his son Louis the Pious. But Louis allocated parts of the empire to different sons, and this led to strife among the brothers and revolt against his rule. Louis died in 840, and in 843 at the Treaty of Verdun in northeastern France, the empire was divided among Louis's three sons: Charles the Bald, Louis the German, and Lothair. Lothair was given the imperial title, most of Italy, and a strip of land from the Netherlands to Switzerland; Charles was given West Francia, roughly modern France; and Louis received the German lands east of the Rhine River.

Regensburg became the capital of the new German kingdom. The Franks had traded with the Slavs for decades, but now they began to claim territory to the east, notably in Moravia (Slovakia) and Bohemia (Czechoslovakia). In 845 a group of Bohemian chieftains traveled to Regensburg, asking to receive Christian instruction. Their motives were no doubt as much political as religious. Eastern missionaries had been active in Bohemia, but for the Bohemians there was more to be gained by cultivating political ties with the neighboring German kingdom than with Constantinople far to the east. At the end of the ninth century, two leaders from Bohemia were baptized in Regensburg, and in the early tenth century Duke

Wenceslas (907–935) turned Bohemia toward the West by recognizing the authority of the German king.

Wenceslas has become famous in the English-speaking world because of the nineteenth-century hymn "Good King Wenceslas," written by John Mason Neale. Wenceslas was not a king, but he was a leading figure in the establishment of Christianity in Bohemia. He built a church in Prague dedicated to Saint Vitus, an early Christian martyr venerated at the great monastery of Corby in the Frankish empire. The German king Henry the Fowler presented Wenceslas with relics of Saint Vitus that were deposited in the new church in Prague. Wenceslas, however, lacked the martial virtues necessary to rule; he may also have moved too fast in establishing Christianity. In 935 he was assassinated by his brother and eventually was celebrated as a Christian martyr. As in other lands, Christianity met resistance in Bohemia, but the direction had been set and in 967 a bishopric was established in Prague.

From Bohemia, Christianity made its way to Poland. There the key figure was Mieszko, a Polish prince who came to power about 960. It was no secret that the German kingdom was pushing to extend its realm eastward, and Mieszko had a keen sense of the political realities he was facing. So he arranged a dynastic marriage with the daughter of the Bohemian king Boleslav. Her name was Dobrava, and they were married in 964. When she arrived in Poland she was accompanied by Western priests with Latin books. Two years later Mieszko was baptized by a priest from Prague. Like Bohemia, Poland adopted Christianity in its Latin form. In 968 a bishopric was established at Poznan, and the first bishop, Jordan, was commissioned directly by Pope John XIII. Apparently the pope was wary of allowing the German king, Otto I—who had been crowned as emperor in 962—to have control over the new Church in Poland. In the year 1000, Otto III made a trip to Poland and recognized Boleslav, the son of Mieszko, as brother and friend of the German empire. Gniezno was established as the primary episcopal see in Poland, with three bishoprics in other parts of the country. Poland was recognized by Rome and the German emperor as a Christian state alongside other Christian countries.

For centuries the Greeks had had mercantile ties with the people living along the great rivers that emptied into the Black Sea. In the early ninth century a group of Rus merchants made a journey to the glittering city of Constantinople, with its grand palaces, magnificent churches, artistic treasures, and wealth. The splendor of the capital impressed them deeply, and other Rus would return, not, however, to trade, but to plunder. In 860 two hundred Rus ships sailed into the Bosporus and attacked the city, which had been left largely defenseless. The emperor was at sea with the imperial navy in the Mediterranean, fighting the Arabs. To a terrified populace gathered in the church of Hagia Sophia, Photius portrayed the new invader with the biblical imagery of Gog and Magog (Ezekiel 38–39). "A dreadful blow has fallen on us from the north. . . . A people has crept down from the north, as if it were attacking another Jerusalem."

But the siege ended swiftly, and the Byzantines sent an embassy to the Rus to sue for peace. In 874 a treaty was signed, and within months some Rus had begun to be baptized. Not long afterward an archbishop was sent to Kiev, the principal city of the Rus, the most southerly of a string of fortified cities on the Dnieper River and an active trading center. It was destined to become the center of a Slavic civilization.

The actual evidence for Christianity among the Rus in the late ninth century is, however, slim. In the middle of the tenth century Olga, the widow of the Rus prince Oleg, made a journey to Constantinople, called Tsargrad in *The Russian Primary Chronicle,* our source for the early history of the Rus. So taken was Constantine the emperor by the beauty and intelligence of the Rus princess that he urged her to be baptized. She consented and was baptized by the patriarch and given the name of Helena, the mother of Constantine the Great. She was then received with great pomp and ceremony by the imperial court, a notable honor and a sign that she was now admitted to a very select company of non-Greek Christian rulers who were part of the Byzantine commonwealth.

But Olga was shrewd enough to realize that she had another option—to turn to the West. In 959 she made a journey to the court of Otto I, the German king who had restored the Western empire. Western Christianity was expanding to the north, into the Scandinavian lands and the Baltics, and to Poland and Czechoslovakia (Prague). She saw advantages in an alliance with the West, but nothing came of her interest. She died in 969, and her son Svyatoslav had no interest in Christianity. It was left to her grandson, Vladimir, who became ruler in 980, to bring the Rus people fully into the Christian world.

An account of Vladimir's conversion to Christianity is told in a colorful story in *The Russian Primary Chronicle,* a work made of different sources from the eleventh and twelfth centuries. According to the *Chronicle* Vladimir received visits from representatives of the several religions practiced by neighboring peoples. First came a group of Muslims from the Bulgars. When Vladimir asked them to explain their faith to him they said they believed in God, practiced circumcision, ate no pork, and drank no wine. When he heard what they had to say, he told them that circumcision and abstinence from pork were disagreeable to him. As for drinking, that "is the joy of the Rus. We cannot exist without that pleasure." Then came the Germans, Latin Christians, who in the narrative are peremptorily dismissed without explanation.

Next a group of Jewish ambassadors arrive from the neighboring Khazar kingdom. They explain that they believe in the God of Abraham, Isaac, and Jacob, practice circumcision, do not eat pork or hare, and keep the Sabbath. The shrewd prince asked where their native land was, and they said it was Jerusalem. But when he asked why they were living elsewhere they explained that their land had been given by God to the Christians. To which the prince said: How can you teach others when you are cast out? "Do you expect us to accept the same fate?"

Finally a loquacious Greek "scholar," an envoy from Constantinople, arrived at the court. In a very long speech to the emperor he refuted the Muslims, Latins, and Jews and narrated in detail biblical history to explain Christian teachings. He even brought along pictures to illustrate his lecture. But at the end, when the envoys urged Vladimir to accept baptism, he "took counsel with his heart" and decided to wait. Then he sought the advice of nobles and elders of his people. They said that in a matter of this sort words and arguments will not do; he had to have first-hand information on how the several religions were practiced. So they suggested he send ten "wise and good" men to visit the several countries and report back how they "worship God."

First his envoys went to the Muslims and observed how they prayed in a mosque. They came away unimpressed. Then they went to the Germans and saw their services, but "we saw no beauty there." Then they made their way to Constantinople. On arrival the emperor sent a message to the patriarch and asked him to prepare the church and the clergy to celebrate the Divine Liturgy. They were taken into the "place where they worship God," the great cathedral of Hagia Sophia, and made to stand—Eastern Christians worship standing—in a "wide space," the area beneath the large central dome. So overwhelmed were they by what they saw that on returning they told Prince Vladimir: "We knew not whether we were in heaven, or on earth; for on earth there is no such vision nor beauty, and we do not know how to describe it; we know only that there God dwells among men."

After listening to their reports Vladimir asked his counselors whether he should accept baptism. The decision rested with him, they said. He was, however, not ready and turned to other matters. A year later his army attacked Cherson, a Byzantine city in the Crimea on the northern shore of the Black Sea, and cut off its water supply. Then he sent an embassy to the emperor Basil II, demanding that he give his sister Anna in marriage. Basil said it was not right for a Christian to marry a pagan, especially for someone born to the purple like Anna. If, however, you are baptized, he said, you will have her as your wife. When Vladimir heard this he said he was willing to accept baptism. Anna, however, was understandably cool to the idea of being carried off to the far north to live among "barbarians," but in that society she had no choice; so "after tearfully embracing her kinfolk," she was put on a ship sailing to Cherson. When she arrived, Vladimir was baptized by the bishop, he and Anna were married, and the couple made the journey up the Dnieper to Kiev, where the prince had the Kievan people baptized in the river.

The account in the *Primary Chronicle* is clearly written from the perspective of the Byzantines, or Rus who belonged to the Byzantine tradition, and is embellished with details that are difficult to verify on the basis of contemporary writings. The tale of teachers from four different religions arriving at Vladimir's court one by one, like suitors in a fairy tale, is unlikely. Yet taken as a whole the story gives a reasonable, if stylized, picture of the course of events and the principal actors. For geographical, cultural, and commercial reasons the Rus were more inclined to Byzantine Christianity than to that of the West. Vladimir understood the advantages of becoming part of the Byzantine commonwealth, with its higher culture and more developed commercial life. His decision was as much political and diplomatic as it was spiritual. On the other hand there is no question that the stately ceremony, vestments and incense, and the haunting music of the Byzantine liturgy worked powerfully on the minds and hearts of those who witnessed them in the grand cathedral in Constantinople. There was—and is—something celestial about Eastern Christian worship, and to this day the Byzantine liturgy is an enduring inheritance among the Slavic people.

Vladimir died in 1015, but in the decades after his conversion he energetically promoted the establishment of Christianity among his people. He oversaw the building of churches and set up bishoprics. He promoted the Slavonic tongue as the language of Christian worship and education. By the beginning of the new millennium the Slavonic liturgy was firmly in place, though Greek was still used alongside Old Church Slavonic. In the mid eleventh century Ilarion, the metropolitan (archbishop) of Kiev, described Kiev as "a city glistening with the light of the holy cross, fragrant with incense, ringing with praise and holy, heavenly songs." And his sermon on "saint" Vladimir is considered one of the finest writings in Old Church Slavonic.

The conversion of the Slavs in the Balkans and among the Rus living along the rivers north of the Black Sea inaugurated a new era in the history of Christianity. A vast new territory, larger than the Byzantine Empire itself, was now poised to build a Christian civilization different from that of the Latin West and the ancient Christian lands of the Middle East.

Afterword

After a thousand years the scope of early Christian history comes into full view. Geography gives the clearest picture. Christianity began in Jerusalem and spread east to Syria and Mesopotamia and on to India and China; in the first decades churches were established in Egypt, Asia Minor, and Greece, later in the Balkans and among the Rus; in the West the new faith took root in North Africa, Italy, Spain, and later in northern Europe, the British Isles, and Scandinavia (including Iceland); far to the south it was adopted in Nubia and Ethiopia. By any measure the movement that began among a small company of Jews in Jerusalem had become a global religion.

The breadth and diversity of peoples and places make it hard to see things whole. Yet there is a pattern, and it is defined by geography, language, and culture. By the end of the first millennium, Christians lived (with some notable exceptions like Armenia and Ethiopia) in three large geographical and cultural areas: the Syriac and Arabic Middle East; the Greek and Slavic East; and the Latin West. As each region had a different past and gave birth to distinctive forms of Christian life, art, architecture, worship, piety, and law, so the Christians living in each of these three large regions would have different futures.

Christianity began in the Roman Empire, but as one looks down the span of the Christian past, the horizon shifts to lands beyond the imperial frontiers. Already in the second century the gospel had been carried to Syriac-speaking Christians in Edessa and in Mesopotamia, and merchants sailing from Roman Egypt had planted a Christian community on the west coast of India. In the fourth century the Armenians embraced the new religion, and on the eastern shore of the Black Sea the preaching of Saint Nino led to the conversion of the Iberian royal house.

By the year 500 the empire had collapsed in the West, and new forms of Latin

Christianity emerged among the Germanic peoples of northern Europe. The Syriac-speaking Christians of the Persian Empire constituted themselves as a distinct Christian communion under their own patriarch, or catholicos, and Syriac-speaking monks traveled the Silk Road to Central Asia and to points east. Toward the end of the first millennium Slavic-speaking peoples embraced Christianity in its Greek dress.

The adaptability of Christianity to diverse linguistic and cultural traditions is remarkable. Christianity brought something new and at the same time received something old. One small example: the painting of Jesus with his arm around the shoulder of Saint Menas, discussed in the chapter on the Copts. The figures are Christian, but Christ's gesture comes from Egyptian funerary art. Christians displayed an impressive openness to the ways of the new peoples who embraced the faith. Pope Gregory the Great advised Augustine, his missionary to the English, not to put an end to the custom of the people to roast animals as sacrifices to the gods. Let them enjoy such celebrations, he wrote, "but in a changed form." Instead of calling these feasts "sacrifices," they should be occasions for thanksgiving to God who gives all things.

The global outreach of Christianity in the early centuries is a testimony to its cultural adaptability and diversity. Christianity as practiced among the Armenians differed from the ways of the Greeks or Ethiopians. Of course the Armenians, Greeks, and Ethiopians had much in common: they were governed by bishops; they fostered monastic life; they baptized in the name of the Father and of the Son and of the Holy Spirit; they confessed the Creed of Nicaea. But the differences in language, customs, liturgical practices, architecture, and art gave birth to distinctive spiritual and cultural forms of life across the Christian world. When the Crusaders arrived in the East to free their fellow Christians from the yoke of Islam, they had great difficulty recognizing and understanding the way Eastern Christians lived and prayed.

The spread of Christianity in the early centuries compels us to shift our gaze to a wider and more diverse world than that of the Roman Empire. Yet any account of Christian beginnings must give a large space to what took shape in the early centuries in the Greek- and Latin-speaking cities close to the Mediterranean Sea, and let it not be forgotten, the surrounding deserts and countryside where monasticism took hold. The vast reach of Roman political institutions, from the British Isles to the Middle East, and the order and stability of Roman rule, made it possible for Christianity to grow slowly and steadily and to build institutions that would endure.

Wherever Christianity was adopted a structure was put in place, through the person of the bishop, that provided continuity with the Christian past and spiritual unity with Christians in other parts of the world. Ignatius was prophetic in the early second century when he wrote that where the bishop is there is the Church. There is no evidence for enduring Christian communities without the office of the bishop. Even in distant lands, when a king adopted the faith, one of the first actions was to send for bishops from more established regions. In other lands, such as in northern Europe, bishops were often in the vanguard of those who brought the faith to the Germanic peoples.

No less important were the monks. Already in the second century the ascetic impulse within Christianity was observed by outsiders. By the end of the third century small groups of men or women lived chaste lives in community, and in the fourth century monasticism exploded across the Christian world. Wherever Christianity was adopted, one found monks. In some cases, in the Syriac-speaking East, in the Slavic world, and in the Latin West, monks carried the gospel to new peoples.

The emergence of monasticism created a new way of life that challenged the ancient urban civic ideal of antiquity and cut against the grain of Jewish tradition. Though retreating into the desert to seek God alone, or joining a community devoted primarily to prayer, may seem to be a world-denying way of life, monasticism became an indispensable part of a flourishing Christian society.

The ancient world was ruled by emperors and kings, and they played a major role in the establishment of Christianity as a global religion. To be sure, kings and emperors were not there from the beginning. Unlike Islam, Christianity began as a community distinct from the body politic, and for the first several centuries it existed independent of political authority. Only with the conversion of Constantine, the Roman emperor in the early fourth century, did Christianity receive the blessing of the ruling powers.

When Christianity made its way outside the empire, in Armenia or northern Europe, Christianization took place in alliance with the king and his counselors. Without the support of the king, Christian beliefs and practices had no entrée to the new peoples. Certainly the alliance between altar and crown would lead to unholy tradeoffs. Kings and princes sought to manage the affairs of the Church and to use its spiritual authority to serve their ends.

Still, even when the Church and the society were one and the king was considered the head of the Christian people, the Church retained its distinctive identity. During the reign of Charlemagne, a king who actively directed the affairs of the Church, Abbot Wala of the great monastery of Corbie in Francia insisted that the Church constituted a parallel sovereignty. The king, he said, should have public properties for the maintenance of his army, and the Church should have "church properties, almost like a second public domain."

From the beginning the Church nurtured a lively intellectual life. This is evident in the great controversies over the doctrine of the Holy Trinity and the person of Christ. As these public debates riveted the attention of clergy and laity alike, Christian scholars went patiently about the task of interpreting the Scriptures and explaining and expounding what was believed. Most were skilled public speakers and accomplished stylists who drew on a rich literary tradition prior to Christianity as well as on the Scriptures. They left behind a large body of writing that gave later generations of Christians an inexhaustible heritage from which to draw.

Translation and transmission of books were essential in the building of new Christian cultures. Among the Slavs and the Armenians, Christian monks were the first to write down the oral language. A written language made possible the growth of a literary culture. In the West, monks taught Latin and copied earlier Christian books as well as ancient works of Latin literature. In the Middle East, monks were responsible for translating the Scriptures and other Christian writings into the new language of Muslim society, Arabic. And in Spain a scholar from England translated the Qur'an for the first time into a Western language, Latin. Wherever there were churches, Christians forged a learned tradition and handed on a cultural inheritance.

Christianity came into the world as an ordered community and made its way as a corporate body with institutions and offices, rituals and laws. Christianity is inescapably social. Its spread among new people had little to do with the conversion of individuals and everything to do with building a new society. Many of the people who became Christians were illiterate; conduct and practices were the coin of the realm, less so preaching or doctrine. What Christianity brought could only be realized in the building of a "city," to use Augustine's apt metaphor in his book *The City of God*.

In the seventh century a great shadow came over the Christian world. When Edward Gibbon introduced the Prophet Muhammad in his *Decline and Fall of the Roman Empire,* he observed that the rise of Islam was "one of the most memorable revolutions, which have impressed a new and lasting character on the nations of the globe." Gibbon saw that Islam did not just inaugurate a religious revolution: its unparalleled expansion changed the course of history by altering the map of the world and creating a new geography.

Textbook accounts of Christianity present its history as a tale of continuous growth and expansion. By a selective choice of periods, events, and geographical regions, the conventional account (seen from the perspective of Europe and North America) gives the impression that Christianity is always moving forward. Seen in global perspective that picture is illusory. If one injects into this sanguine narrative the spread of Islam, things take on a different coloring. Set against the success of Islam and its staying power, the career of Christianity is marked as much by decline and attrition as it is by growth and triumph.

By the middle of the eighth century, a hundred years after the Arab conquest of Jerusalem, at least fifty percent of the world's Christians found themselves under Muslim rule. The great centers of Christian life in the early centuries, Alexandria, Antioch, Jerusalem, Carthage, Seleucia-Ctesiphon, were forced to submit to the dominion of Islam. Many of the major figures in early Christian history, including Origen, Cyprian, Athanasius, Augustine, Cyril of Alexandria, and Isidore of Seville, lived in cities later conquered by the Muslims. The great story of Christian success in the early centuries must be tempered by a melancholy account of decline and in some cases extinction.

It was not only Christians living in the Middle East who suffered under their new rulers. Christianity disappeared in North Africa, and a large part of the Greek-speaking world came under Muslim rule. The Arabs were initially stopped before they could take the cities of Asia Minor, and Constantinople was spared. But in 1071 the Byzantines suffered a crushing defeat at Manzikert, in eastern Asia Minor, at the hands of the Seljuk Turks. Their victory opened the way into central Asia Minor and led to the eventual destruction of Greek-speaking Christianity in the peninsula.

In recent years there has been much moralizing about the Crusades, but it is forgotten that the Crusades ended in failure. For a brief period Christian kingdoms were established in the Holy Land and Syria, but in little more than a century the territories the Crusaders conquered were reclaimed for Islam. The Turkish conquest of Asia Minor was of far greater significance than the Crusades. Consider some statistics: in the eleventh century, the population of Asia Minor was almost wholly Christian; by the sixteenth century Muslims made up ninety percent of the population. During those centuries the Church lost most of its property, its ecclesiastical structures were dismantled, and its bishops were prohibited from caring for their dioceses. As Muslim institutions emerged, the Christian population fled, and those who remained gradually adopted the religion of their masters. Today there are only tiny remnants of ancient Christian communities in Turkey. Eventually Constantinople, Greece itself, and parts of the Balkans came under Muslim rule during the time of the Ottoman Turks.

These developments fall outside the scope of this book, but they are a weighty reminder that after the end of the first millennium, the great period of Christian growth and expansion was over. Christians faced different futures depending on where they lived. Eastern Christianity, in both the Syriac-Arabic East and the Greek-Slavic East, suffered grievously. Only in the West was Christianity able to control its future, and from the perspective of the West, Christianity in the East seems part of a vanished past.

But Christianity is an Eastern religion, and its homeland is in the Middle East. A far better vantage point is Jerusalem. It was located on the western edge of a vast Aramaic-speaking area to the east, and was at the eastern edge of an empire that reached to the British Isles in the west. The prophet Isaiah said that "all the nations shall flow . . . to the mountain of the house of the Lord" (Isaiah 2:2). Jerusalem welcomed people from both East and West, and if one keeps the holy city in mind, the global history of Christianity will not be forgotten.

Chronology and Maps

Plato (429–347)
Aristotle (384–322)
Hasmonean (Jewish) rule of Jerusalem (164–63)
Jerusalem and surrounding regions (Palestine) come under Roman rule (63)
Octavian receives title of Augustus; beginning of Roman Empire (27)
Birth of Jesus of Nazareth (7–4)

A.D.

Conversion of Paul of Tarsus (35)

A.D. 50

Peter and Paul in Rome (60–63)
Fall of Jerusalem and destruction of the Jewish Temple (70)

A.D. 100

Ignatius, bishop of Antioch and martyr (d. 107)
Valentinus, gnostic teacher (100–160)

A.D. 150

Martyrdom of Justin (165)
Irenaeus, bishop of Lyons, writes treatise against the gnostics (178–202)

Birth of Origen of Alexandria, biblical scholar and apologist (185–253)
Victor, bishop of Rome during controversy over date of Paschal festival (189–199)

A.D. 200

Catacomb of Callixtus in Rome (210–220)
Thousand-year celebration of the founding of the city of Rome (248)
Persecution of Christians across the Roman Empire by Emperor Decius (249–251)

A.D. 250

Martyrdom of Cyprian, bishop of Carthage in North Africa (258)

A.D. 300

Diocletian, Roman emperor (284–305)
Persecution of Christians in the Roman Empire begins (303)
Constantine defeats Maxentius at Milvian Bridge outside Rome (312)
Letter of Constantine and Licinius from Milan on freedom to practice religion of
    one's choice (313)
Beginning of controversy over teaching of Arius (318)
Constantine becomes sole emperor (324)
Council of Nicaea (325), original Nicene Creed with anathemas of Arius's teaching
Death of Constantine (337)
Baptism of the Georgian king (337)
Christians in the Persian Empire persecuted (ca. 344–367)
Ulfila, bishop of the Goths (348–383)

A.D. 350

Ethiopians adopt Christianity (350s)
Death of Antony, Egyptian monk (356)
Julian the Apostate, Roman emperor (361–363)
Ambrose, bishop of Milan (374–397)
Basil, bishop of Caesarea, builder of the first hospital (370–379)
Theodosius I, emperor (379–395)
Council of Constantinople I (381), Nicaeno-Constantinopolitan Creed (what is
    known today as the Nicene Creed)
Shenoute, abbot of the White Monastery in Egypt (385 ff.)
Augustine, bishop of Hippo (395–430)

A.D. 400

Cyril, bishop of Alexandria (412–444)

First official council of bishops of the Church of the East (410)

Council of Ephesus (431) condemns the teachings of Nestorius, patriarch of Constantinople

Patrick in Ireland (430s)

Death of Rabbula, bishop of Edessa; Ibas becomes bishop (435)

Theodosian Code (438)

Mashtots, Armenian monk, creator of the Armenian alphabet (d. 440)

Leo, bishop of Rome, author of letter on the person of Christ (440–461)

Council of Ephesus II, the "Robber Council" (449)

A.D. 450

Council of Chalcedon adopts the statement that Christ is known as "one person in two natures"; Jerusalem recognized as patriarchate (451)

Theodoric, king of the Ostrogoths (471–526)

End of Roman Empire in the West; Romulus Augustus deposed (476)

Emperor Zeno's Henotikon, an unsuccessful attempt to end the dispute over teaching about Christ (482)

Gelasius, pope (492–496)

A.D. 500

Christian communities with Persian bishops in Ceylon (Sri Lanka), Kerala in India, and island of Socotra in Indian Ocean

Armenian bishops at the Council of Dvin accept the Henotikon of Zeno

Baptism of Clovis, king of the Franks (508)

Boethius, Christian philosopher (480–524)

Benedict of Nursia, author of *Rule* of Benedict (480–547)

Justinian, Byzantine emperor, builder of the Church of Holy Wisdom (Hagia Sophia) (527–565)

Birth of Muhammad (570)

A.D. 550

Isidore, bishop of Seville and scholar (560–636)

Cassiodorus, monk and scholar (485–585)

Council of Constantinople II, dealing with dispute over the person of Christ (553)

Fulgentius, bishop of Ruspe in North Africa (500–527)

Gregory the Great, pope (590–604)

Augustine (of Canterbury) arrives in England (597)

A.D. 600

Heraclius, Roman emperor (610–641)
Jerusalem falls to the Persians (614)
Columbanus, Irish monk and missionary (540–615)
T'ai-tsung, emperor of China (626–649), Christians in China during his reign
Death of Prophet Muhammad (632)
Jersualem comes under Arab rule (638)
Alexandria falls to Arabs (640)

A.D. 650

Maximus the Confessor, defender of two wills in Christ (d. 662)
Seleucia-Ctesiphon, capital of Sasanid Empire, falls to Arabs (673)
Council of Constantinople III, adopts language of two wills in Christ (680–681)
Synod in Trullo (692)
Carthage in North Africa falls to Arabs (698)

A.D. 700

Muslim invasion of Spain (712)
Battle of Poitiers, Muslim advance halted by Charles Martel (733)
Boniface, apostle to the Germans (680–754)
John of Damascus, defender of veneration of icons (d. 750)

A.D. 750

Beginning of Abbasid caliphate (750)
Black limestone monument with Syriac and Chinese characters about Christianity
    in China (781)
Council of Nicaea II, restores veneration of icons in Byzantine Empire (787)

A.D. 800

Charlemagne crowned emperor (800)
Anskar, apostle to the north (801–865)
Louis the Pious, son of Charlemagne, emperor (814–840)
Theodore Abu Qurrah, first Christian to write treatises in Arabic (d. 823)
Timothy, catholicos of the Church of the East, promotes mission to Central Asia,
    China, and Tibet (d. 823)

A.D. 850

Nicholas, pope (855–867)
Photius, patriarch of Constantinople (858–893)
Cyril and Methodius, missionaries to Slavs in Moravia (863)
Baptism of Boris, khan of Bulgaria (864)
Arabic translations of the Scriptures (870s–880s)

A.D. 900

Wenceslas, Bohemian duke, assassinated (935)

A.D. 950

Bishopric in Prague (967)
Mieszko, Polish prince, baptized (966)
Bishopric in Poznan (968)
Baptism of Vladimir, Rus prince (988)
Bishopric in Gniezno (1000)

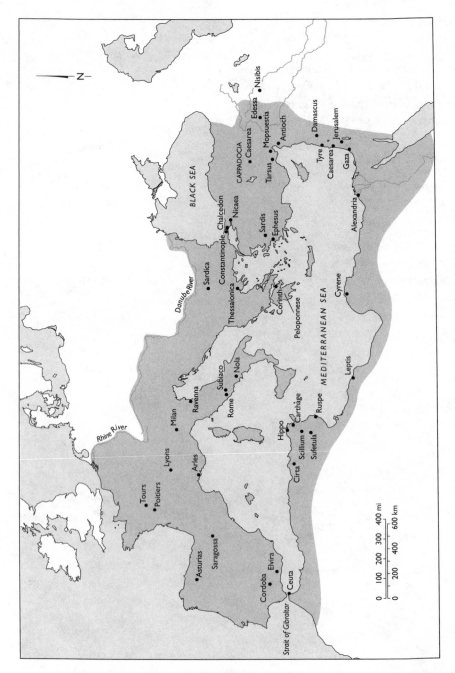

THE ROMAN EMPIRE, CA. A.D. 400

BLACK SEA

MEDITERRANEAN SEA

Danube River

Rhine River

CAPPADOCIA

Nisibis
Edessa
Caesarea
Mopsuestia
Tarsus
Antioch
Damascus
Jerusalem
Tyre
Caesarea
Gaza
Alexandria
Chalcedon
Constantinople
Nicaea
Sardis
Ephesus
Sardica
Thessalonica
Corinth
Peloponnese
Cyrene
Leptis
Subiaco
Nola
Ravenna
Rome
Milan
Hippo
Carthage
Ruspe
Scillium
Sufetula
Cirra
Lyons
Arles
Tours
Poitiers
Asturias
Saragossa
Cordoba
Elvira
Ceuta
Strait of Gibraltar

N

0   100 200 300 400 mi
0   200   400   600 km

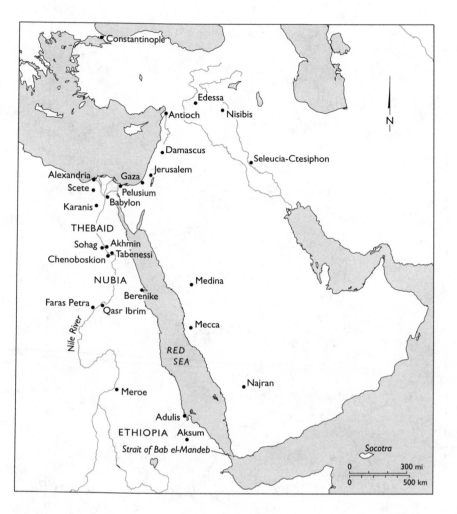

EGYPT, NUBIA, AND ETHIOPIA

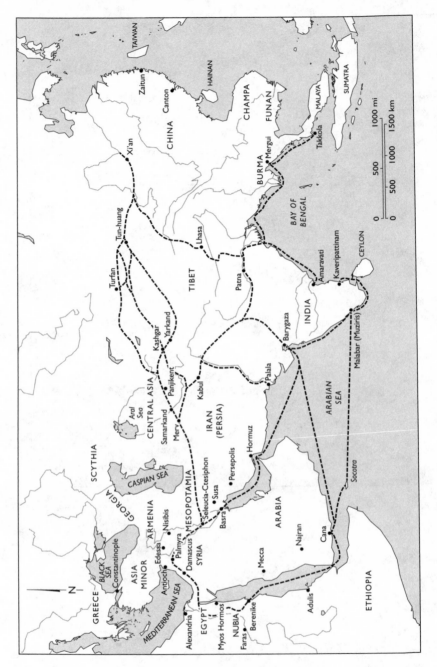

THE MIDDLE EAST AND ASIA. DASHED LINES REPRESENT ROUTES OF THE SILK ROAD.

CHRISTIANITY IN WESTERN EUROPE

THE WORLD OF SLAVIC CHRISTIANITY

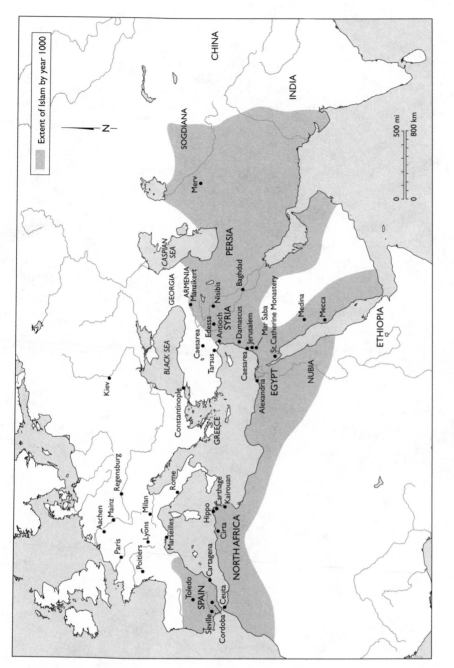

EXTENT OF ISLAM, CA. 1000, AND THE EARLY CHRISTIAN WORLD

Suggested Readings

African Zion: The Sacred Art of Ethiopia. Ed. Roderick Grierson. Yale University Press: 1993.

Asmussen, J. P. "Christians in Iran." *Cambridge History of Iran*. Vol. 3 (2). Cambridge University Press: 1983, pp. 924–948.

Atlas of the Early Christian World. Ed. F. van der Meer and Christine Mohrman. Thomas Nelson: 1958.

Barbero, Alessandro. *Charlemagne: Father of a Continent*. Berkeley: 2004.

Barnes, Timothy. *Athanasius and Constantine: Theology and Politics in the Constantinian Empire*. Harvard University Press: 1993.

Barnes, Timothy. *Constantine and Eusebius*. Harvard University Press: 1981.

Behr, John. *The Way to Nicaea*. St. Vladimir's Seminary Press: 2001.

Bowersock, G. W. *Hellenism in Late Antiquity*. University of Michigan Press: 1990.

Bowersock, Glenn W. *Julian the Apostate*. Harvard University Press: 1978.

Brock, Sebastian. *The Hidden Pearl: The Syrian Orthodox Church and Its Ancient Aramaic Heritage*. 4 vols. Transworld Film Italia: 2001.

Brock, Sebastian. *The Luminous Eye: The Spiritual World View of Saint Ephrem the Syrian*. Cistercian Publication: 1985.

Brown, Peter. *Augustine of Hippo*. 2nd ed. University of California Press: 2000.

Brown, Peter. *Poverty and Leadership in the Later Roman Empire*. University Press of New England: 2002.

Brown, Peter. *The Rise of Western Christendom: Triumph and Diversity*, A.D. 200–1000. Second ed. Blackwell Publishing: 1996.

Brown, Peter. *Society and the Holy in Late Antiquity*. University of California Press: 1982.

Browning, Robert. *Justinian and Theodora*. Thames and Hudson: 1987.

Burman, Thomas E. "Tafsir and Translation: Traditional Arabic Quran Exegesis and the Latin Qurans of Robert of Ketton and Mark of Toledo." *Speculum* 73 (1998): 703–732.

Burns, J. Patout. *Cyprian the Bishop*. Routledge: 2002.

Cambridge Companion to the Age of Constantine. Rev. ed. Ed. Noel Lenski. Cambridge University Press: 2012.

Cambridge Companion to the Age of Justinian. Ed. Michael Mass. Cambridge University Press: 2005.

Cambridge History of Christianity. Vol. 1, *Origins to Constantine,* ed. Margaret M. Mitchell and Francis M. Young, Cambridge University Press: 2006. Vol. 2, *Constantine to c. 600,* ed. Augustine Casiday and Frederick Norris, Cambridge University Press: 2007. Vol. 3, *Early Medieval Christianities,* ed. Thomas F. X. Noble and Julia M. H. Smith, Cambridge University Press: 2008.

Cameron, Alan, "The Last Days of the Academy at Athens." *Proceedings of the Cambridge Philological Society,* no. 195 (new series no. 15) (1969): 7–29.

Cameron, Alan. *The Last Pagans of Rome*. Oxford University Press: 2011.

Chadwick, Henry. *The Church in Ancient Society*. Oxford University Press: 2001.

Christians in Asia Before 1500. Ed. Ian Gillman and Hans-Joachim Klimkeit. University of Michigan Press: 1999.

Clark, Elizabeth A. *Women in the Early Church*. Glazier: 1983.

Collins, Roger. *Early Medieval Europe, 300–1000*. St. Martin's Press: 1999.

Collins, Roger. *Early Medieval Spain*. St. Martin's Press: 1995.

Coope, Jessica A. *The Martyrs of Cordoba*. University of Nebraska Press: 1995.

Coptic Encyclopedia, The. Ed. Aziz Suryal Atiya. Maxwell Macmillan International: 1991.

Cormack, Robin. *Byzantine Art*. Oxford University Press: 2000.

Crislip, Andrew T. *From Monastery to Hospital: Christian Monasticism and the Transformation of Health Care in Late Antiquity*. University of Michigan Press: 2005.

Curtius, Ernest Robert. *European Literature and the Latin Middle Ages*. Trans. Willard R. Trask. Princeton University Press: 1953.

Digeser, Elizabeth DePalma. *The Making of a Christian Empire*. Cornell University Press: 2000.

Drake, H. A. *Constantine and the Bishops*. Johns Hopkins University Press: 2000.

Duffy, Eamon. *Saints and Sinners: A History of the Popes*. Yale University Press: 1997.

Finney, Paul Corby. *The Invisible God: The Earliest Christians on Art*. Oxford University Press: 1994.

Fletcher, Richard. *The Barbarian Conversion: From Paganism to Christianity*. H. Holt: 1997.

Frend, W. H. C. *The Rise of Christianity*. Darton, Longman, and Todd: 1984.

Friedman, Florence D. *Beyond the Pharaohs: Egypt and the Copts in the 2nd to 7th Centuries A.D.* Rhode Island School of Design: 1989.

Gamble, Harry Y. *Books and Readers in the Early Church*. Yale University Press: 1995.

Gibbon, Edward. *The Decline and Fall of the Roman Empire*. Modern Library: 1995.

Griffith, Sidney. *The Church in the Shadow of the Mosque: Christians and Muslims in the World of Islam*. Princeton: 2008.

Harmless, William. *Desert Christians: An Introduction to the Literature of Early Monasticism*. Oxford University Press: 2004.

Herrin, Judith. *Byzantium: The Surprising Life of a Medieval Empire*. Allen Lane: 2007.

Hess, Hamilton. *The Early Development of Canon Law and the Council of Serdica*. Oxford University Press: 2002.

Hodgson, Marshal G. S. *The Venture of Islam: Conscience and History in a World Civilization*. Vol. 1. University of Chicago Press: 1974.

Kelly, J. N. D. *Early Christian Creeds.* Longmans: 1960.

Kelly, J. N. D. *Golden Mouth: The Story of John Chrysostom—Ascetic, Preacher, Bishop.* Cornell University Press: 1995.

Kelly, J. N. D. *Jerome: His Life, Writings, and Controversies.* Harper and Row: 1975.

Kitzinger, Ernst. *Byzantine Art in the Making: The Main Lines of Stylistic Development in Mediterranean Art, 3rd–7th century.* Cambridge: 1977.

Krautheimer, Richard. *Early Christian and Byzantine Architecture.* Penguin: 1979.

Laeuchli, Samuel. *Power and Sexuality: The Emergence of Canon Law at the Synod of Elvira.* Temple University Press: 1972.

Louth, Andrew. *Greek East and Latin West: The Church, A.D. 681–1071.* St. Vladimir's Seminary Press: 2007.

McGuckin, John. *The Ascent of Christian Law.* St. Vladimir's Seminary Press: 2011.

McGuckin, John Anthony. *The Encyclopedia of Eastern Orthodox Christianity.* Wiley-Blackwell: 2011

McGuckin, John Anthony. *The Orthodox Church: An Introduction to Its History, Doctrine, and Spiritual Culture.* Blackwell: 2008.

McLynn, Neil B. *Ambrose of Milan: Church and Court in a Christian Capital.* University of California Press: 1994.

MacMullen, Ramsay. *Chistianizing the Roman Empire.* Yale University Press: 1984.

MacMullen, Ramsay. *The Second Church: Popular Christianity, A.D. 200–400.* Society of Biblical Literature: 2009.

MacMullen, Ramsay. *Voting About God in Early Church Councils.* Yale University Press: 2006.

Markus, Robert. *Gregory the Great and His World.* Cambridge University Press: 1977.

Mathews, Thomas F. *The Clash of Gods: A Reinterpretation of Early Christian Art.* Princeton University Press: 2003.

Miller, Timothy S. *The Birth of the Hospital in the Byzantine Empire.* Johns Hopkins University Press: 1984.

Moule, A. C. *Christians in China Before the Year A.D. 1550.* London: 1930.

Nees, Lawrence. *Early Medieval Art.* Oxford University Press: 2002.

New Oxford History of Music. Vol. 2, *The Early Middle Ages to 1300.* Ed. Richard Crocker and David Hiley. The Oxford University Press: 1990.

Noble, Thomas F. X. *Images, Iconoclasm, and the Carolingians.* University of Pennsylvania Press: 2009.

Noble, Thomas F. X. *The Republic of St. Peter: The Birth of the Papal State, 680–825.* University of Pennsylvania Press: 1984.

Obolensky, Dimitri. *The Byzantine Commonwealth: Eastern Europe, 500–1453.* Weidenfeld and Nicolson: 1971.

Oden, Thomas C. *How Africa Shaped the Christian Mind: Rediscovering the African Seedbed of Western Christianity.* Intervarsity Press: 2007.

Oxford Dictionary of the Christian Church. Ed. E. A. Livingston. Oxford University Press: 2005.

Oxford Handbook of Early Christian Studies. Ed. Susan Ashbrook Harvey and David G. Hunter. Oxford University Press: 2008.

Page, Christopher. *The Christian West and Its Singers: The First Thousand Years*. Yale University Press: 2010.

Quenot, Michel. *The Icon: Window on the Kingdom*. St. Vladimir's Seminary Press: 1996.

Rousseau, Philip. *Basil of Caesarea*. University of California Press: 1994.

Segal, J. B. *Edessa: The Blessed City*. Clarendon Press: 1970.

Sellers, Robert Victor. *The Council of Chalcedon*. S.P.C.K.: 1953.

Soro, Mari Bawai. *The Church of the East: Apostolic and Orthodox*. Adiabene Publications: 2008.

Stark, Rodney. *The Rise of Christianity: A Sociologist Reconsiders History*. Princeton University Press: 1996.

Stevenson, Kenneth. *The First Rites: Worship in the Early Church*. Liturgical Press: 1989.

Swanson, Mark. *The Coptic Papacy in Islamic Egypt, 641–1517*. American University in Cairo Press: 2010.

Taft, Robert F. *The Byzantine Rite: A Short History*. Liturgical Press: 1992.

Vlasto, A. P. *The Entry of the Slavs into Christendom*. Cambridge University Press: 1970.

Von Campenhausen, Hans. *Ecclesiastical Authority and Spiritual Power in the Church of the First Three Centuries*. Stanford University Press: 1969.

Von Campenhausen, Hans. *The Formation of the Christian Bible*. Fortress Press: 1968.

Vryonis, Speros. *The Decline of Medieval Hellenism in Asia Minor and the Process of Islamization from the Eleventh through the Fifteenth Century*. University of California Press: 1971.

Wallace-Hadrill, J. M. *The Frankish Church*. Oxford University Press: 1983.

Weiss, P. "The Vision of Constantine." *Journal of Roman Archaeology* 16 (2003): 237–259.

Western Civilization: The Continuing Experiment. Ed. Thomas F. X. Noble et al. Houghton Mifflin: 1998.

Wilken, Robert L. *The Christians as the Romans Saw Them*. Yale University Press: 2003.

Wilken, Robert L. *John Chrysostom and the Jews: Rhetoric and Reality in the Late 4th Century*. University of California Press: 1983.

Wilken, Robert L. *The Land Called Holy: Palestine in Christian History and Thought*. Yale University Press: 1992.

Wilken, Robert L. *The Spirit of Early Christian Thought: Seeking the Face of God*. Yale University Press: 2003.

Wolf, Kenneth Baxter. *Christian Martyrs in Muslim Spain*. Cambridge University Press: 1988.

Wybrew, Hugh. *The Orthodox Liturgy: The Development of the Eucharistic Liturgy in the Byzantine Rite*. St. Vladimir's Seminary Press: 2003.

Translations

Acts of the Christian Martyrs. Introduction, texts, and translation by Herbert Musurillo. Clarendon: 1972

Alcuin of York, c. 732–804: His Life and Letters. Trans. Stephen Allott. William Sessions: 1974.

Ambrose. Trans. Boniface Ramsey O.P. Routledge: 1997.

Apostolic Tradition, On the. By Hippolytus. Trans. Alistair Stewart-Sykes. St. Vladimir's Seminary Press: 2001.

Armenian History Attributed to Sebeos, The. Trans. R. W. Thomson. Liverpool University Press: 1999.

Art of the Byzantine Empire, 312–1453. By Cyril Mango. University of Toronto Press: 1986.

Athanasius. *The Life of Antony and The Letter to Marcellinus*. Trans. Robert C. Gregg. Paulist Press: 1980.

Augustine, Works of Saint. A Translation for the 21st Century. New City Press: 1990ff. A new translation in progress of all the works of Augustine of Hippo.

Basil, Saint. *The Letters*. Trans. Roy J. Deferrari. 4 vols. Harvard University Press: 1961ff.

Bede. *The Ecclesiastical History of the English People*. Ed. Judith McClure and Roger Collins. Oxford University Press: 1999.

Benedict, The Rule of Saint. Ed. Timothy Fry. Liturgical Press: 1982.

Besa. *Life of Shenoute*. Trans. D. N. Bell. Cistercian Publications: 1983.

Boethius. *The Consolation of Philosophy*. Translated with an Introduction by V. E. Watts. Penguin: 1978.

Brock, Sebastian. *Syriac Fathers on Prayer and the Spiritual Life*. Cistercian Publications: 1987.

Cassiodorus. *Institutions of Divine and Secular Learning*. Trans. James W. Halporn. Liverpool University Press: 2004.

Charlemagne and Louis the Pious: The Lives by Einhard, Notker, Ermoldus, Thegan, and the Astronomer. Trans. Thomas F. X. Noble. Pennsylvania State University Press: 2009.

Christology of the Later Fathers. Trans. Edward Rochie Hardy. Westminster Press: 1954.

Cirta, text of hearing of Christians before mayor. Translation in O. R. Vassall-Phillips, *The Works of Optatus, Bishop of Milevis, Against the Donatists*. Longmans, Green: 1917.

Clement of Alexandria. *Ante-Nicene Christian Library: Translations of the Writings of the Fathers down to A.D. 325*. T and T Clark: 1868.

Confession of Saint Patrick and Letter to Coroticus, The. Image Books: 1998.

Cyprian of Carthage, The Letters of. Trans. G. W. Clarke. 4 vols. Ancient Christian Writers. Newman Press: 1984ff.

Cyril of Alexandria. Trans. Norman Russell. Routledge: 2000.

Early Christian Fathers. Trans. Cyril C. Richardson. The Westminster Press: 1953 (translation of the Didache, letters of Ignatius, Justin Martyr's Apology, selections from Irenaeus of Lyons, and others).

Early Christian Latin Poets. Trans. Carolinne White. Routledge: 2000.

Early Church Fathers, The. A series of volumes of translations of major Christian writers in the early centuries ed. by Carol Harrison and published by Routledge.

Early Latin Theology: Selections from Tertullian, Cyprian, Ambrose, and Jerome. Trans. S. L. Greenslade. Westminster Press: 1956.

Early Sources of the Liturgy. Ed. Lucien Deiss. Alba House: 1963.

Egeria's Travels: Newly Translated with Supporting Documents and Notes. By John Wilkinson. Society for Promoting Christian Knowledge (S.P.C.K.): 1971.

Ephrem, Saint: Hymns on Paradise. Trans. Sebastian Brock. St. Vladimir's Seminary Press: 1990.

Ephrem the Syrian: Hymns. Trans. Kathleen E. McVey. Paulist Press: 1989.

Eusebius: The History of the Church from Christ to Constantine. Trans. G. A. Williamson. Augsburg Publishing House: 1975.

Gnostic writings. *The Nag Hammadi Library in English*. Trans. by Members of the Coptic Gnostic Library Project. Gen. ed. James M. Robinson. Harper and Row: 1977.

Greek Christian Hymn on CD. *Music of the Ancient Greeks*, Ensemble De Organographia. Pandourion PRCD1001: 1995.

Gregory the Great. Trans. John Moorhead. Routledge: 2005.

Gregory the Great, The Letters of. Trans. John R. C. Martyn. 3 vols. Pontifical Institute of Medieval Studies: 2004.

Gregory Nazianzen. "Panegyric on St. Basil." In *A Select Library of Nicene and Post-Nicene Fathers of the Christian Church*. Trans. Philip Schaff and Henry Wace. William B. Eerdmans: 1974.

Gregory of Tours. *The History of the Franks*. Trans. Lewis Thorpe. Penguin Books: 1974.

History of the Monks of Syria, by Theodoret of Cyrus. Cistercian Publications: 1985.

Holy Women of the Syrian Orient. Trans. Sebastian Brock and Susan Ashbrook Harvey. University of California Press: 1987.

Irenaeus of Lyons. Trans. Robert M. Grant. Routledge: 1997.

Isidore of Seville, The Etymologies of. Trans. Stephen A. Barney. Cambridge University Press: 2010.

John of Damascus. *On the Divine Images*. Trans. David Anderson. St. Vladimir's Seminary Press: 1980.

Kontakia of Romanos, Byzantine Melodist. Translated and annotated by Marjorie Carpenter. University of Missouri Press: 1970–1973.

Lacatantius. *Divine Institutes.* Trans. Anthony Bowen and Peter Garnsey. Liverpool University Press: 2003.

Lives of the Desert Fathers, The. Ed. Benedicta Ward, trans. Norman Russell. London, 1980.

Lives of the Monks of Palestine, The. Trans. R.M. Price. Cistercian Publications: 1991.

Martyrs of Najrân, The: New documents. Trans. Irfan Shahid. Bollandiste: 1971.

Maximus the Confessor. Trans. Andrew Louth. Routledge: 1996.

Medieval Handbooks of Penance: A Translation of the Principal Libri Poenitentiales. By John T. McNeill and Helena M. Gamer. Columbia University Press: 1990.

Noble, Thomas F. X., and Thomas Head, eds. *Soldiers of Christ: Saints and Saints Lives from Late Antiquity and the Early Middle Ages.* Pennsylvania State University Press: 1995.

Origen. Trans. Joseph Trigg. Routledge: 1998.

Origen. *Contra Celsum.* Translated with an introduction by Henry Chadwick. Cambridge University Press: 1953

Pliny. *The Letters of the Younger Pliny.* Trans. Betty Radice. Penguin: 1963.

Procopius. *On Buildings.* Trans. H. B. Dewing and Glanville Downey. Loeb Classical Library. Harvard University Press: 1940.

Prudentius. With an English translation, ed. H. J. Thomson. 2 vols. Loeb Classical Library, Harvard University Press: 1969, 1979.

Sahas, Daniel. *Icon and Logos: Sources in Eighth-Century Iconoclasm.* University of Toronto Press: 1986.

Sayings of the Desert Fathers, The. Trans. Benedicta Ward. Mowbray: 1975.

Tacitus. *The Annals.* Trans. A. J. Woodman. Hackett: 2004.

Three Byzantine Saints. Trans. Elizabeth Dawes and Norman H. Baynes. St. Vladimir's Seminary Press: 1977.

Timothy, Catholicos of the Church of the East. Translation of the dialogue with the caliph al-Mahdi, in Alphonse Mingana, *Woodbrooke Studies: Christian Documents in Syriac, Arabic, and Garshuni.* Vol. 2. W. Heffer & Sons: 1928, pp. 1–162.

Vita of Constantine and the Vita of Methodius, The. Translated with commentaries by Marvin Kantor and Richard S. White. University of Michigan Slavic Publications No. 13: 1976.

Index

Aachen, 339–340

Abbasids, 309, 315, 327

Abgar (king of Edessa), 25

Academy of Athens, 252–254

Acts of the Apostle John, 301

Acts of the Scillitan Martyrs, 319

Acts of Thomas, 243–244

Aedesius, and Ethiopia, 215–216

Alban (martyr), 273

Alcuin, 337

Alexandria, 24–25, 196, 206; Muslim capture of, 316

Allegory, 62

Al-Maqdisi (geographer), 296

Ambrose (bishop of Milan), 127–135 passim; and Augustine, 185; as author of hymns, 148–149

Ammonius Saccas (philosopher), 57

Anastasis, Church of the (Church of the Resurrection, Church of the Holy Sepulcher), 27, 110–112, 113, 117, 212, 279, 282, 293, 296

Anastasius (emperor), 170–171

Anthony David of Baghdad, 312–313

Antony (monk), 100–102

Apostles, 13–14; and Jewish heritage, 18; as witnesses of resurrection, 17–18

Apostles' Creed, 45

Apostolic Canons, 180

Apostolic Tradition, The, 34, 48, 175–176

Arabian peninsula, Christianity in, pre-Islam, 217–218

Arabic language, 307–308, 310, 314, 318, 328, 331

Aramaic language, 7, 17, 25, 26, 229, 230. *See also* Syriac language

Architecture, Christian: Armenian, 235; basilica, 84, 137–138; chapel of Charlemagne at Aachen, 340; churches as public buildings, 112; Church of Holy Wisdom, 249; Church of the Resurrection (Anastasis), 112; Coptic, 210; Ethiopian, 220; influence of icons on, 306; innovations by Justinian, 249; liturgical use, 137; mosaics, 138–139; St. Catherine at Mount Sinai, 251

Arius of Alexandria, 89–94

Ark of the Covenant, in Ethiopia, 220

Armenia, Christianity in, 229–335

Armenian language, alphabet for, 230–232

Art, Christian: beginnings, 49–51, 53–54; Clement of Alexandria on, 49–51; creation of Christian artistic tradition, 143–144; crucifixion, 140; Daniel, 53;

Art, Christian (*cont.*)
fulfillment of Old Testament in New,
140; icon of Christ and St. Menas, 210,
356; Jonah, 52; lamb bearer, 50–51;
Madaba mosaic, 116; mosaics, 138–139;
mosaics of San Vitale, 141–143; narrative nature, 140; Nubian frescoes, 212;
orant, 51–52; Orpheus, 51; Sogdian, 241
Athanasius of Alexandria, 95, 100–102, 216
Augustine of Canterbury, 172, 272–275
Augustine of Hippo, 183–195 passim; on
care for the poor, 157; *The City of God,*
184, 189–190, 220, 246, 331, 343, 358
Augustus (emperor), 6, 333
Auxentius, bishop of Milan, 128

Baptism: in the *Apostolic Tradition,* 176; of
Clovis, 259–260; controversy over
rebaptism, 71–72; in Didache, 175; early
practice, 32–33; of Jesus, 8, 32; John the
Baptist and, 8; of Saxons, 336
Barbarians, 258–259
Basilica, Christian use of, 84, 137–138, 249;
Santa Maria Maggiore, 139; Santa
Sabina, 138
Basilica Euphrasiana, 138–139
Basil of Caesarea, 154–162 passim; canoni-
cal letters, 179; on cantors, 150; on the
Holy Spirit, 95; on the monastic life,
104–105
Bede, 271, 273–274, 276
Benedict of Aniane, 263
Benedict of Nursia, 252, 260–263
Benjamin (Coptic patriarch of Alex-
andria), 317–318
Bible, formation of canon of, 43
Bishop, office of, 30–32, 356–357; and celi-
bacy, 299; at Nicaea, 91–92, 94; relations
with emperor, 132, 135, 170–171, 324
Boethius, Anicius, 264–265
Bohemia, 350–351
Boniface (bishop), 276–278, 327
Boris (khan), 346–349
Brown, Peter, 156

Bulgaria, 346, 349–350
Burial practices, Christian, 48

Caelestius (disciple of Pelagius), 191
Caesarea, 61–62
Canon law, 174–183 passim; codification
under Justinian, 254; on iconography,
300
Cappadocia, 154
Cassiodorus, 265
Catacomb of Callixtus, 47–48, 50, 53–54
Catholic, meaning of term, 29–30, 179
Catholicos of the East, 227
Celibacy, of clergy, 181–182, 227–228, 299
Celsus, critic of Christianity, 63
Charlemagne, 333–343 passim
Charles Martel, 334
Childeric (Frankish king), 259
China, Christianity in, 241–243
Chosroes I (prince), 253
Christ, great controversy over, 194–204
passim, 254–256; divine and human will
of, 284–287
Christianity: in Arabia, 217–218; Arme-
nian, 230, 234; Bohemian, 350–351; Bul-
garian, 346–350; Chinese, 241–243;
Coptic, 317–319; corporate nature of,
23, 35–36, 358; and culture, 2; Ethio-
pian, 219–221; Georgian, 236–237; hier-
archy and governance, 30; Indian, 238;
North African, 319–323; Polish, 351;
relationship to Islam, 294–296, 308–
312, 318, 322, 328–331, 358–359; relationship to Judaism, 18, 20, 22, 39, 121–123,
125, 325–326; Roman view of, 17, 63;
Russian, 351–354; Spanish, 324–332
Church: Augustine on unity of, 187–188; as
City of God, 190
Church councils and legislation, 177
Church of the East, 3, 222–228 passim,
233–234; missionary activity, 239, 245
Church of the Resurrection (Church of
the Holy Sepulcher, or Anastasis), 27,
110–112, 113, 117, 212, 279, 282, 293, 296

Church-state relations, 170–171, 357; Ambrose and, 132–135; in Armenia, 237; coronation of Charlemagne, 340; Donation of Pippin, 334–335; and Donatists in Augustine, 189–190; in Georgia, 237; Hosius of Cordoba and, 325; under Islam, 318, 331; under Justinian, 255; at the trial of Maximus, 286

Cicero, Marcus Tullius, 67

City of God (Augustine), 184, 189–190, 220, 246, 331, 343, 358

Clement of Alexandria, 49–51, 146

Clovis (king), 259–260

Colman (bishop), 276

Columba, 271

Columbanus, 271–272

Confessors, 69–71

Consolation of Philosophy (Boethius), 264–265

Constantine, 75–87 passim; convocation of Council of Nicaea, 90–91; and the Church of the Resurrection, 110–111; letter on behalf of Christians in Persia, 226; death and succession, 118

Constantinople: Arab assault on, 297; culture, 248; founding of, 86–87; geography, 247; loss of importance, 298; relations with Charlemagne, 341; relations with Rome, 180, 182, 203–204

Constantius II (emperor), 118

Constantius Chlorus (emperor), 80

Coptic language, 206–207, 318–319

Cordoba, 327–328

Corpus Iuris Civilis, 251–253

Cosmas Indicopleustes, 238

Council of Carthage: of 251, 70–71; of 256, 72; of 411, 188

Council of Chalcedon, 201–204; absence of Armenians, 234; aftermath in Alexandria, 205–206; defense of by Maximus, 283–285; Tome of Leo and, 169–170

Council of Constantinople, First, 96–97

Council of Constantinople, Second, 256

Council of Constantinople, Third, 287

Council of Elvira, and legislation, 177–178

Council of Ephesus, 198–199

Council of Heira, 302

Council of Nicaea, First, 90–94; canon law and, 178; date of Easter, 179

Council of Nicaea, Second, 304–306

Council of Sardinia, 166

Council of Seleucia-Ctesiphon, 227

Council of Whitby, 276

Cross, 267–268, 279–270, 300. *See also* Crucifixion

Crucifixion, in Christian art, 140

Cyprian of Carthage, 64–75 passim; in comparison to Ambrose, 129; on canon law, 178; on care for the poor, 156; conflict with Rome, 165; on reading of scripture, 150

Cyril of Alexandria, 196–200 passim

Cyril and Methodius, 345–346, 349

Cyrus (patriarch of Alexandria), 317

Damasus, 167

Decius (Roman emperor), and persecution of Christians, 66–68

Dhu Nawas (prince in Arabian peninsula), 218

Didache, 174–175

Didascalia, 175, 176

Diocletian (emperor), and persecution of Christians, 76–79

Dionysius Exiguus, and date of Christ's birth, 180–181

Dioscorus of Alexandria, 200–201

Docetism, 37

Dome of the Rock (Jerusalem), 293–296

Donation of Constantine, 335

Donatism, 186–189

Drake, Harold, 83

Duffy, Eamon, 166

Easter: early Christian celebration of, 38; controversy over date of, 37–39, 94, 164–165, 179, 276

Edessa, 25, 222–223

Edict of Milan (so-called), 85

Egeria (pilgrim to Holy Land), 112–115

Emperors, 357; relation with bishops, 132–135, 170–171, 324

Ephrem the Syrian, 147–148, 150, 223, 225

Epistle to Diognetus, 47

Ethelbert (English king), 274

Ethiopia, 214–221 passim

Etymologies (Isidore), 266, 325

Eucharist: in Didache, 175; early practice of, 33–34; as fulfillment of the sacrifices of the Old Testament, 143; as sacrifice, 34–35

Eunuch, Ethiopian, 215

Europe, Charlemagne as father of, 338

Eusebius, 60, 90, 136

Euthymius, Armenian monk, 231–232

Fasting, 39, 58, 107, 176, 181, 221, 231, 236, 299

Filioque, 338–339

Flora and Maria, Spanish martyrs under Islam, 330

Frumentius (bishop of Aksum in Ethiopia), 215–216

Fulgentius of Ruspe, 320–321

Galen, on early Christian asceticism, 100

Galerius (emperor), 81

Geez language, 214, 217

Gelasius (pope), 170–171, 255

Georgia, Christianity in, 235–237

Georgian language, 237

Gervasius, discovery of relics in Milan, 130–131

Gibbon, Edward, 58, 251, 327, 358

Gloria in Excelsis, 151

Gnosticism, 39–41, 44–45, 57

Gospel of Truth, 40

Grammar, Latin, 266

Gregory the Great (pope), 171–173; missions under, 269, 273–275

Gregory the Illuminator, and Armenia, 229–230

Gregory of Nazianzus, 95

Gregory of Nyssa, 95

Gregory of Tours, 259–260

Greek language, 7; in Holy Land, 232; in Jerusalem, 113–114; and Justinian, 247; at Nicaea, 92; Origen and, 59

Guido of Arezzo, and musical notation, 152–153

Hadrian I (pope), 304, 338

Hadrian II (pope), 349

Hebrew language, 58–59, 349–350

Henotikon of Zeno, 234

Heraclius (emperor), 283

Hexapla, 59–60

Holy Land: as Christian land, 116; Armenian monastic communities in, 231–232

Holy Sepulcher, Church of the (Church of the Resurrection, or Anastasis), 27, 110–112, 113, 117, 212, 279, 282, 293, 296

Holy Spirit, 24; Augustine on, 192; Basil of Caesarea on, 95; as God, 97; John Chrysostom on, 111; in Nicene Creed, 97

Holy Wisdom (Hagia Sophia), Church of, 249

Homoousion, 93, 97

Hosius of Cordoba (bishop), 324

Hospital, 159–161

Ibas of Edessa and Syriac language, 222–223

Ibn al-As, Amr (Muslim critic of Christianity), 316

Ibn Antonian, Gomez, 328–329

Ibn Ishaq, Hunayn (Christian philosopher), 315

Iconography, 300–301; icon of Christ and St. Menas, 210, 356; and Quinisext, 300; ban on, 301–302; council of Heira and, 302; John of Damascus on, 302–303; Hadrian I on, 304; council of iconoclasts, 304; Tarasius on, 304; Second Council of Nicaea on, 304–305; Theodore of Studium on, 305; impact on architecture, 306; Carolingian view of, 306, 338

Ignatius (bishop of Antioch): letters, 29–30; martyrdom, 28; and docetism, 37

Illness, destigmatizing, 159

Inculturation, 275–276, 356

India, Christianity in, 238–239

Innocent I (pope), and Pelagian controversy, 168, 192

Irenaeus (bishop): early life, 41; on gnosticism, 41–42, 44–46; on primacy of Rome, 165

Isaac (monk), 329

Islam: beginnings and spread of, 288ff; biblical roots, 290; calendar, 291; conquest of Syria, 292–293; political nature of, 291–292; relationship to Christianity, 294–296, 308–312, 318, 322, 328–331, 358–359; Shahadah, 290; and submission to God, 290; Timothy I, 239–240

Isidore (bishop of Seville), 266, 325

Jacob of Sarung, Syriac writer, 148

Jerome, biblical scholarship of, 60

Jerusalem: Armenian monastic communities in, 231–232; as Christian city, 109ff; Christian view of, 279; Church of the Resurrection, 110–111; early Christian community in, 27; fall of Jewish city, 26–27; Holy Week liturgy, 113; Jews living in, 117; Madaba mosaic, 116; Muslim rule of, 292–293, 295; Paulinus of Nola on, 115; as pilgrimage site, 109, 114–116; and rebuilding of Jewish temple, 124–125; Sasanid conquest of, 280–283; and stational liturgies, 114

Jesus, 6–16 passim; divinity of, 23

Jews: fall of Jerusalem, 26–27, 110; history of in land of Israel, 8; living in Holy Land under Christian rule, 117; rebellion against Rome, 26; in Roman Empire, 121; as teachers of Origen, 57–58

Jizyah, 294–295

John VIII (pope), 350

John Chrysostom, sermons against Judaizers, 122–124, 126

John of Damascus, 302–303, 308–309

John Scholasticus, and Greek canon law, 181

Joseph, in Qu'ran and Bible, 290

Judaism, 7–8; Passover (Pesach) and Christian Paschal festival, 38; Origen and, 58; in Roman Empire, 121; relationship to Christianity, 20–22, 39, 121–122, 125, 325–326

Julian (Roman emperor), 118–126 passim; compared to Justinian, 253

Justinian (emperor), 246–256 passim

Kebra Nagast (Glory of the Kings), 219–220

Kingdom of God, Jesus' preaching of, 8–9, 11–12

Kings, anointing of, 335

Krauthammer, Richard, 235

"Labarum," 83

Lactantius, 82, 85

Latin language, 257–258; in Africa, 319; under Charlemagne, 342; in Ireland, 270; in Jerusalem, 113–114; and Justinian, 247; Muslim use of, 322; in Spain, 330–331; in West, 217

Leo the Great (pope), 168; and Attila the Hun, 169; and Council of Chalcedon, 201; identification with St. Peter, 169; sermons, 169; Tome of, 169–170, 201

Library, first Christian, 60

Licinius (emperor), 90; letter on religious freedom, 85–86

Liturgy: architecture required for, 137; Armenian, 234; Byzantine, 249–250, 353; Carolingian, 342; Holy Week in Jerusalem, 113; role of Byzantine emperor in, 250; stational, 114

McLynn, Neil, 131
Macrina, 105
Madaba mosaic, 116
Manichees, 186
Marcian (Roman emperor), 201, 203, 205
Marcion, and Old Testament, 40, 45–46
Maronites, 224
Martin I (pope), 285–286
Martyrdom: of Alban, 273; of Christian soldier, 77; Crown of Martyrdom by Prudentius, 324; Cyprian on, 71; of Cyprian, 73–74; of Ignatius of Antioch, 28; Martyrs of Cordoba, 329–330; Origen on, 56; of Peter, 163; of Pope Martin I, 286; of Wenceslas, 351
Mashtots, Armenian monk, 230–231
Material culture, 2, 54, 112
Mathews, Thomas F., 143–144
Maximus the Confessor: collaboration with papacy, 285; on the two wills of Christ, 283–286; travels to Carthage, 284; trial and exile, 286; torture and death, 297
Medicine, 158–159
Melito of Sardis (bishop), 281
Melkites, 224, 294, 298
Menas and Christ, icon of, 210
Miaphysites, 205–206, 211, 224–225
Milan, city of, 77, 85, 127–131, 134, 138, 167, 185
Military service, Christianity and, 77, 170
Mission, Christian, 3–4; to Britain, 272–275; to China, 241, 243; to Gaul, 271; to Germany, 277; under Gregory the Great, 269; to Iceland, 278; to India and the Far East, 238–240, 243–245; to Ireland, 270; to Poland, 278; to Scandinavia, 278; to Scotland, 271; to Slavs, 345–346
Monasticism, 357; anchoretic, 102; Armenian, 104, 231–232; Antony and, 100–102; Basil of Caesarea on, 104; Benedict and the Rule, 261–263; care for the sick, 159; cenobitic, 102–103; in China, 241–

242; Coptic, 319; Egyptian, 99–103; female monasticism, 105–106; Irish, 271; John Chrysostom on, 108; and love, 107; Macrina and, 105; and mission to the West, 271–278; Monte Cassino, 261; and prayer, 106; relation to Christian communities, 103–104; St. Catherine at Mount Sinai, 250–251; sayings of the desert fathers, 106–107; Shenoute, 207–209; Syrian, 103; and translation, 312; and work, 107
Monophysites. *See* Miaphysites
Mosaics, 138–139; Madaba mosaic, 116; Santa Maria Maggiore, 139–140, 143; San Vitale, 141–143
Muhammad (the Prophet), 288–296 passim; relations with Ethiopia, 218
Music, Christian: Carolingian renaissance and, 152; Clement of Alexandria on, 146; Coptic, 147; early Greek hymn, 145; Ethiopian, 147; Gloria in Excelsis, 151; later Greek, 149–150; Latin, 148–149; Sanctus, 150–151; Syriac, 147–148, 225–226; Trisagion, 150, 232; Venatius Fortunatus, 266–268

Najran, Christians in, 218
Narsai (Syriac writer), 223, 240
Nature, term in controversy over Christ, 200, 202–203
Nestorius, 195–196, 198, 207
Nicene Creed, 93–94, 96–97
Nicholas I (pope), 347–348
Nino, missionary to Georgia, 235–236
Nisibis, school of, 225, 240
Nubia, Christianity in, 211–213
Nubian language, 212

Obedience (monastic), 261
Olga (Rus queen), 352
Origen, 55–64 passim; on medicine, 158–159
Our Father, 11–12
Ousia (substance, or being), 93, 97

Pachomius, monastic founder, 102–103
Pange lingua (Sing, My Tongue, the Glorious Battle), 267
Panjikent, 240–241
Papacy, 165–167, 170; Columbanus and, 272; Donation of Constantine, 335; papal states, 172, 335; pope as Peter, 169; teaching office, 168; term pope, 168
Patrick (bishop), 270–271
Paul (apostle), 18–23 passim
Paulinus of Nola (bishop), 115
Pelagius (monk), 180–183
Penance, individual, 135, 272
Persecution, 65; in Carthage, 69; Diocletian and, 75–79; Sasanid, 226–227
Peter (apostle), 18, 21–22, 163
Philoponus (Christian philosopher), 254
Philosophy, 104, 254, 314–315
Photius (patriarch of Constantinople), 347–349, 351–352
Pilgrimage: Egeria, 112–115; to Fulda, 278; to Jerusalem, 109, 114–116; to tomb of Cyprian, 323
Pippin the Short (king), 334–335
Plainchant, 152–153, 342–343
Poetry, Christian, 282–283
Poitiers, Battle of, 326–327
Poland, Christianity in, 351
Poor, care for the, 157–158
Possidius (biographer of Augustine), 193–194
Presbyter. *See* Priest, office of
Priest, office of, 31–32; celibacy of, 181–182, 227–228, 299
Proclus (patriarch of Constantinople), 233
Procopius (historian), 248, 250–251
Protasius (martyr), discovery of remains, 130–131
Prudentius (poet), 133, 165
Psalms, 262
Pulcheria (empress), 198, 201, 203
Purgatory, seeds of later teaching, 61

Quartodecimans. *See* Easter: controversy over date of

Quinisext Council, 181–182, 298–300
Qu'ran, 290, 332

Ratislav (Moravian king), 346
Religious freedom: Christian justification of, 85
Robert of Ketton, 331–332
Romanos the Melodist, 149–150
Rome: Church in, 24, 68; churches built under Constantine, 166; city of, 83; relations with Constantinople, 180, 182, 203–204. *See also* Papacy
Rufinus (historian), 215–216, 235
Rule of Benedict, 261–263, 278, 341
Rule of faith, 44–45
Rus, 351–352

Sacrifice: ancient practice of, 35; emperor Decius and, 67–68; Eucharist as, 34–35; fulfillment of Old Testament sacrifices in Eucharist, 143; Jewish under Julian, 120
Sahak (catholicos of the Church of the East), 232–233
Saint Catherine, monastery of (Sinai), 250–251, 312, 313
Saint John Lateran, church of (Rome), 84, 110, 129, 136, 166
Samarkand, 241
Santa Maria Maggiore (church), 139–140, 143
Santa Pudenziana (church), 138
Santa Sabina (church), 138, 140
San Vitale (church), 141–143
Sasanid Empire, 223, 224, 225, 226–227, 229, 233, 235, 253, 280, 283, 288, 316
Saxons, 336–337
Schools: under Charlemagne, 342; in Ireland, 270; under Julian, 119–120; Justinian and the academy of Athens, 252–254; Nisibis, 225, 240
Scriptures, seized by Roman authorities, 79–80
Shapur II (Persian king), 226

Shenoute (Coptic monastic leader), 207–209

Sian-fu, monument of, 242

Silk Road, 239

Siricius (pope), 167–168, 179

Slavic language, 345–346, 349, 354

Slavs, 344–346

Sogdiana, 240–241

Solomon, in Ethiopian epic, 219–220

Sophronius (patriarch of Jerusalem), 282–283, 288, 293

Stephen I (pope): conflict with Cyprian, 72, 165

Stephen II (pope), 334–335

Stephen of Ramla (monk), 313

Strategos (monk), 280–281

Substance, or being (*ousia*), 93, 97

Symeon the Stylite, 103

Symmachus (senator): Memorial, 133

Syriac language, 113–114, 240, 308, 310

Tacitus, 17

T'ai-tsung (Chinese emperor), 241

Tarasius (patriarch of Constantinople), 304

Temple, Roman, 136–137

Tertullian, 43

Thaddeus (apostle), 25

Theodora (empress), 211, 248

Theodore Abu Qurrah (Arabic Christian writer), 311–312

Theodore of Mopsuestia, 223–224

Theodore of Studium (monk), 305

Theodoret (bishop of Cyrrhus), 125, 200

Theodosius I (emperor): convenes First Council of Constantinople, 96; conflict with Ambrose over Jewish synagogue, 134; decree on Catholic Christianity, 130; favors Nicene bishops, 95–96; massacre of Thessalonians and penance, 134–135

Theodosius II (emperor), 198–199

Theodulf of Orleans, 338, 342

Theophilus (bishop of Alexandria), 196–197

Theotokos, 197, 202

Thessalonica, 344

Thomas (apostle), 243–244

Thomas of Marga, 240

"Three Chapters," 255

Tibet, 240

Timothy I (catholicos), 239–240, 309–310

Translation of religious texts, 358; Arabic, 312–314; from Arabic into Latin, 331–332; Armenian, 230–232; Chinese, 242–243; Coptic, 206–207; Geez, 217; Gothic, 258; Slavic, 346, 350

Trinity, doctrine of, 98, 145

Ulfila (Arian bishop), 258

Umar (caliph), 293

Umayyads, 327

Valentinus (Gnostic teacher), 40

Vandals, 320

Venatius Fortunatus, 266–268

Vespasian (Roman emperor), 26

Vexilla regis prodeunt (The Royal Banners Forward Go), 267–268

Victor (pope), 164

Vigilius (pope), 255–256

Vladimir (Rus prince), 352–354

Wenceslas, 351

White Monastery (Egypt), 207–209, 317

Zachariah (patriarch of Jerusalem), 281–282

Zacharias (pope), 334

Zoroastrianism, 226